The Politics of Documentary

Michael Chanan

To my brothers David, Noel and Gabriel

First published in 2007 by the
BRITISH FILM INSTITUTE
21 Stephen Street, London W1T 1LN

The British Film Institute's purpose is to champion moving image culture in all its richness and diversity across the UK, for the benefit of as wide an audience as possible, and to create and encourage debate.

Cover design: Eureka!
Cover illustrations: (front) *Boca de Lixo* (Eduardo Coutinho, 1993, CECIP) ; (back cover) Nabokov (left) to Stravinsky in *Stravinsky* (Wolf Koenig & Roman Kroitor, 1962, Canadian Broadcasting Corporation/ National Film Board of Canada)

Set in the UK by Fakenham Photosetting Limited, Fakenham, Norfolk
Printed in the UK by The Cromwell Press, Trowbridge, Wiltshire

British Library Cataloguing-in-Publication Data
A catalogue record for this book is available from the British Library

ISBN 978–1–84457–226–7 (pbk)
ISBN 978–1–84457–227–4 (hbk)

Contents

Preface and acknowledgments

Unexpectedly and without anyone predicting it, as the centenary of cinema came and went, documentary returned to the big screen. Accompanied by the growth of digital video (cameras and desktop editing, DVDs and now the internet) the result has been a swell of interest on different fronts and a growing number of books – critical, vocational and popular. This book falls into the first category, but is written by a documentarist who is now an academic, aimed at anyone seriously concerned with the issues.

The new wave documentary is very different from the way documentary used to be. It is hardly at all like the 1930s, which saw the first great wave of documentary film, when the camera was taken as unimpeachable witness of public events. Nor is it very much like the early postwar years, before it became easy to shoot with synchronous sound, when documentary often took the form of the visual essay, with or occasionally without a verbal commentary. And then documentary split into two. On television, it became one of the principal strands of public service broadcasting, a remit providing positive opportunity limited by political constraints. Beyond the confines of the television screen, the language was more forthright, as documentarists aligned themselves to political causes and their films circulated on 16mm among diverse and sometimes international audiences.

As the centenary of cinema approached, however, two alterations produced enormous shifts. First, the arrival of video had the contradictory effect of greatly expanding participation while also seeing off 16mm distribution, and a new generation grew up for whom even the recent history of documentary had disappeared from view. But the displacement of film by video has made it ever easier to make films of all sorts, and because of technological convergence, digital video has produced new forms of dissemination. However, all this activity has been profoundly shaped by the second big shift, in the political culture which documentary addresses, either directly or indirectly. On the one hand, the heartlands of capitalism saw the demise of traditional class politics and the gradual demoralisation of the organised left in the face of neoliberalism; on the other, came the rise of second-wave feminism, identity politics and the new social movements, all of which have global resonance. In the middle of this process came the unthinkable (no one expected it, either left or right): the collapse of Communism and the end of the Cold War, leading to the intensification of the hegemony of globalising capitalism. In the course of these momentous changes, documentary widely abandoned its formerly all-knowing tone of voice, acknowledged the susceptibilities of the camera and its own subjectivity, discarded sobriety and modernised its language to match the loss of the old sociopolitical certainties and the articulation of new preoccupations. Parallel developments have taken place in many parts of the world: a radical new documentary cinema first appeared in Latin America in the 1960s, while the 90s have seen the rise of notable documentary movements in countries like India and China, although the different sociopolitical imperatives of these countries means that they have not simply followed Western models, but evolved according to their own dynamics.

The political context is always crucial, even where films do not engage or contest it. The underlying premise of this book is that documentary is a fuzzy genre (if genre is the right word) which defies definition but remains distinct from fiction in various ways. One of the crucial differences is that fiction addresses the viewer primarily as a private individual, it speaks to the interior life of feelings, sentiments and secret desires; whereas documentary addresses the viewer primarily as a citizen, member of civil society, putative participant in the public sphere. But in that case, it is always strongly influenced, in certain ways structured in advance, by the conditions which govern the public sphere in each country. In China, for example, independent documentary escapes censorship when it is shot on video because it falls outside the regimes which apply to either film or television, and judging by the two or three examples I've been able to see, film-makers are able to press against the limits of what is publicly utterable, partly by being observational and factual, and remaining politically opaque.

China may seem an odd example to mention in connection with the public sphere. Conventional wisdom has it that if there is no freedom of the press, constitutionally or *de facto*, then there *is* no public sphere. On closer examination, this often turns out to be a reductive argument primarily motivated by ideological posturing. In fact there is no form of modern society without access to a space where ideas and opinions are voiced and exchanged, however coded, and nowadays this includes those which reach them from elsewhere. The public sphere, as the theatre or arena of debate in which ideas are discussed and public opinion is formed, is not an ideal and uniform domain, but a network of social spaces, ranging from the physical to the virtual. From the spaces of public gathering where dialogue is direct, to the mass media (the press, broadcasting, cinema and music), where, as the term indicates, it is mediated, to a greater or lesser degree. (The newest domain, that of cyberspace, looks like a strange mixture of both.) The composition of this network varies in different countries according to their own political histories and complexions. On this reading, where free speech appears from outside to be restricted or disallowed, this doesn't have to mean that it has been driven underground; it may, however, become heavily coded, like the hidden national allegories of Soviet artists under Stalinism, or the artistic expression of dissent that developed in Brazil under the generals. These, of course, are very difficult conditions for documentarists. But the technological conversion to digital video means that nowadays documentary can be found practically everywhere, often in the form of local movements and festivals, or beamed in on satellite television; and it provides a crucial gateway through which new ideas and attitudes, novel social trends and tendencies, enter wider circulation. In short, documentary makes a vital contribution to public debate, and without it the public sphere isn't functioning properly. This book is focused on this political role.

The book also asks why the history of documentary, with a prehistory that goes back to the beginnings of cinema, remains largely unknown, and reconsiders how documentary arrived where it is now. It comprises three parts and fifteen chapters. Part One, 'Mapping the Field', consists of three chapters which look at the current scene, the problems of defining documentary, and the question of the veracity of the documentary image. Part Two, 'Historical Moments', has seven chapters. This is a historical survey, but each chapter has a double aspect: a period and a theme. The time frame goes from the beginnings of cinema to the 1960s. The themes can be summarised as the prehistory of documentary;

documentary's discovery of its own representational space; the nature of documentary authorship; the arrival of sound (and the challenge of music and spoken commentary); the social documentary and its alternatives; the essay film; and the problematics of cinéma vérité. Part Three, 'Contemporary Themes', contains five chapters. The first two shift the perspective away from the West, to Japan, Iran and Latin America. The next two chapters are also a pair, looking at questions of the documentary subject and the self-interpolation of the film-maker in their own film. The last chapter stands back to consider the testimony of the archive, its fragmented record of a century's history, and its relation to social memory.

A word or two of qualification seems in order. Since this is not a history of documentary as such, it is therefore a little arbitrary in those genres, individuals and films which are included or not included. There is nothing here about docudrama, nor the fake documentary, although there should have been. Some of the omissions I think of as more regrettable than others – I originally intended to write something about two of the most creative early television documentarists at the BBC, Dennis Mitchell and Philip Donnellan; I meant to include more than passing reference to Emile de Antonio, Errol Morris, Ross McElwee, Chantal Ackerman and Agnès Varda, and there should have been something on Raymundo Gleyzer (whose magnificent *México, la revolución congelada* – Mexico, The Frozen Revolution – made in 1970, has only just had its Mexican première). Many readers will find other names which are missing or only referenced in passing. I wanted to write more about Chris Marker, and should have included something about Nick Broomfield, Michael Moore and Molly Dineen; there is nothing on documentary in India or China. All that, however, would have near doubled the length of the book, so they had to be left out.

This book has been a good many years in the writing and is based on a certain pattern of accumulated experience. In many ways the first people I have to thank are the student film-makers I've taught at various higher-education institutions, first in the late 70s (when I felt like an unemployed film-maker employed to teach people how to become unemployed film-makers) and then in the 90s until now. It was they who elicited my first thoughts on how to understand documentary without regimenting creativity, imagination or political critique. This teaching experience has been enriched by invitations to teach sessions in film schools in Spain and especially at the EICTV, the International Film and Television School in Cuba, which I've been privileged to visit on several occasions over the last few years; this appreciation extends to the staff of the school, especially Julio García Espinosa, Luciano Castillo, Jorge Yglesias, Enrique Colina and others.

I also owe hearty thanks to all the interlocutors, unfortunately too many to mention here, at the various Visible Evidence conferences I've attended (including, of course, the one we hosted in Bristol in 2003), and the three symposiums on First Person documentary sponsored by Bristol Docs and convened by Alisa Lebow in Bristol and Tony Dowmunt at Goldsmith's College, in 2004, 2005 and 2007. For conversations and assistance while writing the book, my thanks go to John Adams, Alex Anderson, Holly Aylett, Terryl Bacon, Josetxo Cerdan, Gabriel Chanan, Noel Chanan, Peter Chappell, Simon Clarke, Guillermo De Carli, Josie Dolan, Jon Dovey, Josep Lluis Fecé, Stanley Forman, Ambrosio Fornet, Fredric Jameson, Pat Kahn, Eamonn Kelly, Clara Kriger, Jerry Kuehl, Thomas Lahusen, Alisa Lebow, Margarita Ledo, Martin Lister, Susan Lord, Angela Martin, Laura Mulvey, Maria Luisa Ortega, George Steinmetz, Michael Uwemedimo and Andrea Zimmerman. For information and/or copies of their films my special thanks to Peter Chappell, Eduardo Coutinho, Andrés di Tella, Jill Godmilow, Roger Graef, Patricio

Guzmán, Avi Mograbi, Chris Marker, Anthony Simmons and William Raban. Many thanks also to staff at the BFI and the National Film Archive, especially Patrick Russell for his help in locating some of the illustrations, and Roger Smither at the IWM, ditto. Thanks also to Humberto Perez Blanco for preparing the index. Finally, for institutional support, I am grateful to the British Academy and the University of the West of England.

Some passages in the book have appeared in earlier forms in a number of conference papers or previously published essays, to wit: 'On Documentary: The Zapruder Quotient', *Filmwaves* no. 4, 1998; 'Documentary and the Public Sphere', in John Izod and Richard Kilborn (eds), *From Grierson to the Docusoap: Breaking the Boundaries* (University of Luton Press, 2000); 'The Documentary Chronotope', *Jump Cut* no. 43, July 2000; 'Uses and Abuses of Documentary', *Journal of Media Practice* vol. 2 no. 2, 2001; 'Talking Film with Fredric Jameson: A Conversation', in Douglas Kellner and Sean Homer (eds), *Fredric Jameson: A Critical Reader* (Palgrave, 2004); 'Documentary, History, Social Memory', *Journal of British Cinema and Television* vol. 1 no. 1, 2004; 'El documental y la esfera publica en América Latina', *Secuencias* no. 18, 2004, pp. 22–32 (reprinted in *Cuadernos de Cine Argentino* no. 3, 2005, pp. 76–89); 'Documentary, Public Sphere and Education: New Video Documentary in Argentina', *Journal of Media Practice* vol. 6 no. 2, 2005; 'Documentary in Latin America' and other entries in the *Encyclopaedia of the Documentary Film* (Routledge, 2006), 'Performing the Occupation: The Films of Avi Mograbi', SCMS, London, 2005; 'An Argentine Take on Television: A Typically Unusual Story', First Person Symposium, Bristol, 2007; 'On William Raban's *Thames Film*', *Literary London*, 2007, <www.literarylondon.org/london-journal/chanan.html>.

Michael Chanan, London, 17 July 2007

Part I Mapping the Field

1 The New Documentary Wave

On the return of documentary to the big screen in the times of digital video

I

The most unexpected turn in cinema over the last ten to fifteen years has been the return of documentary to the big screen. No one predicted it, but a stream of new feature documentaries has entered the cinema in small but growing number. Suddenly it seemed that documentary didn't just belong on television any longer, and that documentaries in the cinema weren't just oddities any more, and they didn't only consist of nature spectaculars or 'rockumentaries', but a whole range of subjects: America's predilection for gun violence (*Bowling for Columbine*), the practices of gleaners in France (*Les Glaneurs et la Glaneuse*), the portrait of a philosopher (*Derrida*), a children's spelling competition (*Spellbound*); a rural French primary school (*Être et avoir*), a bus hijacking in Rio de Janeiro (*Bus 174*), a dysfunctional family in New York (*Capturing the Friedmans*); a game between two Danish film-makers (*The Five Obstructions*), a story of British mountain climbers in the Andes (*Touching the Void*).[1] The different countries these titles come from – the USA, France, Brazil, Denmark and the UK – point to the international character of this new wave of films, and the phenomenon is even wider than this, with many films, through no fault of their own, failing to attain international distribution. Spain is a case in point, because here, for more than a decade, there has been a wave of documentaries entering the cinema which only achieve foreign distribution very selectively, but nonetheless include some of the finest and most interesting examples of the new documentary anywhere in the world – like *El sol del membrillo* (The Quince Tree Sun), the study of a painter at work on a canvas; *Monos como Becky* (Monkeys Like Becky), about the treatment of psychiatric disorders; and *En construcción* (Under Construction) about urban redevelopment in Barcelona.[2]

The re-emergence of documentary can be traced in the press. In Britain, for example, notwithstanding the success over the preceding few years of films like *The Thin Blue Line*, *Roger and Me*, *In Bed with Madonna* and *Hoop Dreams*,[3] the leftwing weekly *New Statesman* was still writing back in 1996 about documentary as a 'fringe pursuit for a few consenting adults'.[4] Two years later, the liberal daily the *Guardian* was reporting that documentaries were emerging into cinema.[5] Jump forward another five years and in 2003 a writer in the *Telegraph*, a rightwing daily, is asking 'Why Truth Is Stronger Than Fiction'; and a year later, an editorial in the *Guardian* concludes that 'Real Life Doesn't Need a Script, Just Good Editing'.[6] This is a real change in attitude, since not long earlier, in the first flush of postmodernist thought, sceptics and doubters were widely given to disparaging documentary on the grounds that its claims to authenticity rested on what was no more than an illusion of objectivity – and objectivity, it seemed, was no longer what it used to be, but rather another form of subjectivity. Hence it was said that documentary was actually biased and manipulative, and really just another form of fiction.

But this won't do – it's much too simple. First, because the reality effect of documentary is not just an illusion (or only in the trivial sense which is true of all cinema – the play of light on a screen). The documentary image has a quality or dimension that is different from fiction, because it carries a determinable link with the historical world. Fiction we know to be invented and set up for the camera, whereas documentary consists of scenes drawn from the social and physical world that exists independently of the camera – that is to say, the same world that the viewer moves around in and belongs to, not its imaginary double. In semiotic terms, the afilmic world. This, of course, is too schematic, because what you see in documentary is often contrived. Nevertheless, you can go and visit Michael Moore's Flint, Michigan, but not Charles Foster Kane's Xanadu; and indeed you can encounter Michael Moore, but Citizen Kane you could never meet face to face even when Orson Welles was alive. The Michael Moore you meet in the flesh may not be quite the same as the one on the screen – perhaps better for you if he isn't – but if you visited the studio when Welles was on set, you would not be meeting Kane but Welles dressed up as Kane, who only exists on the screen. As Walter Benjamin wrote in 'The Work of Art in the Age of Mechanical Reproduction', in the studio, the 'equipment-free aspect of reality . . . has become the height of artifice; the sight of immediate reality has become an orchid in the land of technology'.[7] The camera is a mechanical (or now electronic) eye which automatically records whatever it's exposed to – the profilmic scene – but in itself it cannot distinguish between a profilmic scene that is fictional and one that isn't, a scene specially prepared or already existing. Certain documentary techniques depend on this lack of discrimination, which allows the practice of various forms and degrees of staging or reconstruction, and yet the referentiality of documentary is still of another order to fiction: it has historical reference. When you stage a fiction, in the studio or on location, you are suspending time and day and entering a temporality belonging to the narrative to which the scene belongs. When you film a documentary, what you capture in the camera is a moment grabbed from the day and time given by the calendar and the clock. Although it's true that this is frequently manipulated and often obscured in the course of editing to fit the temporality demanded by the argument of the film.

Of course the documentary representation is imbued with all sorts of filmic qualities brought to it by the film-maker. It is always already subject to the film-maker's angle, perspective and artistry, which is to say that John Grierson, founder of the British documentary movement, wasn't wrong to call it 'the creative treatment of actuality'. But to discount the automatic function of the camera altogether and emphasise only the subjective part – the film-maker's conscious and unconscious choices – is to fall into error. For one thing, in semiotic terms, this opposition between objective and subjective is false. The photographic image (we'll come back to this) is both index and icon at the same time: an automatic rendering of the scene and a pictorial resemblance full of associations and connotations.

The documentary idiom, in the view of Dai Vaughan – a film editor reflecting on his medium – encourages us to believe that the fact one is seeing something amounts to evidence that it must have existed in the first place.[8] In the case of fiction, this 'existed in the first place' is of the second order: it's been placed there in order for the camera to capture it and make what it will of it. We know this as we enter the cinema, or wherever we nowadays settle down and invite the illusionism of the screen to envelop us. But with documentary, this illusionism is unstable. The scene spills out beyond the frame, it has no fixed place from which it has to be pictured, the camera jumps around, the editing displays little respect for continuous action and, worst of all, the film often insists on reminding us of the outside world we just left behind. It is partly a question of who and what is in front of the camera and how they behave – in fiction, an actor playing a character in a prepared setting according to a script; in documentary, social actors as themselves, generally in an unprepared environment and situations which are preferably unrehearsed.

The viewer can usually tell the difference pretty easily, but again it's not quite as simple as that, and this is not a definition but a generalisation – and an expression of the documentarist's desire. A watertight definition of documentary is effectively impossible – many people have tried to provide one and they all come unstuck, often because a film comes along which breaks the rules while clearly remaining documentary. It would be better to think of documentary in the same way that Wittgenstein taught us to think of forms of life like games, which come in families and are related by family resemblance. In one of the key concepts of the *Philosophical Investigations*, Wittgenstein urges us to look at how the members of a family share their features in various ways, yet none of these features is the single defining characteristic of family resemblance. Any two members of a family may share features with a third member – two grandchildren of different parents, say, who both have the same nose as their common grandfather – without looking anything like each other. What makes them members of the same family is their common genealogy. Wittgenstein applies the analogy to games, showing that there need be nothing in common between a cardgame, say, and a game in the playground. As you move from one type of game to another their attributes shift: 'In ball games there is winning and losing; but when a child throws [a] ball at the wall and catches it again, this feature has disappeared.' As we go through different examples, he says, we see how similarities crop up and disappear, '[a]nd the result of this examination is: we see a complicated network of similarities overlapping and criss-crossing: sometimes overall similarities, sometimes similarities of detail'. There is 'no better expression', he concludes, to characterise these similarities than 'family resemblances', 'for the various resemblances between members of a family: build, features, colour of eyes, gait, temperament, etc. etc. overlap and criss-cross in the same way'.[9] It needs only a moment's reflection to see that the same can be said of artistic genres. A genre doesn't consist of a set of rules but a family of works, some of which are treated as models or paradigms of the genre in question. But different examples of the genre may follow the same or different features in the same paradigm, and like the children of the same parents, they may not always resemble each other. Documentary, on this reading, comprises an extended family with its own different branches, where the films can be quite unlike each other – as different, for example, as the patient and impeccable observation of a Nicolas Philibert (*Être et avoir*) from the association of ideas which governs the montage in a characteristic film by Chris Marker, like *Sans Soleil* (Sunless, 1984), with its essayistic narration, or the performative political buffoonery of a Michael Moore (*Roger and Me*). Yet clearly none of these films is fictitious, and we readily call them all documentary.

In any case, the sceptic's disparagement of documentary as peddling false objectivity is nowadays off target, because documentary has shifted its ground and become more individual and personal. There are still film-makers who practise rather strict forms of observational filming or third-person narrative – *Être et avoir* and *En construcción* are both examples – but many new-wave documentarists are given to flouting the traditional documentary stance of impersonality, and frequently insert themselves into their own films in a whole variety of ways, from Moore's buffoonery, by way of the voice asking questions from behind the camera of Molly Dineen, to Varda's pensive self-reflexivity. Consequently the truth they insist on telling no longer pretends to omniscience as it used to, and is no longer delivered as if from on high, but is told from an individual or personal point of view – which if anything makes them not less, but more persuasive.

The move towards subjectivity has been a growing trend since the 1970s, at any rate among the 'consenting adults' of the independent documentary movement which was mostly marginalised by television and rarely impinged on the working film critic except occasionally at film festivals. It is almost a mystery how this independent movement survived, since documentary was never at home in the major cinema circuits, and even shorts disappeared from the art-house circuit after the 1960s. Commercial interests generally regarded the form as either a filler or an interloper, best left to little alternative distributors who serviced the film-club minorities. Television, after initial hesitancy, had adopted documentary eagerly but imposed its own codes of compliance, especially in the matter of political 'balance', a code word for not upsetting the applecart of an assumed consensus. And yet, although mostly excluded from both cinema and television, works of artistic experiment and political agitation circulated through alternative distribution in 16mm throughout the 60s and 70s, and then began to move onto video, finding audiences of aficionados, students and political groups wherever there was half a chance. (In my own case, I first worked on video in the early 70s, using a reel-to-reel Sony Portapac, doing a piece for a youth group in central London, but we had no proper means of editing, and when we wanted to make a promotional film, we did it on 16mm. The second time, more than ten years later, it was a video for the Chile Solidarity Campaign, incorporating dramatic footage of repression and resistance shot clandestinely in Chile for this purpose. This was when I began to realise that grassroots political video was developing faster in certain places where conditions were more difficult than it was in the heartlands of democracy.)

A crucial element in postwar documentary before television took it up, to be found in the work of independent film-makers like Joris Ivens, Alain Resnais and Chris Marker, was the poetic expression of oppositional and dissident opinion. The 1960s brought politics back into centre frame, and a strong case can be made that following the innovations of cinéma vérité and Direct Cinema in the 1960s, it was alternative film-making, and not the televisual forms, which sustained the critical spirit of documentary and led it into new territory. This raises the question of the role of documentary in the public sphere. If the public sphere is the arena of free speech, the network of dialogue in which public opinion is formed and those in authority are held to account, then the history of documentary – first its exclusion from the cinemas and then the split between television and independent documentary – is a clear demonstration that this is not a single and unitary space of free and equal debate, but a network of parallel and overlapping zones, often of limited extension, and with unequal access to the mainstream forms of publication and broadcasting. There are central media and peripheral ones, but they're not disconnected, they overlap and rub off on each other. The small publics of the latter often consist in the most active members of civil society, organised in trades unions, campaigns and pressure groups, nowadays often employing their own publicity officers and political lobbyists to create a presence in the wider arena. In short, the mainstream media which serve both the state and civil society as the central means of communication are never entirely closed off but, on the contrary, always to some degree permeable to ideas and opinions arising in the interstices, the margins and from below. Documentary is one of the forms through which new attitudes enter wider circulation, through the form of its advocacy and the articulation of the social actors who participate as subjects.

In the mainstream model, subjects and subject matter are mediated by the impersonal director, who hides behind the voice of the commentary and serves as both intermediary and gatekeeper. But where this mainstream paradigm is weaker and especially when the documentary adopts the stance of the first-person testimony, it becomes the direct expression of novel social trends and tendencies, like those of feminism, the gay and lesbian movements, and other strands of extra-parliamentary, solidarity and identity politics. It is not an accident that these movements have used the documentary as one of the primary means of expression and assertion, often creating their own film festivals to provide a showcase, or that they shifted the voice of documentary in the process. It is a shift with complex aesthetic ramifications, since a film may speak in the first-person singular but imply a first-person plural, and this has implications for the way the viewer is situated, as one of the 'us' who are pictured on the screen, or as the other from whom this 'we' wishes to differentiate itself.

II

Although aficionados, politicos and students still make up an important part of the documentary public, there have been radical changes in the forms of distribution and consumption. The 16mm format has now been entirely replaced by video and DVD, which have changed the patterns of both distribution and viewing; patterns that are further altered as the internet also becomes a new and novel means of distribution, creating new genres of short video films with little respect for formal distinctions. Why, at the same time, documentary has returned to the cinema, and people are willing to pay to see it projected on the big screen, has yet to be explained, although the journalists struck by the phenomenon have made several suggestions. These boil down to three main reasons: it's either a reaction to the inadequacies of mainstream cinema, or to the inanities of television, and either way it has something to do with the costs of documentary production decreasing because of digital video, which is also a much more accessible medium of dissemination.

In the first case, it's a reaction against the fantasy worlds which have increasingly come to dominate commercial cinema. In other words, while the dominant culture of the multiplex has become mired in a special-effects cornucopia of puerile wish-fulfilment, full of bully-boy violence and conspicuous destruction, fairytale romance and the obligatory happy ending, an answer to this loss of reality is found at the margins in a restoration of documentary, which deals in the actuality of the social and historical world of everyday life, in all its postmodern ambiguity and confusion. Indeed David Gritten in the *Telegraph* commended *Être et avoir* and *Spellbound* as by far the best films he'd seen that year 'because both are honest attempts to engage our brains and emotions. . . . These two documentaries work for me in ways that no schematic, "well-plotted" Hollywood drama has done in a long time.'[10] This was echoed by Blake Morrison in the *Guardian* when he said that the stories these documentaries choose to tell aren't determined by committees or focus groups, so they become 'a place for surprising things to happen and for difficult issues to be explored'. But this is also, he added, about bucks. *Touching the Void*, for example, cost a modest £1.5 million. A fictionalised Hollywood version with big-name actors would cost ten times as much, and 'the bigger the budget, the less control for the auteur – and the fainter any semblance of reality'.[11] (Note the assumption here that documentary is an authorial form of cinema.)

The New York independent documentarist Emile de Antonio once advised against making a film that cost more than a million dollars – above that level, he said, you lose control to your backers. The figure he cites is relative. At the start of the twenty-first century, £1.5 million is a very low budget in comparison to Hollywood, but high for a documentary. Except for the big prestige series, television expects its documentaries to come in very much less. Even so, in recent years television documentary has been faring badly. In Britain, where it was previously protected by a public service remit which has been progressively watered-down and abandoned, traditional documentary has been increasingly diverted into the niche-market channels of cable, satellite and now digital television, to be replaced by lavish series, formulaic docusoaps, and so-called reality shows. During the 1990s, in Morrison's view, with television increasingly governed by the competition for ratings, the space for documentary on the terrestrial channels was largely given over 'to programmes about self- or home-refurbishment – how to improve your cooking skills or your life'.[12] For Gritten, this kind of television is so transparently bogus, with participants shamelessly playing up to the camera and producers nudging them towards some executive's notion of 'good TV', that many viewers, repelled by such machinations, yearn for real stories with no agenda or predetermined outcome.[13] This explanation corresponds with the findings of a recent survey of documentary audiences in two small countries, Holland and Scotland, which suggested that people who go to see documentaries in the cinema watch less television than average, and are willing to pay to see independent films on the big screen.[14]

Television's relation to documentary has been Janus-faced. On the one hand, TV is a medium with a kleptomaniac nature which jumps at new opportunities, eager to feed the viewer with novelty; on the other, it is compelled to tame innovations and, where necessary, to evacuate the results of politically dissident critique (the scope for critique depends in part on the general political culture, which varies, of course, from country to country). This tendency was already apparent thirty years ago. Writing in 1976, Dai Vaughan mentioned the ironic remark of a fellow film editor about the exciting innovations of the 60s: 'In those days we were developing the conventions. Now we merely apply them.'[15] The introduction of a new model of television broadcasting in the 1980s, pioneered by Channel 4 in the UK, which functions as a kind of television publishing house putting out work that is independently produced, promised to extend the boundaries, and for eight or ten years it did so. But Channel 4 operated on the basis of a public service remit, on a model that was undermined by the growth of cable and satellite transmission, where general purpose schedules are replaced by themed channels intended to cater for various niche markets. While this explosion in television channels implies a growth in demand for all sorts of factual programme-making, conditions were contradictory, and terrestrial broadcasters responded by reconstructing their schedules in the attempt to keep hold of their audiences. (Channel 4 itself bears very little resemblance today to its original self.) For independent documentarists, it has become very difficult to evade the logic of the channel controllers, since television is a buyers' market – although paradoxically, nowadays a contracting one, since documentary viewers are now forsaking it in favour of DVDs and the internet. This means there is constant pressure to keep production costs down, another factor inducing conformity because it discourages risk-taking. As the veteran documentarist Roger Graef recently put it, the film-maker is pulled in conflicting directions. 'Even as channels ask for innovation, they are retreating to safer, more controllable formats. TV executives exhort the creative community to "think big", "out of the box", to come up with "landmark ideas that will punch through the schedules". They want to be surprised. But they want to be surprised in predictable forms.'[16] Creative film-making, however, requires the opposite ethos: no formulas with guaranteed numbers of viewers and no imitation of given models. It needs a willingness by commissioners to take risks, to fund and stay with projects that may not bear fruit for years.

In this situation, one of the reasons digital video makes a difference is that production can be achieved on highly economic budgets by small agile units with highly flexible skills and working practices. But television has been squandering the potential of digital video on formulaic formats like the docusoaps, which cater to a suspect dialectic between exhibitionism and voyeurism. This is seriously to distort the ideals of public service broadcasting to which documentary traditionally answered. The dumbing down of documentary lies behind the complaint of another columnist in the *Guardian* in 2001. Under the headline 'Know Nothing about Afghanistan? Blame the Death of the Documentary', Charlotte Raven argued that the account of events provided by the news is too constrained by its own agendas and clichés to be 'adjusted to the subtlety of real situations', and 'the only group of media workers with the patience and inclination to give us a real idea of what foreigners get up to when they're not under the cosh are the documentary makers'.[17] But television executives have abandoned 'the unspectacular business of showing us how other people live', a job which needs no computer animation, or five-year voyages to film the fish that no human being has seen. The result was summed up by the headline. Behind the journalese is a crucial accusation: television documentary is not being allowed to fulfil the potential of its educative and sociopolitical role of speaking to the public sphere about things that matter. (Five years later, there's a stream of documentaries on television about the problems and sufferings of the people of Iraq, but it's too late.)

Outside television, however, video began to succour a new kind of documentary which was effectively impossible to shoot on film, because much too costly, but at the same time, as the technology for video-to-film transfer was developed, could now end up in the cinema. An early example, released in 1994, was *Hoop Dreams*, a study of black high-school basketball players in Chicago for whom sport is one of the few means of social escape, which was shot over a period of seven years and became a worldwide box-office success. Not on the scale of your average fiction movie, but as Gritten noted in the *Telegraph*, it 'easily made its money back, a signal to investors that documentaries were worth a punt'.[18] At the same time, the new technology of digital cameras and desktop editing has made it possible for the independent documentarist, working at the edges of the system and disposed to cutting all sorts of corners, to bring their film in for considerably reduced costs. Or even, if you believe the hype, next to nothing: if you don't count the cost of the gear, don't include rent and electricity, and no one's time is paid for, then you get Jonathan Caouette's extraordinary *Tarnation* (2003), a highly personal meditation on the film-maker's dysfunctional family, which the film's publicity tells us was made on his own Macintosh computer for $218. Another example, *The Yes Men* (2004), a political spoof against the World Trade Organisation, was filmed in several different countries for less than $40,000 (with the help of friends in appropriate places who managed to provide much of the travel involved).[19] Of course you then have to ask about what these figures don't include. *Tarnation* interweaves Caouette's footage of his own family with snippets taken from film and television. Clearing the rights, transferring the video to film, budgeting for publicity and marketing, took the total cost to $400,000.[20] The same process for *The Yes Men* added about $350,000.

If these figures are indicative, what they point to are the workings of the market through which a film must pass to find its audience. The peculiarities of this market, which is divided and fragmented between many different outlets, and no longer confined to traditional commercial operations, is a crucial but largely overlooked factor in the encounter of documentary with its public. The resurgence of the documentary is driven by the hunger of the cinema audience, or at least a significant part of it, everywhere in the world, or wherever they get the chance, to see something of what is ordinarily called the 'real world' on the big screen, although nowadays many seem aware that reality is not necessarily what it seems. The numbers are not huge. We are speaking of a large minority of the *gros publique* which is frustrated by the narrowness of mainstream television and entertainment cinema alike. Not the millions who go to cinema for nothing more than entertainment, but in a good-sized country, it can amount to a few hundred thousand. And this, it turns out, is enough to make documentary distribution in the cinema a going concern. For the moment, at least, the market has taken a form where small-scale production is re-valorised and, just as important, is now comprised of a multiplicity of voices.

III

The journalists' suggestions diverge and contradict each other. For one it's a return to reality, a reaction against the fantasy worlds which increasingly dominate mainstream commercial cinema. For another, it's because documentarists have learned how to tell individual stories the way Hollywood does, with strong characters and narrative drive. Both things are partly true, but most documentaries remain quite un-Hollywood-like in their insistence on the legitimacy and integrity of the film-maker's encounter with a certain segment of reality. If documentary necessarily happens outside the studio, it is also beyond the reach of the movie culture of Hollywood and its imitators.

On this reading, documentary hardly belongs at all to the studio model of film production or, nowadays, the corporate production of feature movies according to strictly (and cynically) commercial criteria – the industrial system that the Argentinian film-makers Fernando Solanas and Octavio Getino, in a famous manifesto of 1969, called 'first cinema'.[21] It is more in line with what they called 'second cinema' – the 'artistic' type of film with psychological and social leanings characteristic of European production models, which values the director as an artist and author. (How authorship functions in the cinema is an issue that's been debated for fifty years; exactly how it works in documentary is hardly considered – a question we shall return to in a later chapter.) Second cinema, they said, is individualistic, bourgeois and politically reformist. But there was also a third cinema, the militant film of opposition, for which one of the models was their own documentary epic, *La hora de los hornos* (The Hour of the Furnaces) of 1968 – according to one account, a film made 'in the interstices of the system and against the system . . . independent in production, militant in politics, and experimental in language'.[22] The scheme they proposed in the manifesto is politically dated, but the distinctions somehow remain.[23] First cinema in documentary is the anonymous made-for-television look-alike output of Discovery Channel and National Geographic, where the credits roll by at the end too quick to be read, and authorship is a byword for corporate anonymity. The new wave documentaries which nowadays get international distribution are mostly independent examples of second cinema, clearly carrying their author's name. (In the television version, this is usually a high-profile figure from academia or journalism in the role of presenter or reporter.) When free speech, the prerogatives of public service broadcasting and investigative journalism combine, the results can be politically powerful stuff (for example in the work of John Pilger or Adam Curtis). But there remain independent films which television refuses to broadcast and conventional distributors decline. One example is Franny Armstrong's *McLibel* (2005, original version 1997), which shows how you can defend yourself in the courts without lawyers against a libel action by a multinational corporation and win, a David-and-Goliath story which no one would commission. Another is *Injustice* (Ken Fero and Tariq Mehmood, 2001) about black deaths in police custody. These are much closer to third cinema (let's say two-and-a-half).

Third cinema was never limited to Third World countries – Solanas and Getino spoke of First World examples like the Newsreel Collective in the USA, the *cinegiornali* of the Italian student movement, the films made by the États Généraux du Cinéma Français, and those of the British and Japanese student movements – films distributed widely in the 60s and 70s in the alternative film circuits of the day. This model was eclipsed by two main factors. One was political, that is to say, a loss of political direction in the face of the ideological offensive of neoliberalism in the 1980s, compounded by the fall of the Berlin Wall and demise of the socialist bloc, the end of the Cold War and the erasure of a whole revolutionary tradition. The second factor, as already intimated, is technological, involving the demise of 16mm and the rise of video. The demise of 16mm robbed the films of the infrastructure of distribution; the rise of video worked over the course of time in the opposite direction, to create a new alternative mode of circulation, often sponsored by non-governmental organisations and supplied by a new generation of film-makers, working in the margins and interstices around the world, and creating a range of new forms and styles and modes of address.

Video also replaced the home movie, which began in the 1920s on 16mm and shifted in the post-war boom to 8mm and Super-8. A number of experimental film-makers had used these formats to produce diary films, which video, with its greater ease of use, now proceeded to democratise. The late 1980s saw the adoption of the video diary as a new televisual format, nurtured by the BBC's community programmes unit, at the same time as the emergence in Brazil and other Latin American countries, and among the aborigines of Australia, of the indigenous video movements. Although these examples appear to pull in opposite directions – the video diary succours individualism, the indigenous video is communitarian – they share a common element, to which video seems especially prone: the camera acquires its own voice, and that voice speaks in the first person. In the more political versions of first-person documentary the pronoun is plural, implicitly or explicitly, and the point of view is collective. Needless to say, videos like this, which are very close to third cinema, don't usually make it to either cinema or television.

If the new wave documentary of recent years mostly corresponds to second cinema, it has also developed new modes of filmic speech and new forms of address. One kind of result, where the director is regarded prima facie as an author and the film is allowed to have an open ending, is described by

Jonathan Romney in the *Guardian*: the documentarist readily becomes an autobiographical essayist who ponders the state of the world on a minimal budget, less interested in simply showing us the world than encouraging us to rethink it.[24] (Actually this already serves to describe films of the 80s like Marker's *Sans Soleil*, or Ross McElwee's *Sherman's March* [1986].) Sometimes there is subjectivity without autobiography, sometimes the film-maker goes further and makes quasi-fiction out of their own life. (Here a paradigm would be Nanni Moretti's *Caro Diario* [Dear Diary, 1994].) It is difficult and risky to generalise, because this movement is multi-stranded and divergent in its tendencies. It is also easier now to make films within the interstices of the system and find them taken up, albeit modestly, than in the period of revolutionary militancy in the 60s and 70s, since the outlets have diversified and multiplied. Indeed we can hardly speak of a movement in the traditional sense, which is bonded together by shared stylistic tendencies, the way we think of Italian neorealism, for example, or American Direct Cinema of the 1960s. The new documentary of the past ten or fifteen years is not an artistic movement but a wave of activity. Nonetheless, what has emerged in so many of these films is a new kind of documentary discourse which asserts the prerogative of the film-maker to have their very own take on the world. The documentary camera remains rooted in social reality, declaring the film-maker's citizenship of this, our world, and their right to assert their perspective on it.

The huge variety of subjects and styles of new wave cinema documentary makes it difficult to pin down different genres (however hard both film critics and marketing people may try). Some are about ordinary people in ordinary situations, like the schoolroom of *Être et avoir* or the folk in *Suite Habana* (2003) by the Cuban director Fernando Pérez. Or in special situations which they've chosen themselves, like the public competition of *Spellbound*. Others concern ordinary people in situations of extremity, like the hijacking of *Bus 174*, or the dysfunctional family of *Capturing the Friedmans*. In terms of style, some are controlled, formally restrained, almost 'classical': *Être et avoir*, *Touching the Void* and *Suite Habana* are examples – here the film-maker remains outside the frame, concentrating fully on the characters. Others take a more anarchic or postmodernist approach to both visual style and narrative: examples here include the profusion of imagery in *Les Glaneurs et la Glaneuse* (2000), *The Five Obstructions* or *Tarnation*, and these films are not only highly self-reflexive, but make constant play on the frisson of juxtaposing the most diverse kinds of images. The films of Nick Broomfield and Michael Moore, as well as titles like *Super Size Me* (2004) and *The Yes Men*, represent a mode of political reportage in which the film-maker's personality invades the film, which consequently becomes highly performative; the style, which has strong resonance in the US, is highly gendered but also adopts a satirical and ironic stance. Everywhere there are also films – some of the most inventive and delightful – which challenge the concept of documentary altogether by mixing up documentary and fiction in such a way that the film is both and neither at the same time: paradigmatic titles here include *Dear Diary*, Abbas Kiarostami's *Close Up* (1990), Patrick Keiller's *London* (1994) and Avi Mograbi's *Happy Birthday Mr Mograbi* (1999).

Despite these divergences, there is a common thread running through many of these films in their emphasis on performance. This has a double aspect, that of the subject, and in many of these titles, also that of the film-maker. On the one hand, there is the question of the subject's relation to the camera, the form and degree of self-projection, the idea of the photogenic to which the subject tries to appeal, the readiness to speak, or to speak out. On the other, the figure of the film-maker in person, on screen, self-projecting, sometimes in the role of a clown. The old bugbear in the critique of documentary was that the camera isn't to be trusted because it doesn't just capture what's there, it elicits performances from people. (When Don Pennebaker was criticised for this over his portrayal of Bob Dylan in *Don't Look Back*, he replied, if I recall correctly, that of course Dylan was performing, 'he was playing himself, and doing it very well'.) In the new mode the objection is mitigated by the sight of film-maker and subjects interacting. In *Derrida*, for example, the impeccable performance of the French philosopher trying not to perform, but nonetheless revealing his narcissism (of which he is perfectly aware), is matched by the constant self-reflexive interventions of the film-makers, which repeatedly reveal their naivety (which is partly cultivated for the benefit of the camera). If the film-maker's performance on screen often parodies the reporter or the presenter at the helm of the prestige television series, it can also become a critique of their presumptuous certainties; although when Michael Moore, employing a persona designed for the camera, makes a practice of bumbling buffoonery, he is more manipulative than may first appear. Sometimes it doesn't work out so well: Oliver Stone's *Comandante* (2003), where multiple cameras film his encounter with an ageing Fidel Castro, ends up little more than one megalomaniac interviewing another. On the other hand, there is Agnès Varda filming *Les Glaneurs et la Glaneuse* (2000) by herself, in which the film-maker with her hand-held digital camera composes a thoughtful and reflective dialogue with what she gleans about gleaners, making it a marvellous metaphor for the documentary endeavour as such.

With today's video stores beginning to stock a few independent documentaries, there are also new digital carriers – tape, disc, the internet – which are stimulating a variety of initiatives, new means of reaching the public and finding or creating audiences. Although swamped by the entertainment movie and popular television shows, these new networks of dissemination provide space for documentary work of many different kinds, long and short, ensuring that documentary not only refuses to die but even flourishes. The question arises: can the documentary idiom remain the same in these different scenarios of production and consumption? Or do these migrations have something to do with the way the idiom of documentary has changed while film theory wasn't looking?

Clearly, documentary has undergone a series of shifts in both the technology of production and the spaces of reception, to which there corresponds a multiplication of modes of address and orientation towards the audience, in which different ways of shooting and different spaces of viewing imply offerings of different types, and the cultivation of different expectations on the part of the viewer. This would suggest that meaning and significance depend on the viewer's situation: they are not inscribed behind the emulsion or in the pixels, and cannot be measured like the silver quotient or the disk space required; we are not talking of physical but of semiotic properties, and of the cultural systems and social and political movements to which they belong. Semiotic analysis enjoins us to remember that the screen is not a window, what we see on it are signs, and signs are always – in large part – already culturally encoded. If documentary begins in what Kracauer called 'the seizure of reality', then afilmic reality – the world that exists independently of the camera – should not be confused with profilmic reality – the scene to which the lens is exposed. The one is not a direct translation of the other but a necessarily incomplete segmentation, which is coded (or partly coded) through the double function of index and icon. As index the moving image renders natural or literal meanings, the forms and configurations we readily identify as they reach our eyes. As icon the picture is subject to stylistic predilections, cultural conventions, social norms, aesthetic ambiguity, symbolic connotations. Associations and connotations are combined according to the quasi-linguistic rules of attraction between successive images which we know as montage, but these are rules that are constantly being broken, transgressed and, just as importantly, re-invented. But in this way we learn to see the world around us afresh.

IV

The trends sketched out in these paragraphs have been multiplied by digital video: compact cameras with competent sound, computer editing, the internet as a medium of publicity and now dissemination, video projectors and screens which allow the public exhibition of documentaries in many different kinds of space, from big cinemas to small art galleries – spaces which imply different forms of attention and thus elicit different kinds of documentary. The art gallery, big or small, is not a comfortable place to watch a screen, but the last few years have seen major installations, by both film-makers and gallery artists, of impeccable but original documentary quality, some of them multiscreen, which provide a form of space and time for their subjects which is unusual and unlikely in more traditional settings. Indeed the gallery environment induces a different way of looking, of seeing screens as pictures which move and speak, rather than the film as a complete work to be watched from beginning to end. Kutlug Ataman's installation at London's Serpentine Gallery in 2003 comprised seven videos of many hours' length of a whole variety of people talking about themselves: the visitor moves around the gallery, watching and listening to each for a while in turn, assembling their own montage as they go; however long or short the time spent in the gallery, the result is a very different impression of modern Turkey from the stereotypes of the mass media. Aleksander Sokurov's account of a Russian army unit stationed at the Afghan border, *Spiritual Voices* (1995), consists of five segments of differing lengths (the shortest 33 minutes, the longest 90) playing alongside each other, which mesmerise the viewer into a unique evocation of the peculiar suspension of time in conditions of war. Susan Hiller's *J-Street Project* (2005) includes an hour-long video consisting of nothing but street scenes of all the roads in Germany which still carry names like 'Jew Street' or Lane or Place or what-have-you; here the temporality is that of the submerged historical memory.

   In short, digital video has been hugely enabling, for both economic and aesthetic reasons, and has been accompanied by huge growth in minimal cost production, which circulates in the world outside television, and since the launch of YouTube in 2005, has exploded onto the internet (where agents are now searching for the next big talent). But none of these developments are quite straightforward. For example, the films that enter international cinema distribution are limited by the predilections of the same monopolistic distributors who dominate both entertainment and art cinema. Film and video work which eschews these values in favour of unusual demands on the viewer rarely find favour. But theatrical dissemination has also been impeded because this requires the video to be transferred to 35mm film. Although the job can now be done very effectively, relative to the low production costs it's also expensive. (In the case of my own film about Detroit (*Detroit, Ruin of a City*, 2005), a transfer to 35mm would have cost more than our £15,000 production budget, so we opted for a DVD edition which only cost a third of that.) The independent producer can rarely afford such expense, and therefore needs a distributor, but finding a distributor means entering a marketplace which is in a state of confusion, precisely because digital video introduces new channels of sales and distribution.

According to recent reports, DVD sales in countries like the US and UK are beginning to outstrip cinema admissions and it turns out that the benefits are not limited to the likes of Blockbuster. The growing circulation of DVDs which can be easily purchased over the internet has also benefited independent production, including documentary. A few big successes have raised the stakes and there are now more feature documentaries entering the cinema than ever before; even more are turning up at film festivals without achieving the goal of cinema distribution, many of which will circulate by alternate means. According to one report, between 1996 and 2002 an average of fifteen documentaries were distributed theatrically in the US each year.

> With limited releases and little advertising, a box-office gross of a million dollars was considered good business, a figure achieved by roughly four films in any year, but still only a quarter of what was deemed respectable for an independent narrative film.[25]

But in 2003, the number of releases nearly tripled, and climbed to fifty the following year, amounting to roughly 10 per cent of the total number of releases. Nine of these films exceeded a million at the box office, led by Michael Moore's *Fahrenheit 9/11*, but this was exceptional in the scale of its release, opening in over 850 theatres.

If documentary cinema exhibition is held back by the cost of 35mm prints, in some places exhibition practices are beginning to change, as art houses install video projection. This still only covers a small circuit, but it hugely reduces the costs of distribution. The numbers seem fairly insignificant compared to the commercial mass market, yet the new documentary plays a vital role in a public sphere denuded and distorted by the negative tendencies of the mass media to contain debate within the narrowest limits. When the real exchange of ideas is replaced by the mere semblance of discussion, delivered with the authority of the broadcaster to an audience unable to take part in it, the result is what Jürgen Habermas has called the pseudo-public sphere. In this perspective, it is striking that in the US – where the mass media are the most thoroughly dominated by corporate interests and usually disciplined into promoting the administration on duty – some of the biggest recent documentary successes have been explicitly political. Michael Moore is only the most prominent of these film-makers; other recent titles include *The Corporation* (Mark Achbar and Jennifer Abbott, 2003), *Outfoxed* (Robert Greenwald, 2004) and *Unconstitutional* (Nonny de la Peña, 2004). In a discussion of the documentary phenomenon in a recent issue of the independent New York film magazine *Cinéaste*, while one contributor suggested 'three negative reasons for the current popularity of political documentary – Bush, Hollywood and television', another reported that when Morgan Spurlock, the director of *Super Size Me* (2004), told a festival audience, 'We live in a world where independent documentary film has truly become the last bastion of free speech', he won a round of applause from a packed house.[26] While this is not a return to the militancy of the 60s and 70s, it animates the critique of neoliberal hegemony, contesting authority and catalysing debate, and a good part of the new documentary audience represents a growing constituency of ideological resisters.

Documentary is ready to take up the political challenge because politics is in its genes, though not always expressed. But the documentary camera is always pointing directly at the social and the anthropological, spaces where the lifeworld is dominated, controlled and shaped by power and authority, sometimes visible, mostly invisible but often palpable. This also means that documentary addresses itself to the spectator quite differently from fiction. Fiction movies, inheriting the narrative paradigms of nineteenth-century novel and drama, bourgeois forms modified by cinema's populist vocation, appeal directly to the spectator's emotional and sentimental life, their private subjectivity – even when dealing with public, historical or political subjects. Documentary, on the other hand, speaks to the viewer as citizen, as a member of the social collective, as putative participant in the public sphere. The public sphere is its home ground. Or as Paula Rabinowitz puts it, classical Hollywood narrative binds its spectators through psychologically motivated characters and conventions which enhance verisimilitude and invite the viewer's identification. The apparatus situates the viewer as the subject of a desire which is private and internal. By contrast, the documentary mobilises the viewer as a social subject, situated in history. 'This subject clearly desires too, but the desire is directed toward the social and political arenas of everyday experiences as well as toward world-historic events shaping those lives,' and away from the psychological manifestations 'which characterize the fetishistic forms of narrative desire'. She adds that this is not to pose a clear-cut distinction between inner and outer forms of desire,[27] but to suggest that these are interpolated differently in fiction and in documentary, which make different kinds of claims about reality.

There is an important rider: to be political in this sense is not a question of advancing an ideological position, militating for a cause or campaigning for anything, it isn't even necessary to mention politics – because what the documentary can do is to call public attention to its subjects and concerns sometimes just by bringing them to light, without being wrapped in the narrative plots of fiction and drama, but turning stereotypes back into real people with their own names and in their own living environment. In a world dominated by fantasy images, the return of documentary is therefore a healthy sign of a return to reality – although once again it's not so simple. For example, first-person political documentary is liable to encourage the narcissism of a Michael Moore or a Nick Broomfield, and the result is a form of enquiry which betrays both the political impotence of the enquirer and the loss of an organised radical political culture to orient their critique.

Yet the fact remains that documentary represents an intervention in public debate which because of new technologies is capable of escaping both prescription and proscription. Another important thing about this effect is that it also operates on the local level. A report by Amy Hardie cites an example in Italy where the producer has developed his own distribution strategy: to 'put some small amounts into local television advertising, because this is a local film, in a local dialect, of Padua, and arrange screenings just in this area. We will get an audience of 10,000 and that will be enough.' Hardie concludes that the development of digital technology encourages the ambitions of low-budget feature documentaries; the low break-even point allows the small box-office returns to become a viable option. Another example of how this works is Phil Grabsky's *The Boy Who Plays on the Buddhas of Bamiyan* (2002). Grabsky, an experienced professional, had been approached to make a one-hour television film about the possible reconstruction of the Buddhas of Bamiyan which had been destroyed by the Taliban, but then he decided 'that wasn't the story': the story was those people who still lived alongside the destroyed statues. So he took off by himself and, working with only a fixer, ended up with a documentary feature which no one had commissioned, but which was then picked up for both television and cinema.[28] Another instance is *West of the Tracks* (2002) by Wang Bing, a young film graduate making his first film, an extraordinary three-part epic, running in toto some nine hours, about the abandoned industrial district of Tiexi in Shenyang. According to one writer, who calls it 'without question the greatest work to have come out of the Chinese documentary movement', 'digital video, freeing the director for a one-man working style, allowed Wang Bing to complete his film in total independence, without obligation to studios, the state or any other institution'.[29] In Iran, an independent documentary by Masoud Dehnamaki, *Poverty and Immorality*, dealing sympathetically with Tehran's prostitutes, was officially banned but circulated in the form of 'bootleg' copies, and excerpts were broadcast by an opposition satellite television channel operating from outside the country.[30] In short, even in countries where access to official screens is strictly controlled, digital video and alternative dissemination make the new documentary possible.

Digital video is not always used, however, for the purpose of free debate and social advocacy. Convergence is not about the convenience of the independent film-maker but the construction of a global consumer market, where people discover other uses, and not just those traditionally promoted by the consumer press and television shows of people's video funnies. On the back of this market came the 'camcorder' and the 'handicam' – a video camera you can hold with one hand – and most recently, video cameras incorporated into mobile phones. The results include amateur pornography and brief glimpses of the scene of natural disasters or bomb attacks which make their way onto the television news. They include the videos which various terrorist groups nowadays shoot of their activities and disseminate through the internet and on videocassette, and then again, those filmed by the occupation troops. One of these, which appeared on British television in February 2006 but was shot in 2004, shows an incident in which British troops are seen chasing a number of Iraqis into a military compound where they kick, punch and head-butt them. The soldier behind the camera gives a running commentary, laughing and shouting obscene encouragement.[31] This is not just a bit of snatched footage, but a fashioned piece of work to which the videographer has added, on the soundtrack, the bombastic strains of Wagner.

At the opposite end of the ideological spectrum, there is the reflorescence of documentary in Argentina in the midst of the country's nightmare collapse in 2001. This was a case of poetic justice, since it was partly the product of the film schools which mushroomed in Argentina during the 1990s – both private and public – which in turn were a product of the same neoliberal economic policies that eventually produced the collapse of the banks, but only after allowing people to buy the latest video gear relatively cheaply and pay for courses in how to use it. With the *Argentinazo* of December 2001, the banks put up shutters, the country defaulted on its international debt and got through five presidents in twelve days, and the result, as Guillermo De Carli wrote to me, was that 'documentary has been boosted by an explosive reality', as young film-makers, now in full possession of the means of production, needed no funding or commissions to go out on the streets and film. The movement became known as *cine piquetero*, after the *piquetes* – the picketers who make their voices heard by blocking roads and bridges. The most interesting things were happening, from spontaneous videos which recorded the popular mobilisations and the *cacerolazos* (the extraordinary protest marches of house-wives and old women bashing their pots and pans), which were then sold on the streets from stalls piled with copies, to 'film-makers who are turning to documentary, and who discover a know-how, even a certain Argentinian tradition, going back to the work of Raymundo Gleyzer in the 1960s, in the way of presenting or narrating what is going on'.[32]

Fernando Solanas, the old man of third cinema, went to speak at meetings of the new movement, praising them for their passion, and for showing what never gets seen on television, even calling them the heirs of third cinema. Wishful thinking? It is not as if the new documentarists themselves claim such allegiance, in part because their knowledge of the 60s and its models is limited, and in part because the political conjuncture has shifted, but a year after the *Argentinazo*, as many as forty groups of video film-makers were working alongside the local assemblies, the workers' cooperatives who took control of bank-rupt firms and the women's groups, all of which came to function with a dynamic which is not usually found under capitalism. Ranging from short reportage to full-length documentaries, *cine piquetero* shares the popular dynamic, and presents a vivid panorama of both the extent of popular action and its sheer inventiveness. The work was shown at factories, community movement assemblies, local cafés and street festivals, but not on television or in the cinemas. Screened in meetings and assemblies, in parks and on the streets, bypassing the official media entirely, it entered a parallel and alterative public sphere outside the channels and tributaries of parliamentary democracy, which is rooted instead in the popular move-ment itself. In short, the people in these videos are representing themselves (and telling their elected rep-resentatives to leg it: '¡Que se vayan todos!' – 'Let them all go!') with consequent effects on the form of address which these videos elaborate. Where Nichols has summarised the conventional form of docu-mentary address as 'I talk to you about them',[33] here, even those which have individual credits take the form 'we talk to each other about us'. This is not unlike the indigenous video movement which began in Brazil in the late 1980s and now encompasses several countries, where indigenous communities use video to speak to each other, and sometimes to their Others, in a direct mode of address.

Like the indigenous video movement, the new political video in Argentina covers a wide range of forms and styles, from short reports on particular events to the music video, but the basis is what might be called 'participant reportage': fluid hand-held camera, direct sound, street interviews, the same ingre-dients as television reportage but put together differently: often without commentary, cross-cut with found images taken from television and the press, edited with a sense of irony and deconstructive intent, and often backed by the new Argentinian rock music. In short, the pervading spirit of the dynamic of popular protest on the streets, especially the *escrache*. This is a *lunfardo*, or slang word, for a kind of fiesta of public shaming and denunciation. The practice was begun by the organisation HIJOS (Children of the Disappeared), who would suddenly turn up outside the house of a former military torturer, for example, and mount a kind of performance in the street, with several hours of drumming and slogans, music, parades, pamphlets, even street theatre. Some of those being denounced, the *escrachados*, hid themselves away, others fled; some responded with bullets. After December 2001, *escraches* began to be mounted against politicians, banks and the mass media. The extraordinary spectacle of the *escrache* can be seen in several videos and its spirit pervades the whole movement, so that it could perhaps be called *video escrache* – a style which brings to the screen the same energy and popular feeling, the same mixture of elements and symbolic gestures. The world's eyes, the global media, soon turned away from Argentina's plight, but not the new documentarists, for whom their cameras were once again weapons in a struggle for survival which testifies to resistance in the face of adversity. This kind of production has yet to circulate easily across the national boundaries, even though these can now be overcome in cyberspace. Here video is a medium which functions very well precisely at the local level, where exhibition and distribution can be carried out with few resources, and the work can most directly challenge national television and its hegemonic ideologies of consensus politics. However, the local level is to be found everywhere, and alternative circuits of video distribution are opening up all over the place, on every continent. In the various scenarios which are now evolving for video, including its migration to the internet which is just beginning, the old canons of the institutional documentary are once again being thrown into question, and new methodologies and ways of working are emerging, there in the interstices, where they are always born.

Notes

1. *Bowling for Columbine* (Michael Moore, USA, 2002); *The Gleaners and I* (Agnès Varda, France, 2001); *Derrida* (Kirby Dick and Amy Ziering Kofman, USA, 2002); *Spellbound* (Jeffrey Blitz, USA, 2002); *Être et avoir* (Nicolas Philibert, France, 2002); *The Five Obstructions* (Lars von Trier and Jørgen Leth, Denmark, 2003); *Bus 174* (José Padilha, Brazil, 2004); *Capturing the Friedmans* (Andrew Jarecki, USA, 2003); *Touching the Void* (Kevin Macdonald, UK, 2003).

2. *El sol del membrillo* (Victor Erice, 1993); *Monos como Becky* (Joaquin Jorda, 1999); *En construcción* (José Luis Guerín, 2001).

3. *The Thin Blue Line* (Errol Morris, USA, 1988); *Roger and Me* (Michael Moore, USA, 1989); *In Bed with Madonna* (Alek Keshishian, USA, 1991); *Hoop Dreams* (Steve James, USA, 1994).

4. Boyd Tonkin, *New Statesman*, 30 August 1996, p. 38.

5. Michael Atkinson, 'Fact Finders', *Guardian Guide*, 2 May 1998.

6. David Gritten, 'Why Truth Is Stronger than Fiction', *Telegraph*, 28 June 2003; *Guardian*, 23 July 2004, third editorial.

7. Walter Benjamin, 'The Work of Art in the Age of Mechanical Reproduction', in Hannah Arendt (ed.), *Illuminations* (New York: Shocken Books, 1969), p. 233.

8. Dai Vaughan, 'The Broken Trust of the Image', *Vertigo* no. 4, 1994/5, pp. 16–20.

9. Ludwig Wittgenstein, *Philosophical Investigations* (Oxford: Blackwell, 1963), p. 32e, § 66.

10. Gritten, 'Why Truth Is Stronger than Fiction'.

11. Blake Morrison, 'Back to Reality', *Guardian*, 5 March 2004.

12. Morrison, 'Back to Reality'.

13. Gritten, 'Why Truth Is Stronger than Fiction'.

14. Amy Hardie, Docspace Report, March 2002.

15. Dai Vaughan, *Television Documentary Usage* (London: BFI, 1976), p. 19.

16. Roger Graef, 'Reel Life Changes', *Guardian*, 27 November 2006.

17. Charlotte Raven, 'Know Nothing about Afghanistan? Blame the Death of the Documentary', *Guardian*, 30 October 2001.

18.   Gritten, 'Why Truth Is Stronger than Fiction'.

19.   *The Yes Men* (Dan Ollman, Sarah Price, Chris Smith, USA, 2003). Personal communication from Andy
       Bichlbaum and Mike Bonanno.

20.   Pat Aufderheide, 'Copywrongs', *In These Times*, 25 January 2005, <www.inthesetimes.com>.

21.   Fernando Solanas and Octavio Getino, 'Towards a Third Cinema', in Michael Chanan (ed.), *Twenty Five
       Years of the New Latin American Cinema* (London: BFI/Channel 4, 1983). First appeared in *Tricontinental*,
       published in Paris in October 1969.

22.   Robert Stam, '*The Hour of the Furnaces* and the Two Avant Gardes', in Julianne Burton (ed.), *The Social
       Documentary in Latin America* (Pittsburgh, PA: University of Pittsburgh Press, 1990), p. 253.

23.   See Michael Chanan, 'The Changing Geography of Third Cinema', *Screen* vol. 38 no. 4, 1997.

24.   Jonathan Romney, 'What's Up, Doc?', *Guardian*, 19 August 1997.

25.   Paul Arthur, 'Extreme Makeover: The Changing Face of Documentary', *Cinéaste* vol. 30 no. 3, Summer
       2005, pp. 18–23.

26.   *Cinéaste* vol. 30 no. 3, Summer 2005: Thom Andersen on p. 32, Pat Aufderheide on p. 27.

27.   Paula Rabinowitz, 'Wreckage upon Wreckage: History, Documentary and the Ruins of Memory',
       History and Theory vol. 32 no. 2, May 1993, p. 129.

28.   See <www.theboywhoplaysonthebuddhasofbamiyan.co.uk/director.htm>.

29.   Lu Xinyu, 'Ruins of the Future', *New Left Review* no. 31 (second series), Jan/Feb 2005, pp. 126, 127.

30.   *New York Times*, 26 November 2005,
       <www.nytimes.com/2005/11/26/international/middleeast/26dehnamaki.html?8hpib>.

31.   See <news.bbc.co.uk/go/pr/fr/-/1/hi/uk/6230711.stm>.

32.   Personal communication.

33.   See Bill Nichols, *Introduction to Documentary* (Bloomington, IN: Indiana University Press, 2001),
       p. 13f.

2 The Documentary Field

On the problems of defining the documentary

I

A few years ago at a conference, a Polish scholar who had participated in the Solidarity movement fifteen years earlier, captured the paradoxical quality of the documentary in an autobiographical comment on the changing look of the films which portrayed the events of the day. 'By contrast with the tight control over television news exercised by the Communist regime', said Wieslaw Godzic,

> the documentaries of Solidarity really represented to us the truth. But all these years later, I can also say that they represent a series of myths, about notions like 'the man in the street', which we experienced at the time as the reality.[1]

Bound up in this conundrum are certain questions about the nature of documentary that have come to the fore in the period since the Solidarity films were made – doubts, confusions and misgivings which it seems that the ethos of postmodernism has made into a constant liability. There has been a loss of faith in the legitimacy of the documentary claim on the real, in which the form has succumbed to a general disbelief in the possibility of objective truth, at least as formerly understood. In plain terms, the documentary film appears to assert the veracity, the truth value of its images, yet considered over a period of time, the documentary genre – if genre is the right word – gives the impression that truth is always already relative. What the remarks of the Polish scholar suggest is that the reason is not necessarily to be found within the documentary itself, but is a consequence rather of the changing perspectives of lived experience – or in a word, of history, and the way it positions and repositions the viewer. One of the symptoms of this condition is that documentaries tend to suffer a problem of dating, as if the older the film, the more quaint it looks – and often the more apparent the ideology which informs it. The corollary is that documentary also becomes a strange new form of historical evidence with an elusive character, in which the immediate sight of the past (or the present which becomes historical through the act of filming it) is mediated by the contexts in which it is made and then seen – a shifting relationship between the subject, the apparatus, the film-maker, the medium, the viewer and the viewer's situation, which may well produce unexpected effects. As Laura Mulvey has recently written, to look back into the reality of lost worlds by means of the cinema 'is to have the sensation of looking into a time machine. However clichéd the concept, the presence of that reality, of the past preserved, becomes increasingly magical and uncanny.'[2]

But these effects are hardly accidental. To begin with, the production of documentary is constantly affected and reshaped by a process which cultural theorists Jay David Bolter and Richard Grusin have called remediation, whereby the formats of the media which carry the representation are constantly evolving, thereby altering the character of the representation. New or modified formats present themselves as improved versions of old media, and old media, rather than disappearing, refashion themselves in response to the challenge of the new.[3] So it happened that the idea of documentary had scarcely been formulated when the coming of film sound in the late 1920s changed the groundrules – but not initially to the advantage of documentary. Then, at the end of the 50s, when the difficulties of location sound recording were swept away by a new generation of equipment – hand-held 16mm cameras synchronised with portable magnetic tape recorders – and documentary acquired a new power of direct speech, it was as if it re-invented itself. The effects of video two decades later were less dramatic, given the poor technical quality of the first generation of equipment, until the arrival of digital video and computer editing in the 90s managed almost totally to displace the technology of cinematography just as it approached its centenary. One of the effects of this unfolding process is that the old images preserved in the archives not only tend to reveal their historical character but also their materiality – which renders their mediation evident – while new formats are experienced as re-creating immediacy, 'getting closer' to the reality which they record, or apparently even capturing it for the first time in its fullness. This is half the history of documentary.

The logic of remediation, however, is not the same as technological determinism – the notion that technological development is the principal agent of these changes, or as Brian Winston puts it, 'What the technology *can* deliver is what the technology *will* deliver and users will adopt'[4] – a position that reduces the aesthetic to the effect of technical possibilities or constraints; this is a mechanical argument which always overstates the case and from which many commentators shy away, although it often returns through the backdoor, so to speak. But as the age of film blurs into the age of video, it becomes increasingly difficult to deny that all media representation is the product of technologies which are in continuous flux, and which therefore play havoc with our sense of what is represented. In 1898 one Boleslaw Matuszewski argued that perhaps the cinematograph doesn't give the whole story but at least it's unquestionable. 'Ordinary photography allows retouching which can go as far as transformation, but try retouching in an identical way' every one of thousands of frames.[5] A hundred years later, after the arrival of digital video and computer editing, this argument is no longer persuasive. However, there are limits. In 2001, when technicians at Industrial Light and Magic were asked if the video of Osama bin Laden transmitted on Al-Jazeerah Television could have been faked, John Dykstra, who shared the Oscar for the special effects in *Star Wars*, admitted:

> No, we could not possibly fake that tape. We can show you alien planets, make dinosaurs walk the earth, perfectly lip-sync a talking pig, have Forrest Gump shake hands with John F. Kennedy and make Harry Potter play airborne racquetball on a goddam broomstick, but there's no imaginable way we could fake a conversation between two men in a plain room with soft focus and fuzzy sound. There's just no way.[6]

And the other half of the history? There is another implication in the Polish scholar's remarks, namely, that documentary is a battleground of social and historical truth, and this is one of the main reasons why people make them. The official reportage was contested and impugned by the films made on behalf of Solidarity itself, which, like other political and social movements before and since, considered having films to represent and propagate their views to be a valuable enterprise. Does this mean that the Solidarity films only amount to propaganda? Is the term counter-propaganda any better? Independent documentary has always been driven by engagement, either political or social. As Louis Menand puts it in a review of Michael Moore's Bush exposé *Fahrenheit 9/11* in 2004,

> It's not surprising that documentary-makers have usually worked in a spirit of advocacy. They are people sufficiently committed to a point of view to go to the trouble of obtaining expensive equipment, carting it into the field, shooting miles of film under often unpleasant or dangerous conditions, and spending months or years splicing the results into a coherent movie. It's easier to write an editorial. It's easier, even, to write a book . . . They make movies because they are passionate about their subjects and they want to arouse passion in others

– and this, he adds, has 'something to do with the nature of documentary'.[7] Should these contestatory documentaries not be considered something more than half-truths in the name of political rhetoric? Or is it that documentary is a form that turns truth and truth-telling into propaganda's tools and weapons? Does this mean that all truth is thus revealed as relative? What about documentaries that are intended not as propaganda at all but, say, as essays in poetic expression or didactic demonstrations of scientific findings? There are traps in these questions, like the assumption that poetry, truth and propaganda are mutually exclusive categories, which of course is no more true of documentary than it is of fiction. Only that in documentary, precisely because of its implicit truth claims, it becomes more problematic.

Undoubtedly, at the beginning of this history, documentary was widely greeted by a simple trust in the veracity of the image which is nowadays adjudged naive, and not only by critics, but as if every postmodern viewer has learned that the empirical is not always what it seems. (There is also a suspicion among theorists that film and its effects, and the media system to which film belongs, has something to do with this condition of uncertainty.) In fact the first tentative critiques of the transparency of the image already arose in the 1920s, especially in revolutionary Russia where film-makers coming to the art from theatre, literature and other fields – Eisenstein, Kuleshov, Pudovkin, Vertov, Shub, Shklovsky, Brik and the rest – engaged in intense debate about the new medium in a spirit which questioned the ideological assumptions to be found in nineteenth-century notions of realism. Here were film-makers not afraid of theoretical argument – on the contrary, they considered it an integral element of research into the nature and potential of the new artform – who thus occupy a singular position in both the history of cinema and its theoretical investigation. While the division of cinema into fiction and non-fiction was something they took as elementary, a symposium organised by the journal 'New Lef' in 1927 heard the writer Sergei Tretiakov argue that even in what he called the 'raw material' of the newsreel there are gradations of distortion (and in particular, Vertov's work could hardly be called pure newsreel). Apparently the Russians didn't yet have the term 'documentary', and Viktor Shklovsky thought that instead of dividing cinema into newsreels and fiction films, it would be more useful to speak of story and non-story films; others spoke of staged and unstaged.[8] Such distinctions, once posed, will never go away, but as yet the debate is caught up in the same concept of reality that it means to critique, since to speak of distortion is to remain within the notion that there is such a thing as the undistorted. As we shall see, however, talk of distortion renders documentary a hostage to a different kind of fortune than it deserves.

That problems like these make the documentary a highly awkward form to evaluate is probably one of the reasons it is under-represented both in orthodox versions of film history and, until recently, in critical film theory. If the sudden explosion of studies on documentary in the last few years demonstrates that nevertheless these are signal problems in contemporary culture – indeed nothing shows more emblematically the growth of scepticism over the course of the twentieth century than our attitude towards the documentary – on the other hand, discussion has been hampered by poor historical knowledge of its evolution. Thus it comes about that ten years after Bill Nichols brought out his influential book *Representing Reality*, more or less the first of these new critical studies, he would be criticised for providing documentary with a false genealogy which has been too readily accepted.[9] In the view of Stella Bruzzi, he had imposed a theoretical model on documentary history in which what he calls the classic expository style comes first, rather arbitrarily attributed to the 1930s.[10] To speak only of that same decade, this model lumps together films as various as Buñuel's parody of a travelogue *Land without Bread* (1933), the artful public service documentary *Night Mail* (1936), the equally artful militant political reportage of *The Spanish Earth* by Joris Ivens, and the swish *March of Time* newsreels, the corporate voice of *Time-Life* – even though the fact that they all use commentary is practically the only thing they have in common. It also fails to recognise what came before that, especially the 'city' films of the likes of Paul Strand (*Manhatta*, 1921), Walter Ruttmann (*Berlin, Symphony of a City*, 1927), Alberto Cavalcanti (*Rien que les heures*, 1926), Dziga Vertov (*Man with a Movie Camera*), Joris Ivens (*The Bridge* and *Rain*) and Jean Vigo (*À propos de Nice*), all made before the coming of sound.

One explanation for this forgetfulness, of course, is precisely that these examples from the 1920s belong to silent cinema and the prehistory of documentary, which was long ago relegated to the archives from which a few films occasionally emerge for special screenings; this was certainly true until recently, when some of them have appeared on DVD. Much lip service is paid, for example, to the pioneering work of Soviet film-makers of silent days, yet only one or two of Vertov's films are ever seen nowadays and Esfir Shub earns hardly more than a footnote in the histories. But the problem is the same after the introduction of the sound film. A few famous titles from the 30s and 40s (*Night Mail*, *Listen to Britain* [1941], etc.) stand in for the celebrated British documentary movement, while important documentaries from the 50s by subsequently well-known feature directors like Georges Franju or Alain Resnais or Lindsay Anderson are mostly known only by repute (sometimes one of their documentaries is included as an extra on a DVD release of one of their features). Both Ivens and Jean Rouch are known, if at all, by only the smallest fraction of their immense and crucial work spanning many decades. However, it is not as if we need a new 'great figures' version of history: the point is that if this history is in a sketchy and hapless state, then it is evidence of another basic fact about documentary: its marginalisation from cinema as a commercial institution, its enforced absence from the entertainment film market as the exhibitors excluded it, a trend already evident in the 1920s, which nowadays has another consequence. Despite the growing number of new wave documentaries now being released on DVD, the catalogues remain mostly bare of those from earlier periods (except for big-budget television series, especially on natural history and war), a state of affairs which reinforces historical ignorance in all but a small tribe of aficionados. If it would only be aesthetic justice to restore these film-makers to their historical place, the importance of doing so would be to rediscover the significance of their films as paradigms in the evolution of documentary language and form, not as the 'masterworks' of old-fashioned talk, but as 'exemplary texts' for analysis. Since this is spirit of the accounts given here of individual films, a rider is necessary: these films are not generally found in the mainstream, which is where experimental departures in style and technique are recuperated and codified.

In this perspective the coming of sound indeed represents a break, but of a kind and significance that remains to be ascertained. The history of cinema is interrupted by what Fredric Jameson has called this embarrassing 'fact', which seems to divide film into 'two distinct evolutionary species or sub-species – *silent* and *sound* – of which the latter, like the Cromagnons, drove the former out and made it extinct'.[11] Whether this discontinuity has the same repercussions on documentary as on fiction should not be assumed, and we shall investigate it in due course; on the other hand, one thing remains the same: the history of documentary after the break remains just as obscure. The result is a particular kind of historical unfolding in which major films, with strong influence on the next generation, quickly get forgotten and fall out of circulation, leaving almost no time for the formation of the kind of canon which usually operates in any artistic field. The effect was exacerbated by the migration of documentary to television in the 1950s, where it became part of the evanescent flow of programmes, as ephemeral as journalism and again rapidly disappearing into the big black hole of the archives, from which a few are only just now beginning, very selectively, to emerge; in Britain alone, major film-makers lost in this way include names like Dennis Mitchell and Philip Donnellan. One of the symptoms of this amnesia is that new generations of documentary film-makers are less in touch with the history of documentary cinema than their counterparts in fiction, and documentary is fated, as we shall see, to be continually re-inventing itself, for both good and bad.

II

The marginalisation of the documentary seems to have gone with a prejudice against it even on the part of the most astute of theorists. Christian Metz, for example, one of the first cine semiologists – hence one of the founders of modern critical film theory – argued in the 1960s that narrative was privileged. We know, he said, that when cinematography was invented in 1895,

> critics, journalists, and the pioneer cinematographers disagreed considerably among themselves as to the *social function* that they attributed to, or predicted for, the new machine: whether it was a means of preservation or of making archives, whether it was an auxiliary technography for research and teaching in sciences like botany or surgery, whether it was a new form of journalism, or an instrument of sentimental devotion, either private or public, which could perpetuate the living image of the dear departed one, and so on. That, over all these possibilities, the cinema could evolve into a machine for telling stories had never really been considered.

But the merging of cinema and narrativity, said Metz, 'was a great . . . historical and social fact, a fact of civilisation', with the effect, among other things, that

> all nonnarrative genres – the documentary, the technical film, etc. – have become marginal provinces, border regions so to speak, while the *feature-length film of novelistic fiction*, which is simply called a 'film' – the usage is significant – has traced more and more clearly the king's highway of filmic expression.[12]

Although in broad terms this is obviously correct, it is worth prising this argument apart a little, because the consequence is not only the neglect accorded to documentaries but also to documentary film language. It is notable that the early uses of film that Metz mentions are all effectively forms of documentation, as if to say that the first impulse of film was not storytelling but an instinct for the record of empirical observation. It is no accident that these uses are all modelled on functions already fulfilled by both photography and the phonograph, as if the cinematograph were merely another – at the time, ultramodern – form of mechanical reproduction. If the link with photography seems obvious, John Tagg has argued that the increasing use of photography towards the end of the nineteenth century by the police and other agencies of social control served to strengthen the idea of the photograph as a form of objective record.[13] The connection with the phonograph is equally significant. Speaking of his invention of the 'talking machine' in 1877, Edison considered what would subsequently become its principal use, the reproduction of music, as merely one possibility among many, which included a dictation machine, a talking book for the blind, teaching languages and elocution, preserving the voices of the departed, speaking the time – and since Bell invented the telephone the year before, recording telephone conversations.[14] One of Edison's intentions in developing the kinetoscope, the forerunner of the cinematograph, was to provide images to go with the phonograph – a trick he was unable to realise, and which would not be accomplished for more than a quarter of a century. The film medium was thus born in the gap between a notion of the complete reproduction of sight and sound, and the technical reality of one or the other, but not both at the same time. Moreover, initially perceived as an extension of photography, the idea that moving pictures would primarily come to mean fiction was no more obvious at the moment of invention than thirty years earlier that the phonograph would develop with music.

These, then, are the seeds of documentary as a function of the medium, or as what Metz called one of the 'dialects' of cinema. This is not so far from the kind of picture we get from a previous generation of film theorists like Siegfried Kracauer, who contrasted the 'realism' of Lumière with the 'fantasy' of Méliès as if they represented alternative and fundamentally distinct modes of apprehension. Méliès himself, in his first prospectus of 1897, announced that he specialised 'mainly in fantastic or artistic scenes, reproductions of theatrical scenes, etc. . . . . thus creating a special genre which differs entirely from the customary views supplied by the cinematograph – street scenes or scenes of everyday life'. Kracauer thought that Méliès's tremendous success would seem to indicate that he catered to demands left unsatisfied by Lumière's 'photographic realism', and considered the two of them as thesis and antithesis in a Hegelian sense, in other words, as a dialectical opposition whose synthesis lies at the root of film as art.[15] Kracauer's brand of dialectics may be out of fashion, but it still contains a critical core. The screen as a representational space offers a constant interplay between different modes of appearance which present themselves conventionally as ontological antinomies: reality and illusion, realism and fantasy, story and non-story, staged and unstaged, etc. It was probably inevitable that when documentary emerged in the 1920s this dualism would be reinforced. If it was rapidly perceived as fiction's other, this is first of all because it involved the repudiation of fiction in the name of the real. Such indeed was the position taken up by Vertov and Ivens, and after them the British documentarists of the 30s – Grierson, Rotha and others – of whom Nichols observes that they 'drew harsh and unflattering comparisons' between the 'escapist, meretricious spectacles' of the fiction film industry and the social purpose and aesthetic potential of documentary.[16]

This can be seen, however, not as some inevitable contradiction – an inescapable antagonism between aesthetic absolutes – but as a prime example of what Pierre Bourdieu called the space of positions and position-taking which characterises every field of cultural production.[17] In Bourdieu's account, a cultural field is structured by conflict between different positions within it which present themselves in the shape of antinomies – like Romantic versus Classical, abstract as opposed to realist, or, in this case, fiction as against documentary. The positions within any field are several, and always imply differences from other positions in respect to questions of aesthetics and style, but they may also reflect external factors like social context and political values. Mapping these differences is an intricate affair which requires great sensitivity to what Bourdieu, borrowing the concept from medieval philosophy, calls the *habitus* – roughly speaking, the characteristic demeanour adopted by the modern social subject depending on their social identity. Where Thomas Aquinas defined 'habitus' as a mental habit or ingrained way of thinking, Bourdieu broadens it out to the stance of the individual which is conditioned by their location within the social structure, and the way this shapes their attitude. Participants in a field have a point of view on the social space of their activity which stems from their position within it; in everyday life, this is internalised and converted into corresponding dispositions. The agents of this kind of position-taking are not just the artists and writers and film-makers who adopt a particular form or style or genre, but the whole community of critics, publishers, curators, gallery directors, programmers, teachers and scholars who mediate the consumption of cultural creation in the public sphere. In short, the habitus provides a 'feeling for the game', it generates a form of practical knowledge which is not usually formulated discursively but remains largely unconscious. This is the same kind of knowledge that Marx referred to in a well-known letter to Engels, where he mentions 'learned non-guild handicraft knowledge' like sixteenth-century clock-making, which comprised an elaborate oral lore, a body of knowledge which is passed orally from master to apprentice.[18] Or in a more contemporary context, this is the 'expert knowledge' which software engineers try to extract from experienced practitioners and translate into computer language. Bourdieu's focus is the internalisation of social structures that produces appropriate behaviour in a given social context, behaviour which appears spontaneous and natural but in fact is socially conditioned, and dependent on what he calls *doxa* (here the word comes from ancient Greek): the taken-for-granted, the presuppositions and conventional wisdom which go along with the habitus.

On one level, then, everything in the following pages is a description of the positions, counter-positions, habitus, dispositions and doxa belonging to the field of documentary over its hardly 100 years of existence. The history of documentary in this perspective is a criss-cross between external and internal position-taking, beginning as an aesthetic and intellectual rebellion against the populism of commercial cinema in the 1920s which articulated the claim of documentary against both fiction and the newsreel. In the 1930s, as its practice spread, it acquired a rationale – the social conception advanced by Grierson – and a doxa in the form of a craft lore which is learned through apprenticeship in the métier. Later, when documentary migrated to television, institutional pressures required the articulation of this lore, or a good part of it, in the form of official codes of practice. At the same time, the advance of documentary quickly generated the rival claims of different types of documentary against each other, rehearsed in the polemics of film-makers, critics and columnists; these are governed by the same kind of dynamic as Bourdieu finds in the cultural field as a whole between traditional and avant-garde, conformist and iconoclast, orthodoxy and heresy. But as Bourdieu adds, 'the choice of the moment and sites of battle are left to the initiative of the challengers, who break the silence of the *doxa* and call into question the unproblematic, taken-for-granted world of the dominant groups'[19] – a role that successive generations of documentarists happily embrace.

III

The first lesson of the Polish experience – what we can call the Solidarity syndrome – is simply this: that how a film is received and read depends on where and when the screening takes place and who the viewer is. The space of viewing changes the way the symbolic representation on the screen is apprehended. A film may look very different when the space between the screen and the viewers' eyes is dissimilar, a church hall as opposed to a comfortable cinema, for example; and perhaps the study of cinema should begin with a phenomenology of the act of viewing itself, its varying qualities and modes in different spaces and circumstances. I have written elsewhere of how I once saw a work of underground cinema, Carolee Schneeman's *Fuses* (1967), first of all on a large screen at the ICA in London, and then not long afterwards, projected on the wall of her home at a party.[20] I had not much liked it the first time, but very much the second, and in retrospect it seemed clear to me that this was because of the kind of film it was: the neutral dull space of the cinema deadened something in the image, which came alive on the domestic wall. Which suggests that although the film strip remains the same, the picture contained in the image is not as stable as its chemistry. (By the way, is this autobiographical non-narrative experimental film a species of documentary, because it uses images seized from a non-fictional reality? If not, why not?)

The documentary is not just remediated by changes in the technology of production, but also by variations and changes in that of reproduction, that is, the form of consumption. The documentary has always been highly adaptable to different viewing spaces. It was born, as an artistic form, in the film clubs and art cinemas which spread across Europe in the 1920s, whose appearance constitutes the first counter-movement against the capture of cinema by the commercial criteria of big business; but this divide wasn't total, and Flaherty and Ruttman, in the USA and Germany respectively, are among those who made feature-length documentaries for commercial distribution. Meanwhile, in the Soviet Union, Vertov and his comrades were using the trains of the agitprop movement to take films to audiences in places without cinemas, holding outdoor screenings for revolutionary soldiers engaged in the civil war, and in rural villages and towns around the country. In the 30s, after the introduction of 16mm sound projectors, the British documentary movement employed 'non-theatrical' distribution, which also catered for a growing quantity of educational and sponsored films, with screenings in spaces like works canteens and church halls as well as classrooms and lecture theatres. In the 1950s, the documentary began migrating to television and thereby entered the home, although it is quite untrue that television immediately killed off documentary on the big screen – on the contrary, 16mm exhibition did service in the political resurgence of the 60s, even conquering new social spaces wherever groups and communities had use of them. Indeed Latin America at this time saw the emergence of a new documentary movement which rapidly spread throughout the continent, where there was previously no such activity to speak of. Brazil, for example, at the start of the 1980s, had an alternative circuit of some 500 film clubs. Only after television had spawned consumer video would 16mm begin to decline, to be replaced by the videocassette. Video quickly entered new spaces, like art galleries, where documentary video art is nowadays a regular feature; or in Latin America, where by the late 1980s the camcorder was being employed in Brazil to create an indigenous video movement, producing its own work dedicated to the strengthening of community-level politics, shown in the villages with the players and monitors powered by car batteries. This range of diverse exhibition practices and viewing sites speaks of the evolution of the public realm in which the idea of documentary originally took root as a discourse of the factual and the real, and which it has helped to configure, with the effect that the modern public sphere is in part defined by its practice. In this perspective, documentary is more like a moral and political force than just an artistic practice. Without it, the public sphere isn't functioning properly.

IV

What emerged in the 1920s was a range of films distinguished from fiction by their imagery of a veridical reality, films of a distinctly different ilk, looking for a term to describe them in all their diversity. If 'documentary' is the rough and ready word that came to be adopted for this purpose, then it is pertinent to enquire how this came about. When Grierson applied the word 'documentary' to Robert Flaherty's film of South Sea islanders, *Moana*, in a newspaper review in 1926, he used it as an adjective, speaking of the film's 'documentary value' as 'a visual account of events in the daily life of a Polynesian youth and his family'.[21] Within two or three years, however, it had turned into a noun, and a subtle shift of meaning took place.

Brian Winston has rehearsed the derivation.[22] As an adjective, the word 'documentary' entered the English language surprisingly late, in the early 1800s, and even 'document' as a noun, meaning 'something written, inscribed, etc., which furnished evidence or information', only dates from 1727. This word is derived from *documentum*, meaning lesson or proof, which in turn is derived from *docere*, to teach, and therefore carries the sense of demonstration or proof by inscription, like a geometrical theorem. But according to Winston, it also captures another meaning, another point of reference, since the term replaced the medieval 'muniment', from the Latin for fortification, meaning 'title deed'. The word 'document', says Winston, therefore 'speaks to the modern growth of legal rights grounded in contracts', and 'the swamping of the emerging industrial world in paper': a whole series of legal terms, 'muniment', 'affidavit', 'charter', 'memorandum', 'brief', 'writ', etc., are all incorporated under the new generic term 'document'.[23]

Not only that. In the sense of an official record giving evidence or proof, the concept effectively elided pedagogical and legal authority into one. But the legal document is different from a proof in the mathematical sense, an inscription which can be reiterated whenever necessary; it is not a universal but a particular, a unique object which represents an historical act, event or occurrence. This is the meaning which transfers to the photograph and later the moving pictures: in the process, the photographic image is taken as a guarantee of the ontological integrity of the object it portrays; the photograph indexes what actually existed. The result is an ambiguity, a slippage between two senses of evidence, evidence as demonstration, and evidence as trace, which will henceforth become constantly confused because the documentary film is both.

In French, the word *documentaire* was put to use very early, as Grierson acknowledged in the very first paragraph of his 'First Principles of Documentary', for the travelogue.[24] The designation suggested a stance of disinterested observation, a slice of real life in distant or quaint or exotic places. Films of exotic locales with an element of melodrama or adventure added in, like Edward Curtis's single production, *In the Land of the Headhunters* (1914), would be described as *documentaires romancés*, or 'romance travelogues', a term that can clearly also be applied to the films of Flaherty where the story of individual struggle for survival amid nature's hardships is indeed highly romanticised; these are the films which broke through to establish the documentary as a minor genre of the new standard type of feature film. The lesser travelogue, however, was often considered a species of *actualité*, a word which as Winston observes, 'originally meant nothing more than the conversational topics of the hour', but when applied to the cinema, 'moved from meaning "factual film" in general to obtain its current more limited sense of "newsreel"'.[25] In English, the word 'actuality' had its own derivation, first recorded in 1675, as a synonym for 'reality'; it dropped out of use as a film genre when 'newsreel' took over (only to reappear in a new guise many decades later in the television classification of 'factual', which returns us to the topics of the hour). The English term travelogue – a contraction of 'travel monologue' – was introduced by a photographer called Burton Holmes, who made his début in a slides-and-anecdotes show at the Chicago Camera Club in 1890, thus confirming the genres of early cinema as the remediation of preceding forms of popular entertainment like the magic lantern show (and perhaps a new American way with the English language).

If this small exercise in deconstruction points to some of the sources of the conceptual confusions around the term documentary as the name of a genre, it also reminds us of the diversity and impurity of its origins. When Grierson, who knew something about the endeavours of the Russians, wrote his 'First Principles' in the early 30s, he sought to distinguish 'higher' and 'lower' forms, to downgrade both bread-and-butter journalistic examples like travelogues, newsreels and magazine films, as well as the didactic form of the scientific, educational or 'lecture' film, and instead to reserve the proper use of the term for those that aspired to the virtues of art, where the film-maker moves beyond the mere collage of unthought-out material and the servile accumulation of fact to seek the relationships which hold the facts together. 'Here', he wrote, 'we pass from the plain (or fancy) descriptions of natural material, to arrangements, rearrangements, and creative shapings of it.'[26] Clearly a normative distinction, Grierson's aim was to advance a certain attitude to documentary production rather than, in practice, a particular kind of documentary. The films produced by Grierson and his unit in fact comprise a wide range of subgenres. They allowed themselves almost everything; nothing was excluded because it was done in the manner of reportage or travelogue or even enactment, as long as it had the required dose of civic purpose; such exclusion was anyway impossible, since the skills required are in every case the same, but applied in slightly different ways. The result is a body of work with the same degree of diversity already found in the 1920s, when documentary ranged from Vertov's political newsreels and Shub's historical compilations to Flaherty's ahistorical romanticisations, by way of the city films of Ruttmann and others, and at the end of the decade, the surreal scientific observation of the natural world by Jean Painlevé. But if these all comprise exemplars of the same genre, then what do they have in common to justify this appellation?

Grierson's famous definition of documentary as the 'creative treatment of actuality' is not to be dismissed as merely the motto of a gifted phrasemonger – it indicates a necessary tension which is a constitutive element of the documentary project. But it needs to be seen in context. Grierson himself called the 'First Principles' 'a minor manifesto' and like all manifestos it has a rhetorical tone and a prescriptive intention, for which the phrase has a useful elasticity. If it fails to provide an adequate definition of documentary as such, the difficulty lies elsewhere, in Grierson's notion that the documentary can be distinguished from other genres of factual or non-fiction film. The problem here is the slippery and ambiguous word 'genre'.

V

The concept of genre, the term that classifies works of art according to shared thematic or stylistic features, has a history going all the way back to Greek antiquity, but no one any longer believes that the classic prescriptions, which deal in fixed categories and rules, are adequate to account for the evolving nature of genre – Adorno thought that 'the effects emphasised by Plato and Aristotle were probably fictitious even at that time'.[27] Classical theories, which have nothing to say about how genres change or new ones appear, lost their force, he says, because the principle of individuation which arose with the Renaissance 'not only runs counter to genres but also opposes the subordination of art to a prevailing praxis' in which genre thus becomes unstable.[28] In hindsight genres are indeed historical – they go in cycles, they are fluid and porous, they steal from each other and mix up elements from diverse sources, above all they tend to break their own rules. And historically, says Adorno, 'genre has gone through several phases: from legitimation (of old genres) to creation (of new genres) to destruction (of genres *per se*)'.[29] But Adorno is speaking from the position of high modernism, where he believes artistic individualism has done away with genre altogether. Problem: this is not what happened in mass culture, which instead has come to regenerate the conventions of genre in the supervening interests of moulding the market. As indeed Adorno knew perfectly well – this is the basis of his critique of commercial popular music, which he lumped together inaccurately under the term 'jazz'.

Adorno wished to advance the claims of modernist critique against the false ideological pleasures of the culture industry; cultural critics of a later generation, wishing to shed the elitist mantle, sometimes ended up losing sight of the ideological moment altogether. This should not be allowed to disguise the dialectic of cinema: it is not an accident that as modernism entered on the negation of genre, the cinema screen gives it new life. Movies are not produced using the same individualistic aesthetic labour as the premodern high art forms, but under a regime of industrially organised labour, in which, as the studio production system gets into its stride, artistic authority is dissolved into a team that has its own internal hierarchy. The labour process itself generates genre as a solution to the common endeavour, by providing a series of models or paradigms that tell everyone in the team (behind the camera and in front of it) what they're supposed to be doing (more or less). It also satisfies the requirements of the producers and financiers by enabling them to get what they're expecting (more or less). And it hooks the audience (more or less) for similar reasons, an audience whose predominant cultural tutelage and susceptibilities came from the collective traditions of nineteenth-century popular culture – music hall and melodrama – rather than the privileged individualism of high art. The documentary, however, as it emerges in the 1920s, occupies a peculiar position in this scheme. By definition, it is not a studio picture: it has to be shot wherever it has to be shot. It doesn't have actors and scripts, and only requires a small production team. It is difficult for a producer to control. It also displays a tendency to re-establish individual aesthetic authority and, in the early period, readily aligned itself with modernism. In short, documentary is what Ivens somewhere described as a creative no-man's land, an interloper in the genre system.

The problematic nature of genre in mass culture can be illuminated by turning to Raymond Williams. It is true, Williams thought, that the concept of genre lost its neoclassical abstraction and sense of regulation, 'but new kinds of grouping and classification, of an empirical and relativist tendency, became habitual', in which the variety of practice was recognised by the proliferation of 'genres' and 'subgenres' of a new kind: not the formal categories of epic, lyric and dramatic, 'but (to quote from a current encyclopaedia) "novel, picaresque novel, romance, short-story, comedy, tragedy, melodrama, children's literature, essay, humour, journalism, light verse, mystery and detective stories, oratory, parody, pastoral, proverb, riddle, satire, science fiction"'. This, said Williams, is the reduction of classification to absurdity; it is also the intellectual debris of mixing up 'at least three types of classification: by literary form, by subject matter, and by intended readership'. The last gives the game away, for the whole approach is actually governed by the imperative of meeting the market. Strictly speaking, said Williams, 'this is not genre theory at all'.[30] Much the same can be said of the genres of cinema, a confusion that film genre theory has repeatedly tried to sort out, without, it must be said, ever arriving at consensus. In the view of Oswald Ducrot and Tzvetan Todorov, 'first we must stop identifying genres with the names of genres'.[31] We cannot define genre solely on the basis of denomination: certain genres have never been named; others have been merged under a single name in spite of differences in their properties. Instead they propose to apply the notion of dominance put forward by the Russian formalists. If a certain work is to be declared a tragedy, for example, the elements of tragedy must not only be present but dominant. But with this, the terrain of the enquiry shifts away from formal qualities as such, towards the susceptibilities of authors, who always entertain a certain model of writing even if only to violate it, and of audiences, who approach the work with certain expectations and dispositions. And since these susceptibilities vary at different times and places, we are obliged, they think, to give an historical rather than analytical account.

On this reading, when the documentary emerged in the 1920s it behaved like a genre without a name, whose name, when it was adopted, effectively merged into one category a range of films with quite different characteristics, except for the one dominant aspect which is captured only negatively in the term non-fiction. The word documentary caught on partly because it reversed this negativity, offering a home to films in danger of being orphaned. But this doesn't quite solve the problem. The term clearly covers a great variety of divergent forms and practices, from observation to compilation, from the testimonial to reconstruction, which makes it difficult to define 'in and of itself', so to speak. But if we follow Wittgenstein and speak of family resemblance, then there are clusters of conventions but no single defining characteristic or set of attributes which all documentaries satisfy. What is there in common, for instance, between two classic postwar examples, like *Momma Don't Allow*, made by Tony Richardson and Karel Reisz in 1955, a cool, Free Cinema observational portrait of a jazz club in London, and a dozen years later, *LBJ* by the Cuban film-maker Santiago Alvarez, a biting montage of satirical political propaganda composed almost entirely of found material? Maybe nothing, apart from an absence of commentary and the fact that neither of them are fiction. What remains in evidence is the sheer variety that the term documentary encompasses, which always overspills any attempted definition, whether by Grierson or anyone else.

VI

It might be instructive to pursue the etymology of the word forwards beyond the moment when Grierson first employed the term. Consider the following usages given in the Oxford English Dictionary Online:

1926 *N. Y. Sun* 8 Feb. 18/1 'Moana', being a visual account of events in the daily life of a Polynesian youth and his family, has documentary value.

1930 P. ROTHA *Film till Now* I. ii. 65 The Documentary or Interest Film, including the Scientific, Cultural and Sociological Film.

1932 *Cinema Q.* I. I. 67 Documentary is a clumsy description, but let it stand. The French who first used the term only meant travelogue.

1932 *Film in National Life* (*Rep. Comm. Educ. & Cult. Films*) viii. 115 §174 A deliberate documentary film must be a transcript of real life, a bit of what actually happened, under approximately unrehearsed conditions.

1934 *Punch* 26 Dec. 720/1 Most documentary films seem to hinge upon the exposition of some staple industry.

1935 R. SPOTTISWOODE *Gram. of Film* 288 The documentary as he defines it is still flourishing.

1936 *Times Lit. Suppl.* 25 Jan. 72/3 The documentary film – or, *tout court*, 'documentary'.

1941 [see ACTUALITY 4b].

1947 J. HAYWARD *Prose Lit. since 1939* 32 'Mass-Observation', whose intriguing 'documentaries' of the British people at work and play contain the crude substance of innumerable novels, biographies, and essays.

1957 V. J. KEHOE *Film & T.V. Make-Up* i. 17 Some producers do not like the smoothness of the face created by the use of make-up. They strive to achieve what is termed a *documentary* effect . . . by the lack of make-up on men (even at times, on women).

1957 *Listener* 18 July 103/1 Mr. Owen's 'documentary', as he calls his attractive book, reveals him as an acute observer.

1962 *Observer* 8 July 20/4 Henry Cecil's light legal documentary fiction.

The first of these is Grierson's review; the second shows Rotha writing not as a polemicist but a popu-lariser. The third is Grierson's 'First Principles', the fourth a government report struggling to define the indefinable. The next three (1934–6) represent the full acceptance of the term in both the press and the intellectual community, and its transformation from adjective to noun. The four last items tell another story. Here the term begins to overflow its filmic identity in a most peculiar way. If 'documentary' is used in the make-up item to mean 'naturalistic', for the rest, a word whose original meaning, according to the dictionary, is 'of the nature of or consisting in documents', is being projected back onto written texts in order to accord them a special status on the model of the documentary film. The last of these, being almost postmodern in its mixture of genre categories, suggests that by the early 60s, the Griersonian ideal had become fatally weakened.

Grierson's ideological influence spread far and wide, and lasted well into the postwar period – he was always an honoured guest at documentary festivals in places like Montevideo and Leipzig, wherever an international community of documentarists gathered – but no one then or since has escaped the fate of any attempt to define the object at the centre of their attention. Several decades later, the cultural bureau-crats of the European Union have no more effective definition to offer of what they term the 'creative documentary', which they need to define in order to give it funding. The definition provided in the first Media Programme at the start of the 1990s is cod Hegelian, being once again entirely negative. It says what it isn't (it isn't corporate production, or current affairs, or instructional, or 'programmes where the image is not essential') but not what it is, as if it were some kind of mythical beast which no one has ever seen, but everyone would recognise immediately if they saw it. To put it crudely, documentary comes in all sorts of shapes and sizes and possesses a range of subspecies quite as varied as those of fictional cinema, and this multiplicity impedes the search for a satisfactory definition. As the writer Patricia Hampl nicely puts it, documentary is like 'a big, frayed umbrella, with a motley crew sheltering under it'.[32] There are too many different styles and techniques, it becomes impossible to find any particular technical or sty-listic feature which is either necessary or sufficient to guarantee even the vague principle of veracity implied by 'a transcript of real life, a bit of what actually happened, under approximately unrehearsed conditions'. Some of these subgenres (if that's what they should be called) even overlap with fictional cinema – what exactly is docudrama? – and make it difficult to establish clear criteria for the difference between the two.

Wittgenstein, who described the aim of philosophy as showing the fly the way out of the fly-bottle, advises us to abandon the search for clear distinctions and definite differences, and not to fall back into an idealist mode of thinking by looking for definitions, or the 'essence' of anything, the single defining characteristic, the necessary and sufficient condition. A genre, on this reading, is not to be defined by any set of fixed categories, conventions, conditions either necessary or sufficient, but belongs to the realm of family resemblance. Let us see documentary as a family, or better, an extended family or maybe network of families, even a whole tribe, with a genealogy that stretches from the Lumière actualities to the latest *Panorama* reporting from Afghanistan; from travelogue to ethnography to *cinéma vérité*; from the newsreel to the public service documentary; from the city film to the solidarity film; from the scien-tific films of Painlevé, or the poetic propaganda of Humphrey Jennings, to the television docudrama, the docusoap, and the varieties of 'alternative' or 'new wave' documentary shown in independent screen venues up and down the country. The main branches of this genealogy would represent particular traditions or even subspecies, each with its own classic examples, which serve as models, paradigms, exemplary instances. Different examples might then follow the same or different features in the same paradigm, but in the same way as the children of the same ancestry, they may not always resemble each other. Moreover, on this reading it is normal for films to conjoin features from different types and styles, and there would also be cases of intermarriage or marrying out. This is what happens in fiction, where you get crosses between genres which normally don't mix – the musical Western, for example, such as *Annie Get Your Gun* (1950) – so why not in documentary? Here I think of *Latcho Drom* by Tony Gatlif (1993), an ethnographic musical road-movie if ever there was one. In short, if we look at documentary in genealogical terms, the puzzle begins to evaporate, the fly finds a way out of the bottle. The question then becomes, where is it going to land?

Notes

1. Visible Evidence, Cardiff, 1996.
2. Laura Mulvey, *Death 24x a Second* (London: Reaktion Books, 2006), p. 52.
3. Jay David Bolter and Richard Grusin, *Remediation, Understanding New Media* (Cambridge, MA: MIT Press, 2000).
4. Brian Winston, *Technologies of Seeing* (London: BFI, 1996), p. 86.
5. 'Boleslaw Matuszewski and the Documentary Idea', in Kevin Macdonald and Mark Cousins (eds), *Imagining Reality: The Faber Book of Documentary* (London: Faber and Faber, 1996), p. 14.
6. 'Osama bin Laden Video: Behind the Scenes', <yorick.infinitejest.org:81/1/obl-video-makingof.html>. The example is mentioned by Jane Gaines, who adds:

   > In a perverse way, bin Laden, raising the issue of 'which is which', calls our attention to the difference between the real historical figure – alive, not dead – and the videotape image . . .
   > In a weird way, the videotape in question recapitulates the history of the actuality as it becomes documentary. After the end of the century of the ascendance of actuality, this most notorious actuality image no longer produces the earlier kind of wonder but is caught in a game of cat and mouse between desperate but malevolent groups on the margin and a highly resourceful and also malevolent superpower. This is the rhetoric of the image with a vengeance.

   Jane Gaines, 'Switched at Birth: Documentary as Not Fiction', Visible Evidence XI, Bristol, 16–19 December 2003.
7. Louis Menand, 'Nanook and Me, "Fahrenheit 9/11" and the Documentary tradition', *The New Yorker*, 9–16 August 2004, p. 90.
8. S. Tretyakov *et al.*, in Lewis Jacobs (ed.), *The Documentary Tradition* (New York: Norton, 1979), pp. 29–36.
9. Bill Nichols, *Representing Reality: Issues and Concepts in Documentary* (Bloomington: Indiana University Press, 1991).
10. Stella Bruzzi, *New Documentary: A Critical Introduction* (London and New York: Routledge, 2000), p. 2.

11.   Fredric Jameson, 'The Existence of Italy', in *Signatures of the Visible* (New York: Routledge, 1992),
      p. 157. Italics in the original.

12.   Christian Metz, *Film Language: A Semiotics of Cinema* (Oxford: Oxford University Press, 1974),
      pp. 93–4. Italics in the original.

13.   See John Tagg, *The Burden of Representation, Essays in Photographies and Histories* (London and
      Basingstoke: Palgrave Macmillan, 1988).

14.   See Michael Chanan, *Repeated Takes: A Short History of Recording and its Effects on Music* (London:
      Verso, 1995).

15.   Siegfried Kracauer, *Theory of Film: The Redemption of Physical Reality* (Oxford: Oxford University Press,
      1960), pp. 30–3.

16.   Nichols, *Representing Reality*, p. 4.

17.   See Pierre Bourdieu, *The Field of Cultural Production* (Oxford: Polity Press, 1993).

18.   Marx to Engels, 28 January 1863, *Marx-Engels Selected Correspondence* (Moscow: Progress Publishers,
      1975).

19.   Bourdieu, *The Field of Cultural Production*, p. 83.

20.   Introduction to Michael Chanan, *Cuban Cinema* (Minneapolis: Minnesota University Press, 2004).

21.   Forsyth Hardy (ed.), *Grierson on Documentary* (London: Collins, 1946), p. 11.

22.   Brian Winston, *Claiming the Real: The Documentary Film Revisited* (London: BFI, 1995), pp. 8–13.

23.   Winston, *Claiming the Real*, p. 11.

24.   John Grierson, 'First Principles of Documentary', in Hardy, *Grierson on Documentary*, p. 78.

25.   Winston, *Claiming the Real*, p. 13.

26.   John Grierson, 'First Principles of Documentary', in Hardy, *Grierson on Documentary*, p. 79.

27.   Theodor W. Adorno, *Aesthetic Theory* (London: Routledge and Kegan Paul, 1984), p. 289.

28.   Adorno, *Aesthetic Theory*, p. 289.

29.   Adorno, *Aesthetic Theory*, p. 288.

30.   Raymond Williams, *Marxism and Literature* (Oxford: Oxford University Press, 1977), pp. 182–3.

31.   Oswald Ducrot and Tzvetan Todorov, *Encyclopedic Dictionary of the Sciences of Language* (Oxford:
      Blackwell, 1982), p. 149.

32.   Patricia Hampl, 'Memory's Movies', in Charles Warren (ed.), *Beyond Document, Essays on Nonfiction
      Film* (Hanover, NH: Wesleyan University Press/University Press of New England, 1996), p. 76.

3 Rules of Evidence

On the semiotics of the documentary image

I

The documentary claim on reality is not just a theoretical question but a matter of practical concern to authority, at times a matter of law, and even of state. Authority naturally responds to the provocations of documentary with suspicion, even within actually existing democracy. The more liberal the state, the more it tolerates the inconvenience, as long as the documentarist remains within the bounds allowed by legality. But was documentary ever completely free from censorship and control? And not just in totalitarian countries of right or left but also under parliamentary democracy? In postwar France, for example, where in 1953 a film by Alain Resnais and Chris Marker, *Les statues meurent aussi* (Statues Also Die) was banned for its criticism of colonialism. The statues which die are African, and they die when they are removed by the colonial power and enter museums and Art History, or become curios for the Western art market, which robs them of their original symbolic functions. The Centre National de la Cinématographie considered this an attack on government policies and kept the film back for ten years. This is an interesting example because such views would hardly have been censored if they'd appeared in an academic journal, but a film is considered more dangerous because it might be seen by the uneducated. Or take the US, where in 1967 Frederick Wiseman's *Titicut Follies* occasioned a series of trials which culminated in the State of Massachusetts imposing restrictions on its exhibition (but only, of course, within their jurisdiction). Supposedly the film offended public morals; in fact it exposed the appalling conditions in a state mental institution. The country of the mother of parliaments doesn't come out of this too well either. According to one account, between 1959 and 1993, more than 100 television programmes on Northern Ireland were banned, censored or delayed by the broadcasting companies themselves. The government rarely intervened directly, but under Mrs Thatcher did so twice: first in 1985 to stop a BBC documentary called *At the Edge of the Union* because it included a humanised portrait of Martin McGuinness, thought to be the IRA's commander-in-chief; and second in 1988, with the imposition of the Broadcasting Ban, intended to deny the terrorists 'the oxygen of publicity' by banning their voices from television and radio, or those of anyone expressing sympathy or understanding towards terrorism. The Ban was badly framed, and producers exploited loopholes by means of subtitles or dubbing by actors, leading to unaccustomed Brechtian moments. In one example, *Inside the Maze* (1991), an IRA prisoner in the Maze is allowed his own voice when he's just a prisoner, but not when he's a prisoner's representative in a meeting with prison officers about food and the size of sausage rolls. The ban lasted until 1994, when John Major withdrew it.[1]

We shall encounter other historical examples later, but the potential danger posed by documentary to those in power in the democratic state was recently confirmed in the US by Michael Moore's *Fahrenheit*

9/11, which in 2004 became the first documentary to win the top award at the Cannes Film Festival in nearly fifty years, while back home it was subjected to attempts to keep it from commercial distribution, although there were no grounds for legal action. When Moore, on the eve of the Festival, accused the Disney Corporation of stifling free speech by blocking its subsidiary Miramax from distributing his exposé of the second President Bush, he was accused by the right of a publicity stunt in keeping with his performative style of self-promotion on screen, but in the view of a serious film critic like Jonathan Rosenbaum, the achievement of the film was in 'delivering to American moviegoers many facts about George W. Bush and the wars in Afghanistan and Iraq that our TV news has downplayed or ignored. (Sure, it's manipulative and slanted – but transparently so, unlike Fox News or CNBC.)'[2]

Like the contours and ecology of the public sphere, the forms of censorship and regulation depend on each country's own particular history, but everywhere they become elements shaping the documentarist's habitus. There are rules of evidence, and rules of engagement. If the public sphere is an arena of rational discussion, a theatre for debate and deliberation, then it is not just a space of discursive relations but also of the norms of decorum which govern those relations and the debate engaged therein. In theory the public sphere is all inclusive, an open commons where hegemony is contested, in reality it develops mechanisms to maintain a proper sense of social order and thus defend the body politic which owns it (or thinks it does). It is therefore both permissive and normative – on the one hand, a space where dialogue is encouraged, on the other, where convention, compromise and legal authority are brought to bear in order to discourage and restrain over-independent thinking. The norms function as a kind of homeostatic mechanism which operates to exclude what is not acceptable to the establishment consensus, the doxa of liberal democratic society, or what J. K. Galbraith called the 'conventional wisdom'. Yet the public sphere is not a homogeneous expanse but a series of overlapping domains with their own particular interests – political parties, professional bodies, quangos, campaigns and pressure groups – which each tolerate different degrees of independent thought, novelty and challenge; even the conventional wisdom is therefore not a given, but a field of constant skirmishes between different strategies of debate and contestation, where documentary is sometimes found on the frontline and often takes up the position of a sniper.

The rules of contestation and engagement vary between the different media. Since freedom of the press is one of the defining conditions of democracy, the print media are usually the closest to enjoying freedom to publish without prior constraint. Cinema and broadcasting are in slightly different situations. Cinema, which the social and political establishment originally perceived as a scientific curiosity or a form of entertainment but not a form of speech, was subjected to regulation in order to curb its potential for sinful indecency, but otherwise it was left to the regulation of the market and the industry's self-regulation. Broadcasting was a different proposition again, because of the novel way in which it reached its audience. Unlike the sale of conventional cultural goods, or the box office in the performing arts or cinema, the public didn't pay for broadcasting directly (until the recent arrival of pay TV). At the same time, the wavebands were a limited resource and broadcasting was therefore perceived as being in need of regulation by its very nature (always in a manner varying according to country). Under actually existing democracy, regulation doesn't usually amount to direct censorship, but comprises institutional codes of practice and legal limits (albeit balanced by legal protection), conditions which foster self-censorship and conformity with approved codes of representation (not to mention the fear of losing your job).

I draw again from my own experience for an example of how this affects the independent documentarist in British television. In 1983, I was involved in the production of a documentary for Channel 4 about the South Atlantic war of the previous year, *Malvinas, Historia de traiciones* (Malvinas, Story of Betrayal), directed by Jorge Denti, an Argentinian film-maker living in exile in Mexico. Denti was a politically engaged Latin American making films for alternative distribution who had been forced into exile by a military dictatorship. He was aware that British television required something called 'political balance', but had never worked in an environment where this was part of the habitus and had little idea of what this meant in practice, and he therefore left it up to the English members of the team to select the appropriate participants from the English side of the conflict to match those he had selected to present the Argentinian side. In addition, we made sure the British participants included politicians of both right and left, as well as car workers, journalists and historians, again to match their Argentinian counterparts. The plan succeeded. Channel 4 accepted the film as edited, and after a little negotiation, the supervising authority (the IBA) approved it with only one small cut. (This was a comment by an Argentinian about Ghurkhas who cut off the ears of captured combatants. A British army spokesman had said – but too late to include in the film – that of course it wasn't true, but it was good psychological warfare.) Reviewing the film in *The Times*, David Robinson found it very leftwing (in Argentina it was criticised in some quarters for being too Peronist) but commended it for its attitude of 'a plague on both your houses'.[3] Reflecting on the experience more than twenty years later, I would say that our comportment towards the regulators was a mixture of the considered and the instinctive; the habitus tells you what to expect, but certain subjects or approaches push you closer to the limits and force you to analyse your choices more carefully.

II

Britain is a pointed example because of its exemplary school of documentary in the 1930s and the reputation of its television documentaries in more recent decades. While theatre censorship dated back to the eighteenth century (and only came to an end in 1968), film was first brought under indirect control by the 1909 Cinematograph Act, followed by the creation of the British Board of Film Censors (BBFC) in 1912, which still exists, renamed the Board of Classification; although much weakened, video has been included in its remit since 1985. These measures illustrate the evolution of a tendency to avoid direct intervention, preferring what the economist J. M. Keynes, in helping to create the Arts Council in the 1940s, defined as 'the arm's length principle': that government should not administer such affairs directly, in order to be free of any possible charge of partisan interference or political patronage, but should delegate responsibility to special agencies, of the kind nowadays called quangos (quasi-autonomous non-government organisations). The same hesitancy to interfere directly explains the reluctance of government in the early days of cinema to answer calls for the introduction of censorship by direct measures which could be seen to conflict with the principles of free speech that governed the press. The 1909 Act was introduced for reasons of safety – cinemas had suffered fires, there was legitimate concern over the inflammability of celluloid – but it allowed local authorities to attach conditions as they saw fit, effectively handing censorship over to local worthies up and down the country. Inevitably the film trade objected to being pushed around by moralising town councillors and local Watch Committees, and came up with a plan for self-regulation by their own board of censors. Since the government on duty lent the scheme support but left the existing legislation unaltered, local authorities retained the *de facto* power to ensure that the industry censors would behave with due responsibility; it also meant they had the power to allow the exhibition of films that were banned by the BBFC, a loophole which would facilitate the emergence of the film society movement between the wars.

From the start, the Board took exception to films for reasons such as 'indelicate sexual situations', 'scenes suggestive of immorality', 'scenes tending to disparage public characters and institutions' and 'the irreverent treatment of sacred or solemn subjects'.[4] Apart from initially banning nudity and the representation of Christ, the BBFC never issued an explicit etiquette like the infamous Hays code in the United States, but in discouraging producers from indulging in social criticism, it did no more than articulate the inherent conservatism of those who controlled the business, who were equally hostile towards outlandish kinds of artistic experiment. (One story recounts the board's rejection of a French avant-garde film of the 1920s with the comment, 'we cannot understand this film, but if there is anything in it to be understood, it is undoubtedly offensive'). When certificates were denied to Soviet films like Eisenstein's *The Battleship Potemkin* (1926), a small but active band of cinephiles found the solution in the loophole left by the legislation, and escaped the problem by screening films to members-only audiences on premises licensed by the local authority. The London Film Society, launched in 1925, owed its official consent to its respectable, predominantly intellectual supporters,[5] but it provided a model for the workers' film societies which began to emerge before the end of the decade, in parallel with similar movements in countries like Germany and France. (With Communists playing a crucial role in the movement, local authorities were often reluctant to concede, and there were still attempts to ban *Potemkin* as late as 1934.[6])

The introduction of 16mm sound projectors in 1933 increased the scope of activity, since the legislation covered inflammable film and the film stock employed for 16mm was non-inflammable. The result was a growing non-theatrical sector, ranging from schools to church halls, which provided a major part of the sphere of circulation for an alternative cinema. Similar developments in other countries allowed the small-scale international distribution of new political documentary, especially around issues like the Spanish Civil War. But this hardly affected the situation of those who depended on official sponsorship like Grierson's team at the GPO Film Unit, where a degree of self-censorship was practised and the films remained politically timid. As Harry Watt, co-director of *Night Mail*, later admitted, 'The truth is that if we had indulged in real social criticism to any extent, we would immediately have been without sponsorship and our whole experiment, which was artistically a fine one, would have finished. So we compromised.'[7] Ironically, newsreels were exempt from censorship, but as the film historian Bert Hogenkamp comments, 'Afraid of losing their privilege of not having to submit their films (issued twice weekly) to the BBFC, the newsreel companies tried to avoid controversy as much as possible and concentrated instead on "safe" topics like sport, fashion and royalty.'[8] As a leftwing columnist of the day put it, 'Always militarism, jingoism, sabre-rattling or sport – never internationalism, peace, scientific advance or any matters likely to raise the intellectual and moral standards of the people.'[9]

Broadcasting produced a different kind of regime, since it was a different kind of medium, a live form of ephemeral content available to anyone with a receiver and generally enjoyed in domestic privacy. Radio, as a form of wireless telegraphy, came under the control of the Post Office as the competent body for the issue of licences to operate. As a medium, it began to take off after World War I – a consequence of its wartime development by the military.[10] By 1921 there were 127 radio stations operating in the UK according to the enthusiasts' magazine *Wireless World*, which considered the provision of 'wireless time and telephony' as a public service.[11] The BBC – company not corporation – was originally formed the following year as a cartel of manufacturers with Post-Office encouragement. The problem was how to finance this activity, since a radio broadcast is not a commodity which could be sold to the listener, who only had to purchase the set. This was exactly why the manufacturers set up their own radio stations in the first place, as a loss leader, to encourage the sale of receivers. The commercial solution, adopted in the United States, was to make a commodity out of airtime and sell it to advertisers and sponsors, whose interests would ensure the acceptability of the content to authority; in the old cultures of Europe, especially with the example of revolutionary Russia on its borders, high military and civic echelons concerned with certain facts about mass susceptibilities preferred keeping radio under tighter, more direct control and retained the monopoly on broadcasting for the state. The British solution was more subtle – the monopoly was given to the BBC which was turned into a public corporation, to be financed by a licence paid by the listener. In return, the system would be run as a public service, as interpreted by its directors (and its first director general, John Reith). The structure of governance and the licence fee meant that the BBC operated at arm's length to government. (The licence fee remains to this day a unique form of hypothecated taxation, separately collected and dedicated to a single purpose, and in my view is a perfectly sensible way to finance public service broadcasting – the alternatives, like advertising or subscription, would quickly threaten the integrity of the service.)

This was a system where self-regulation was built in, and thereby inculcated self-censorship. It gave every appearance of government defending the freedom of speech while actually handing control to a committee of 'the good and the great' – a euphemism, according to Stuart Hood in his firsthand account (he was controller of BBC Television in the early 1960s), for the list of names maintained by a department in Whitehall to be 'recommended to successive governments as trustworthy enough to be called upon' to serve as members of royal commissions, public institutions, quangos and the like (he adds that only a small percentage are women).[12] The true habitus of the good and the great is found in the plush clubs of the establishment. Their task as BBC governors was to see that the corporation's policies reflected a gentlemanly consensus in politics and of 'taste' in entertainment and the arts; but this is not an easy balancing act, and the BBC's history, says Hood, has been prey since its earliest days to a contradiction between its duty to inform and the pressure from the governors 'not to rock the boat'.[13] The very constitution of the BBC thus produces a potential clash between the professional habitus of its staff and the dominant ideology which the governors personify and perpetuate. The latest example to expose the real balance of power behind these arrangements was the crisis of 2004 and the rapid fallout from the Hutton Inquiry into the death of the government weapons expert David Kelly. The official inquiry would be widely criticised as a whitewash, but its immediate effect was to add to government pressure and force the resignation of the BBC's chairman, Gavyn Davies, closely followed by its director general, Greg Dyke. Dyke's resignation provoked a walk-out by hundreds of BBC staff in his support, but BBC news and documentary became pretty cowed in the aftermath.

Documentary, which entered this milieu during the 1950s, was treated as a branch of journalism, which brought with it the responsibilities of the exercise of freedom of speech within the public service ethos – not so very different from Griersonian principles. As Brian Winston puts it, the Reithian 'contract with the listener/viewer' is already a form of regulation, even though it has no more legal force than the parallel notion of 'a breach of public trust'.[14] Inevitably, the growing sophistication of documentary over the 1960s, which introduced new scope into the representation of public issues, produced a good deal of nervousness on the part of the confraternity of controllers, regulators and politicians, leading to the BBC's introduction in 1972 of its *Principles and Practices in Documentary Programmes*. Winston calls this a 'rehashing of Grierson's principles in a Canute-like attempt to turn the tide' of the new trends of Direct Cinema and cinéma vérité. The first of several subsequent codes of practice elaborated by successive waves of regulators responsible for overseeing either the BBC or its commercial rivals, these texts acquire a peculiar status. Like Grierson's 'First Principles of Documentary', they remain largely unread, but are diffused by osmosis through the community of documentary producers to become the doxa.

Notwithstanding the codes and the regulators, in corners where liberal management allowed a degree of experimentation, even reportage was allowed to challenge established codes of representation. The most remarkable work came from a commercial broadcaster, Granada Television, whose current affairs weekly *World in Action*, launched in 1963, demonstrated, according to Stuart Hood, 'that it was possible to inject passion into the television documentary'.[15] Indeed the slot generated several clashes with the broadcasting authority over 'due impartiality',[16] and had a history of breaking stylistic norms. A couple of examples appear on a recent reissue of several episodes on DVD. *Mick Jagger* from 1967 is billed as 'an exclusive interview with Jagger after his jail sentence for drug possession was quashed'.[17] An introductory sequence sets the scene as the Rolling Stone is released on appeal, holds a press conference and then, courtesy of Granada, flies by helicopter to a rural spot outside London, a quiet location requested by Jagger himself, where he sits down to talk to four representatives of the Establishment (the editor of *The Times*, a retired politician, a Jesuit theologian and a bishop). The format is that of the television current affairs magazine, with a filmed introduction followed by a discussion recorded on videotape by multiple cameras, except that there is no presenter here, and instead of a studio, it takes place on a sunny terrace in the home counties, recorded by an outside broadcast unit and with the panel, which is without a moderator, relaxing on garden chairs. This setting creates a conversational quality to the exchanges in which the wild rock musician in hippy dress proves himself more than capable of matching the reasonable tones of the official guardians of morality. This hybrid piece of reportage deserves to be set alongside the classic rock documentaries of the time as a counterweight to their excesses.

The second example, *The Demonstration*, is a report on the demonstration against the Vietnam War in March 1968, when protestors attacked the US Embassy in London's Grosvenor Square. Transmitted hardly more than forty-eight hours after the event, only careful planning could have produced such a remarkable feat of editing. Again the film is divided into two halves, the set-up and the demonstration in progress. Commentary is minimal. We begin in Trafalgar Square, where the recorded voice of a tourist guide at a push-button information point speaks of the history of the Square as a traditional site of political protest. The protestors are represented by a coach-load of students on their way down to London from Manchester, and an interview with their spokesperson, talking of the general political crisis as well as Vietnam. Both narrative development and the obligations of 'balance' are satisfied by a short sequence of police preparations (including the mounted police), but when we get to the rally, the film introduces an ironic new narrative device – a US radio commentator, Gerry Landy, out with his tape recorder. Here, and at the very end of the film, Landy's unctuous comments allow the film-makers to avoid their own editorialising, while the distancing effect of the irony raises questions about the clichés and stereotypes which govern the standard representation of such events. The really remarkable part of the film, however, is the riot which followed in Grosvenor Square, which comprises fully ten minutes *without a word of commentary* – only the sync sounds of chanting and jeering, police whistles, snatches of verbal exchange, the cries of the arrested. To accomplish this gripping sequence, the film marries the techniques of film and television, approaching the event like an outside broadcast but using film cameras, shooting from different vantage points around the Square and within the mêlée. If this fulfils the promise of the opening commentary, that 'Tonight, *World in Action* allows you to judge for yourself', the final irony is that while the report is implicitly anti-Establishment in its politics, in treating Grosvenor Square like a sports stadium, it turns the political demonstration into a prime phenomenon of the society of the spectacle.

III

Television norms and regulation have greatly loosened up since the period when the codes were first introduced. In 1998, following an exposé by the *Guardian* newspaper, Britain's Independent Television Commission (ITC) levied a fine of £2 million against the television company Carlton 'for grave breaches of the programme code' in the case of a documentary called *The Connection*, about Colombian heroin trafficking to Britain, directed by one Marc de Beaufort, which was broadcast in 1996.[18]

De Beaufort and his team had apparently uncovered a new heroin route from Colombia to London and could reveal how the Cali cartel was targeting British schoolchildren with a superior grade of heroin. They had filmed an 'exclusive interview' with the number three man in the cartel, and even managed to covertly film a drugs mule swallowing fingers of heroin and catching a British Airways plane to Heathrow airport. It turned out that the Cali number three was nothing of the kind, but as the newspaper described him, 'a retired bank cashier with low-level connections to the drugs underworld'. The film-makers claimed that in order to film the interview they had been blindfolded and taken to an unknown location; the newspaper revealed that it had been filmed in the producer's hotel room (a hotel maid showed the journalists which room it was after watching a copy of the film with them). Nor was the 'loader', who is seen helping the mule swallow the heroin, working for the Cali number three, as claimed in the film's commentary, but he was a parking attendant and friend of the character playing the mule. He told the newspaper he thought they were filming a reconstruction of a drug run in which he would be paid for acting a part with a disguised identity. Furthermore, the mule hadn't swallowed heroin, and his ticket to London, as revealed by credit card records, had been paid by the producers (although he was indeed a mule, and later ended up in prison in Spain). He told the newspaper how the sequence in the plane had been filmed:

Marc asked me how a mule acts in a plane. I said, 'Film me and I will act as if I had heroin in the stomach'. They filmed me and I did what mules do to show they don't eat food. I put it in my pocket and deposited it in the toilet of the plane. . . .

Needless to say, there was no new heroin route to the UK either. In short, the report was a fake from start to finish – but not in the same way as 'fake' or 'mock' documentaries' like *David Holzman's Diary* (Kit Carson, 1968) or *This Is Spinal Tap* (Rob Reiner, 1983), which were satirical fictions posing as documentaries. *The Connection* pretends to be a real documentary. The mock documentary only pretends to pretend.

The débâcle of this film raises a whole number of issues, not least because it had won eight international television awards for 'risk-taking investigative reporting' and was screened on fourteen television stations around the world. A few days after the *Guardian*'s exposé, a former Channel 4 executive, John Willis, wrote in the same newspaper that people like himself would be put to wondering 'how one of British TV's most experienced content lawyers . . . and one of our most trusted documentary executives . . . could have found themselves in the middle of such a story', but they would recognise it was part of a deeper malaise. According to Willis, 'The line between fact and drama in documentary has grown increasingly blurred and in the struggle between journalistic truth and dramatic excitement, drama is winning.' This was happening, he said, because in the process of what the newspaper called 'the lust for ratings, fame and prizes', proposals 'are oversold to the commissioner and then the producers are afraid they cannot deliver', implying that when they then bend the rules, the commissioner turns a blind eye rather than pull an expensive programme from the transmission schedules.[19] While this is not an explanation, it illuminates the problem as it appears from the habitus of the television executive.

According to the *Guardian*'s media correspondent Kamal Ahmed, 'A straightforward documentary, revealing something that the public doesn't know but should do, is no longer considered enough for ratings hungry executives. Programmes now have to "make a noise" and create headlines.'[20] He pointed out that the trend had been criticised the year before by Martin Bell, the former TV correspondent who entered Parliament as an independent anti-sleaze MP. 'The accolades are part of the problem,' said Bell. 'The . . . calendar is bespangled with a string of prize-givings and award ceremonies. It might be that we have now reached a point where prizes are no longer a badge of professional integrity but even a threat to it.' Another illuminating comment by a television professional, moreover a man of proven integrity, which again is however, no explanation.

Willis alleged that it was worse in the US, where the ratings wars had undermined the journalistic integrity of the news:

America's totem pole of truth, Dan Rather, was embarrassed when a freelance cameraman had apparently recreated scenes, for his programme, of Afghan rebels sabotaging electricity pylons days after the real action took place. Even more spectacularly, NBC rigged car-crash footage to illustrate the alleged propensity of GM trucks to catch fire in side collisions. For filming purposes NBC had fixed incendiary rocket devices to the truck.

Or in Germany,

> where the arrival of new private TV channels sparked off audience wars in 1996. A journalist called Michael Born exposed the German Ku Klux Klan with his all-seeing hidden cameras. When the police investigated they discovered the Klan were in fact friends of the producer dressed in sheets.

Born ended up in prison. For his part, Bell described the fakery he himself had observed before leaving TV: 'I know there is fraud in TV . . . I have seen it happen.' In Chechnya, one reporter had himself filmed running back and forth across an empty road, and intercut it with scenes of gunfire. In the Balkans, a TV journalist filming in a helicopter nudged his cameraman, and then in the script described the jolt as the moment they were hit by fire. The invasion of Iraq in 2003 produced another crop of examples.

There is little reason here to accept the conventional wisdom, going back to Grierson, that documentary and journalism are different animals, since they both turn out to be engaged in the same dodgy practices. Another columnist recalled that at the previous year's documentary festival in Sheffield,

> there was barely a murmur when the new generation of docusoap makers freely admitted that they mixed fact and fakery to achieve their ends. The producer of a series about village life said her work was 'loosely based on the real lives' of her subjects. Reasons were offered – it was all in the Grierson tradition; the audience were mature and could tell the real from the fake. In any event, said one programme head, the schedules meant that you didn't have time to hang around to film everything actually happening.[21]

It is worth taking this report apart a little, since it conflates the positions taken by producers and executives. Sheffield's annual documentary festival is Britain's major annual gathering of professional documentarists, where you are liable to find, if you repair to the bar between screenings, debating sessions and receptions, that reasons uttered in public are often rationalisations, which betray the cynicism with which it seems the television game is now being played by executives and film-makers alike. Nevertheless, the habitus and doxa of the executive is of a different order, in which an appeal to 'the schedules' as the controlling factor is a euphemism. But you cannot hide an economic regime geared to privileging the sensational and the titillating over judgment and imagination, and which disallows documentarists the properly funded time for research of the kind needed to ensure care and accuracy.

How this sad situation came about takes us back to the start of a new model of television broadcasting in the early 1980s with the introduction of Channel 4, the first instance of what French commentators called 'third generation television' – neither the public service television channel, nor commercial television, but the station as a television publishing house (with or without a public service remit); a system in which programme-making is subcontracted to private production companies. In Channel 4's first year alone, commissions were handed out to some 350 'independent producers' of varying size (who in turn would often subcontract the crewing within the so-called freelance sector, which thereby came to serve as a reserve army of what the advertising industry calls 'creatives'). The new model produced a huge gain in the diversification of television production beyond the traditional narrow aristocracy of labour. At the same time, it created a buyer's market which put pressure on producers to stick to both the budget and the rules (though Channel 4 itself encouraged experimentation). Pressure increased with the expansion of television and the progressive advance of video technology which lowered the costs of tooling up for production, and allowed the entry into the labour market of a growing number of graduates from the expansion of film and video courses in higher education. In the end, the results seemed to justify the pessimism of cultural critics who warned that the privatisation of television was a two-edged sword. As Brian Winston sees it in *Lies, Damn Lies and Documentaries*, his study of what he calls 'The Great British Documentary Scandal', it is no wonder, given that TV documentaries are largely made by 'small (and desperate)' independent production companies, 'that so many documentarists are playing fast and loose with reality'.[22]

The Great British Documentary Scandal was not, then, a singular disgrace but a whole wave of misrepresentations, misdemeanours, unlabelled reconstructions and outright fabrications across the spectrum of documentary, current affairs and reportage. As another writer in the newspaper noted, *The Connection* was the 'third scandal about veracity in British TV documentaries' to break in a matter of weeks.[23] Channel 4 admitted there were scenes in a film called *Rogue Males* that 'misled the audience and should not have been included', including one where two men were filmed supposedly stealing building supplies; then the BBC admitted that there were 'invented' scenes in the highly successful docusoap *Driving School* from 1997. Nor did examples stop coming; Winston chronicles more than half a dozen other cases. Questions were asked about another docusoap, *The Clampers*, and a documentary called *Much Too Young: Chickens*, of 1997, where men seen picking up rent-boys in Glasgow were revealed by a disgruntled researcher to have been members of the production team (on this occasion Channel 4 was fined £150,000 and told the producer she would never work for them again).

Winston observes that these deceptions are not all of the same kind, and criticises both the press and the ITC itself for conflation, for failing to distinguish mendacity from the orthodox grammar of documentary film-making. When *The Connection*, for example, was criticised because the mule's journey was actually two separate trips cut together to appear as one, it was not the cut which made it false but the spurious nature of the action represented in the shot. De Beaufort claimed in reply to the charges that 'The film never pretends to be an observational film about one trip. It is a representational film about the trade.'[24] Quite apart from his untruth over details, this is hardly a proper defence, either intellectually (a fiction may also be representational in this sense) or legally. The code may be ambiguous but is clear enough in general terms: reconstruction is allowed in well-defined circumstances, it must not 'distort reality' and must be clearly labelled on the screen. For programmes dealing with criminal and antisocial behaviour, like drug smuggling, additional rules apply: there must be no payments to people filmed committing criminal acts, and they must not commit these offences for the camera. There are also guidelines on the use of secret cameras, and payment to people involved in programmes. Part of the *Guardian*'s case against Carlton was that they failed to take heed when they were warned, and the episode raised wider questions about the pressures on today's documentary makers to come up with hard-hitting, dramatic, populist programmes for peak viewing.

But the television community was caught in a double bind. Within the trade, says Winston, there was a certain amount of sincere professional condemnation of the film's mendacity, but a reluctance to mount a public defence of documentary practices for fear of appearing to defend the indefensible. Willis was standing on similar terrain. Shortening an hour-long meeting to a three-minute sequence is a basic documentary technique. Shooting sequences from different angles and cutting them together is a long-established process.

> We . . . need to differentiate between the accepted grammar of television and dishonesty. TV plays with the truth. It always has done. The selection of shots, editing, lighting, camera angles – all involve choices made by the director. They should reflect reality but are not reality itself.

Winston concludes that 'The primrose path leading to fraud starts with the lies of the images, not with the edit.'[25]

IV

So, a paradox. It seems that questioning the integrity or authenticity of a documentary sooner or later comes down to the truth value of the individual image, the fragment seized from reality, even though, at the same time, the fragment is given its meaning only through combination with other such fragments, through montage, the process of editing.

Back in 1920s' Soviet Russia, one of the sites where documentary was born, this was readily understood as a dialectical phenomenon; in Vertov's formula, life-facts become film-facts which have to be combined by montage into film-truth. A theoretical formulation with practical implications. The theory posits that the scene in front of the camera, which semiotics later calls the profilmic scene, this scene, once filmed, is no longer identical with itself, and only reveals its new identity when combined with other such non-identicals. If this was an insight derived from applying the Marxist dialectic to the new art of cinema, it also holds true from the very different intellectual discourse of semiotics, at least according to Barthes. In the early 1960s, when the journal *Cahiers du cinéma* asked him about the relevance of linguistics to film, he replied that a linguistically informed analysis of film was not concerned with the image as such, but only with the combination of images into narrative sequences.[26] For the analysis of documentary, however, this apparently universal and fundamental proposition, which no one seriously denies – that montage is precisely what makes cinema possible – carries the danger of assuming that the syntagms of documentary – the syntactic forms of the combination of successive images – are the same as in fiction, or derive from them. This is to fall into error. Documentary frequently borrows the tropes of diegetic fiction but it doesn't need to, and there are innumerable films throughout the history of documentary which effectively dispense with them – we shall come to some examples later. But in that case, we need to understand more about the properties of this slippery 'fragment seized from reality', the individual shot, which seems to present the issue of the truth-value of the image in its elementary or basic form.

The shot as elementary form raises a key question for any semiotics of documentary, that of the minimal unit of signification employed to build the communicative system. In the case of film, it would seem logical to nominate the individual shot, which serves as the minimal unit of editing, as the basic building block of all film language, whether fiction or documentary. From the perspective of the editor, however, this move quickly turns out to be both ambiguous and problematic. Are we speaking of the shot as it comes out of the camera, or as the editor cuts it up? What if the camera shot is cut in two and used in different places – is this one shot or two? What of continuous shots taken with a mobile camera, long takes which appear to combine several different shots connected by camera movement, which the editor may choose to leave as one shot or divide up by means of cuts?

Better perhaps to think of the shot as a temporal unit of varying length and a certain duration, which on the screen comprises an organic whole, a Gestalt, like a melody, within the flow of the montage. This is the approach of Gilles Deleuze, who has analysed the representation of movement and time as the movement-image and the time-image. According to Deleuze, there are three levels of temporality in the shot: the frame, which is immobile, like a snapshot; the movement-image, delimited by cutting, which comprises a mobile section of duration; and the time-image, the image of time which flows from the montage which links one movement-image to another (but which can also take the form of the long take or sequence shot). For his understanding of duration, Deleuze draws heavily on the work of an earlier French philosopher, Henri Bergson, who found its epitome not in film but in music. (Bergson's comments on film are naive, but then he made them at the time of cinema's infancy.) To interrupt a rhythm, says Bergson, to dwell on one note too long, is to bring about a qualitative change in the whole musical phrase, and something similar is true of the rhythms of both filming and editing. Here, to say that the shot is the minimal unit is also to say that editing is about rhythm, and every editor knows that to alter the length of a shot is to change its feel and import (which of course is true for both documentary and fiction). It is not an accident that Henri Lefebvre found the same difficulty in deciding the 'minimal unit' in the case of music. 'Where', he asked, 'can you find the atom, the elementary sign, the musical unit? . . . is it the sound? The "note"? The pure sound produced by the tuning fork or the sound with its harmonics?'[27] What exactly is the musical equivalent of the morpheme or the phoneme? Should the signifying unit be the interval? Or the chord? Or the musical phrase? Better to abandon the assumption that the relation of signifier-signified works the same way in both verbal and non-verbal systems – a warning which also applies to film.

Nevertheless, since semiology seeks to understand film on the model of language, another temptation is to consider the shot as the equivalent of the word. But the shot is quite unlike this. It is first of all a concrete visual sign, not an arbitrary and conventional symbol, and not an item in a vocabulary. There is no lexicon of shots, no dictionary of images, as Pasolini put it (one of the few film-makers since the Russians in the 1920s to engage with theoretical issues). There are only libraries and archives – a question we shall come back to later. It is true that words are malleable, they can be broken apart and put back together in new combinations ('travelogue', 'docudrama', 'infotainment'), they can be inflected this way and that – but in this the similarity with the shot is only superficial. The word can only be broken up into a finite number of specific sub-units (which have no meaning in themselves: they are phonemes or morphemes, depending on the scheme of analysis). Whereas the shot can be cut anywhere *and still remain a minimal unit of editing*, like the worm which is cut in half and wriggles away in opposite directions. In other words, it retains its fundamental quality as a segment of time, a movement-image. Even down to a single frame, with the duration of a flash – whereas a frame-still on a page is not a shot, it's a photograph, reduced to immobility.

Moreover, there is montage between shots, and montage within the shot. The shot is a complex signifier, multiple and simultaneous, made up of the elements depicted within the frame, their relationships, and their movement and alteration. In comparison to language this is more like the equivalent of a sentence or even a paragraph – and then some: even the most exhaustive verbal description of the image necessarily leaves something out; there is always something left over which cannot be rendered into words. Indeed film is what Raymond Bellour used to call 'the unattainable text', which escapes at the very moment the critic tries to seize it. This of course is true for both documentary and fiction, but there is also a critical difference, neatly explained by Dai Vaughan:

> In fiction, the elements are exhausted in the production of the overall meaning of the text; and anything which cannot be read as contributing to this meaning is consigned to a limbo of insignificance. In documentary, by contrast, the elements are seen as always exceeding their contribution to any given meaning; and they remain always open to scrutiny either for their own sakes or for their potential in the generation of new meanings oblique, peripheral, or even antagonistic to the text as understood.[28]

V

The peculiar character of the fragment seized from reality is posed in the singular example of the Zapruder footage, the twenty-two seconds of 8mm film of the assassination of J. F. Kennedy taken by an amateur cameraman which forms the principal visual material evidence of the event. For many years the footage was suppressed, only to be seen by researchers visiting the government archive where a copy was held; it had been purchased by *Life* magazine the day after the assassination and published only in the form of still images, minus the frame which shows Kennedy's head being blown apart. Although bootleg copies were circulating by the end of the 60s, it was seen publicly for the first time only in 1975, when a US television journalist defied the risk of legal action to show it on network television. Nowadays available quite readily, everyone can confirm for themselves what the footage shows: Kennedy thrown to the rear by a bullet which, according to the Warren Commission, came from behind.

The significance of the Zapruder footage is multiple. It not only offered an exemplar of the fragment seized from reality, but became a standard of *what the fragment seized from reality looks like*. Not only an icon of the event, also an icon of historical event-ness, a rare moment when contrary to Matuszewski's reasonable assumption, history happens where one waits for it. Largely because of this, and despite the effort of numerous documentarists (and of Oliver Stone's major effort at dramadocumentary in the highly tendentious *JFK*), the Zapruder footage somehow resists all attempts to divide it up or even insert it into a narrative context; especially when every narrative context on offer still leaves the case unproven, and just who killed Kennedy remains a matter of speculation. The Zapruder footage is thus a signal example precisely because it isn't a documentary, or even newsreel in the usual sense, but the simplest kind of minimal filmic unit, the filmic equivalent of the snapshot. As Pasolini put it, Mr Zapruder didn't choose his camera angle, 'he simply filmed from where he happened to be'.[29] It is not devoid of point of view, but there is a crucial sense in which it isn't authored, the sense in which authors have intentions that go beyond the immediate; Mr Zapruder, the legal author, is not an author in this aesthetic sense.

A BBC television documentary about cinéma vérité some years ago described the Zapruder footage as 'a home movie taken from the position a Hollywood movie crew would have set up' if they had been staging the event.[30] Not quite. As Stella Bruzzi points out, Mr Zapruder's view of the motorcade 'was partially obscured by a large road sign, tantalisingly blotting out certain details of the assassination'.[31] One might add that the Hollywood movie would also have complemented the shot with others, for example a reverse to show the gun being pointed, though not necessarily by who, since this would give the game away. (This is more or less what Santiago Alvarez does in his satirical *LBJ*, where he cuts from a frontal photograph of Kennedy in the car to the supposed assassin – an image from a movie of a medieval soldier pointing a crossbow.)

On top of that, the Zapruder footage is shaky and poorly framed, the lens jiggles in response to Mr Zapruder's reaction to hearing the shot and Kennedy's head momentarily drops out of the image. However, on close and repeated examination it, it seems to show Kennedy being shot at least twice, and the second bullet, which splits his head open, seems to come from somewhere out in front of him. Researchers who saw the footage in the 60s believed that it impugned the Warren Commission's conclusion that there was a single assassin.[32] At New York University in the early 70s, the footage began to acquire the properties of a fetish. Among film-makers like Mike Wadleigh and Martin Scorsese there was talk of the Zapruder quotient; according to Wadleigh, 'if you had a very high quotient of total amateurism in terms of technique, but the content was superb, what you were filming was absolutely riveting, that was 100% on the Zapruder curve'.[33]

The BBC documentary, using this interpretation of the Zapruder footage as an emblem of the putative truth value of the documentary image, skirts around what Metz called 'a certain crazy optimism that has sprung up around cinéma vérité: the belief in a kind of innocence of the image, which is somehow mysteriously exempt from connotation'.[34] On the one hand, there is the idea that as a naive reality-fragment, the footage is devoid of any imposed interpretation or narrative purpose, it has no hidden authorial intention or discernible bias. On the other, it is brief and incomplete and the truth it reveals is restricted to the verisimilitude of the image. No one denies that what is shown is what happened – Kennedy was assassinated in Dallas by person or persons unseen – but as Bruzzi puts it, 'its mimetic power cannot stretch to offering a context or an explanation'; however, she falls back into hyperbole when she says that it 'shows us everything and shows us nothing'.[35] Similarly, the American documentarist Errol Morris becomes misleading when he says in the BBC film that because the documentary image cannot tell the whole truth, it is therefore a lie. I am relieved to discover, on subsequently meeting him at a film festival, that his thinking is more subtle than this; ironically the television documentary misrepresented him. In conversation he agrees that the issue is more complicated, and the documentary image is indeed evidentiary, it contains a veridical aspect which is filtered through the particular point of view of the observer filming it, and the skill and craft and artfulness with which the camera is operated – or lack of it in the case of the Zapruder footage. It is one thing to recognise this dose or dimension of subjectivity in the image. It doesn't follow that it is therefore not a true image. For that would be to assume an equation in which the subjective is opposed to the objective, and the objective is identified with truth. The two are not opposed in this way, they are both present at the same time. As the Zapruder footage, in its own way, very clearly shows.

Watching the Zapruder footage there is no room for thinking that the event portrayed is staged, or to imagine that those who appear in it are actors. However, its veridical quality rests largely on the viewer's extra-filmic knowledge of the represented event. The representation is corroborated by public knowledge, and in more than one way. The faces are already publicly known, the event itself was publicly witnessed. This is not at issue. Nor is its subjectivity in dispute, being so obvious. What niggles is the limited and contingent nature of what appears within the frame; or the other way round, everything the image is missing because it lies outside the frame and we know it must be there. But if Mr Zapruder's camera wasn't pointing the other way, and therefore cannot show what we really want to know and nobody saw, this is simply an elementary condition of all such filming of non-fictional reality. As Pasolini put it, 'It is impossible to perceive reality as it happens *if not from a single point of view*, and this point of view is always that of a perceiving subject.'[36] Unless there is another camera, the documentary editor's raw material always represents only one possible version of what could have been shot, because the camera could always have been positioned differently, or pointing in another direction; and whichever way it's pointing, it can never shoot what's going on behind it (unless of course in a mirror). But this tells us something about the particular qualities of documentary images, for it is not a concern which arises with fiction, with its orchidean reality, and where the editor usually has several different versions of the same scene to choose between. Why? Because fictional action is repeatable, whereas the documentary image, in seeking to capture the moment on the wing, is unique and unrepeatable.

The Zapruder footage tells the (or a) truth, but not the whole truth, because the whole truth lies off screen, and the greater part of it remains invisible. This is where the 'fragment seized from reality' differs from fiction – in the character of off-screen space. This is not to say that there is no off-screen space in the fictional narrative – on the contrary, it can easily be created by a glance or a sound – but rather that Benjamin's orchidean reality is an exclusion zone, whereas the documentary image is always open to the non-orchidean reality which hangs around outside the frame all the time and constantly threatens to invade it, or to pull the camera away. Indeed, the space of which the segment isolated by the camera is but a part, is a sphere of contingency and accident. This is also implicitly recognised by Benjamin when he remarks that 'the newsreel offers everyone the opportunity to rise from passerby to movie extra', adding that in this way anyone might even find themselves turning up in 'a work of art, as witness Vertov's *Three Songs of Lenin* (1934) or Ivens' *Borinage* (1933)'.[37]

VI

The semiological puzzle persists. The philosopher asks: 'When I see JFK being shot, do I see JFK? Do I see a representation of JFK? Do I see an accurate or inaccurate representation?' The semiologist answers:

> What appears on the screen, which our sensibility works on, is not reality, but a sign. The great error which has been committed regularly, is to embark on the study of film as if the spectacle of cinema placed us in the presence of a double of reality. It should never be forgotten that film is constituted by images, that is to say, objects which are fragmentary, limited and fleeting like all objects. What materializes on the screen is neither reality, nor the image conceived in the brain of a film maker, nor the image which forms itself in our brain, but a sign in the proper sense of the term.[38]

Thus the art historian Pierre Francastel in the middle of last century. The sign is the intermediary between the reality contained in the profilmic scene, the film-maker's appropriation of it and the image created in the brain of the viewer. What kind of sign exactly? The answer has been well rehearsed, ever since Peter Wollen first published *Signs and Meaning in the Cinema*: both index and icon.[39] Index, because it's the automatic product of a mechanical and chemical process; icon, because it's a graphic likeness which encodes a symbolic response. As index, the image refers directly to the profilmic scene; as icon, it has the capacity to evoke a host of secondary meanings – connotations, associations, nuances, overtones, undertones – which in turn are themselves often iconic. Indeed it cannot fail to do so. Moreover, these associations are multiplied and organised by the process of montage. In short, index and icon are not two different kinds of sign but two aspects of any cinematographic image whatever.

'Profilmic', indicating what is found in front of the camera and leaves its impression on the film, is one of a series of terms introduced by Étienne Souriau in the 1950s, in the preface to a collection of essays by a group of French scholars, followers of Francastel, who decided that to advance their discussions they needed to agree on a clear vocabulary. Two of these terms were to pass into general currency in subsequent film theory – the other being diegetic, belonging to the narrative. They also introduced 'afilmic', for the reality that exists independently of any relation with film, unselected reality, the world about us which exists independently of the camera being pointed at it. In Souriau's conception, the afilmic includes the stuff of documentary: 'A documentary is defined as presenting people and things that exist in the afilmic reality.'[40]

If only – unfortunately it's not quite so simple. First, the indexical attributes of the photograph are tamed by the subjective control of the photographer, whose stylistic choices can so inflect the image as to imbue it with all sorts of artistic hues (what Tretiakov called 'distortions'). It is perfectly possible to transform the ugly into the beautiful – this is what Ivens called 'the error of exotic dirt', describing how in filming *Borinage*, they 'sometimes had to destroy a certain unwelcome superficial beauty that would occur when we did not want it'. The wrong kind of shadow, for example, from the light streaming in at the window of a hovel, could destroy the effect of dirtiness, so they deliberately adopted a raw style of the filming

> to prevent agreeable photographic effects distracting the audience from the unpleasant truths we were showing . . . Without this sort of precaution there was always a danger that these tiny dilapidated barracks (sometimes covered with ivy) might look picturesque instead of appalling.[41]

If the documentary image, despite this plasticity, nevertheless commands our accedence, then in the opinion of Dai Vaughan, this is because its visual idiom reassures us not only that this is the way it looks, but 'more fundamentally, that an object of which this is a representation must have existed in the first place.'[42] Roland Barthes speaks of this as the 'real unreality' of the photograph, real because the photograph is not experienced as an illusion, unreal because what it presents is a 'having-been-there', not a 'here-now' but a 'there-then'.[43] For Barthes the camera is a recording device: 'the scene is *there*, captured mechanically, not humanly (the mechanical is here a guarantee of objectivity).' The acceptance of this guarantee is sometimes referred to as trust, sometimes as the contract between film-maker and viewer, and the truth is that both can be broken (which in that case returns us to the question of how this trust is regulated, and in whose interests).

But observe the logic of Souriau's scheme. On the one hand, it says the afilmic world can become filmic material, and this is basically what documentary consists of (or better, aspires to). But in the process it becomes imbued with a whole range of filmic qualities. Souriau considers these qualities under four rubrics, *creatoriel, filmographique, filmophanique* and *spectatoriel* – difficult words to translate but corresponding to the film as intended by the film-maker; as the physical object manipulated by editing; as projected on the screen; and as perceived by the viewer. The film-maker begins by isolating and fragmenting elements of (afilmic) reality, and then comes the editing by which these fragments are recombined according to narrative or poetic requirements. The screen is flat but interpreted as having depth; it is in constant movement; here 'the proportions, arrangement and contrasts of light and shade, the dynamic axes of movement and other screen properties . . . may acquire an expressive value distinct from their representational significance'.[44] In short, whatever is in front of the camera is profilmic, while the filmic indicates the domain of human agency which photographs, directs and edits the film, and cannot avoid making all sorts of aesthetic and subjective, conscious and unconscious choices in the process. These choices are partly a matter of style and technique, and partly stem from other factors, sociological or ideological, or simply lack of skill, as in the case of the Zapruder footage. For here the filmic is present in a negative form, as amateurism, meaning lack of filmic control in the way the camera is handled.

The Zapruder footage, insofar as it conforms to Souriau's definition, is a paradigm of the afilmic, or what Tretiakov called 'raw material', but not of the method of documentary, which relates the individual shot to others through montage, as a movement-image to be combined with others. The Zapruder footage stands alone. Yet precisely for this reason it also exemplifies the properties of the image as icon, presenting itself as an emblem of history. The literal denotation of the image is singular and referential but iconic meanings belong to what Barthes calls the plane of connotation, which has a tendency to proliferation. Denotation is what anchors the image in perceptual identity – it is what you see it is – giving the photograph the quality Barthes describes as 'the paradox of a *message without a code*'.[45] Connotation proceeds in the opposite direction, accumulating symbolic associations which the perceptual image evokes, both intentionally and unintentionally, and with the passage of time. The index is particular, limited and fragmented; the icon is polysemous, but the consequent variation in readings, says Barthes, is not anarchic, because it depends on the different kinds of knowledge which the viewer brings to bear on the image, and such knowledge is always culturally coded. Nevertheless, the multiplication of connotations leads to ambiguity and uncertainty, because it opens the sign up to the very question of meaning. In the cinema, says Barthes, traumatic images are in this way bound up with uncertainty and anxiety.

VII

Our analysis has shown that the fragment seized from reality is always already both index and icon, and that equally, objective and subjective should not be regarded as mutually exclusive categories – they are both present at the same time. Nor is it usually possible to separate them out. However, there are certain circumstances in which this is done, for example, in a court of law, society's ultimate arbitrator of evidence and veracity.

Here I can cite another experience of my own, dating from 1978, when we filmed a big anti-Fascist demonstration in London. We had shots of people being arrested and showed the material to the defence committee. One shot clearly showed a policeman rushing towards a line of demonstrators standing their ground shouting, who then grabbed one of them by his frizzy hair, pulling him some distance to the open door of a police van, where he was bundled inside; the shot was continuous and the defendant was not, as alleged, resisting arrest. We ended up in court showing the film on his behalf. The only requirement was that we showed the footage (16mm) unedited, which required a special projector (the double-headed kind usually only found in dubbing theatres, capable of running the separate sound track in synchronisation with the picture). In the courtroom, the *mise en scène* was beautifully ironic – the only place where we could put the projector so that everyone could see the screen was by placing it in the witness box itself, while I had to stand beside the box and reach over to turn it on. The film was taken as unimpeachable evidence of the arrest with which the testimony of the arresting officer simply did not tally, and the result was a happy one. Since I hardly needed to watch the footage, I turned the projector on and looked at the policeman in question, who went white as a sheet. As soon as the projection came to an end, the magistrate looked round the courtroom and announced 'Case dismissed'. Here, of course, it was only the indexical element which counted, not the iconic at all.

Is the faith of the court in the objectivity of the filmic evidence to be considered naive? It has to be said that everyone there was content to consider it indisputable. Is this merely the result of a disposition to believe? Are there certain limits to what would be considered admissible evidence in such circumstances? What are the mechanisms by which the multiple nature of truth – indexical, cultural, legal, consensual – is here pinned down and fixed? These questions direct us inexorably to another example of snatched footage, George Holliday's casual video recording of the beating of Rodney King by a bunch of Los Angeles policemen in March 1991, which he sold the next day to a local television station for $500. A year later, four policemen were acquitted by a white jury from the suburbs of assaulting a black man in the city and black Los Angeles responded to the verdict with several days of rioting, in which fifty-four people were killed, more than 2,000 injured and over 13,000 arrested. Clearly these riots were the result of an enormous amount of pent-up tension, for which the accidental video served as a kind of telescope through which millions of people around the world were able to glimpse not tinsel-town but the real LA, and the real LAPD. 'What was so frustrating for the black community in L.A.,' says one commentator, 'was the sense that the truth had been validated through the video, and that this consensus was being denied its legitimacy.'[46]

As a traumatic image, the trauma was multiplied several times over by the global traffic in images of the age of satellite television – at least a billion people saw it worldwide according to Michael Renov, a film theorist working in California, who explains that despite the apparently universal assumption of the footage as undeniably 'damning' evidence, the defence contrived to give it their own preferred reading.

The meaning of every tortured movement of King's body during the 81 seconds of tape was interpreted by the defense through a variety of analytic techniques (reframing; repetition; reversed, slowed, or arrested movement). These techniques proved capable of 'defamiliarizing' the tape's subject matter which, in this case, amounts to dehumanizing the victim.[47]

Bill Nichols, another Californian film theorist, picks up the analysis:

> The defense lawyers for the four LAPD officers charged in the beating turned Rodney King from victim to dangerous provocateur and converted police response from raw brutality to panicky self-defense. Their skill testifies to the malleability of footage that may document what happened on one level but not guarantee its meaning on another. The historical imprint may attest to authenticity, but meaning remains the result of interpretations applied and accepted.[48]

But who had the authority to interpret this fragment seized from reality? Film theorists have tried to recover their intellectual claims from the shysters, but certain critical facts remain. Like the minimum content of the Zapruder footage, there was no argument whether Rodney King was beaten. Unlike the Zapruder footage, which was suppressed, the Holliday footage became material evidence in court. Here it turns out the image can be challenged in the same way as a witness, says Ron Burnett, 'to the same degree and using similar premises', except that it cannot answer. As Carl Plantinga puts it, 'though the video clearly showed that man's beating, it remained mute about his or the policemen's intentions and motivations'.[49] Burnett believes the defence introduced 'so many levels of interpretation to the image that the jury was dissuaded from taking the beating at face value'.[50] Renov sums up: 'No longer ought we as a culture to assume that the preservation and subsequent re-presentation of historical events on film or tape can serve to stabilize or ensure meaning.'[51] But it would be wrong for anyone to conclude that if it could be made to mean anything, its truth is therefore merely relative. The problem is rather that in certain usually extreme situations, the indexical content fails to limit the interpretation of the image and the iconic and ideological values that accrue to it. But if the image is wrenched out of true, there may well be a social cost to pay, and here it was precisely through a kind of legalised denial, a refusal to acknowledge the obvious indexical content of the image, its evident reality, that the video became the trigger that released the rage of a community.

We might settle for saying (at least for the moment) that the truth in the image is objective in being what the lens sees, and at the same time subjective, in corresponding to a particular and necessarily partial point of view. But then there is the domain of what Souriau called the spectatorial axis, the space between the screen and viewer's eyes, which includes a series of sociological and psychological factors which affect the viewer's disposition towards the film. Indeed different viewing spaces – the cinema, the domestic television screen, a courtroom – are conducive to different types of attention, and the same viewer is liable to see the same piece of film differently if the space of viewing is different. This is not to impugn the documentary endeavour, because it's only the obverse of what happens in the space between the profilmic scene and the viewfinder – in both cases, it partly depends what one is looking for. But it leads to the conclusion articulated by Fernando Birri, one of the pioneers of the Latin American new wave of the 1960s, that the documentary is a process of approximation towards reality, but a reality the camera can never fully grasp.[52] This idea is beautifully expressed by a recent contribution to an email discussion on the subject of cinematic truth. It is not necessary, says Sean Cubitt, to abandon truth in favour of relativism, but merely to abandon it as 'a full presence':

What we have to do is defer the arrival of truth, on the principle of Zeno's paradox. Representation – or any other process of adequate description – approaches its object in the same way Achilles approaches the tortoise, by infinitesimals. By the time we have described the real, it has moved on fractionally, and we must follow it across the diminishing gap, without ever seizing it. Documentary operates by Zeno's paradox, constantly approximating but never seizing a real which flees before it.[53]

Notes

1. See W. Rolston and D. Miller (eds), *War and Words: The Northern Ireland Media Reader* (Belfast: Beyond the Pale, 1996); and D. Miller, *Don't Mention the War: Northern Ireland, Propaganda and the Media* (London: Pluto Press, 1994). On *Inside the Maze*, personal recollection by the film's editor, Noel Chanan.

2. Jonathan Rosenbaum, 'The Screed We Need', *Chicago Reader*, 2004, <www.chicagoreader.com/movies/archives/2004/0604/062504.html>.

3. Quoted from memory.

4. See Michael Chanan, *The Dream That Kicks, The Prehistory and Early Years of Cinema in Britain* (London: Routledge, 1996), 2nd edn, p. 211.

5. Including Anthony Asquith, Lord David Cecil, Roger Fry, J. B. S. Haldane, Julian Huxley, Augustus John, J. M. Keynes, George Bernard Shaw, John Strachey, Dame Ellen Terry and H. G. Wells.

6. See Don Macpherson (ed.), *Traditions of Independence: British Cinema in the Thirties* (London: BFI, 1980), p. 112.

7. Harry Watt, *Don't Look at the Camera* (London: Paul Elek, 1974), p. 192.

8. See Bert Hogenkamp, *Deadly Parallels: Film and the Left in Britain 1929–39* (London: Lawrence and Wishart, 1986), p. 44.

9. Quoted ibid.

10. See Michael Chanan, *Repeated Takes: A Short History of Recording and Its Effects on Music* (London: Verso, 1995), Chapter 3.

11. Cited in Asa Briggs, *The BBC: The First Fifty Years* (Oxford: Oxford University Press, 1985), p. 16.

12. Stuart Hood, *On Television* (London: Pluto Press, 1987), 3rd edn, p. 39. Hood joined the BBC at the end of World War II and rose to become BBC-TV, controller of programmes, 1962–4.

13. Stuart Hood, 'News from Nowhere?', *International Socialism* no. 68, 1995, <pubs.socialistreviewindex.org.uk/isj68/hood.htm>.

14. Brian Winston, *Lies, Damn Lies and Documentaries* (London: BFI, 2000), pp. 95–6.

15. Stuart Hood, *A Survey of Television* (London: Heinemann, 1967), p. 119, quoted in Stephen Heath and Gillian Skirrow, 'Television: A World in Action', *Screen* vol. 18 no. 2, Summer 1977, p. 12.

16. See Norman Swallow, *Factual Television* (London: Focal Press, 1966), pp. 84–90, and Peter Black, *The Mirror in the Corner* (London: Hutchinson and Co. Ltd, 1972), pp. 164–5.

17. Mick Jagger, transmitted 31 July 1967.

18. See Winston, *Lies, Damn Lies and Documentaries*, pp. 10–11 and *passim*.

19. John Willis, 'The Faking of Real TV', *Guardian*, 11 May 1998.

20. Kamal Ahmed, 'Drugs, Lies and Videotape', *Guardian*, 7 May 1998.

21. Steve Boulton, *Guardian*, 6 May 1998.

22. Winston, *Lies, Damn Lies and Documentaries*, p. 32.

23. Steve Boulton, *Guardian*, 6 May 1998.

24. *Guardian*, 6 May 1998.

25. Winston, *Lies, Damn Lies and Documentaries*, p. 19.

26. See Victor Burgin, *The Remembered Film* (London: Reaktion Books, 2004), p. 23.

27. Henri Lefebvre, 'Musique et sémiologie', *Musique en jeu* no. 4, 1971.

28. Dai Vaughan, *For Documentary* (Berkeley and London: University of California Press, 1999), p. 80.

29. Pier Paolo Pasolini, 'Observations on the Long Take', *October* no. 134, 1980, p. 3.

30. *Late Show Special* (Tim Kirby, BBC2), 22 November 1993.

31. Stella Bruzzi, *New Documentary: A Critical Introduction* (London and New York: Routledge, 2000), p. 13.

32. There is another television documentary I remember seeing, which added a sound recording of the event that also survived, not in this case an amateur piece of work but the sound picked up through the open microphone of a motorcycle cop on duty close by; married up, the clip jumped alive with a synchronous soundtrack on which one heard and seemingly saw the report of three shots, not two.

33. *Late Show Special*.

34. Christian Metz, *Film Language: A Semiotics of Cinema* (Oxford: Oxford University Press, 1974), p. 195.

35. Bruzzi, *New Documentary*, pp. 17–18.

36. Pasolini, 'Observations on the Long Take', p. 3.

37. Walter Benjamin, 'The Work of Art in the Age of Mechanical Reproduction', in Hannah Arendt (ed.), *Illuminations* (New York: Shocken Books, 1969), p. 231.

38. Pierre Francastel, 'Espace et Illusion', *Revue Internationale de Filmologie* no. 2 vol. 5 (1951).

39. Peter Wollen, *Signs and Meaning in the Cinema* (London: Secker and Warburg, 1969).

40. See the Preface to Étienne Souriau, *L'Univers Filmique* (Paris: Flammarion, 1953).

41. Joris Ivens, *The Camera and I* (Berlin: Seven Seas, 1969), p. 88.

42. Dai Vaughan, 'The Broken Trust of the Image', *Vertigo* no. 4, 1994/5.

43. Roland Barthes, 'Rhetoric of the Image', in *Image-Music-Text* (London: Fontana/Collins, 1977), p. 45.

44. Souriau, *L'Univers Filmique*, p. 8.

45. Roland Barthes, *Camera Lucida* (New York: Hill and Wang, 1981), p. 195.

46. Ron Burnett, *Cultures of Vision: Images, Media and the Imaginary* (Bloomington: Indiana University Press, 1995), pp. 21–2.

47. Michael Renov in M. Renov (ed.), *Theorising Documentary* (London and New York: Routledge, 1993), p. 9.

48. Bill Nichols, in Renov, *Theorising Documentary*, pp. 188–91.

49. Carl Plantinga, *Rhetoric and Representation in the Nonfiction Film* (Cambridge: Cambridge University Press, 1997), p. 57.

50. Burnett, *Cultures of Vision*, p. 22.

51. Renov, *Theorising Documentary*, p. 8.

52. Fernando Birri in *New Cinema of Latin America*, dir. Michael Chanan, 1983.

53. Sean Cubitt, posting to <film-philosophy@mailbase.ac.uk>, 20 April 1998; quotation slightly edited.

EARLY YEARS

1913: pointing at the camera in *With Captain Scott, R. N. To the South Pole*

1920: *Trials and Tribulations of a Cameraman*: loading the camera in the Arctic cold (above and below)

1927: Joris Ivens behind the camera in the opening shot of *The Bridge*

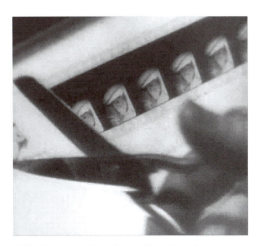

1929: *Man with a Movie Camera* (Dziga Vertov)

1932: *K.Sh.E* (Esfir Shub), the sound camera in the opening sequence

1932: *K.Sh.E*, the camera filming from a cradle hanging from a construction crane at the Dnieper Dam; a similar image occurs in *Man With a Movie Camera*

1930s: Workers Film & Photo League van on the street

1940S FILMING PRACTICES

1940/41: amateur film-maker Rosie Newman using her 16mm Cine Kodak Model K (Courtesy of the Imperial War Museum, IWM 65393)

1941: Humphrey Jennings (left) shooting in Westminster Abbey (IWM D1861)

1943: training military film
cameramen at Pinewood
Studios on De Vry cameras
(IWM H 30989)

1947: Richard Leacock (left) and Robert Flaherty, shooting *Louisiana Story*

1940S SCREENING PRACTICES

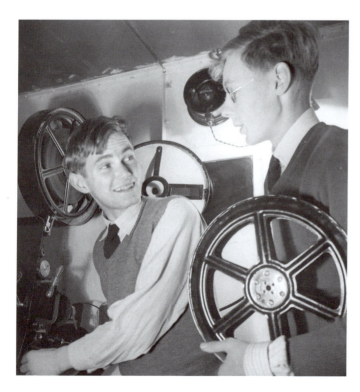

1943: public schoolboys at Ampleforth College run their own cinema (IWM D 17369)

1943: setting up 16mm projection for a Ministry of Information screening in a village hall (IWM D 22620)

1943: British WWI propaganda films being screened in an Arab village in Palestine ('Men and boys watch conventionally from the projector side of the screen; a smaller group of women and girls watch separately on the "wrong" side') (IWM K 4164)

PART II Historical Moments

4 Documentary before Documentary

From the first Lumière films to *Nanook*

I

At the beginning, when documentary was not yet documentary (but then fiction wasn't fiction yet either), when the medium was mute and each film ran only a minute or two, moving pictures hardly amounted to more than a miscellany of visual titbits, which made no demands on literacy and thus spread easily and rapidly far and wide. The world on the screen exerted a magical attraction but remained anecdotal and predominantly iconic. In terms of public discourse, it was practically inarticulate, other than to reinforce already stereotypical images or create some new ones; in short, intensely fascinating but apparently ill-adapted to serving intelligent purposes. Indeed, early cinema fed on the same popular cultural appeal as the new illustrated press, of which Siegfried Kracauer somewhere remarked that in the illustrated magazines the public sees the world whose perception of it is hindered by the illustrated journals themselves.

The icons of early cinema were often torn out of context – like the *Indian War Council* and *Sioux Ghosts Dance* filmed by William Dickson in Edison's kinetoscope studio in 1894, or the Berber woman making a pot which Félix-Louis Regnault filmed at the Colonial Exhibition in Paris the following year – short films which set the tone for such 'exotic' scenes but failed to humanise their subjects. On the contrary, images like this tended to signify only an otherness shorn of any articulate content (which is one of the definitions of the exotic). They may even resist signification altogether and remain thoroughly mystifying. But this didn't bother Regnault: a physical anthropologist who adopted the cinematograph with scientific pretensions, he held typical racist views about 'inarticulate savages' whose 'language is so poor it does not suffice to make them understood'.[1] This, however, would do better as a description of the lack of sustained expressive power of early film than of its subjects.

As a scientific aid, the cinematograph promised to reveal an 'Unseen World', the title of a series launched in Britain in 1903 by the film dealer Charles Urban, where the subject matter is filmed through a microscope, with individual titles such as *Birth of a Crystal*, *Cheese Mites*, *Circulation of Blood in the Frog's Foot* and *Anatomy of the Water Flea*. (Cecil Hepworth, caught up in early cinema's penchant for self-satire, immediately produced a parody, *The Unclean World*, in which a scientist inspects his food through a microscope and discovers two large insects; two hands appear in the frame and pick them up, revealing them to be clockwork toys.) The technique of microscopic filming produces a double magnification, first through the microscope and then the projector, which appears to reveal an entirely new spatial dimension. A similar discovery in the dimension of time takes place through time-lapse photography, originally known as 'speed magnification'. These so-called scientific films transformed the dimensions of time and space through cool empirical observation, but while the story they told about science was dramatic, it was devoid of context and totally lacking in plot, which could only help to foster a thoroughly mystifying notion of science.

If the scientific film has remained a subgenre of documentary ever since, there is also a wider connection between documentary and science, in which science as an ideology of knowledge lends its authority to the camera as an instrument of objective observation. The link is forged, as Brian Winston reminds us, at the founding moment of photography, when Arago presented the new invention to the French parliament in 1839 not as an artist's aid but as a scientific instrument, which produces evidence and truth.[2] The attribution of objectivity seems to imply that the camera obeys the Galilean principle by which scientific instruments guarantee that observation and measurement are independent of human discrimination – except that the camera, still or moving, isn't quite like this. For one thing, precisely as an instrument and not a machine, its results depend on the skills and imagination of its user. Umberto Barbaro, the first theorist of Italian neorealism, cited the argument of the Soviet writer Lebedev, that the machine is indifferent to its operator and the product of twenty different workers will be identical, but not so with the camera; allow twenty operators to shoot the same scene and the results of each will be different, according to their different mentalities, states of mind, wishes, expressive capabilities and intentions; and these, of course, are the elements or determinants of aesthetics and style.[3] But this doesn't mean that aesthetics and style overwhelm the content denoted by the image. We know that the indexical and the iconic are always present together, opening out the image to connotation – associations, nuances and undertones, often themselves iconic – beyond the immediate denotation, but this doesn't mean the documentary image cannot represent veridical truth or count as evidence, though somewhat different and rather more complex to unravel than Arago supposed back at the beginning. It does mean that documentary can only develop through learning to exploit the inflection of the denotative image by the connotations it summons up, and this lies in the discovery of the properties of montage.

II

Writing about the relation between ethnographic and avant-garde film traditions, Catherine Russell has observed that while scholars of early film have been much preoccupied with the emergence of storytelling and narrative, the dominant mode of cinema for its first ten years or so was the actuality. This is not a genre but a broad-ranging field of subject matter, from native cultures to military conflicts, royalty to sports matches, everyday activities and urban panoramas. Nominally 'unstaged', many were simple moving photographs of socially staged events like processions and parades, dancing and public performance. In this world of documentary before documentary, the cinema, she says, 'provided its own logic of the spectacle: whatever it captured became an attraction by virtue of being filmed'.[4] In a similar vein, Tom Gunning has spoken of the early days as a 'cinema of attractions', whose heritage passes to the avant-garde of the 1920s, in which display predominates over narrative absorption.[5] In France, several writers begin to speak of this magnetic sense of attraction as *photogénie* – the photogenic – in cinema.

It is the burgeoning world of the story film that first produces a sense of narrative progression in the succession of shots. This is already true of the first multiple-shot story films, in which the mature language of the cinema is no more than embryonic; but even here, where narrative articulation is crude, the screen already constitutes a representational space sufficient unto itself – for as Metz himself says, enclosure is the basic requirement of narrative – with characters playing parts in a simple plot with beginning, middle and end. In the case, for example, of Cecil Hepworth's *Rescued by Rover* of 1905, the cast is led by a dog, and the representational code employed is one of continuity of action (or grammatically speaking, direction matching) which requires little or no actual acting, and certainly no character psychology. The minimum requirement of a film plot is that somebody does something to someone or something which produces a reaction or response – a gypsy steals a baby from a pram and a dog comes to the rescue; there is an identifiable agent, and an alteration which carries from one scene (or shot) to another until resolution. This is different from the films which form the prehistory of documentary. Here the projected world is not imaginary, the people in it are not fictional characters caught in a plot but social actors in the public world, and these fragmented attempts at what Kracauer called the seizure of reality remain precisely that: fragments – however beautifully shot and composed, like the very first Lumière films – but with no relation of cause and effect between them and certainly no resolution.

The difference is this: the narrative yields up everything the viewer needs to know in order to follow the story. (At least in principle; but there were also early story films which assumed prior knowledge of the tale – indeed this is why the Passion and boxing matches are both among the earliest subjects, as Nöel Burch pointed out, precisely because in these cases the story was already known; otherwise they relied on the accompaniment of a spoken commentary to fill in the gaps.)[6] The proto-documentary is not so forthcoming. Its significance is mostly limited to the surface of the reality it seizes, largely comprising familiar and ready-made symbols, the icons of the world it reproduces. In the exemplary case of the spectacle provided by royal and state occasions, the act of observation became complicit with the function of the event itself, magnifying the political message which is always communicated by such display, for as Thomas Hobbes once observed, power is the reputation of power. Or as Walter Bagehot put it in *The English Constitution* in 1867, the use of 'theatrical elements' is necessary in order to induce reverence on the part of the 'ruder sorts of men' towards the 'plain, palpable ends of government' – which clearly anticipates the ideological service that authority expected (and still expects) the moving pictures to render to the state.

In the domain of actuality, certain subjects were able to grow in length by a simple process of accretion. State occasions and royal processions could be filmed by several cameras along the route. Several typical scenes of a foreign country strung together became a travelogue (or in French, *documentaire*). Boxing matches were ideal for the limited length of film carried by the early cameras, since they were conveniently divided into short segments which could then be strung together. Another variant is represented in a thirty-minute title made by Cricks and Sharp in 1906, *A Visit to Peak Frean and Co.'s Biscuit Works*. An early instance of company sponsorship, the film consists in a series of long takes of the process of manufacture from raw materials through to finished product. Later examples sometimes take the form of 'a day in the life of . . .', like *A Day in the Life of a Coalminer* (1910) and *At Messrs Pilkington's Glassworks* (1913). There is a clear ideological purpose behind these films, which are intended to demonstrate how modern and efficient are the companies concerned. The same year as the Pilkington Glassworks film in England, the leading force in modern industrial practice in the United States, Henry Ford, bought a film camera, encouraged by his friend (and erstwhile employer) Edison, and within a few

months instructed his advertising department to embark on the production of factual films for promotional purposes. If films like these signal the beginnings of a new idea of public relations, they also
have value for later investigators, like the social historian studying the conditions of labour in the period.
And they also produced a new visual iconography. The film of Peak Frean's biscuit works ends with an
amazing shot of hundreds of workers streaming out through the factory gates – undoubtedly modelled
on the early Lumière film of workers leaving the factory, it goes on for so long that it transcends the
merely empirical to become an icon of the mass of workers required for mass production. There are similar scenes in the Ford films – one of them even shows the workers driving away in their own identical
Ford automobiles – and of course it was the Ford films which established the icon of the moving production line, which was elevated in their films into the very symbol of progressive capitalism, and hilari-
ously satirised by Chaplin in *Modern Times* (1936).

If only for lack of any standard of comparison, early cinema was susceptible to fakery. Albert Smith,
returning in 1898 from Cuba to New York during the Cuban–Spanish–American War, boasted that he had
taken footage of the Battle of Santiago Bay when he hadn't, so he faked it, using models and cigarette
smoke. It was a hit, which the public did not apparently suss.[7] Then when he went to South Africa, he felt
no compunction about dressing up British soldiers as Boers and passing it off as footage of the Boers in
action. James Williamson filmed *Attack on a China Mission Station* in the back garden in the English resort
of Hove in 1900 and then staged scenes from the Boer War on a local golf course. Barnouw comments
wryly that such activity was not regarded in the competitive ethos of the time as 'deceit' but as 'enterprise'.[8]
Sometimes these simulations were indeed exposed as fakes, but mostly a peculiar contract seemed to operate between film-makers and audiences, in which the one didn't tell and the other didn't ask. In 1907 came
a successful fake by William Selig of Chicago, *Hunting Big Game in Africa*, which purported to be a film of
one of Roosevelt's hunting trips and used a double to impersonate him, though carefully avoiding mention
of his name. The upshot was that the following year Roosevelt had the English cameraman Cherry Kearton
accompany him on a real hunting trip. The resulting film was one of the first of an extended form of travel
documentary in which British cameramen, schooled in the nineteenth-century tradition of empirical observation and amateur scientific investigation, excelled (Kearton himself went on to film in India, Borneo and
South America). With the ostensive purpose of making a scientific record, explorers travelling to remote
corners of the globe took on such cameramen as official photographers, who then came back with titles
like *Hunting Hippopotamus on the Blue Nile* (Pathé, 1907), *Abyssinian Marriage* (Roberto Omenga, 1908)
and *Life and Events in Tangka* (Deutsche-Bioskop, 1909), in which audiences vicariously experienced the
thrills of the veldt and the jungle, or the hardship of the desert and the wilderness.

Here again the documentary instinct for 'the seizure of physical reality' turns out to carry ideological implications, which were perfectly obvious to historians of documentary like Barnouw. Since the leading film-producing countries were nations with colonial empires, not surprisingly, he says, their films
reflected the attitudes that made up the colonial rationale: 'natives' were generally shown as 'charming,
quaint, sometimes mysterious; generally loyal, grateful for the protection and guidance' of the Euro-
peans, who were 'benevolently interested in colourful native rituals, costumes dances, processions'.[9]
Or as Russell puts it, the tendency in early cinema to put otherness on display enacts a fascination hidden
within a scientific discourse which betrays a power relation. Early cinema is both an allegorical form of

the colonial discourse and a site of construction of racial stereotypes.[10] But if the 'native' was encouraged to exhibit their exotic habits in the name of the camera as a scientific instrument of ethnographic
observation, the effect was to reduce exotic peoples to racist inferiority while turning the hunters and
explorers who embodied the idealised man-of-action abroad in the Empire into celebrities. A similar
effect would later transfer to war reporters, as Adorno would observe: 'cameramen in the first tanks and
war-reporters dying heroic deaths, the mish-mash of enlightened manipulation of public opinion and
oblivious activity'.[11] Thus the war cameraman came to represent the heroism of war, while the com-
batant soldier died anonymously. It's different now: reporters are embedded and there are names
attached to body bags sent back from Iraq and Afghanistan.

III

No major expedition would be considered complete without a cameraman (they were always men at
that time) who would often end up presenting the resultant film standing beside the screen delivering
their lecture (or a substitute, elaborating on lecture notes provided by the film dealer). If expeditions constituted ideal subjects for extended visual narratives, nevertheless a commentary was indispensable to
sustain interest and render the succession of images intelligible. Thus prolonging the model of the nineteenth-century magic lantern show, the genre retained an element of performance in front of the screen
which the story film folded into the screen itself. When the lecturer was in due course replaced by intertitles, the quotient of factual content went down.

The genre reached its climax in 1912, with Herbert Ponting's celebrated film of Scott's Antarctic expedition, whose unwieldy title announces its straightforward intent: *With Captain Scott, R.N. To the South Pole*.
First seen in Britain before the tragic outcome of the expedition became known, the film acquired a second
life when it was learned that Scott and his comrades had perished, and Ponting delivered his lecture for over
a year in London before taking it on tour.[12] In this version, incorporating photographs which Scott himself
had shot on the last fateful part of the expedition, the film turned the explorer into one of the first popular
tragic heroes of modern times, and it was twice reissued – once in 1924 following the success of Flaherty's
Nanook of the North (1922), and again in 1933 with a soundtrack. In the 1990s, under the title of the sound
version, *90 South*, it was one of the few non-fiction films of the early period available on video.

In Ponting's hands, the expedition film not only provided the audience with figures of identification
up on the screen, but included the trace of the film-maker. One begins to see here the articulation of a
coherent point of view, that comes and goes during the film, which is not imposed by the narrator's
semantic domination but belongs to the camera-eye, the eye at the viewfinder. If the diegetic camera of
the fiction film behaves like a disembodied and seemingly invisible observer, able to adopt any angle and
framing, Ponting's camera performs differently, to produce a different kind of construction of space, not
through continuity of action but around the corporeal point of observation. Instead of disembodiment,
what you get is the sustained inscription of the physical presence of the camera at the scene that it pictures, describing the space as it changes from one shot to the next. At one moment Ponting even delivers what looks a little like one of the first moments of deliberate documentary self-reflexivity, when we
get a shot of him in the act of filming, as if to say 'Look, I'm here, in the middle of all this'. But the shot
is paradoxical. It occurs twice, at the head and tail of a sequence in which the explorers take exercise by

playing football on the ice. It is obviously taken by a second camera which remains invisible, disembodied and unremarked. In the sound version the scene is accompanied by a curious piece of commentary in which Ponting refers to himself at the camera in the third person, while still not identifying the second cameraman. The same paradox turns up in a curious US documentary of 1920 called *The Trials and Tribulations of a Cameraman*, which portrays the difficulties of filming in the Arctic: the whole process, from transporting the gear to threading the camera in the freezing cold, is shot by another camera which is never acknowledged.[13] But you can feel the cold as you watch.

The power of Ponting's film lies in the beautifully photographed variety of imagery – the bows of the vessel ploughing through the icy sea, the expedition team erecting their tents, huddling together in the freezing cold, playing football on the ice, scenes of penguins and whales – in which the camera is a palpable participant in the scene, juxtaposed with the terrible beauty of the frozen continent which overflows the frame. This is documentary as the discovery of the photogenic world, the aspect of the world which lends itself to the pictorial prospect of the composed image, inviting the viewer to wonder at its visual arraignment. But this sensation, once again paradoxical, of the camera capturing a reality which remains beyond its capacity, can also be seen as an early example of the phenomenon of excess, the sense of a meaning or import which emanates from the screen and seems to lie beyond its confines, even beyond our ability to account for it. In Ponting's film, the excess we are confronted with has a familiar Romantic ring – the grandeur of the landscape which was theorised by Kant, in his *Critique of Aesthetic Reason* more than a century earlier, in the difference between the beautiful and the sublime, where the latter is the excess of nature in all its awesome glory. In cinema, this aura of meaning-beyond-meaning, which is often what we take away from the film afterwards, is experienced as excess because it seems to spill out of the screen uncontrolled and ungoverned, and therefore tends to defy analysis. Or as Nichols has it, excess in documentary is whatever remains beyond the organising principles of narrative, exposition, argument, and which falls 'outside the web of significance spun to capture it'.[14]

IV

The early development of documentary form also took place in Mexico during the Revolutionary years following the uprising of 1911, where the immediate success of topicals depicting the momentous events of the day helped to stimulate the early growth of Mexican cinema, and there was a marked increase in both the number of films and cinemas to show them in. In the absence as yet of a dominant international cinematic model for political reportage – the French *Pathé Journal* started in 1909, and newsreel production in the USA only in 1911 – these actualities developed along their own distinctive lines. In the account of Aurelio de los Reyes, film-makers stimulated by an eager urban audience took to the battlefields, where their instinct was to pursue a positivist belief in the camera's objectivity and to eschew a political agenda of their own. A film of 1912 by the Alva brothers, for example, *Revolución orozquista* ('The Orozco Revolution') attempts to report the events from both sides of the battle lines – the film-makers were even caught in crossfire which damaged their equipment – and it is difficult, says de los Reyes, to tell where the authors' sympathies lay; an objectivity which he adds does not survive the imposition of censorship by the Huerta regime in 1913. But in this brief period, de los Reyes holds that Mexican film-makers quickly developed greater skill than film-makers north of the border in the construction of a documentary narrative, and what he calls 'a local vernacular form of representation of contemporary happenings'.[15]

The film people in the north mostly treated the 'Mexican War', whose intricacies, factions and changes of leadership bewildered them, as an exotic background for love stories and adventure films where a central theme, according to Margarita de Orellana, was 'the heroism and superiority of the United States, whose citizens alone were portrayed as capable of bringing peace, order, justice and progress to a country like Mexico'[16] – a superiority complex which has bedevilled the gringo portrayal of Latin America throughout the history of cinema.[17] One producer, however, was particularly enterprising, and followed the journalists in beating a track to Pancho Villa. Villa was induced to sign a contract for $25,000 with the Mutual Film company granting them exclusive rights to film his battles. But the film people, led by Raoul Walsh earning his first director's credit, approached the reality as something to be organised for their convenience, requiring Villa to fight in daylight and reconstruct scenes from the battle if satisfactory pictures were not obtained in the heat of the conflict. Walsh even had him postpone daybreak executions until there was enough light to film by. When the results were not considered appealing enough, the battle scenes were restaged back at the studio.

The vernacular representation of the Mexican films depends on vernacular knowledge, which by definition is lacking in the viewer distant in either space or time. At the remove of almost a century, these images, presenting general views of the visible effects of political forces – including mass demonstrations and political meetings as well as the battlefield – are reduced to general icons of mass political upheaval which need specialist knowledge to be properly intelligible. Without it, what remains is merely the spectre of a narrative, of events unfolding in parallel, articulated through the sequence of spatial representations which strongly communicate, like Ponting in the Antarctic, the camera's palpable presence at the scene. Yet even today this spectre is capable of arousing the viewer's astonishment, thereby signalling another form of excess, which is particularly embroiled in documentary, which Nichols suggests has a simple and familiar name: history. History is the referent of documentary which always stands outside the filmic text, 'always referred to but never captured'.[18] This is partly because the film is always made up of images that are never more than fragments, and partly because history itself is anyway invisible, an absent cause (as Fredric Jameson calls it) accessible only through textual reconstruction. Nevertheless, these early documentaries announce a shift in the register of history. From now on, history will also become its own image, it will not now simply disappear but will leave a direct visual trace offering palpable evidence of its existence, or its having existed. Yet this will always be an image of excess which remains beyond our grasp, as if it were always just outside the frame, or happening just after the camera stops running.

Death is another form of excess, which will later criss-cross the history of documentary, repeatedly raising questions about the limits of representation. These limits are already approached by the photograph which punctures time. Barthes writes about this in *Camera Lucida*, describing a photograph of 1865 of a young man waiting to be hanged for an attempted assassination, in which one reads *he is going to die*, and shudders with horror at a catastrophe which has yet to occur and has already occurred.[19] Béla Balázs has a similar response remembering Ponting's film and the poignant effect of the photographs taken by Scott himself in the last days, which come across with the chill of the already dead, when he wrote his *Theory of the Film* over thirty years later: 'Who could forget Captain Scott's film, which is almost as if he had shot his own death . . .'.[20] Soon, this is what started to happen: cameramen filming their own deaths. Balázs also remembers in the same passage a couple of images from World War I in which 'we see the cameraman dying for the sake of his picture' – or rather, the shot comes to a sticky end as the cameraman is killed 'but the automatic mechanism ran on'. The camera wobbles and the image goes out of focus, signalling where the camera was overturned as the cameraman expired. The shots occur in a French film called *Pour la paix du monde* made at the end of the war from material in the army archives, and dedicated to six cameramen killed on active service while shooting it. (Exactly the same thing is seen more than fifty years later in the shot which Patricio Guzmán uses in *La batalla de Chile*, his account of the last year of Allende's Popular Unity government; this time it was taken by an Argentinian cameraman filming the attempted coup of June 1973, who is shooting a soldier on the streets who is shooting at him.) The significance of such shots, says Balázs, lies in more than 'the death-despising courage to which they bear witness', but in something quite novel: unlike every other form of visual representation, the image presented by the movie camera is that of a reality not yet completed, but which is 'still in the making while the presentation is being prepared. . .. It is this tangible being-present that gives the documentary the peculiar tension no other art can produce.'[21]

It was just such uncontrollable candour that government and the military most feared, and to which they responded with restrictions and censorship. Typically, say the authors of a study of British World War I propaganda, the images were carefully staged: apparently realistic shots of wounded soldiers at the front were usually stage-managed to present fatigue accompanied by cheerfulness, 'wounds were always freshly dressed and there were rarely pictures of Allied dead', although dead Germans featured more often.[22] World War I had a powerful effect on the subsequent practice of publicity and propaganda, but the progress of film through the trenches was halting, inconsistent and often paradoxical. The Germans entered the war favouring the use of new media, both the film camera and radio, but they ended up losing it, which they attributed at least partly to the enemy's superior propaganda effort. Britain and France at first kept cameramen away from the front, fearing demoralisation at home from revelations about the true face of war (and perhaps, according to Furhammer and Isaksson in their history of film and politics, that it would be 'handing information on a plate to enemy espionage');[23] their attitude changed when faced with the effect of German newsreels which were being widely distributed in the United States. By the time German propaganda had been trounced, America and its own cinema had performed an about-turn – the overwhelming pacifism of 1914 turned into equally overwhelming militarism. But, was this only because of British and French counter-propaganda? Furhammer and Isaksson report that the US film industry began making films leaning towards American intervention as early as the middle of 1915, well before government moved away from its isolationist position.

> One reason was certainly that several film companies had intimate financial connections with businesses that would welcome American participation in the war. There were film companies with pro-German sympathies, but for the great majority an English victory was a matter of vital economic importance.[24]

But they also argue that 'propaganda films are usually as much a means of exploiting a given climate of opinion as of exerting an influence. The public pays for the satisfaction of having its attitudes confirmed and reinforced.'[25] Whether the films had any effect on the war, the war certainly had a major effect on films. For the first time, the cinema managed to shake off its cultural inferiority complex as it transcended cheap entertainment to achieve patriotic prestige. Or to put it another way, World War I is when film first properly enters the political public sphere, when it is first officially recognised by the guardians of the public sphere as a force to be reckoned with when it came to the shaping – intentional or unintentional – of public opinion.

The reception of these films was grounded in the iconography of the newsreel, a format first launched by the French company Pathé a few years before the war. Combining short topicals into a magazine format better able to compete with the growing popularity of the short-story film, the newsreel quickly caught on, but its visual language remained disconnected. The formula was simple enough and remained unchanged for decades: a string of unrelated stories and regular appearance (weekly or twice weekly). According to evidence given to the Board of Trade by the Newsreel Association of Great Britain in 1938, apart from special editions, newsreels are 'mainly composed of items of "up-to-the-minute" news or matters germane thereto'[26] – a euphemism for royal personages and celebrities, society weddings and traffic jams, ship-launchings and big sporting events. Virginia Woolf described what they were like in her essay on the cinema of 1926, in which a literary intellectual finds she can only look upon film disparagingly:

> at first sight, the art of the cinema seems simple, even stupid. There is the King shaking hands with a
> football team; there is Sir Thomas Lipton's yacht; there is Jack Horner winning the Grand National.
> The eye licks it all up instantaneously, and the brain, agreeably titillated, settles down to watch things
> happening without bestirring itself to think.[27]

To begin with, this magazine format was a device for packaging exactly the same kind of topicals as before, and did nothing to enhance their communicable content, or deliver what counted as news in the serious newspaper – the agenda they followed was closer to that of the yellow press. But with the war, the urgency of history began to invade the screen, which became a parade-ground of rhetorical associations. A picture of 10 Downing Street would no longer signify merely the residence of the Prime Minister but national emergency; the launch of a battleship became a sign of more than naval pride, but the promise of victory at sea. A shorthand visual imagery took over, not unlike the synecdochic form of newspaper headlines.

Whether public interest was based, in the words of British film historian Rachael Low, on morbid or sentimental curiosity, it was readily exploited by both trade and government for propaganda purposes. If the language of the newsreel remained undeveloped, this was partly due to the limitations of the early film apparatus, which imposed severe restrictions on both style and technique. Accordingly there were attempts to develop equipment like long-focus lenses and lightweight cameras better suited to the requirements of war filming. Matuszewski had thought it easy to imagine the camera being carried on the same shoulders that bear rifles, but in the event it was mostly still too cumbersome for non-combatants, in Low's description, 'to risk their lives carrying heavy cameras into dangerous hiding places thirty yards or so from German snipers'.[28] Without more articulated and dynamic images, the resulting films were tied down by the constant need for intertitles that were 'sometimes heavily loaded with emotion'; they displayed little by way of continuity. Nevertheless, says Low, they 'conveyed an entirely new understanding of the complexity of modern warfare'.[29]

V

When a new kind of film emerged after the Great War for which the term documentary provided a useful label, there is no single point of origin, no unique foundational model. Documentary emerged as a distinctive genre by differentiating itself from fiction, on the one hand, and on the other, from the newsreel and the 'interest' film. It emerged in different countries and varied settings over the following years in a process fashioned by a dialectic between entertainment and propaganda, escapism and reality, which played out differently in the democracies of the West and Russia after the 1917 Revolution.

In the US, the production of factual shorts was not led by the film industry but by another branch of industry altogether. Although it has somehow, until very recently, escaped the attention of film historians, including historians of documentary, the Department of Motion Pictures established by the Ford Motor Company in 1914 emerged by the early 20s as the largest producer of such films in the country. With his well-known suspicion of conventional advertising, cinema struck Ford as an ideal instrument for the right kind of publicity. It was not the typical hyperbolic claims of advertising which he thought would sell cars but a combination of the right price, a network of dealers and service centres, and reputation, which was generated in the social space of consumption where commodities are enjoyed and consumed, by publicity which created the right associations with the product. Ford's thinking was cousin to that of Edward Bernays, pioneer of the public relations business and, accordingly, these were not just advertising films, or actualities of how the cars were made. The strategy included what is nowadays called product placement, with the Model T making subtle (or sometimes not so subtle) appearances in films about how to raise better livestock or keep the boys on the farm, following the principles articulated by one Watterson R. Rothacker, a prominent producer of such films at the time, that 'Advertising apparently without advertising is decidedly more potent than a direct commercial announcement' and 'the moving picture play which entertains the consumer while his buying instinct is being aroused' is 'the most subtle advertising ever conceived'.[30]

Typical editions of the newsreel format *Ford Animated Weekly*, which ran from 1914 to 1921, might cover anything from car races and campaigns for better roads to Henry Ford meeting President Wilson or his mentor Thomas Edison. The *Educational Weekly* (1916–21) favoured topics that would give the films a longer circulation period, like modern agricultural methods, or the manufacture of consumer goods such as lightbulbs and chewing gum. There were films on safety at work and on the road, with titles like *Safety First* (1920) and *Hurry Slowly* (1921), films about history, civics and citizenship, portraits of great cities, the benefits of electrification, modern sanitation, and education for immigrants. The last was one of Henry Ford's pet projects, and as Lee Grieveson has written, these films explicitly sought to promulgate norms of behaviour allied to the 'Americanisation' of the immigrant worker on Ford's own production lines and, in general, the establishment of the moral and social conditions that would contribute to increased efficiency and the goal of governing a mass population of workers.[31]

Ford had a clear idea of his market. Because the films were being offered for only a nominal rental fee, they were shunned by the majors who considered them unfair competition, but they were seen each week at over two thousand outlets by some three million people who were mainly located in small-town and rural communities, including non-theatrical settings like churches, YMCAs and schools. This made good sense, since rural viewers were far more likely to purchase Model Ts and Fordson tractors than the urban middle class (who preferred more expensive and sophisticated automobiles) or the urban work-ing class (who used public transport). The films employed simple prosaic intertitles peppered with con-ventional rhetoric, boasted excellent photography, photogenic in a superficial way, emphasising clarity and light and devoid of any kind of moody artistry; wherever appropriate, they employed conventional continuity cutting. One contemporary reviewer commented that 'the viewer is entertained so interest-ingly that he forgets that he is witnessing one of the cleverest advertising plans of these times'.[32] If these films represent a precocious awareness of the power of cinema in moulding public opinion, then they clearly belong to what Gramsci meant by Fordism, which was not just an industrial method ('scientific management') but an ideological project to maintain hegemony. They promulgated an ideology of mod-ernization and mediated the public response to industrial transformation of the kind pioneered by Ford in his own operations. As Grieveson remarks, we could call this Fordism via film.

In this perspective, there is no avoiding the obvious implication that Soviet documentary was intended to do the same job, and advance the hegemonic project of Communism. In that case, the dif-ferences that emerge are more than just aesthetic, but speak of the way that aesthetic options were put to work in the two systems, capitalism and Communism, and their contrasted approaches to the newly mediatised public sphere. The October Revolution had an explosive effect, liberating the imagin-ation and opening the doors to modernist experimentation, a freedom that was not brought under control for a good many years. But the gestation of documentary was a paradoxical process, which began, because of limited resources, with the promotion of the newsreel to the front rank of ideo-logical struggle. Dziga Vertov and the group who called themselves, in Vertov's neologism, the *Kinoki* or 'Film-eyes', with their aim of capturing 'life-as-it-is' worked in this arena. Here, the experimental development of the newsreel became the bridge to the full-grown documentary form of subsequent films by Vertov and others. At first, in the years of civil war and armed foreign intervention, almost no other kind of film-making was possible, but even later, when fiction films began to reappear, the ideo-logical imperatives of the Revolution provided a continuing rationale for documentary endeavours. Lenin himself famously told his Cultural Commissar Lunacharsky that he thought the production of films 'imbued with Communist ideas and reflecting Soviet reality should begin with the newsreel'.[33] And in his 1922 directive on cinema, Lenin wants every programme to contain a proper proportion of the two types of film, entertainment and propaganda. He imagines a series called *From the Life of the Peoples of the World* on subjects like 'the colonial policy of the British in India, the work of the League of Nations, the starving in Berlin, etc., etc.' Entertainment films had to be monitored and censored for obscenity and counter-revolutionary content, but within these limits, producers should be allowed broad initiative.

But if Lenin set the agenda for cinema, the forcing ground was the Revolution itself, which was nothing less than a new kind of totalisation of society that involved rethinking everything from the ground up. The overthrow of the old order gave licence to iconoclasm, experimentation and re-evaluation in all the arts. Outright class enemies abandoned the country, others who found themselves abroad, stayed away. At home, the artistic community argued the need to repudiate bourgeois ideas and forge a new universal and proletarian culture. Great hopes were pinned on cinema precisely because of its originality, its dynamic potential and the fact that it was not encumbered by the norms of bourgeois aesthetics. Here, for the first time in its short life, cinema was taken seriously by intellectuals, politicians and artists alike. Debate was accompanied by experiment, and Vertov developed his methods and ideas in dialogue with critical currents in the avant-garde to which he belonged: he was close to both the Lef group, the revolutionary wing of Russian Futurism, led by the poet Vladimir Mayakovsky, who declared that 'art is not a mirror which reflects the historical struggle, but a weapon in that struggle';[34] and the constructivists, who compared the fabrication of the work of art to the tasks and methods of building and engineering.

Constructivism celebrated the machine as an organising metaphor for the production of a new society, and Vertov's theory of documentary derives from the material qualities of the camera itself as a 'machine for seeing'. The passage is frequently quoted:

I am [the] cinema-eye – I am a mechanical eye. I, a machine, show you a world such as only I can see. From now on and for always I cast off human immobility, I move constantly, I approach and pull away from objects, I creep under them, I leap onto them, I move alongside the mouth of a galloping horse, I cut into a crowd, I run before charging troops, I turn on my back, I take off with an airplane, I fall and rise with falling and rising bodies.

The film-eye, according to Vertov, is a machine which surpasses the limitations of unaided human observation, but the concept, as befits a Leninist, is a dialectical one: the film that is shot is raw material for production, which acquires significance through the process of editing. The *kinok* records 'life-facts' which the camera turns into 'film-facts', which are combined through montage into 'film-truth', *Kino-pravda* – a term that later, when translated into French as cinéma vérité, becomes, through insertion into a different context, somewhat problematic.

Number Eight in the *Kino-pravda* newsreel series opens with the image of a roll of film being taken out of its box for projection. It ends with a self-advertisement: a travelling film team arrives in a town square, unpacks the gear, sets up the screen for an open-air showing, and a caption gives instructions for arranging a visit by such a film show. The effect is to create a loop from screen to audience, an orbit which connected the images to the audience's world. Or nowadays marks our separation from it, because today a film like this has long been overtaken by the Solidarity syndrome – it has become an historical document, a representative and representational piece of history. Not just on account of the assortment of 'life-facts' that it contains, but as an historical object in itself, which speaks to us as a voice from the moment when it was created, telling us how it felt living then and there.

From this perspective, the self-advertisement is more than a filmic gambit, but symbolises *the transformation of the space of film itself* to include the place where it's shown; here the screen is continuous with the viewer's own world. If Lenin told Lunacharsky that 'of all the arts for us the most important is cinema', the reason is obvious enough: its ability to reach a widespread and largely illiterate population with a vivid portrayal of great propaganda value. The country was vast and heterogeneous, people spoke dozens of different languages and dialects; cinema was a terrific instrument for the enormous job of educating them in the basic tenets of the Communist state. It was also and necessarily more than that. Cinema participates here in a transformation of the public space in which it is seen, the domain of common knowledge of the historically existing world which underpins political life; a transformation which, like everywhere else, it both promotes and reflects, as agent and instrument, source and effect, vehicle and catalyst. Its self-multiplication produces a redefinition of the public sphere, which extends both geographically and culturally beyond the traditional literate domain (even as that domain is extended by literacy campaigns and universal education).

This talk of the public sphere in the context of Communism will sound odd to many ears; conventional wisdom has it that the two are incommensurable. This is not the way it appeared to those involved in the process, who saw an expanding field of activity – just like everywhere else. Vertov conceived the *kinoki* as the centre of a national network of local cine-amateurs (which failed to materialise) providing a continuous flow of newsreel footage; he even imagined it being supplemented by an equivalent 'radio-ear'. Brecht had similar thoughts about radio, of which he wrote in 1932 – back in the West – that it had the capacity to become 'the finest possible communications apparatus in public life, a vast system of channels [of communication]'. That is, it could be if it were organised to transmit as well as receive, 'to let the listener speak as well as hear . . . to bring him into a network instead of isolating him'. This was not a technical dream, but an inherent capability of the technology, 'the natural consequence of technological development'. If this potential were realised, it would become possible to

transform the reports of those who govern into answers to the questions of those governed. Radio must make exchange possible. It alone can organize the major discussions between business sectors and consumers about the norms for consumer goods, the debates about raising the price of bread, the disputes in municipalities. Should you consider this utopian, then I ask you to reflect on the reasons why it is utopian.[35]

It is still utopian, but this utopia has been imagined over and over again. It is also part of the history of documentary. It fed the aspirations of the workers' film movements which appeared between the two world wars, and then the community video movements which appeared in the 1980s. It does so again today, when new promise is found on a global scale through the internet, which is also a space for conducting debates of precisely the kind that Brecht suggested.

VI

The film which in most film histories announces the beginning of the documentary as a genre, Flaherty's *Nanook of the North*, is perhaps better thought of as the culmination of the prehistory we have just surveyed. The ideological roots of Flaherty's approach are found in the travelogue and explorer films which follow a model going back to the nineteenth-century magic-lantern lecture, with its thoroughly paternalistic style of address. Flaherty is the very personification of the tradition, a member of the tribe of explorers, the son of a prospector who scoured the Canadian wilderness for United States Steel and other corporations, sometimes taking young Robert with him on his trips. The boy became a prospector in turn, winning his spurs on four expeditions for William Mackenzie, builder of Canadian railroads, during one of which he first filmed the daily life of a family of Inuit. This material was notoriously consumed by flames in the cutting room and *Nanook* is the product of his second attempt, sponsored by the fur traders Revillon Frères.

The film's breakthrough was largely due to the introduction of an individual protagonist for audience identification. As one of the early US film critics put it, in a volume called *The Best Moving Pictures of 1922–23*, this gave the film a 'personal touch': 'Another producer, attempting to do the same thing, would have been content to photograph "A Native Spearing Fish" or "Another Native Building His Igloo". . . Mr Flaherty made Nanook his hero – and a fine, stalwart hero he was.'[36] In the absence of a dramatic plot, Nanook's co-star, and the villain of the piece, was the North, the Arctic, which Nanook and his folk must battle against in a desperate struggle for survival.

This model of documentary is composed of a series of scenes and shots in which the actions and activities on view were performed for the camera, not according to a script but played out by a group of social actors who took on the roles of a family. According to Flaherty himself, in an interview near the end of his life, it was precisely to enable such a way of filming that he took with him not only the camera but also laboratory equipment and projector, in order to develop and show the film to the Eskimos 'so that they would accept and understand what I was doing and work together with me as partners'.[37] As a recent commentator puts it, 'The filmmaker actively involved his subjects in the filming, telling them what he wanted them to do, responding to their suggestions, and directing their performance for the camera'; in short, they were 'knowing actors in the movie and active collaborators in its making'.[38] Fifty years after *Nanook*, Jean Rouch would call him 'a geographer-explorer who was doing ethnography without knowing it'. When Flaherty, he said,

> built his developing lab at Hudson Bay and projected his images for Nanook, he had no idea that he was inventing, at that very instant, 'participant observation' (a concept still used by ethnographers and sociologists fifty years later) and 'feedback' (an idea with which we are just now clumsily experimenting).[39]

What made this possible was Flaherty's closeness to his subject, a familiarity built up over a long period of time (the equivalent, in anthropology, of field work). In his own words,

> In so many travelogues you see, the filmmaker looks down on and never up to his subject. He is always the big man from New York or from London. But I had been dependent on these people, alone with them for months at a time, travelling with them and living with them. They had warmed my feet when they were cold, lit my cigarette when my hands were too numb to do it myself; they had taken care of me on three or four different expeditions over a period of ten years. My work had been built up along with them; I couldn't have done anything without them. In the end it is all a question of human relationships.[40]

What Flaherty doesn't say is that these human relationships occur between unequal partners, and the camera represents a form of power which is only possessed by one of them. The picture he gives us of Inuit life is his, not theirs, and some of what he has them enact is not always quite genuine. First, he had to contend with technical limitations. Famously, for example, due to the limitations of his lenses and film stock, he had to build a special half-igloo, open to the sunlight, in order to film its interior. The resulting shots are thus the performance of being inside an igloo. But then he goes further, in the interests of dramatising their plight, and calls on his cast to revive a traditional and dangerous method of hunting walrus with harpoons, a practice Nanook's people had abandoned as soon as they became able to trade pelts for guns and ammunition – the business of the company that financed the film. The old method is here reconstituted from the memory of his 'actors' ('informants' in ethnographic terminology). He would do the same with the tattooing in *Moana* (1926) and again with shark-fishing in *Man of Aran* (1934), of which he said, 'I should have been shot for what I asked these superb people to do for the film, for the enormous risks I exposed them to, and all for the sake of a keg of porter and five pounds apiece.'[41] There is re-creation here not only of the action, but also of an image of a way of life, but what these narratives enact is an imaginary construct imposed from outside the community.

Flaherty's central thematic in all these films harks back to the Rousseauesque 'noble savage', man in direct relation to nature, a world of hostile forces (or a lost paradise) that has not been overwhelmed by industrialisation. In *Nanook*, the Eskimo world of human existence at the edge of the world is a powerful symbol of this condition (*Moana* represents the paradise). But the intense naturalism of the film disarms the viewer, who is rendered almost schizophrenic, superior but awed, knowing but also naive. Lacking knowledge of Inuit life, one is faced not so much with a concrete social reality as a condition abstracted from history; this is the same picture classically constructed by early ethnography as the form of temporal experience of 'primitive' societies, before they enter into history and become 'civilised'. Flaherty portrays Nanook's way of life as natural – unchanging, timeless – when it was already threatened and succumbing to the supposedly 'civilising' forces of Western 'progress'; a process in which the film is implicated and inevitably suppresses, (just like *The Trials and Tribulations of a Cameraman*), as every classic ethnographic film regularly suppresses its own process of fabrication. As William Rothman puts it, *Nanook* consistently underplays the extent to which Western civilisation had already encroached upon the traditions it depicts, 'the extent to which modern society gives Nanook and his family no choice but to accommodate themselves to it, to become part of the modern world, not a self-contained universe separate from it'.[42] Grierson himself criticised the film on this account, describing Flaherty as a romantic. Consider the problem of the Eskimo, he wrote: 'His clothes and blankets most often come from Manchester, supplied by a department store in Winnipeg . . . They listen to fur prices over the radio, and are subject to fast operations of commercial opportunists flying in from New York . . .'.[43]

Flaherty credits the 'kindliness, faithfulness and patience of Nanook and his family', while omitting any reference to his corporate sponsor, who thus occupies the position of a structuring absence. According to another commentator, this 'explicit absence' also disguises the fact that Nanook is not a real historical person but a created figure, acted by someone standing in as a model for just such a character, an archetype rather than a person, without much individuality.[44] The most contentious scene in this connection, which occurs early in the film and thus has a strong effect on the way we read the character of

Nanook, is the clowning with the phonograph record, preceded by what Rothman correctly calls a con-descending title: 'In deference to Nanook, the great hunter, the trader entertains and attempts to explain the principle of the gramophone – how the white man "cans" his voice.' In the shots that follow, we see Nanook peering at the machine and bending forward to listen to it better. He laughs with pleasure, directing a big, broad grin to both the trader and the camera. The clincher comes when he picks up a record and puts it to his mouth, presumably licking it in order to feel the grooves. The moment has a comical edge, says Rothman, because in our own culture someone who had never seen a record would hardly try to figure out what it was 'by putting it in his mouth and biting it; only a baby would do that – or a dog'.[45]

For many viewers the scene clearly produces a strong sense of Nanook being set up, of the film-maker and the trader conspiring to expose the naivety of this 'great hunter' who does not comprehend 'how the white man "cans" his voice'. However, I once had the opportunity to discuss this scene with Richard Leacock, Flaherty's cinematographer on his last film, *Louisiana Story* (1948), who vehemently defended Flaherty's integrity (and Nanook's). What he said is true: in a freezing climate the touch of your tongue is more sensitive than numbed fingertips. And indeed, viewing the scene again in this light, one can even imagine the unheard conversation, as the trader points to the grooves to explain how the sound is recorded. Is Rothman simply mistaken, then, if he feels that Flaherty in this sequence seems to disavow the humanity of his subject? Is this perhaps an effect of the Solidarity syndrome, the historical distance of the modern viewer who projects their own susceptibilities into the old images?

At all events, Rothman concludes that Flaherty's treatment of his subjects was not so very different from the way fiction films treat their actors, and he calls *Nanook* a film 'poised between documentary and fiction'.[46] The film was not an instant success when it first appeared in the States, and was only taken up by US critics after recognition in London and Paris, Berlin and Rome, places where it ran for many months. Meanwhile, Allakariallak, who played Nanook, died of starvation a year after the film was premièred. The news of his death, according to Flaherty himself in an interview many years later, 'came out in the press all over the world – even as far away as China'.[47] In short, with *Nanook*, the documentary not only came of age, but it did so as a global discourse.

Notes

1. Quoted in F. T. Rony, *The Third Eye: Race, Cinema, and Etnographic Spectacle* (Durham, NC: Duke University Press, 1996), p. 3.
2. Brian Winston, *Claiming the Real* (London: BFI, 1995), pp. 130–6.
3. Umberto Barbaro, *El film y el resarcimiento marxista de la arte* (Havana: Ediciones ICAIC, 1965), p. 236.
4. Catherine Russell, *Experimental Ethnography* (Durham, NC: Duke University Press, 1999), p. 51.
5. Tom Gunning, 'The Cinema of Attractions: Early Film, Its Spectator and the Avant-Garde', *Wide Angle* no. 3, 1986, pp. 56–62.
6. Noël Burch, *Life to Those Shadows* (London: BFI, 1990).
7. For a full account of the episode see Michael Chanan, *Cuban Cinema* (Minneapolis: University of Minnesota Press, 2004), pp. 41–3.

8. Erik Barnouw, *Documentary: A History of the Non-Fiction Film* (Oxford: Oxford University Press, 1974), p. 24.

9. Barnouw, *Documentary*, p. 23.

10. Russell, *Experimental Ethnography* pp. 55–6.

11. Theodor W. Adorno, *Minima Moralia* (London: New Left Books, 1974), p. 55.

12. See Rachael Low, *The History of the British Film, 1914–1918*, vol. 3 (London: Allen & Unwin, 1948), p. 20.

13. My thanks to Patrick Russell for drawing this film to my attention.

14. Bill Nichols, *Representing Reality: Issues and Concepts in Documentary* (Bloomington: Indiana University Press, 1991).

15. Aurelio de los Reyes, 'The Silent Cinema', in Paulo Antonio Paranagua (ed.), *Mexican Cinema* (London: BFI, 1995), p. 71.

16. Margarita de Orellana, 'The Circular Look, The Incursion of North American Fictional Cinema 1911–1917 into the Mexican Revolution', in John King, Ana López and Manuel Alcarado (eds), *Mediating Two Worlds, Cinematic Encounters in the Americas* (London: BFI, 1993), p. 6.

17. See, for example, DeeDee Halleck's compilation film, *The Gringo in Mañanaland* (1995).

18. Nichols, *Representing Reality*, p. 142.

19. Roland Barthes, *Camera Lucida* (New York: Hill and Wang, 1981), p. 96.

20. Balázs in Kevin Macdonald and Mark Cousins (eds), *Imagining Reality: The Faber Book of Documentary* (London and Boston, MA: Faber and Faber, 1996), pp. 31–2.

21. Balázs in Macdonald and Cousins (eds), *Imagining Reality*, p. 31.

22. M. L. Sanders and Philip M. Taylor, *British Propaganda During the First World War* (London: Macmillan, 1982), p. 155.

23. Leif Furhammer and Folke Isaksson, *Politics and Film* (London: November Books, 1971), p. 12.

24. Furhammer and Isaksson, *Politics and Film*, p. 9.

25. Furhammer and Isaksson, *Politics and Film*, p. 12.

26. Quoted in Anthony Aldgate, *Cinema and History, British Newsreels and the Spanish Civil War* (London: Scolar Press, 1979), p. 26.

27. Virginia Woolf, 'The Cinema', first published in *Arts*, June 1926.

28. Low, *The History of the British Film 1914–1918,* vol. 3, p. 154.

29. Low, *The History of British Film 1914–1918*, vol. 3, p. 157.

30. Kathryn H. Fuller, *At the Picture Show, Small-Town Audiences and the Creation of Movie Fan Culture* (Charlottesville and London: University Press of Virginia, 2001), pp. 83–4.

31. Lee Grieveson, 'Watching Henry Skate: The Films of the Ford Motor Company', <www.mchanan.dial.pipex.com/detroit>.

32. Quoted in Fuller, *At the Picture Show*, pp. 83–4.

33. Anatoli Lunacharsky, 'Conversation with Lenin', in Richard Taylor and Ian Christie (eds), *The Film Factory* (London and New York: Routledge, 1988), p. 57.

34. Quoted in Masha Enzensberger, 'Dziga Vertov', in *Screen Reader 1, Cinema/ Ideology/ Politics* (London: SEFT, 1977), p. 395.

35.   Bertolt Brecht, 'The Radio as a Communications Apparatus', in Marc Silberman (ed.), *Brecht on Film and Radio* (London: Methuen, 2000), pp. 42–3.

36.   Robert Sherwood, 'Robert Flaherty's *Nanook of the North*', in Lewis Jacobs (ed.), *The Documentary Tradition* (New York: W. W. Norton, 1971), p. 16.

37.   Robert Flaherty, 'Robert Flaherty Talking', in Roger Manvell (ed.), *The Cinema 1950* (Harmondsworth: Penguin, 1950), p. 14.

38.   William Rothman, *Documentary Film Classics* (Cambridge: Cambridge University Press, 1997), p. 1, quoting Gilberto Perez.

39.   Jean Rouch, *Ciné-Ethnography* (Minneapolis: University of Minnesota Press, 2003), p. 32.

40.   Flaherty, 'Robert Flaherty Talking', pp. 18–19.

41.   Quoted in Rotha, 1983, p. 116.

42.   Rothman, *Documentary Film Classics*, p. 2.

43.   Barnouw, *Documentary*, p. 45.

44.   Marc-Henri Piault, *Antropologia y cine Documentary* (Madrid: Cátedra, 2002) (trans of *Anthropologie et Cinéma*), pp. 91, 95.

45.   Rothman, *Documentary Film Classics*, pp. 11f.

46.   Rothman, *Documentary Film Classics*, p. 6.

47.   Flaherty, 'Robert Flaherty Talking', p. 18.

5 Discovery of Space

The 1920s: The city and the wilderness

I

Thom Andersen's film essay *Los Angeles Plays Itself* (2003) presents us with the paradox of the city which is probably the most photographed on earth yet also one of the most invisible, because it is only usually there as background and we are not supposed to notice it. This long (almost three hours) and mesmerising montage of clips of Los Angeles places and scenes taken from almost 200 Hollywood movies, combined with Andersen's essayistic text, is not fiction, but as one critic puts it, 'qualifies as social history, film theory, personal reverie, architectural history', not to mention a 'bittersweet meditation' on the automobile, a critical history of the city's public transport, a song of nostalgia for lost neighbourhoods, and most of all as 'film criticism on the highest level'.[1] A veritable history of Hollywood cinema, it is also like a 'city symphony in reverse', because it's a strange documentary which (with one or two exceptions) is made up entirely of fictional images. But Andersen shifts the way we look at these images, defamiliarising them by deconstructing the language of screen space which produced them.

In the early part of the film he demonstrates the Hollywood movies' habitual disregard for geographical integrity – as when a car turns a corner on a cut and finds itself ten miles away. As another reviewer puts it, 'Even when they are shot in real places, movies create fantasy spaces – streets are renamed, buildings are moved, one city stands in for another.'[2] This is nothing new, of course – Kuleshov demonstrated how to do it in his famous experiment on 'creative geography' around 1920: in one version, two characters walking along different streets in Moscow catch sight of each other, their meeting is filmed in a third street, they shake hands near the White House (taken from an American film), and they mount the steps of St Saviour's Cathedral.[3] For Kuleshov, the experiment demonstrated that 'the whole power of cinematographic effect is in montage', but Andersen's point is that Hollywood, by these and the further means he goes on to lay before us, has systematically betrayed its home city and told lies big and small about its history. For example, he shows us one by one the way certain sites and buildings repeatedly stand in for fictional locations, like the Bradbury Building, dating from 1893, which cropped up as a Burmese hotel in *China Girl*, a London military hospital in *The White Cliffs of Dover* (1944) and an apartment house of the future in *Blade Runner* (1982). These are the small lies that are the bread-and-butter of fictional cinema. He goes on to discuss Los Angeles as both a character and a subject in films like *Chinatown* (1974), *Who Framed Roger Rabbit* (1988) and *L.A. Confidential* (1997), which trade on certain myths about the city; in contrast to African-American film-makers like Charles Burnett and Billy Woodberry, whose neorealism provides the antithesis of studio fakery.

If all cities, as Rosenbaum says in his review, are palimpsests – made up of layers which have been altered over time yet still leave traces of their original form – what Andersen shows is the way cinema is another way of overwriting the city, in a city where this relationship is especially intimate. But as the Kuleshov experiment suggests, it is also the very condition of cinema. Indeed the editor of a recent book on cinema and the city writes of cinema as a peculiarly spatial form of culture. A follower of the 'spatial turn' in recent critical thinking, Mark Shiel wants us to speak of both 'space in films' and 'films in space'.[4] 'Space in films' concerns the space of the shot, the settings, the mapping of a diegetic world, the grammar of narrative cinema. 'Films in space' is about the cinema as a place of modern urban entertainment, and the industry to which it belongs: the geographies of production, distribution and exhibition; including the signs and symbols of this industry, the posters on the streets, the pages in the press and the magazines, the books on the shelves, the shows on television and nowadays the pages on the internet.

Shiel takes his cue from Henri Lefebvre. In Lefebvre's scheme,[5] cinema is both a representational space – the symbolic space of the screen lit up in the projection beam – and a spatial practice – the spatial organisation of a major sector of cultural production. As a representational space, the screen is constituted by a system of non-verbal signs, partly but never wholly coded, which makes symbolic use of physical representations of place. It is also ambiguous, offering the simultaneous impression of seeing the world around us differently, and of really seeing a different world. As a spatial practice, the industrial geography of cinema raises questions about the way that forms and modes of production are implicated in forms and modes of representation. Where is production located – is it centralised or dispersed? Are the films shot in studios or on location? How does distribution operate: what transport is needed for shipping prints, and where does their distribution reach? And exhibition, the space of encounter with the audience: who does the audience comprise demographically speaking, with what kind of sensibilities and susceptibilities? All these are factors that impinge on the screen as a representational space, acting together to situate the worlds that come to life in the projection beam. But the answers are not always the same for fiction and documentary. For one thing, documentary is not shot in studios but on location, and thrives on the ability of the camera, from the very beginning, to freely roam the world. In the process, documentary creates its own cognitive map of the world it goes out to meet. Like all cognitive maps, the places are real but the angles from which they're seen and the ways of moving around between them derive from the map-maker's own criteria – cultural, social, imaginary and symbolic.

The location of the screen – the physical place where the film is watched – is a space of representation. As a space of representation, the cinema quickly came to mean discrete works, individual films codified in a variety of ways according to genre, and experienced by visiting the cinema or place where they are shown (until television brought them into the home, and then the introduction of the video-cassette further extended their circulation). The darkened hall is a collective site of aesthetic consumption governed by the economic rules of exhibition as a form of mass consumption. Hence the architectural design of the cinema itself, the dream palace of the 1920s and 30s which provided an environment of plush fantasy, an escapist environment for escapist entertainment, where documentary reality was an interloper, and which was also designed, like the shopping mall, to control the movement of crowds on entering and leaving the premises. (This, according to Douglas Gomery's history of movie presentation in the United States.[6] As for the shopping mall, I am thinking of Harun Farocki's film, *The Creators of Shopping Worlds* [2001], which patiently documents the planning process of a new shopping mall by a team of architects, designers, managers and social scientists: a dry and didactic but fascinating report which shows us the lengths that capital goes to in order to control the movement of the shopper, individually and *en masse*, how they circulate and where they stop, down to where the shopper's gaze falls and a how a 'spontaneous' purchase may be induced.)

Lefebvre declines to celebrate the power of film. This is odd. He knows that film is more than simple visual reproduction, and its essential quality is that of montage ('cutting things up and rearranging them, decoupage and montage – these are the alpha and omega of the art of image-making'[7]) – in short, that it calls on the recombination of images which in the process generates new meanings. He claims that film is nevertheless an 'incriminated' medium because 'images fragment' – 'they are themselves fragments of space' – although he immediately adds that in this the image is like all signs, a necessary abstraction. For this very reason, of course, the argument can be turned around. Just because the shot is indeed an abstraction, it becomes possible, through the recombinations of montage, to transgress and transcend its limits by conjoining images. Film thus becomes a way of reconstituting and reconstructing space. Indeed the articulation of a cogent discourse of spatial representation is the very condition of cinema. In a manner comparable to the process in Deleuze which transforms the movement-image into the time-image through montage, recombination also becomes a way of reconceptualising space: a form of symbolic spatial production which creates, through re-appropriation, a new lived relationship with the space inhabited by the subject. (Always given that the more mobile the camera and longer the take, the more that montage is contained within the shot itself.)

The construction of space involves a critical difference between fiction and documentary. (Perhaps one should call this, after Derrida, *différance*, because it is not something given and predetermined, but to be constantly re-created at every turn.) In simple terms, the world of fiction is parallel to our own, but separate, other and phantasmal, while that of documentary belongs to the same material world as the one we actually inhabit. The space of fiction is contained and closed off; we cannot physically enter it and any connection with it is imaginary (like Buster Keaton walking into the screen at the beginning of *Sherlock Jr* [1924], or Jeff Daniels walking off it in Woody Allen's *The Purple Rose of Cairo* [1985]). Documentary, on the other hand, represents a world that is continuous with the one we live in, it invokes a space which is isomorphic with the physical reality in which we live our everyday lives, at least in principle, and sometimes quite palpably – as in Benjamin's remark that the passerby might become a film extra, 'part of a work of art', in films like those of Vertov or Ivens. Again this tells us that off-screen space is different. In fiction, off-screen space is only there to the extent that what is visible or audible points to it. In documentary, it is always there on the edges, threatening to break in. In short, documentary becomes the generic term for a particular mode of spatial discourse about the real world, a form of symbolic spatial production which creates, through re-appropriation and recombination, a new lived relationship with the space-image, not through identification with the figure of the star but empathy with the social subjects of a world we inhabit ourselves.

II

As the film industry became institutionalised after World War I, following commercial principles everywhere except Soviet Russia, and as the proper fare for the dream palace was deemed to be the fiction of adventure and melodrama, fantasy and escapism, so the urge towards documentary was reduced to secondary status and progressively marginalised from the cinema as a site of mass entertainment. Even if the relegation of social reality was a side-effect of the studio system, this was no mere accident. Fiction tames the ambiguity of the screen by adopting the side of the imaginary. Documentary is less compliant. Even in the early days, when its powers of articulation were still limited, in certain cases the image of the actual was liable to invoke an excess of reality: a sense of immediacy, the 'tangible being-present' that so impressed Balázs, which is potentially unsettling, because unfinished, or in Bakhtin's word, unfinalised.

With the normalisation of the fictional feature film as the dominant form of cinema, the occasional long documentary, like those of Flaherty, took on the appearance of a new but minor narrative genre. Ruttmann was able to make *Berlin, Symphony of a City* for the cinema, a remarkable film which stood quite outside the norms of genre, because Weimar Germany was wide open to artistic experiment. Mostly, however, the 'factual' film did not aspire to compete with the feature in the cinema, and for the most part was rapidly reduced to marginal status as a 'short', and treated by exhibitors as mere filler. Yet there were those who took it seriously, like Ford in the United States, or in Britain, the city of Glasgow, who began sponsoring short films on municipal topics in 1920, which researchers are only now beginning to recover from the archives.[8] Above all, however, it was the film club movement and arthouse circuits which took shape during the 20s where the documentary found its real encouragement alongside the experimental short, and this is therefore the birthplace of documentary as an artistic movement. Despite the very different milieux, there is one feature which is shared by the Ford films, the municipal film-makers and the avant-garde: all three show a marked predilection for the contemporary city as the prime subject matter.

In Soviet Russia, documentary thrived because its fresh-eyed construction of reality fed into the ideological priorities of the Revolution. Elsewhere, the potential openness of the documentary hardly recommended it to commercial interests, and non-commercial sponsors required it to observe the proper decorum. In other words, the images had to be contained within a clear interpretive scheme corresponding to the sponsor's interests. The easiest way to do this was through explicit language, applied by means of intertitles, whose use was generalised during World War I to replace the showman-lecturer. The intertitle is a device that interrupts the flow of images with a linguistic inscription, thereby subjugating the photographic picture to semantic domination, or, in other words, instructing the viewer how to perceive what they are seeing (a function that would pass back to the voice when sound came along and incorporated a spoken commentary). Exceptions came in the shape of a handful of films which created their own space of reception by dint of their own aesthetic force, the cogency of their own symbolic ordering, much in the same way as the paradigmatic works of the modernist revolution in painting and music by the likes of Picasso and Kandinsky, Schoenberg and Stravinsky. In a similar vein, films of the 1920s like Ruttmann's *Berlin, Symphony of a City* or *Man with a Movie Camera*, are first and foremost exemplars of modernism. This is also to say that here the documentary was conceived as a modernist venture, a very different kind of endeavour from that of Flaherty. These are films that abandon the props of narrative encoding and eschew the use of intertitles, in order to develop other strategies of address, thereby becoming the outstanding paradigms of another kind of cinematic space: almost a kind of hyper-reality, let's say, compared to ordinary realism.

Different economic conditions in Soviet Russia, Europe and the United States, as well as different cultural susceptibilities, had a determinable effect on the shape of what could be attempted. In Europe, where the aesthetics of the Russian avant-garde resonated strongly, the 20s saw the advance of documentary mainly on the cinematic margins, where it was allied with the plastic arts and associated with the emergence of what was known sometimes as 'art cinema' and sometimes as 'independent cinema'. The designation *cinéma d'art* had been introduced by the French before the Great War to legitimise a new genre of dramatic pictures, mainly consisting in filmed theatre, which aimed to attract a more middle-class audience. In the 1920s, the term shifted to include a range of films, both fiction and non-fiction, which fell at the margins or even outside the emergent genre system. On the one hand there were movements like German Expressionism or Soviet montage cinema – in other words, narrative films which eschewed the norms of the commercial mainstream. On the other were the non-narrative experiments of the avant-garde, a motley tribe largely consisting of artists who turned to film because it offered a terrain for the renewal of vision which they took as their vocation to pursue. Names include Hans Richter, Fernand Léger, Man Ray and Laszlo Moholy-Nagy. Some of their experiments were entirely abstract, the exploration of light and shade, shapes and patterns in movement, or else they treated fragmentary images of objects in the world somewhat in the manner of the Cubist collage. Since the 1920s was a highly politicised decade, there was soon a third current, a social avant-garde, which avoided abstraction and cultivated the documentary especially for its powers of observation, particularly of aspects or sectors of society that were normally hidden and ignored.

What was common to these positions was the primacy they gave to the photogenic and visual poetry, as against the subservience of the image to the narrative logic of commercial cinema. In the silent era, when language was no barrier, visually heightened films like these might achieve an audience as international as genre cinema, if nowhere near as large, and a screening circuit developed which included the first 'art houses' and newly appearing film societies in cities like London, Paris, Berlin and Warsaw. (These circuits would also support independent work arriving from the US, like the films of Flaherty.) The artistic wing also relied for the dissemination of their work on the radical art journals of the day, like *G* and *De Stijl*, which were numerous if often short-lived, supplemented by a number of magazines dedicated to film art, like *Close Up*. But producing such films was a precarious business, and art films of any kind were nearly always one-off ventures. Many of the artists' films were funded by the makers themselves; sometimes projects would be supported by film clubs; and in France, several important films, by Cocteau, Buñuel and Man Ray, were commissioned by an old-style patron with progressive tastes, the Comte de Noailles. As a recent historian of experimental film puts it, there were two basic choices. The endeavour needed a range of skills requiring special facilities, including shooting, processing and editing. Either you had to depend on a network of helpers, professional and amateur, or you had to do it yourself; a choice, says A. L. Rees, 'which appealed especially to painters and photographers with craft skills and a hands-on aesthetic'.[9] Inevitably, the more experimental the film, the more small-scale. This, in principle, is still the same today, only the ground rules have been altered, in ways we shall discover later, by video and digital technology.

The same considerations apply to the documentary, except that a documentary could hardly be made at home in the artist's studio. Indeed, it was born precisely in the turn outwards to discover the quintessential site of modernity – the city. The city, with its acceleration and mechanisation, the

automatism of everyday life, its rendering of privacy and anonymity, its opposition of crowd and individual, freedoms and constraints, becomes an *idée fixe* of documentary for a decade. Antecedents of
the city documentary can be found in early films about motor cars speeding through the streets, career-
ing out of control, running people over, crashing and even exploding. Indeed early cinema fed off fascination with other new technologies whose birth belongs to the same period as cinematography, the
whole panoply of scientific and technological marvels of the times, from aeroplanes to X-rays, often
going awry, and in this way, as the vehicle which disseminated its reputation, film became the medium
par excellence of the modern age and its everyday anxieties. But these things are only symptoms.
The emergent documentary of the 1920s responds to a deeper need for the portrayal of the city as both
metaphor and embodiment of the modern world. In the process, the city pictured is more than the
appearance of its physical locations and the activities that go on there, but the networks that conjoin
and feed them, and which the city dweller feels and senses as much as sees.

The silent city documentary of the 1920s explores the spatiality of the city under various guises and
in the full gamut of styles. It enters as living subject with Paul Strand's short and impressionistic *Manhatta*
of 1921, incorporating Walt Whitman's lyric hymn to New York, to become the protagonist in its own
story in films like Cavalcanti's fanciful *Rien que les heures* (1926), or Jean Vigo's lyrical-metaphorical *À
propos de Nice* of 1930. Ruttmann's 1927 film, *Berlin, Symphony of a City*, is a vast panorama of an hour
and a quarter. At the opposite end of the scale, a film of 1926 called *Cinq minutes du cinéma pur* (Five
Minutes of Pure Cinema) is a delirious high-speed tour of Paris which harks back to the delights of trick
photography in the earliest days of cinema, while the short films of Ivens (*The Bridge*, 1928 and *Rain*,
1929) take moments of special beauty, like rain in the streets or a lifting bridge, and condense them into
barely ten minutes. Another approach is found in a film of 1927, *La Zone* by Georges Lacombe, a sustained portrait of the life of the rag-pickers living in the shanty towns which then girdled Paris. A highly
accomplished film club production which belongs to the social avant-garde, *La Zone* exemplifies an evolving documentary method that is both pragmatic and elastic, and which accomplishes its political task
without any rhetoric. The narrative shape is a simple 'day in the life', from dawn to dusk. Some of it is
staged by taking actors to the locations where the rag-pickers work, where the film meticulously shows
the jobs of sorting rubbish into different types of matter (organic, paper, metals) for recycling, then passing to careful and sympathetic observation of locales like the flea market, and the ethnic diversity and
various personalities who inhabit the zone. Here Lacombe knows how to get social actors to repeat their
actions for the camera as it takes up various different positions, and even once or twice incorporates
'advanced' camera movements, like a hand-held walking shot through the market stalls.

Ivens is a key figure. With something like seventy films over sixty years – his swan song, *A Tale of the
Wind*, was made in 1988 – his oeuvre spans practically the whole history of documentary, and evolved
in dialogue with the times. 'There is nothing surprising about Ivens' presence in Cuba,' said the Cuban
film journal *Cine Cubano* in November 1960:

> Wherever there is a country struggling for its freedom, a people trying to liquidate the old structures
> and forge a sane and healthy future where man can find and reclaim his dignity, Ivens will be present.
> And as a creator, not a tourist.[10]

Ivens had filmed in Spain during the Civil War, in China during the war against the Japanese invader, and then at the end of World War II voiced a cry of alarm over the Dutch government's intentions against the young Indonesian Republic, thus becoming an undesirable in his native country. To the Cubans he represented an ideal they could readily identify with – the participant witness who wielded the camera with the precision of a rifle. The scion of a family of professional photographers, he started out by studying at the vocational college for photography in Berlin before returning to his native Holland to become a pioneer documentarist instead of taking over his father's business. In the early 30s he would distance himself from the avant-garde in favour of the emphatic realism of political engagement, although he would never entirely allow his passionate political convictions to drown out his artistic aspirations, and several of his postwar films are gems of experimentalism or the poetic film essay.

The Bridge, dating from 1928, is a study in cinematic movement, a rhythmic montage of speeding trains, big slow ships, and the mechanics of a new railway bridge in Rotterdam which is raised to allow the ships to pass beneath, described at the time in the film magazine *Close Up* as 'a pure visual symphony' with no tricks or subterfuges.[11] Ivens filmed with a lightweight spring-driven Kinamo camera which allowed him to clamber around the structure of the bridge, with the result, according to his own account, that the construction of the film was 'determined by the functions of the bridge itself'.[12] The film had an immediate appeal and was widely shown in the film club movement, but was also judged by critics like Balázs for yielding to the abstract and formalist. As Deleuze sees it, this rapid montage of 700 shots, which means that different views can be fitted together in an infinite number of ways, is neither the concept of a bridge, nor is it 'the individuated state of things defined by its form, its metallic matter, its uses and functions. It is a potentiality.' He calls it 'the any-space-whatever in which this bridge appeared as pure quality, this metal as pure power, Rotterdam itself as affect'.[13]

Ivens took a similar kind of constructivist approach to filming *Rain*, which although only twelve minutes long, took two years to make, including four months' shooting, when Ivens tells us that he never went anywhere without his camera.

> I lived with it and when I slept it was on my bedside table so that if it was raining when I woke I could film the studio window over my bed. Some of the best shots of raindrops along the slanted studio windows were actually taken from my bed when I woke up.[14]

Once again the film is a composite. For example, 'To achieve the effect of the beginning of the shower as you now see it in the film I had to photograph at least ten beginnings and out of these ten make the one film beginning.' Again Deleuze finds it to be neither the concept of rain nor the state of a rainy time and place. 'It is a set of singularities which presents the rain as it is in itself, pure power or quality which combines without abstraction all possible rains and makes up the corresponding any-space-whatever. It is rain as affect . . .' [15] Indeed Ivens says that the film produced a physical, almost corporeal response.

> I was so happy when I noticed at one of the first screenings of the finished film that the audience looked around for their raincoats and were surprised to find the weather dry and clear when they came out of the theatre.[16]

According to his own account, there were two crucial lessons these films taught him: that 'The screen is not a window through which you look at the world, it is a world in itself',[17] and 'Many artistic problems were actually technical problems, and vice-versa.'[18]

III

It is one of the curiosities of film history that three of the city films were made by three brothers. Dziga Vertov was born Denis Kaufman – his futurist pseudonym means 'spinning top' – older brother by one year of Mikhail, chief cameraman at the same Moscow studios, and his brother's collaborator: Mikhail, who made his own forgotten film called *Moscow* in 1927, is the cameraman who appears in *Man with a Movie Camera*. Vigo's cinematographer was their somewhat younger brother Boris, who had been separated from them during the chaos of the Russian civil war, and ended up going to Paris to study. The family relationships among the film-makers may be read as a metaphor for the family relationships among the films, which is not so much a matter of mutual influences as an extended brotherhood. These films are all the offspring of the modern city of which they offer their various testimonies. Their makers share a coming-to-terms with the city as if it were a condition for their self-invention as documentarists. As if, because film constitutes a new form of cognitive mapping, the city becomes its first natural subject. As if you had to be able to find a way of expressing the space of lived experience as the first condition for making documentary at all. To achieve, through the synthetic power of the screen, a vision of the space of everyday life, the social forces binding it together and pulling it apart. A synthesis which transcended the capacity of the naked eye, or rather, the restricted perspective of the atomised and isolated individual observer, so that making a film like this is a way of transcending your own city-dweller's alienation.

Vertov's *Man with a Movie Camera* is a *tour de force* of sustained filmic speech, a continuous chain of images – uninterrupted by intertitles – constituted by a complex montage of every kind of semantic unit available to the editor. The film synthesises several strands in Vertov's thinking: the emphasis on the machine; the desire to counter the bourgeois vision of the artist as an inspired individual and instead to show artistic creation as a useful job like engineering or dressmaking; the aim of demystifying cinema by representing the way it's made, showing the business of shooting and editing and projecting. His material is everyday life in the modern city. His narrative is a simple 'day in the life' structure. His method induces the viewer to acknowledge the screen as a constructed reality rather than its transparent reflection.[19] The film turns neither on simple spectacle, nor on icons of power, authority and hegemony, but on the everyday life of the city street, places of work and recreation, in which the only individual character whose presence runs throughout the film, and then only as a cipher, is the cameraman who is shooting the film, clambering around to get the shots, who is finally displaced by the camera itself, on its tripod, out in front taking an animated bow.

If images of the cameraman require the same invisible second camera as in Ponting's football scene, the effect is quite different. The reflexivity of *Man with a Movie Camera* fulfils the function which the Russian formalists called *ostrenanie* – estrangement or defamiliarisation – a process aimed at destabilising routine forms of perception, breaking the habit that 'prevents us from really looking at things' (in Fredric Jameson's phrase),[20] and which is in fact the recovery of perception, and therefore potentially subversive. Here the link between aesthetic theory and artistic practice indicates the affinity of this different kind of documentary for the modernist quest, with its tendency towards the break-up of the stable representation, which in the end, as the experimentalism of the 20s gave way to the orthodoxies of Stalinism, made it suspicious to official Communism; and Vertov's views, so fanatically argued, made him troublesome, even before Stalinism took hold. He first came to notice abroad in 1926 with a film called *A Sixth of the World*, which earned him a prize at the World Exposition in Paris but cost him his job in Moscow – the agency which commissioned it took exception to the sequence at the beginning portraying the decadence of Western life, 'that is', says Feldman, 'the lives of their potential customers'. Vertov found work at the studios of the Ukraine, where Feldman believes he conceived *Man with a Movie Camera* as 'an angry response to his dismissal', and an assertion of his independent-minded creative principles.[21]

Ruttmann's *Berlin, Symphony of a City* is a rare example of an avant-garde feature-length documentary made for the cinema – as a quota production for Fox's European operations – which was directed by a painter already known for his abstract films. The title's allusion to music, part of its original conception by the screenwriter Carl Mayer, becomes in Ruttmann's hands much more than a metaphor. The frame is almost never without the internal movement of people, feet, cars, machinery, work, sport, all the bustle of everyday life. When the camera isn't mounted on a moving platform like the train entering the city, which creates a rhythm of objects moving rapidly past, it is generally fixed, or occasionally pans or tracks, but Ruttmann constantly cuts on action within the frame, composing the film through the juxtapositions of movement in the constant activity passing in front of the camera. In Ruttmann's hands the medium of film is polyrhythmic, composed of rhythms of movement both within and between the shots, and through the changing tempo of the montage the film is like a symphony without any breaks between the movements. Much of the effect is due to the camerawork of Karl Freund, who knew he would have to rely on what Kracauer, in a later account of the film, calls 'candid-camera work'.

> Craftsman that he was, he hypersensitized the stock film which was then on the market, so as to cope with poor lighting conditions, and moreover invented several contrivances to hide the camera while shooting. He would drive in a half-enclosed truck with slots in the sides for the lens or he would walk about with the camera in a box that looked like an innocent suitcase. No one ever suspected that he was taking pictures . . .[22]

Boris Kaufman would approach the shooting of Vigo's *À propos de Nice* in the same spirit.

At first *Berlin* unfurls at a tremendous pace, with no shot more than two or three seconds long, until we get to the lazy hours of the afternoon. Speed of cutting is a quality that *Berlin* shares with *Man with a Movie Camera*; both films also adopt the general narrative shape of the unfolding of a day; both employ a technique of shooting that is free from the tyranny of the 180-degree rule, the law of continuity on which narrative grammar is constructed, which plays an even smaller role in Ruttmann's film than in Vertov's. The difference between the two films is not so much that Vertov's is a synthetic city, made up of Moscow, Odessa and Kiev, while Ruttmann sticks to Berlin, but more crucially, the contrast between Vertov's teeming humanity and Ruttmann's distanciation from the individual. Berlin is depicted as a circulatory system of railways, roads, sewers and power plants, and the cycle of activity of the human subjects caught up in its speed and bustle, while objects such as trains, telephones, nylon stock-ings, elevators, typewriters, dishwashers, aeroplanes and store-window mannequins are all equally 'actors' in the drama of modernity made cognisable by the film.

Kracauer identified *Berlin* as a paradigm of the 'cross-section' genre of 1920s' German cinema, whose prototype was another film which Freund produced for Fox Europe the previous year, a tale of the capricious travels of a banknote as it continually changes hands (*The Adventures of a Ten-Mark Note*). Kracauer associates the genre with the contemporaneous artistic movement of *Neue Sachlichkeit* (New Objectivity), and in this light, the very documentary quality of *Berlin*, its abandonment of dramati-sation, becomes a liability, as it piles up thousands of details without connecting them by anything except formal devices: 'The editing . . . resorts to striking analogies between movements or forms. Human legs walking on the pavement are followed by the legs of cows; a sleeping man on a bench is associated with a sleeping elephant [in the zoo].'[23] In the excellent account by Wolfgang Natter,

> Close-ups or medium shots of human subjects are rare. Close-ups are far more often framed on machin-ery or other objects. The most typical framing in the film is the medium-long shot. This framing strategy, along with the absence of an individual point of view perspective, contributes strongly to the distanc-ing effect.

It also contrasts not only with Vertov, but also with Cavalcanti's Paris and Vigo's Nice.[24]

Berlin inevitably aroused considerable controversy. According to Natter, 'A reading of the reviews that appeared following *Berlin*'s release points to the variety of Berlins that in 1927 might have entered cinematic space.' Critics often recognised their own Berlin in the film only to descry the absence of other bits. But there was also a deeper disquiet, because *any* portrayal of the city entered what Natter calls 'a highly contested ideological discussion on modernity, mechanization, and urbanization'.[25] As *the* metropolis of Weimar Germany, Berlin was the locus of both desire and anxiety, aspiration and resent-ment, in the face of modernisation, industrialisation, capitalism, even democracy, and there were some who criticised the film on grounds of what Kracauer at the time called 'its lack of a political stance', its avoidance in the name of aesthetics of any overt political discourse disguised its alignment with political obscurantism: 'At best,' said Kracauer,

> the film is based on the idea that Berlin is the city of speed and work – a formal idea that in no way leads to any content and that perhaps for this reason intoxicates the German petit bourgeois when it appears in society and literature.[26]

The postmodern viewer might well agree with this reading intellectually, but this is a film with a huge excess of energy, which still packs an extraordinary punch.

If *Berlin* initiated a wave of 'street' films, which Kracauer dismisses with the comment that they were cheap to produce and 'offered a gratifying opportunity of showing much and revealing nothing', there is one production of 1929 that has to be singled out for its sheer originality in resolving the problem of the cross-section genre. *Menschen am Sontag* (People on Sunday) has entered film history as a collaboration between a group of young film-makers who ended up a few years later in Hollywood, including Robert Siodmak, Edgar Ulmer, Billy Wilder and Fred Zinnemann, with Siodmak and Ulmer as the directors. Announcing itself as 'a film without actors', it offers an original and unexpected blend of documentary and fiction in which a group of Berliners – a taxi driver, a wine salesman, a music-shop assistant, a film extra and a model – play themselves in the portrayal of a typical weekend (and since they all had weekday jobs, the film was shot over a number of weekends during the summer of 1929). This is recognisably the same Berlin, the same streets and railways and trams, the same trappings of the modern city, but under another aspect. People in Ruttmann's film are completely dominated by the circulation system, here they are brought into the foreground, as (in Kracauer's description) 'they leave their dreary homes for one of the lakes near Berlin, and are there seen bathing, cooking, lying about on the beach, making futile contacts with each other and people like them. This is about all.'[27] But this is too dismissive. The interesting thing is the way the narrative is decentred by extended sequences of documentary observation of the everyday life of the city and its bustling inhabitants, which locates the five friends in a very unheroic world. This is much more than scene-setting, but describes a different relationship between the subject and their everyday world than was usual in either fiction or documentary. But Kracauer was right about the political circumstances of the film, with its characters drawn from the ranks of 'lesser employees': in Weimar Berlin, the 'little man' and his plight, the class of white-collar workers and small self-employed, had turned into a political factor. 'They were wooed by the Nazis as well as the Social Democrats, and the whole domestic situation depended upon whether they would cling to their middle-class prejudices or acknowledge their common interests with the working class.' In the end, *People on Sunday* is one of those films which impress themselves on the imagination as pointers towards a different kind of cinema, where the simple opposition between fiction and documentary is transcended. Others include *Kuhle Wampe* by Slatan Dudow and Bertolt Brecht (1932), another vision of Berlin; two films by Jean Renoir, *Toni* of 1934 and *La Vie est à nous* of 1936; and the 1934 Mexican film *Redes*, co-directed by Fred Zinnemann.

Ivens found Ruttmann's film of the city dissatisfying and felt 'that a city film with human interest and content could be done without Ruttmann's virtuosity and superficial effects', but he admitted that similar criticism was made about his own much more modest *Rain*, in which, he said, he subordinated everything 'to the aesthetic approach' and the film was criticised for its lack of 'content'.[28] This happened in Russia, when he showed his films to audiences of workers in 1930. When they saw *The Bridge* they would ask 'Why don't you explain what cities this bridge links? Why don't we see any people on the bridge?'. He would reply that everyone in Holland knows these details and when he made the film he wasn't thinking of a foreign audience seeing it. But the questions stuck in his mind. 'This audience saw a train going over a bridge and wanted to know much more than the mechanical functions of the bridge.' Their reaction to *Rain* was equally 'healthy and disturbing':

It seemed to them that I had fallen in love with reflections and textures. They said *Rain* showed too little of human reactions and concentrated too much on objects. One challenging remark was – 'Why are you afraid of faces? If you could look at a face with the same frankness with which you look at a raindrop you would be wonderful.' [29]

This reaction, he said, made a deeper impression on him than comparisons between the lighting and composition in *Rain* and Dutch genre painting.

What Ivens told the Russian audience wasn't quite true however. Both *The Bridge* and *Rain* were shown across Europe in what he himself describes as 'avant-garde movie theatres and . . . ciné clubs'. While these first efforts set out to address a local audience, they were films conceived in an international perspective, addressed to a public consisting of aficionados of the same kind Ivens knew from Berlin and which could be found all over Europe: bourgeois with bohemian leanings, and international in outlook. If his encounters in Soviet Russia contributed to the shift in Ivens' work to political subjects soon after, where his commitment, energy and talents distinguished him as a force to be reckoned with, then it is because they made him think about audiences, about what they know, what they don't know, what they want to know, and what they need to know. The lessons were particularly important for the genre of foreign political reportage which Ivens would make his métier (like *The Spanish Earth* of 1937) – in other words, films for audiences with very little knowledge, tacit or otherwise, of the places depicted, but a yearning for political identification.

IV

In Soviet documentary of the 1920s, the city was not the only site of modernisation. Victor Turin's feature-length *Turksib* of 1929, a film particularly influential on Grierson who prepared the English version, portrays the drama of the construction of a branch of the Trans-Siberian railway in a form that in Paul Rotha's view, writing in the 1930s, 'defined the line of [the] Soviet approach to pure documentary, for it discarded the story form altogether and in grand style dramatised the economic need' for the railway.[30] This film made a deep impression on audiences. According to Grierson's patron, Stephen Tallents,

> It has no personal story, and no individual actors. Its hero is the slowly advancing railway, its villain the forces of drought and storm, of ice and rock and flood. I have seen its reception by a selected audience of English businessmen and labour representatives, and have heard them describe it as a finer film than any other they had viewed.[31]

In the process, it not only shows the effort of construction but also explains the effect the railway will have on the economy of the USSR; cotton from Turkistan and wool from Kazakhstan will replace materials being imported from Egypt and America. Here, the geographical reach of documentary space is a symbolic inscription of the spread of Communist government through the Russian hinterland, which aims at the modernisation of the entire country, bringing the remotest parts within its orbit. Or as Winston neatly puts it, in *Turksib*, Flaherty's primitives, Nanook and Moana, are inserted into economic development.[32]

Again we have a film that is structured somewhat like a symphony or symphonic suite, with recurrent themes and motifs, and a host of memorable images. A Russian film critic wrote of the camel indifferently gazing at the railway line appearing for the first time in the desert; the Kazak horsemen and camel drivers trying at full gallop to race the first train; the enthusiasm of the workers as they finish laying the last rails at fantastic speed.[33]

Barnouw, who refers to the style of the intertitles as Whitmanesque (he was presumably watching Grierson's version), recalls a sequence introduced with the simple title 'Strangers . . .', which 'shows people in a remote Turkestan desert village watching the arrival of surveyors'; and another, which begins in the snow-capped peaks where the snow is melting under the hot sun, the water flowing in rivulets to join a torrent which supplies the irrigation channels that bring water to the thirsty fields. A sequence, says Barnouw, which has been widely imitated.[34]

Winston explains the influence of this film in the West as the result of its relative lack of politics, which enter only obliquely. As a highly effective (and visually beautiful) documentary with little by way of overt propaganda, it provided the Griersonians with an important example of 'how to deal, or rather *not* deal, with politics in the documentary . . . it showed how a film maker could be unpolitical, even in a highly charged political situation with an overtly political topic'.[35] There is a certain truth in this – Turin's film has none of the stridency of Eisenstein or Vertov – although Grierson was clear why he took it as a model: '*Turksib* is an affair of economics, which is the only sort of affair worth one's time and patience.'[36] But the economics are not abstract, and the film is not controlled by a discourse where images illustrate verbal propositions; here we get the living relationship between concrete social actors and productive forces, traced in a storyless plot (for which one of the scriptwriters was Shklovsky) where politics are not so much discarded but form a structuring absence, while the explicit discourse of the film is spatial and geographical: its actors are not just social subjects, but also water, rivers, lakes and irrigation channels; fields and agriculture and animal husbandry; forests and deserts; the wind which blows the sandstorm that engulfs the camel train; nomads on camels and horse-drawn sleds in the snow; the surveyors at work, the gathering of materials, the laying of lines, the blasting away of rocky outcrops, the first locomotive – all these are offered as signs of different spatial practices which are brought together into the epic span of the film, which thereby provides a vivid depiction of the shape of progress, in a form we could call a cognitive map of the social interdependency of a modernising society. (Winston sums up: 'With its happy Asiatics, heroic Russian surveyors and exhortations to get the job done . . . *Turksib* runs from the social and political meaning of the railroad.'[37] But this I feel is wrong. The evident earnestness and enthusiasm of the film's social actors is not invalidated by the terrors of Stalinism to come, or the ultimate demise of Communism some six decades later. This is how they felt about it in the 20s, when Soviet life was full of hope, and this too is part of what this documentary documents.)

Soviet documentary of the 1920s began to explore several other kinds of space as well. Pudovkin, for example, entered the conceptual space of the scientific laboratory in *Mechanics of the Brain* (1926), about the work of the celebrated physiologist Pavlov, which he started shooting before his rather better known début film, *Chess Fever*. According to Pudovkin himself, Pavlov was originally reluctant to co-operate, fearful that popularisation was tantamount to 'vulgarisation', but was eventually reconciled to the project.[38] Beginning with a demonstration of basic reflexes in animals, including the famous experiments with frogs, the film moves on to show the formation of conditioned reflexes in dogs, monkeys being trained to respond to colour stimuli, the effects of damage to various parts of the human brain and the performance of various tasks by children at different ages. In an account by Pavlov's cinematographer Anatoli Golovnya, the film was composed of

> mad men, idiots, paralytics, a woman in childbirth, newborn infants and not newborn . . . ordinary dogs and dogs without a brain; dissected frogs and undissected frogs, monkeys, lions, bears, eagles, cows, horses, hippopotami, crocodiles. And all this entire ensemble turns around, fidgets, runs off or separates out, seizes our operator or grasps onto the camera.[39]

Behind the joking description, this early endeavour to make a documentary of serious scientific exposition threw up certain problems of observation which go to the heart of the documentary endeavour, now as then.

The space of the laboratory calls up from Pudovkin a suitably sober form of montage, subordinated to the task of scientific exposition, as if each shot in the film is a piece of experimental evidence in itself. But this is a carefully worked up effect. Pudovkin spoke, for example, of the problem of filming a sea-lion. One cannot command an animal to swim in a certain direction or approach the camera. Since certain shots are needed to be able to cut them together, you have to rely on the 'approximate control of chance elements':

> For the close-up the bait was thrown again and again until the sea-lion leaped onto the right place on the bank and made the necessary turn. Out of thirty takes made, three were chosen and these gave on the screen the desired image of continuous movement.

This kind of thing would become a perennial problem decades later in the television natural history documentary and, according to a recent study, explains some of the peculiarities of the genre.[40] The producers have to work with material provided by wildlife photographers which is often little more than a disparate ensemble of shots filmed at different times and locations. Experienced wildlife photographers undoubtedly shoot with particular montages in mind, and are commissioned to 'do' a certain subject, but what is filmed 'in the wild' may still need to be supplemented by shots taken in zoos or even laboratories where conditions for close-ups and detail shots are more controlled. The result is inevitably a synthesis of shots which in themselves represent what Deleuze has called any-space-whatever.

In fact, for *Mechanics of the Brain*, most of the filming was in Pavlov's laboratory, known as the Tower of Silence, which in Deleuze's terms is still any-space-whatever, but was specially designed to eliminate external stimuli that might distract the animals' attention. The film-makers found that their presence affected the conduct of the experiments, and in the pediatric laboratory they took the precaution of building a hide. The resulting shots, where the child subjects appear to be looking at the camera, become problematic, because the look in the eyes of the children is markedly different from that of animals. The film ends with a sequence about the development of children from the unconditioned reflexes of the new-born baby to the emergence of the 'aim' reflex which enables children to play games, and thus to enter culture – but it has nothing to say about the difference between animals and human beings which the camera seems above all to see in their eyes.

There is also Esfir Shub's creation of a space of history in a series of compilation films beginning with *The Fall of the Romanov Dynasty* in 1927, using footage she found in a cellar in Leningrad, including a collection of 'counter-revolutionary film' which turned out to be the home movies of Tsar Nicholas II. She does little more than place these films in historical chronology along with footage of war, strikes, arrests of troublemakers and more, with a few brief subtitles to explain individual shots, or occasionally, as Barnouw puts it, give 'a sharp propaganda stab' (we are told, for example, that the Duma included 241 landowners and seven workers, while a munitions assembly line elicits the comment 'The hands of workers preparing the death of their brothers').[41] The images are often individually striking in their composition or subject matter, and Shub allows them to unfold at their own pace. Since her analysis of these historical traces is of course a Marxist one, in which each fragment is seen as the figurative appearance of the dialectic, the result is an embodied commentary on the truth of Marxist historiography – the forces of history are class relations and ownership of the means of production, the authoritarian power of the State, the profoundly conservative role of the Church. What Shub achieves, here and in other films which followed, is not just the reconstruction of history through documentary footage, but the creation of a film-historical discourse which transcends the simple present tense of the actuality camera which took the original footage.

V

In striking contrast to a film like *Turksib*, the geographical consciousness of American documentary in the same years constructs the world in terms of a gulf between the metropolis, the site of civilisation and progress, and the distant unknown of the periphery, an exotic wilderness of primitive and ancient backwardness. Flaherty found his subjects first in the Canadian Arctic, based on his experience as a prospector, and then in Samoa. Why Samoa? Because of the success of *Nanook of the North*, Paramount was prepared to pay good money to send him there to make *Moana*, the film celebrated by Grierson for its 'documentary value' on its release in 1925. The same year Merriam C. Cooper and Ernest Schoedsack came out with *Grass*, a travelogue which follows the journey of the Bakhtiari people of Persia from their winter grazing to their summer camps (a film that in the country it pictured was banned by an authoritarian government which regarded the subject as incompatible with its self-image as a modernising regime). Two years later they came back from Thailand with *Chang*, which follows the Flaherty model of a dramatic story of a family centred on the human struggle for survival in the face of nature in the raw. Then in 1933, they went on to distil what they'd learned about such exotic places into one of the most famous films in the history of cinema: *King Kong* owes its status, despite the absurd plot and clumsily contrived script, to its spectacular visualisation of a modern version of the old myth of beauty and the beast. But if here they stage a confrontation between the jungle and civilisation, the places portrayed in the earlier films belong to the other side of an invisible divide. They remain unconnected to the viewer, except supposedly through the simple humanity of their inhabitants, who are often rendered as unsophisticated and childlike. These are examples of the imaginary geography with which the West sees the East, subjective visions in which, says Edward Said, the gaze is asymmetrical, because imaginative geography of the 'our land-barbarian land' variety does not require that the barbarians acknowledge the distinction. It is enough for 'us' to set up these boundaries in our own minds; 'they' become 'they' accordingly, and both their territory and their mentality are designated as different from 'ours'.[42]

The result is a mixture of fascination and fear, attraction and repulsion. What cinema brought to this syndrome was a gaze which appeared benign, supposing itself to be objective and scientific, but which carried an ideological agenda, where the jungle or the desert speak of the opposition between wilderness and civilisation, nature and science, barbarism and culture.

This ambiguous gaze is already at work in that first film of Flaherty's, which, as a result, seems (in postmodern retrospect) to manifest practically every original sin ever attributed to documentary. There are also a number of sins, mostly of omission, in another first film of an ethnographic mould – *Voyage au Congo*, made by Mark Allégret in 1925–6 on a trip to French Equatorial Africa in the company of André Gide. Rouch lamented that this film was not 'the cinematic mirror of Gide's classic book bearing the same title – a violent testimony against the excesses of colonialism',[43] though he also observed that old out-of-date films like this have considerable historical value, not only as milestones in the history of African films but also as unique evidence of the outlook and behaviour of an epoch.[44]

This film is in quite a different register from Flaherty. Allégret still reproduces a rather nineteenth-century image of exoticism, revelling in the nearly naked bodies which appear before the camera, especially women (and boys), but his attention to the details of everyday life makes it one of the earliest films from Africa with real ethnographic value. We learn a good deal, for example, about how different foodstuffs are prepared, and the different styles of housing in different regions. Many of the shots appear to be staged, in the sense that Allégret has asked his subjects to repeat actions he has been observing for the benefit of the camera – sometimes this is obvious from the loose cutting. The image is punctuated by frequent intertitles which explain what we're seeing, most of them quite factual and free of tendentious colonialist rhetoric. There is one sequence which sits rather oddly with the film's generally sober approach, where Allégret introduces a storyline about the courtship between a young couple, which allows the film to explain how these things are managed; this is the only point where the film has recourse to the kind of personalisation of ethnographic observation which is Flaherty's hallmark. However, many things are evoked only to remain beyond view. A great number of scenes portray women at their domestic labours, almost none show the work of the men, which we learn only indirectly is hunting. Also missing is almost any representation of the presence (let alone the nature) of French colonialism – for the bulk of the film there are almost no white people to be seen at all. There's a substantial sequence of New Year celebrations on 1 January, but without any comment on why Africans should celebrate the Western new year, especially since the film presents them not as Christians but as 'fetishists'. Allégret himself admitted that they removed any indications of the journey itself, except for the opening which portrays their arrival, and the conclusion, at the orphanage in the city where the children are cared for by nuns, which as a result brings the film to a close with an abrupt return of the repressed presence of colonial rule.

Voyage au Congo reproduces the structure of colonial power without intending anything like an apologia for it. There were precious few models for doing anything else. What is striking about this whole period is that while the metropolitan countries are busy producing visions of the colonial world, no alternate visions are produced by film-makers from the countries concerned. Even in Latin America, there was only spasmodic activity, most of which was confined to minor examples of conventional sub-genres like the travelogue or the scientific documentary. Nevertheless, there is evidence of a more creative documentary instinct at work in isolated examples uncovered by scholars. Agustín Mahieu speaks of an Argentinian film of 1916, *El último malón* (The Last Indian Uprising), shot in the province of Santa Fe by an anthropologist called Alcides Greca, which he describes as a kind of documentary reconstruction of an uprising that took place at the beginning of the century, filmed in authentic locations with the indigenous Indians as protagonists of their own story.[45] Paulo Antonio Paranagua speaks of a documentary made for a copper company in Chile in 1919 by an Italian named Salvador Giambastiani which places on display faces marked by the grim conditions in the mines, including a number of scenes of the men at work. He has also chronicled the existence of a substantial number of newsreels produced in various countries from the 1920s to the 1950s, especially Argentina, Mexico, Brazil and Cuba.[46]

Occasionally new finds appear. A documentary of 1993 by the Venezuelan Alfredo Anzola, *El misterio de los ojos escarlata* (The Mystery of the Scarlet Eyes), affords a rare glimpse of previously unseen images of Venezuela in the 1920s and 30s. This is footage shot by the film-maker's father, who made documentaries and two silent feature films, now lost, in the 1920s, and then acquired a 16mm camera and filmed mostly documentary footage throughout the 30s and 40s, while working as the director of a radio station – a radio serial written and produced by Anzola père provides the title of his son's film about him. The film prompts several questions: how many others among the all but nameless Latin American film-makers of the early years had similar careers? And may have left undiscovered archives? And how many of these aficionados have not even left their names behind? And another thing: Anzola, as portrayed by his son, was clearly no intellectual, but a keen cineaste, an aficionado who took his camera with him to events where he had entry as a radio producer. The point of view is uncritical and marked by his social class. But aficionados of the same class in succeeding decades were the very people whose first film-making efforts represent the initial stirrings of the powerful new movement in Latin American cinema which emerged in the late 50s, in which documentary was to hold a privileged place.

Notes

1. Jonathan Rosenbaum, 'LA Existential', *Chicago Reader*,
   <www.chicagoreader.com/movies/archives/2004/1004/041001.html>.
2. Jason Anderson, <www.eye.net/eye/issue/issue_05.26.05/film/onscreen.html>.
3. Vsevofod Pudovkin, *Film Technique* (London: Newnes, 1933), pp. 60–1. Another version can be found in Jay Leyda, *Kino: A History of the Russian and Soviet Film* (London: Allen & Unwin, 1960), pp.164–5, taken from Lev Kuleshov, *Art of the Cinema* (Moscow, 1929).
4. Mark Shiel, 'Cinema and the City in History and Theory', in Mark Shiel and Tony Fitzmaurice (eds), *Cinema and the City: Film and Urban Societies in a Global Context* (Oxford: Blackwell, 2001), p. 5.

5. See Henri Lefebvre, *The Production of Space* (Oxford: Blackwell, 1991).

6. Douglas Gomery, *Shared Pleasures: A History of Movie Presentation in the United States* (London: BFI, 1992).

7. Lefebvre, *The Production of Space*, p. 97.

8. See Elizabeth Lebas, 'Sadness and Gladness: The Films of Glasgow Corporation, 1922–1938', *Film Studies* no. 6, Summer 2005, pp. 27–45.

9. See A. L. Rees, *A History of Experimental Film and Video* (London: BFI, 1999), p. 32.

10. 'Joris Ivens en Cuba', *Cine Cubano* no. 3, p. 21.

11. *Close Up*, June 1928, p. 30.

12. Quoted in Hans Schoots, *Living Dangerously: A Biography of Joris Ivens* (Amsterdam: Amsterdam University Press, 2000), p. 41.

13. Gilles Deleuze, *Cinema 1: The Movement Image* (Minneapolis, MN: University of Minnesota Press, 1986), p. 111.

14. Joris Ivens, *The Camera and I* (Berlin: Seven Seas, 1969), p. 36.

15. Deleuze, *Cinema 1*, p. 111.

16. Ivens, *The Camera and I*, p. 37.

17. Ivens, *The Camera and I*, p. 30.

18. Ivens, *The Camera and I*, p. 35.

19. Vlada Petric, *Constructivism in Film – The Man with the Movie Camera: A Cinematic Analysis* (Cambridge: Cambridge University Press, 1987), p. 9.

20. Fredric Jameson, *Brecht and Method* (London: Verso, 1998), p. 39.

21. Seth Feldman, '"Peace between Man and Machine": Dziga Vertov's *The Man with a Movie Camera*', in Barry Keith Grant and Jeannette Sloniowski (eds), *Documenting the Documentary: Close Readings of Documentary Film and Video* (Detroit, MI: Wayne State University Press, 1998), pp. 46–7.

22. Siegfried Kracauer, *From Caligari to Hitler* (Princeton, NJ: Princeton University Press, 1947), p. 183.

23. Kracauer, *From Caligari to Hitler*, pp. 184–5.

24. Wolfgang Natter, 'The City as Cinematic Space: Modernism and Place in *Berlin, Symphony of a City*', in Stuart Aitken and Leo Zon, *Place, Power, Situation and Spectacle: A Geography of Film* (Lanham, MD: Rowman & Littlefield, 1994), pp. 216–7.

25. Natter, 'The City as Cinematic Space', pp. 213–4.

26. Siegfried Kracauer, 'Film 1928', in *The Mass Ornament* (Cambridge, MA: Harvard University Press, 1995), also in Kevin Macdonald and Mark Cousins (eds), *Imagining Reality: The Faber Book of Documentary* (London and Boston, MA: Faber and Faber, 1996), p. 75.

27. Kracauer, *From Caligari to Hitler*, p. 189.

28. Ivens, *The Camera and I*, p. 40.

29. Ivens, *The Camera and I*, pp. 56–7.

30. Paul Rotha, *Documentary Film* (London: Faber and Faber, 3rd edn, 1952), p. 94.

31. Quoted in Paul Swann, *The British Documentary Film Movement, 1926–1946* (Cambridge: Cambridge University Press, 1989), p. 46.

32. Brian Winston, *Claiming the Real: The Documentary Film Revisited* (London: BFI, 1995), p. 50.

33. Nikolai Lebedev, quoted in Georges Sadoul, *Dictionary of Films*, p. 385.

34. Erik Barnouw, *Documentary* (Oxford: Oxford University Press, 1974), p. 67.

35. Winston, *Claiming the Real*, p. 50.

36. Ian Aitken, 1990, p. 87.

37. Winston, *Claiming the Real*, p. 50.

38. See Amy Sargeant, *Vsevolod Pudovkin: Classic Films of the Avant-Garde* (London: I. B. Tauris, 2000).

39. Quoted in Sargeant, *Vsevolod Pudovkin*.

40. Nils Lindahl Elliot, 'Signs of Anthropomorphism: The Case of Natural History Television Documentaries', *Social Semiotics* vol. 11 no. 3, 2001, pp. 289–305.

41. Barnouw, *Documentary* p. 66.

42. Edward Said, *Orientalism* (London: Penguin, 1985), p. 54.

43. Jean Rouch, *Ciné-Ethnography* (Minneapolis: University of Minnesota Press, 2003), p. 52.

44. Ibid., p. 73.

45. José Agustín Mahieu, *Breve historia del cine argentino* (Buenos Aires: Editorial Universitaria, 1966).

46. Paulo Antonio Paranagua (ed.), *Cine Documental en América Latina* (Madrid: Cátedra, 2003).

6 The Documented Point of View

On documentary film language

I

In the 1950s, a time of modest low-key poetic essays by directors like Franju or Resnais in France, or the Free Cinema group in England, and then the first experiments of cinéma vérité at the end of the decade, it was possible for a theorist like Metz to get away with the assertion that 'non-narrative films for the most part are distinguished from "real" films by their social purpose and their content much more than by their "language processes"'. Or again: 'Remove "drama", and there is no fiction, no diegesis, and therefore no film. Or only a documentary, a "film exposé".'[1] I hardly wish to contest that a very large number of documentaries are indeed to be characterised by their social purpose and content. I also maintain that many are non-narrative, being primarily essayistic or poetic, pamphleteering or didactic. But this hardly justifies Metz's disparagement of the documentary. That phrase of his, 'only a documentary', suggests that documentary is a denuded form of cinema, weak in what he calls the 'language processes' found on the royal road of diegesis, from which he thinks documentary must therefore borrow the 'basic figures of the semiotics of cinema – montage, camera movements, scale of shots, relationships between image and speech, sequences, and other large syntagmatic units'.[2] But what if this is to prejudge the issue? What if documentary has its own 'language processes', and their lack of recognition stems from its own forgotten history in the face of the hegemony of fiction? And what if these language processes are shared out in different ways in different films, according to Wittgenstein's model of family relationships, in a manner that confuses us when we look for definitions? What if Chris Marker's seemingly anarchic narration by association of ideas in *Sans Soleil* is as much the *ne plus ultra* of documentary as the opposite, the purely observational Direct Cinema sans commentary of Frederick Wiseman?

Even though Metz modified his position and developed a concept of codes which is potentially more congenial to documentary, this attitude of denigration towards the documentary left its mark on film theory. What is distinctly odd about this is that the very same period, the 60s and 70s, was hugely inventive for documentary cinema, a period of aesthetic innovation which also had huge ramifications for the 'privileged' mode of fiction. Documentarists not only reached out and seized the moment again and again with growing agility, but also, following their own creative needs and instincts, developed a whole range of new 'language processes' which, as well as radicalising documentary, also impinged on the narrative movie, sometimes to subvert and disrupt the structures of filmic speech that Metz devoted himself to analysing in detail. (This was already evident in the 60s, with the hand-held, sync-sound location shooting of many a film by the French, British and Latin American new waves.) Documentarists debated the pros and cons, even split into different camps, but Metz thought that an independent semiotics of the various non-narrative genres was hardly possible other than in the form of remarks about their difference from 'ordinary' films. Several scholars since then have set out to prove him wrong by producing theories which attest to the multiple forms of documentary exposition and genres on their own terms (and this book is intended as a contribution to this approach).[3] Another response is also possible, namely, to think of recasting the history of film and its 'language processes' from another perspective, which instead of an antinomy between fiction and documentary, perceives a symbiosis, a hidden dialogue, an underlying exchange, in which the development of film language is also a function of the passage from documentary to narrative and back again. Indeed, according to Dai Vaughan, there is scarcely a documentary device which has not at some time been appropriated by the fiction film, although in the context of fiction, he adds, it becomes an arbitrary signifier not of reality but of real*ism*, which is governed by different codes of representation.[4]

II

If early documentary resisted classical narrative continuity, this is partly because of the pull of the photogenic, already seen in examples like Ponting's Antarctic film and Flaherty's in the Arctic. This is not to say that the photogenic attracted fiction any less, but documentary treated it differently. The significance of the films by Ponting and Flaherty is not just that they delivered something beyond the capability of the studio – the awesome sight of the world's polar extremities – but that in the process, the sites where they were filmed, instead of serving for the background of dramatic action, acquired, through their sheer photogenic power, the presence of characters in the film's dramaturgy.

In 1920s' France, in the writings of Louis Delluc, Louis Aragon and Jean Epstein,[5] where film and modernism came together, photogenic becomes a noun, *photogénie*, which means more than 'attractive to the camera', more than the special beauty of certain faces in movement or certain filmic effects, but also a sense of transcendence which film lends to the phenomena under observation, a shimmering that gives us the impression of seeing things as we've never seen them before, as if they were endowed with a special intensity and inner life, or, as Epstein put it, a personality of their own. It operates not only through people, lending stardom to certain actors independently of their ability as actors (or sometimes lack of it), but also through objects. The close-up, for example, has the power to rescind the distinction between objectivity and subjectivity. A close-up of a revolver 'is no longer a revolver, it is the revolver-character . . . It has a temperament, habits, memories, a will, a soul.'[6] As if the power of the photogenic is what turns the index into an icon. In short, for Epstein the photogenic rediscovers an animistic universe in which every detail of the pictured world comes alive: 'a startling pantheism is reborn to the world and fills it to bursting point'.[7] Furthermore, the photogenic as these writers conceive it is not only produced by the specific qualities of the camera – exposure, framing, focus, angle, composition – but extends to the domain of editing and montage, the process which brings the individual images into mutual relation, and which, as the silent documentary reached its maturity, was growing ever more sophisticated.

It is *photogénie*, as perceived by Delluc and co., that aligned the cinema to a modernist aesthetic, and their agitation on behalf of *photogénie* is a fine example of avant-garde cultural politics. As an act of position-taking, *pace* Bourdieu, it amounted to a proposal for new creative strategies which encouraged the emergence in 1920s' France of experimental and documentary film-making – a position they took up in dissent from the mainstream celebration of genre cinema. These strategies could be enlisted for different stylistic aims, both realist and anti-realist. Epstein himself followed his haunting adaptation of Edgar Allan Poe's *The Fall of the House of Usher*, with its use of cinematic devices like the flashback, slow motion and innovative lighting, with *Finis terrae* (1929), filmed on location on the wild coast of Brittany, with local people as his actors, depicting the harsh life of the Breton fishermen and coastal kelpharvesters in an extraordinary anticipation of the neorealist documentary drama. Epstein gives his documentary instinct a dramatic shape: one of the kelpers is accidentally injured by a knife: will the doctor from the other island reach him in time? *Finis terrae*, which Epstein himself called 'a psychological documentary, the portrayal of a brief drama in episodes that really took place, of authentic people and things', is thus like a remake of *Nanook* in another terrain and with another story but with the same theme of the drama of the human struggle for survival in the teeth of the forces of nature.

On the other hand, because *photogénie* implicates montage, it was equally susceptible to the avant-garde impulse to disrupt, subvert or even suspend the classic unities of narrative economy, and instead to develop, as Richard Abel puts it, 'patterns of continuity that depended on a combination of graphic, rhythmic, and associative or connotative relations'.[8] Here an emblematic film would be Cavalcanti's *Rien que les heures* of 1926, a film about Paris by a young Brazilian tyro abroad which opens with a categorical rejection of narrative, a title which reads 'This film contains no story. It is just a sequence of impressions on the passage of time.' What follows is a disconcerting montage of impressionistic shots which William Guynn has described rather nicely: freed from the demands of narrative sequencing, Cavalcanti produces 'photogenic effects through the unexpected and often ambiguous affinities he creates between shots'.[9] *Rien que les heures* is treated by film historians as both an experimental film of the avant-garde and an early documentary, one of the city films of the 20s in which documentary seemed to discover itself. It was these films which offered the first sustained alternative grammar of construction to what had become by now, in Nöel Burch's phrase, the institutional mode of representation: instead of the economy of narrative fiction, an alternative principle of montage, what Guynn calls 'photogenic continuity', which from this moment on provides an aesthetic logic for the particular *photogénie* of the documentary.

III

The elaboration of photogenic montage is the work of the 1920s. It is hardly yet present in 1922 in *Nanook of the North*, which owes its impact and enduring value to its intense photogenicity. Flaherty aimed for a strong naturalistic illusion, achieved through the performance by social actors of various actions against the backdrop of nature to paint a picture of their lifeworld, but always set up and played for the camera. The 'story' thus amounts to little more than a series of activities unfolding across the passing seasons of the year, one of the simplest shapes a narrative can take, arranged to provide a gradual dramatic build-up.

Despite its historical status, *Nanook* is weak in its treatment of the relationship between shot and montage, the process of cutting separate pieces of film together, bringing them into rapport and creating a consecutive whole. The film is narrated through extensive use of intertitles, in places between every shot; this of course prevents continuity editing, which occurs mainly in three or four extended sequences, like the walrus hunt and building the igloo. Even then, shot matching is rough and imprecise: continuity of activity rather than action. This is even true of the early scene of clowning with the phonograph, where one moment Nanook's woman Nyla is to be seen behind him with the baby, and the next moment disappears (the two shots are taken from the same angle). Sequences like this deliver characterisation but not plot points with causal relations; the duration of individual shots is not determined by narrative weight but by factors like their own internal composition and rhythm. But the lingering camera leaves us with a whole number of iconic images by which the film stays in the memory: small dark figures moving across the dappled whiteness of the snow, or picking their way through ice floes; Nanook licking the phonograph record, or his face appearing in the igloo's window.

What we find in *Nanook* is a set of representations whose visual intensity make them models of mobile illustration, despite amounting to little more than a fragmented succession of typical activities. But what they also inscribe is the encounter between the white man and the 'noble savage', the exotic other who is the projection of the colonial imaginary, and the gaze of the camera inevitably places the viewer, back in the cinema in the civilised city, in a position of cultural superiority to Nanook (even enjoined to complicity in the portrayal of the naïf who licks the phonograph record). In the end, *Nanook* is a problem film precisely because it worked, creating a paradigm for documentary narrative. If Flaherty thus came to be seen as the progenitor of the realist documentary, it was not despite his practices of judicious enactment for the camera, but precisely because of them, because they translated his observations into an intelligible form (but *pace* Vaughan, according to what codes of representation?). It was even considered by many as the original model of the ethnographic documentary, an exemplar of the portrayal of the 'exotic other' – which is precisely what makes the film, for more sceptical eyes over eighty years later, somewhat suspect. It also repeatedly crops up as the model for numerous documentaries over the years, not only Epstein's *Finis terrae*, but also films like *Pour la suite du monde* in 1964, by Pierre Perrault, Michael Brault and Marcel Carrière, in which traditional fisherman on a island near Quebec resurrect the traditional beluga whale hunt; or most recently, *The Story of the Weeping Camel*, by Byambasuren Davaa and Luigi Falorni (2003), which portrays the everyday life of a nomad family in the Gobi Desert.

The same year *Nanook* came out, but at the other end of the cinematic scale to Flaherty, Vertov set about producing the *Kino-pravda* newsreels (which are equally suspect to some). These were short, quickly made, and a laboratory for montage. Vertov elaborated his theories in a stream of manifestos, which were presented, as several commentators observe, with the typographical zest of futurist poetry. These ideas were all tested in practice, forged in the pressure of everyday activity. In the urgency to keep up with social reality, each newsreel was different from the previous one. 'The system of editing changed,' wrote Vertov later,

> The approach to the process of filming changed. The character of the captions and the way in which they were used changed . . . Every day one had to invent something new. There was no-one to learn from. We were exploring unknown ground. Inventing and experimenting.

In this unusual laboratory, 'slowly but surely the alphabet of film-language was built up'.[10] Furhammer and Isaksson get it right when they say that the Bolshevik film-makers started by having to turn out the most persuasive possible propaganda films using the least possible material, and one thing led to another:

Out of the shortage of material grew the necessity to experiment with short fragments of film which often lacked continuity. Out of the experiments grew a realisation of the importance of the cutting in achieving an effect: juxtaposition of two separate images could create contrasts, shocks and unexpected meanings which did not exist in either image viewed separately. And out of these insights grew the principles of montage.[11]

When it came to *Man with a Movie Camera*, Vertov, like Ruttmann in *Berlin*, was utterly opposed to Flaherty's textually constructed narrative, rejecting the use of written text on the screen to provide either a discursive framework or even just a narrative prop. (The only words allowed are those which belong to the profilmic scene, but these, of course, acquire special significance.) These films depend no less than fictional narrative on the properties of montage, which they use, however, to very different purpose. Both depend on elaborate forms of sequencing, but the internal organisation of these sequences follows quite other principles from fictional diegesis – they are not divided into unified scenes. Since the underlying narrative shape of both films is the simple 'day in the life', the sequence functions as a composite segment of time, where successive shots are not governed by the principle of 'this and then that' but rather 'this and also this'. Indeed the passage of time is suspended, until something comes along which makes you realise it must have passed anyway. This does not preclude the inclusion of groups of shots linked by continuity of action or activity, but it allows the trope of parallelism to function quite differently from fiction. Parallel storytelling in fiction functions on the level of alternating scenes of action with a determinate temporal relation to each other. In documentary, parallelism functions between images, singly and in groups, without being tied to temporal succession. It is not dramatic but photogenic, rhetorical, metaphorical and poetic. Successive shots follow a logic of implication where, in place of plot and story, the organising principle is rhythm, rhyme and persuasion in its various modes – assertion, contention, polemic, dialectic – through which, as Nichols puts it, 'elements of the world required as evidence for the text's argument can be herded together from separate points of origin'.[12] Narrative is not excluded, but the grammar of narrative continuity is entirely dispensable.

If the discussion of montage always takes us back to the origins of film theory in 1920s' Soviet Russia, when the process was first analysed, then what we owe to the likes of Kuleshov, Eisenstein and Pudovkin are not merely the particular styles with which their names are variously associated, but what taken together might be called the general theory of montage, a kind of filmic general theory of relativity. On this reading, Metz's royal road of diegetic narrative, with its grammar of continuity and various syntagmatic forms, can be understood as a special theory. Both concern the nature of filmic space, time and what we might call gravity or orientation. The general theory says that screen space is, in postmodern parlance, heterotopic: a comprehensive and relative space capable of holding together several different spaces and times belonging to different orders. The special theory explains the particular laws that produce the unified space and time of narrative fiction – the grammar of continuity, the matching gaze, the 180-degree rule, the graduated scale of shots. Fictional narrative comprises a series of segments conventionally denominated as scenes; as every budding screenwriter knows, the narrative scene in fiction is demarcated by a change in place or time. But this has no ready equivalent in the documentary, with the result that documentary sequences flow into one another like successive passages in a piece of music, or like Ruttmann's *Berlin*, a symphony in one movement.

IV

Another film that observes this kind of musical structure is Jean Vigo's *À propos de Nice*, which comes right at the end of the silent period and condenses the full scope of the city film into twenty minutes of intensely photogenic montage – with attitude; or what Vigo himself called '*le point de vue documenté*', the documented point of view. There is no better summary of the film than the entry in Sadoul's *Dictionary of Films*:

> Vigo outlined his theme in his first synopsis: 'Nice is, above all, a town living a game: the great hotels, the tourists, the roulette, the paupers. Everything is doomed to die.' Vigo found the 'paupers more interesting than the tourists' and as a result his film rests mainly on the contrast between the idlers sprawled in the sun, the Promenade des Anglais, and the poor sections of the old town. In the end, Vigo's theme of the 'game' was less important than his portrayal of the carnival, which he depicted as a kind of dance of death intercut with ridiculous funeral statues and kino-eye improvised shots of idlers. This lyrical, violent, and subversive social polemic is full of black humor and biting sarcasm. Into it are incorporated several visual metaphors: the waxed, naked feet; the woman who suddenly appears naked in a chair; the tourist suddenly 'paralyzed.' It is a short film but a great one: 'An example of true cinema, but also an attack on a particular kind of world.'

'Kino-eye' here refers to the practice advocated by Vertov of using a hidden camera, which was also employed by Ruttmann. According to the classic account by Paulo Emilio Salles Gomes, 'To catch strollers unawares, Vigo and Kaufman built a cardboard box to conceal the camera, and frequently went hunting'[13] – that is, Vigo wheeled Kaufman along the promenade in a wheelchair. Other scenes required official permission, which was not always granted, or imposed restrictions on their camera positions. The camera is hand-held throughout, and in almost constant movement, panning and tilting judiciously to add to the movement within the frame, and sometimes shooting at odd angles. The shooting was preceded by intense research, but there was no script, and the filming itself was improvised around a series of motifs identified through the research. Salles Gomes says that Vigo, an admirer of the Soviet films, had always thought of using both kino-eye techniques and 'montage-attraction', but when they got to the editing table he was more or less forced into the latter by the disparity of the material they'd shot, which comprised 'a mass of fragments and half-sentences which would be difficult to mould into a rational and coherent argument. But then, that had never been the intention.' In short, their method obliged them to link the fragments together 'so that they would enrich each other by creating a series of associations'.[14] The shooting, and therefore the cutting, ignores continuity of action, although it generally maintains consistent spatial orientation, and this allows shots to be grouped by contiguity, on the one hand, and on the other, to be interrupted by displacement. The result consists entirely of a montage of images of the city's daily life designed *pour épater le bourgeoisie*. Moment to moment, the editing follows photogenic properties – similarities and contrasts of the plastic qualities of the image, movement, composition, shapes, textures – but also introduces bizarre disruptions. Montage by association and by interruption; juxtaposition of diverse fragments, thematic linkage at the metaphorical level.

This is the way it begins: a short opening shot of fireworks; aerial views of the city, dissolving to a roulette wheel. A toy train brings toy tourists who are raked in by a croupier (in several shots). Waves on the beach and more aerial shots, a palm tree animated by the camera panning up and down the trunk, then a couple of street cleaners. Interrupted by shots of huge puppets being pre- pared for the carnival, cross-cut with waiters setting up tables on a terrace, the camera following their activity. Sideways glimpses of prominent buildings (the Hotel Rhul, the Palais de la Méditerranée, the Hotel Négresco) – in each shot the camera immediately tilts back to upright. A statue on the parapet of one of the buildings of a dancing naked lady (first hint of eroticism). A tracking shot along the empty Promenade des Anglais and a dissolve to the same view full of promenaders – well-dressed ladies and gentlemen strolling in groups or alone, a workman, a beggar, a gypsy woman with a baby in her arms, a street trader. This is a long sequence of several shots, including, briefly, a movie cam- eraman and a stills photographer. The camera angle rises over two or three cuts from ground level to a top-down view of the scene from a neighbouring rooftop, then we get our first proper view of the beach. Pan to a handful of people bathing in the sea and beyond them a small sea-plane landing. Sea- plane and promenade are cross-cut, then come close-ups of sails and a sequence of small sailing boats, followed by sequences of tennis, boules, more aquatic sports and an automobile race. The racing car gives way to a limousine bringing more rich hotel guests, the camera looking down on the tiny figures from on high. Now the sun is at its apogee, the holiday-makers sitting on the promenade basking appear more and more grotesque, and Vigo allows himself a few deft touches of invention: an elegant woman is followed by a shot of an ostrich; a man turns into a blackface mannequin; and half a dozen shots of a young woman seated cross-legged on the terrace, each time in different dress, ending up naked except for her shoes, whereupon her white flesh cuts to a marble sculpture, this time of a naked male.

We are now about halfway through the film and must ask about the sequencing, an ambiguous term which sometimes refers to large composite segments – like 'early morning', 'the city comes to life', 'the noonday sun', and so forth – and sometimes to small groups of shots, like the sailing boats, tennis, boules, or aquatic sports, which are embedded in the larger sections. Let's go back to the opening. Up to the tracking shot of the empty promenade, amounting to around thirty shots, takes three min- utes. The cutting establishes a rhythm employing shots of three lengths – short (just long enough to be recognisable); medium (allowing camera movement); and long (like the track along the empty prome- nade – at eleven seconds, this is the longest shot so far). This is where Salles Gomes (whose description of the film is more detailed than mine) ends his first paragraph, with the remark that now 'everything is ready', implying that this is where the first main sequence ends. This has been the set-up, the presen- tation of the subject, or better, the overture. But there is no actual break here – on the contrary, the next shot is joined by a dissolve. And the same is true of every other point where the critic, analysing the film and reconstructing 'the narrative' (a kind of plot without a story) might detect a sequence join. (At all events, Salles Gomes did a remarkable job, especially given that he wrote his account, as he tells us, 'from notes taken during screenings at the Cinémathèque Française and in film clubs in Paris in 1950'.)[15]

To resume. We are halfway through and the heat of the noonday sun is portrayed through shots of brilliant white walls, and looking upwards at the sky from narrow streets, coming back to ground level in the domain of the resident population – the old town inhabited by the working people who sustain the city, and their families. Scenes of children playing and life lived in the streets; poverty; a child whose fingers have been eaten away by fire (or is it leprosy?); open sewers, garbage, a cat. Now, at last, comes the carnival. Giant dolls parade through the streets, there is dancing and jollity. The most extended sequence, where imagery with several themes is intertwined: eroticism turning to Dionysian frenzy, animals, waves and, above all, death, statues and bodies young and old. And a final sequence: an epilogue, which is not content to reprise the themes but brings in new imagery of factory smokestacks, symbol of the source of the riches that feeds the city.

Vigo's own description of the film, introducing a screening for the Groupement des Spectateurs d'Avant Garde in Paris:

In this film, by showing certain basic aspects of a city, a way of life is put on trial. In fact, as soon as the atmosphere of Nice and the kind of life lived there – and not only there, unfortunately – has been suggested, the film develops into a generalized view of the vulgar pleasures that come under the sign of the grotesque, of the flesh, and of death. These pleasures are the last gasps of a society so lost in its escapism that it sickens you and makes you sympathetic to a revolutionary solution.[16]

It was this screening where Vigo introduced the term 'point de vue documenté' to describe his intentions. Barnouw interprets this as the 'personal' film, and this is not wrong, but since Vigo entitled his talk 'Towards a Social Cinema', Salles Gomes is closer to the mark in calling it a formula for the social documentary. According to this method, the camera, in Vigo's words, 'should be directed at something which must be recognised as a document, and which during the actual editing must be approached as such'.[17] Of course in practice he stretches this to include moments of invention using specially posed shots (the naked woman on the promenade is presumably one of the acquaintances whom Vigo, says Salles Gomes, asked 'for a pose, an expression, a gesture'). But Vigo, says his biographer, was no theoretician, and shows himself to be torn between the demands of social conscience and the prerogatives of the creative artist. The resulting contradictions, however, are grist to the mill. What Vigo is trying to convey in his speech is something about the documentary that derives its demands from social reality but can only be realised through filmic interpretation. From a theoretical perspective, interpretation is a process that is partly individual, partly collaborative (and À propos de Nice announces itself as Réalisation de Jean Vigo et Boris Kaufman), and partly the work of the text (which ends up placing the demands of interpretation on the viewer). A chain of images taken from the public world, merged into the complex semantic forms of montage and sent into the public sphere. A chain of meanings that passes from the film-makers' encounter with their subject to the eyes of the viewer in front of the screen. A discourse that interprets the lived reality according to the propensities and predilections of the film-makers, which are then subject to a process of public reception. If this is what the documentary has become by the end of the 1920s in the paradigmatic form of À propos de Nice, then point de vue documenté seems a very good term to describe it.

V

The coming of sound had radical effects on the screen as a representational space, a space now expanded by the loudspeaker hidden behind it. We shall come to the details in the next chapter, including the problem that early recording systems remained deficient for the documentarist's primary concern of location filming; how the practice of the film lecturer was reborn in the voice of the now unseen commentator; and the way that music was folded into the soundtrack. Yet the *point de vue documenté* à la Vigo did not disappear. Rather, it was pursued by a number of documentarists for whom sound presented the documentary with a challenge by posing the problem of its relation to the image.

If the GPO films produced by Grierson are famous for their experimental approach to sound, one of the paradigms is *Coal Face* (Alberto Cavalcanti, 1935), which is visually like an animated slide show, while the soundtrack embraces commentary, verse, chanting and singing, instrumental music and various naturalistic sounds including snatches of miners talking, and even whistling. (The verses are by W. H. Auden and the score by Benjamin Britten.) This scheme allows the images to be linked by association and affinity, and the film is practically devoid of continuity cutting. However, as the individual shot becomes embedded in the unfolding montage, it falls under the influence of the impersonal and monotone commentary, which consists of short disconnected sentences like 'Coal mining is the basic industry of Britain', 'The miner works in a cramped position', 'The miner stops to eat', etc. This is a form of construction which drains the shot of practically all indexical specificity, with the result that while the film declares its concern for the hardships and dangers of the miner's life, the miners we see are left in a state of iconic generality, reduced to stereotypes. The effect is sufficiently marked that Auden himself wondered if it didn't reflect the compromised ideological position of the cultured middle-class film-maker (a critique we shall return to in a later chapter). But it is also a property of the documentary film language we are describing – and therefore a liability – to exchange the particular for the general in this kind of way, precisely because the image is always already both index and icon. As Carl Plantinga explains, a shot of a dog depicts a particular dog, 'a Boxer named Bubba, for example', but it also depicts a logical class, 'Boxers, or dogs in general, or dogs that run fast'.[18] The result, this time according to Nichols, is that 'smoke stacks from different factories or towns may be inserted to evoke "industry" or, today, "pollution"'.[19] or as Lindahl Elliot puts it writing about natural history films, a lion is likely to mean 'Africa', 'Wild', and indeed 'Nature' itself.[20] Winston sees this at work in the very titles of classic documentaries like *Drifters*, *Night Mail*, *Man of Aran*, etc., which reinforce the synecdoche:

> One fishing smack is the herring industry. One train is the night mail system . . . On the screen, every last Inuit, industrial worker, and deep-sea fisherman comes to stand both for themselves and for a class of persons of their type. The actual image is of one particular person; the rhetoric of the title and the genre is of a tribe.[21]

It is montage and the rhetorical or poetic context that provide the appropriate level of iconic construal. If the individual image gives up something of its particularity in the process, then this is often the effect of the capture of the image by the verbal discourse, which is always more abstract. Take away the commentary and the concrete reality has room to re-assert itself, as in *Listen to Britain* by Humphrey Jennings (who shares the credit for both directing and editing with his editor Stewart McAllister). This is a celebrated piece of wartime propaganda cinema dating from 1941 which one account describes as (again) 'a "symphony" of the sounds of Britain at war'.[22] The musical epithet is more than apt. Music, for Jennings, was not to be relegated to the background, but belonged to the social space of the film's subjects. Here, Jennings bathed the nation in its music, with the benefit of improved equipment and government propaganda resources which enabled him to film, with synchronous sound, on location.

At the time, the challenge of a film without a commentary prompted the addition of a verbal introduction by a nervous civil servant explaining what the viewer was going to see. This turns out to be a film of eighteen minutes comprising over 200 shots in counterpoint to a collage of different types of music – brass band, dance band, folk songs, male voices, female voices, a children's playground song, music-hall song, a piano concerto – which together represent the sound of 'a people at war'. The rhythms of the film are controlled by the soundtrack: the cutting alternates between montage in counterpoint to either music or other sounds, and musical performance in front of the camera in which there is very little cutting (until the famous final sequence at the National Gallery). The propaganda message is the same as that of a film Jennings completed earlier the same year, *Heart of Britain*, where the commentary declares decisively, over a top-flight amateur choir singing the 'Hallelujah Chorus', 'People who sing like that in times like these cannot be beaten'. (And this is the country known in Germany as 'the country without music'.) But here the absence of commentary leaves space for the images to breathe and resonate independently, across cuts that take us, for example, from a dance hall to civil defence crews looking out to sea; from soldiers enjoying a pint and a song to a railway signal box; from an early morning landscape to factory gates; from the music-hall duo Flanagan and Allen entertaining in the lunchbreak at a works canteen, to a Mozart piano concerto at a lunchtime concert in the National Gallery in the presence of the Queen. If *Listen to Britain* comprises, as Ian Aitken puts it, 'an expression of the connectedness of experience' in the nation at war, then it is music through which this is achieved.

In one of the earliest commendations of this film, an article in *Sight and Sound* in 1951, Gavin Lambert holds that 'the technique of *Listen to Britain* is based completely on the power of association'.[23] Twenty years later, in another classic essay, Jim Hillier argues that Jennings employs a kind of dialectical montage which works in a closely similar way to poetic discourse: 'The meaning of an image, or more frequently the connections between images, are left to the audience's emotions for interpretation.' The rich ambiguity that he finds a constant feature of Jennings' style reminds him that Jennings was a product of the Cambridge school of literary criticism which saw William Empson's classic exposition of the multiplicity of poetic discourse, *Seven Types of Ambiguity*. If *Listen to Britain* can thus be considered a test case for what it might mean to call a documentary poetic, its poetic quality is affirmed by more recent accounts. For Nichols, the film 'fractures the time and space' of its apparently observational scenes, dispersing them 'into a large number of dissociated impressions. The result is a poetic form of exposition' which comprises one of the 'classic forms of subjective editing'.[24] Jim Leach considers that this 'refusal to impose meanings' implies both a respect for the spectator and an awareness that meanings are always complex and plural – like poetry.[25] One thing, however, that none of these accounts point out, is that the same associative and open form of meaning must also apply to the music on the soundtrack, and this has crucial implications for the semiotics of film music.

According to Leach, the film is 'organized into seventeen sequences of varying lengths whose boundaries are, however, often obscured by ambiguous transition shots and overlapping sound'[26]. Both writers observe that the internal organisation of some of the scenes employs a semblance of reverse angle point-of-view shots. In other words, from time to time, when the camera picks out individuals, occasionally alone, more often in twos or threes, this becomes an invitation for the next cut to adopt the subjective point of view of a particular social actor, or occasionally the semblance of a continuity cut. The effect is not to dramatise, however, but to draw the viewer into the 'social subjectivity' that forms the experience of living in wartime Britain. As Geoffrey Nowell-Smith remarks, the film's vision is consonant with Churchillian rhetoric, but by no means equivalent to it, since it is both more inclusive and more ambiguous.[27] And all the more effective for its most unwarlike character.

The model which these examples suggest for documentary syntax remains entirely apposite. In this form of discourse, images may be cut together on the basis of analogical affinity in a manner that ignores local spatiotemporal continuity. Instead, we get an expanded space governed not by *mise en scène*, but by discontinuities, both spatial and temporal, that allow for free association across space and time. Different pieces of space may be joined in a continuous argument that links together quite disparate elements of the social and historical world. Thus, while often borrowing the techniques of spatial continuity, the grammar of documentary overrides them and can also dispense with them altogether. There is an observational style of documentary that emerges in the 1960s, above all in the work of Wiseman, which chooses to respect the unities of time and space, but this is only an option, strongly associated with the technique of the long take. Otherwise, when every other shot might bring a new fragment of space rather than a changing view within the same scene, the value of thinking in scenes loses its point, and the syntax of the film looks different. But if the constant juxtaposition and collision of associations and ideas makes the audiovisual discourse potentially unstable, the filmic space where this happens belongs to general theory of montage, and not the special theory which governs the fictional narrative.

VI

À propos de Nice starts off in the familiar mode of a day-in-the-life, at a time of year when preparations for carnival are in progress, but later in the film, the expectable progression of the day gives way, and suddenly carnival is in full swing. There are implications here for a level of organisation which underlies the *point de vue documenté* and lays down its parameters, namely the construction of temporality.

If the trajectory of a day became one of documentary's preferred ways of capturing the quality of urban life – it is also there, for example, in *Berlin, Symphony of a City* and *Man with a Movie Camera* – this is because it provided a simple and practical solution to what Winston calls the 'big narrative problem' of the early actuality, that of closure, by adopting a period of time of a cyclical nature, which ends when the cycle is completed.[28] On this reading, what Vigo does in *À propos de Nice* is to shift gear from the cycle of the day to the cycle of the year. But this is not just a nice aesthetic solution. If Henri Lefebvre is right when he says, studying the view from his window in Paris, that '[t]he cyclical is social organisation manifesting itself',[29] then this has crucial implications for the symbolic representation of the subject matter. It is not an accident, for example, or merely an aesthetic decision, when a film like *Listen to Britain* is organised around a twenty-four-hour time cycle, thus implicitly asserting the resilience of the country's social organisation even in times of war.

If the cycle of the day serves as an underlying form of construction, it falls under the rubric of what Mikhail Bakhtin, coming from the perspective of literary theory, called the chronotope – the organising structure where 'the knots of the narrative are tied and untied', the distinctive way in which the treatment of time and space are combined, the manner in which 'time, as it were, thickens, takes on flesh, becomes artistically visible', while 'space becomes charged and responsive to the movements of time, plot and history'.[30] Documentary, however, has no requirement for dramatic plotting, which is only one of the options open to it, and the day-in-the-life has the benefit of imposing only the most minimal requirements. The same is true of the other main early solution to the problem of closure, that of the journey, because obviously a journey film ends with the journey ending.

Transferring the concept of the chronotope from literature to film inevitably draws attention to the special properties of filmic discourse, the various temporal and spatial devices that characterise the language of film, like the close-up (a certain way of organising space) and the flashback (a way of organising time). The chronotope is not just a question of grammar, however, but rather the way the grammar is used to create a certain relationship to the historical world, the world external to the artistic utterance. Here, too, fiction and documentary behave differently. The time-space of fiction is always 'as if', bounded by its own internal narrative criteria; it spins an artistic time quite capable of mixing any imagined past, present and future. That of documentary is the here-and-now witnessed by the camera, which has no given narrative closure, only limited access to the past, and no access to the future (except hypothetically).

A number of film historians have pointed to what Winston calls the 'despised but popular' travelogue of early cinema as the site of the hidden beginnings of the art of editing. Even before the first story films discovered the basics of narrative continuity through the process of dividing the story into successive shots, the catalogues of the film dealers were suggesting to purchasers that they could buy several of the travel scenes in their lists and combine them to any desired length. In many cases the order would be arbitrary. In others – a bullfight in Madrid, Queen Victoria's Jubilee procession – it was implicit in the subject itself, and the catalogues therefore indicated the correct order.[31] These earliest of multiple-shot films did not depend on continuity of action – they consisted in a succession of tableaux, unified by the discourse of the lecturer who provided a verbal commentary. It was not long before films came along which were not only constructed in the form of a journey but explicitly took someone's journey as the subject matter, from Teddy Roosevelt going big game hunting, to Ponting's film of Scott's Antarctic expedition, to the journey of the Bakhtiari in *Grass* and many more. This is still a popular and highly functional form. On air as I write is a television series of someone going round the equator in three episodes; a few days ago there was a special report by an exiled Iraqi-Kurdish journalist going back to see what conditions were like in his home town (here the journey ends when he comes to the conclusion that it's not yet safe or practical to consider returning for good).

The journey film bears an interesting relation to the road movie, which in turn evokes a novelistic tradition going back to *Don Quixote*, a tradition that includes various novels by Voltaire, Fielding and Goethe, and ends up in the 1950s in the beat novels of a writer like Jack Kerouac. In Bakhtin, the chronotope of the road is a place of encounter with strangers, in circumstances where the traveller's normal domestic and social arrangements are in suspension.[32] The connection becomes explicit in a film like Ross McElwee's *Sherman's March* of 1986, in which the film-maker sets out to make a documentary about the famous march of Sherman's troops through the South at the end of the Civil War, which turns into an account of his encounters with a number of women along the way, including old friends and new acquaintances. The effect of this double storyline is to foreground what Fredric Jameson has called the second level of documentary narrative, which is normally hidden behind the ostensive story, namely, the drama of the film-maker making the film.[33] This is why McElwee's film has to be autobiographical and self-reflexive, in order to get at what is normally obscured by the naive and unreflexive form in which the genre first developed, and which hides as much as it reveals.

When Bakhtin says that on the road, 'people who are normally kept separate by social and spatial distance can accidentally meet', it is the traveller undertaking such films who has the wherewithal to engineer these accidental meetings, implying a certain perspective, especially in the case of more distant and exotic journeys to the far-flung interiors of the colonies. As Charles Musser tells us about the early days, 'Surviving lectures indicate that these images could be made to carry rich and often disturbing meanings – assumptions about imperialism, racial and cultural superiority, sexism and social Darwinism.'[34] (It seems that unless deliberately questioned, these assumptions have remained a bugbear in a good deal of documentary ever since.)

What are the implications, then, of these two basic documentary chronotopes, the cyclical and the travelogue? In a world where what goes around comes around, what is the nature of time? And how is time understood when the subject of the ethnographic other in front of the camera belongs to a cultural domain implicitly regarded as outside history? One answer would be that simple chronotopes like these, composed of a succession of images with no causal connection, favour synchronic relations, the representation of elements in simultaneous play, as opposed to the diachronic, the sense of succession through which both the fictional plot and history are necessarily articulated. (Hence the impression given by those sequences in *Berlin* remarked on earlier, where the passage of time is suspended until something comes up to shift it along.) Not that these are mutually exclusive categories – synchronic images are perfectly capable of invoking historical associations which evoke the diachronic. But insofar as the documentary adopts a synchronic discourse, it shows how things are, not how they came about.

This effect is intensified by the primary quality of filmic time, which is always manifest first of all through its very transitoriness, but in an opposite way to the photograph. The photograph, as construed by Barthes, presents itself as a trace of what was there in front of the camera then, when it was taken, which is no longer present. But on the screen, due to the representation of movement, this '*having-been-there* gives way before the *being-there* of the thing'.[35] Consequently, as Mary Anne Doane puts it, *the spectator always experiences the film in the present tense.*[36] She adds, however, that this present tense manifests 'a certain instability', and indeed, with documentary, further examination shows it to be slippery, elusive and ambiguous. The ambiguity of the self-displacing present-tense image brings to mind the key tenets of the rival philosophical schools of Tlön, in W. G. Sebald's account of the story by Borges, where in one version.

the future exists only in the shape of our present apprehensions and hopes, and the past merely as memory. In a different view, the world and everything now living in it was created only moments ago, together with its complete but illusory pre-history. A third school of thought variously describes our earth as a cul-de-sac in the great city of God, a dark cave crowded with incomprehensible images, or a hazy aura surrounding a better sun. The advocates of a fourth philosophy maintain that time has run its course and that this life is no more than the fading reflection of an event beyond recall.[37]

In short, the temporality of the screen is a puzzle precisely because the form of projection abolishes the past of the photographed image and uses its own properties to create its own image of time.

We can take this a step further. When we sit down to watch a film, we know that what we are about to see already has a conclusion. This allows us to say that the tense of narration is not the simple present tense, but as Pasolini proposed, the historic present – the use of the present tense to narrate events which have already concluded. Pasolini, like Doane, argued that '[r]eality seen and heard as it happens *is always in the present tense*'. This is the force, for example, of the long take, or the sequence shot, which transcends montage. (Pasolini's example was the Zapruder footage, which is too short to be thought of as a long take, but it's the only take, there are no shots from any other angle, so it qualifies as a sequence shot.) But then he adds that the moment montage takes place, 'the present becomes a past that, for cinematographic and not aesthetic reasons, is always in the present mode (*that is, it is a historic present*)'.[38]

In the case of fiction, we also know that nothing that is not contained within the film, directly or by allusion, has any relevance – the fictive world is self-enclosed, and the plot represents the construction of time through the introduction of dramatic cause (and dramatic pause or suspense), parallel story-telling, the flashback, etc. In documentary there is in principle no such self-enclosure; there are many things beyond what the film portrays that could well be relevant; and what we're seeing doesn't necessarily conclude when the filming stops. We know this before we start watching, because the historical world which we take it that documentary portrays has precisely these properties. (History is something we segment and periodise for convenience, in truth it has neither beginning nor end, and this also applies to any particular genealogy of events within it.)

There are theorists who maintain that cinema has no built-in tense system, and that therefore temporal distinctions can only arise if they're appropriately signalled. Narrative cinema developed a wide range of gambits to allow the narrative to jump back and forth – visual cues like changes in costume or locale; optical effects like fades, dissolves and wipes; iconic devices like turning the pages of a calendar; and later, of course, voice-over narration – all in the interests of plot construction. But what if you're not concerned with plot, which is absent in the early chronotopes of both the natural cycle and the travelogue? History, of course, represents human agency (which in the time of early cinema also meant progress). The cyclical has another quality (on which of course Lefebvre also remarks) which connects with the underlying cycles of biology and the planet: bodily rhythms, the seasons of the year, the rhythms of growth and decay, the manifestations of life as such. The symbolic representation of the cyclical through the agency of the mechanical rhythm of the camera-projector produces a naturalising effect: the world appears in an ideal aspect, as a self-governing perpetual-motion machine, while historical time, time which is unrepeatable because it brings change and interruption, is held at bay. This has long been the favoured chronotope of one of the most popular television documentary genres, the natural history film, where nature herself, and therefore her cyclical rhythms, is the ostensive subject. But this then enters into tension with historical time because nature is now also the subject of the concerns of ecology, the environment that human agency is in the process of disturbing and unbalancing to a degree that might soon prove fatal; which means that the representation of the natural world is more than ever an ideological issue.

If the tense of documentary is the historic present – because film is always experienced in the present tense – then the chronotope is capable of expanding to encompass the temporal span required to explain the subject, the origins and evolution of the problem, and where things are at now. The temporality of this kind of documentary is thus an extended present, leading back into the past and often pointing to an open future. This is the method of another basic chronotope which has evolved over the last fifty years, the scientific documentary, which typically centres on a discovery or problem and its interrogation. This interrogation is conducted through the dialogical presentation of argument and explanation – 'consider this, and then there's this to consider, and then that . . .'. A perfect example, drawn from the BBC's *Horizon* series, is *The Cancer Detectives of Lin Xian* (Edward Goldwyn, 1980), which investigates the efforts of a team of Chinese medics to eradicate a particularly virulent strain of cancer of the oesophagus in a valley in Central China.[39] To explain what they're up to, the film has to show that the Chinese approach to eradicating cancer lies not in basic cell research, as it does in the West, but rather on eliminating the suspected environmental causes of the disease, which have to be isolated and investigated one by one – a perfect synchronic scenario. The film begins in the present, describing where we are and why, and introducing us to the team, only then taking us back to the start of their work in 1958, just over twenty years earlier – here, then, the extended present is as long as the memory of the team's founder members, and it takes in events that they and their work were caught up in, notably the interruption caused by the Cultural Revolution (here the film introduces a few moments of archive footage by way of illustration). The exposition of the film follows the structure of a scientific argument, and the narration is constantly drawn back to the historic present ('Next morning, the barefoot doctor takes the slides to the hospital . . .').

The Cancer Detectives . . . comprises observational reportage, interviews, archives, re-enactment and diagrams, yet what we see is not abstracted in the same way as fiction from chronometric time, which on the contrary, returns as part of its indexicality. Where fiction suspends the real time and date of the filming in favour of its fictive temporality, it is not irrelevant in documentary, but often a material factor which is implicated in what is represented. Fiction operates in narrative time, where each moment is primarily defined by its relationship to other moments within the narrative, whereas documentary time is intrinsically, but not always explicitly, referential, corresponding to the external measure of day and time according to the calendar and clock. But of course it can be manipulated, and is often obscured on the editing table to fit the temporality corresponding to the argument of the film. This is the function, for example, of stock shots stored in film archives and libraries, which represent generic and iconic instances of city scenes and landscapes, industry, personalities, any sights whatever, classified under various headings for easy retrieval. It is a fundamental property of the general theory of montage to be able to use them this way, and depends only on there not being anything in the shot that prevents its incorporation into the time-image of whatever film it's going into.

However, this general level of referentiality (London: West End: Street Scenes: 1930s) is alien to films that foreground the presentness of the profilmic moment. A paradigmatic example of this is Eduardo Coutinho's *Babilónia* (2001), which enquires into the hopes of the people at the turn of the millennium and was shot in a shanty town overlooking the bay of Rio de Janeiro on 31 December 1999, with the hours counted down on the screen till we reach the midnight fireworks. Here there are neither stock shots nor any manipulation of temporality beyond condensing a day into a couple of hours, and the film manifests the utmost testimonial integrity. It's another example of the cycle-of-a-day, but it's a very special day, which makes it a very special film.

The expanded present of documentary time is exemplified in a different way by William Raban's *Thames Film* (1986), where it reaches back some 200 years. The tone of the film takes its cue from the voice of T. S. Eliot on the soundtrack reading the lines from *Four Quartets* about the river as a strong brown god. The river is Raban's focus. The first thing we hear on the soundtrack is its lapping waters. The first thing we see, however, is not the river but a painted skeleton playing a pair of kettledrums, revealed as a detail from a landscape of war and death at the estuary of a river. (This is Brueghel's *The Triumph of Death*, on which Raban comments that if Brueghel painted it with a real landscape in mind, then it seems to fit topographically with the entrance to the Schelde looking south-west from Vlissingen towards the Belgian coast; in other words, opposite the Thames Estuary, which it resembles.)[40] Other ghoulish details of Brueghel's painting will recur at later moments in the film; meanwhile it immediately gives way to shots of the Thames Estuary taken from Raban's own boat, the constant point of view for the film as he sails up and down the river. The film's paradigmatic structure lies in the insertion into contemporary views of the Thames of historical images of the same sites taken from engravings, old photos and archive film footage. These sights invoke in turn a series of texts on the soundtrack, including several snatches of Eliot's voice, and quotations from a manuscript in the library of the Port of London Authority, an account of a voyage from London to Dover in 1787 by a certain T. S. Pennant, beautifully spoken by John Hurt.

The second time we hear Eliot's voice, we are looking at the eighteenth-century brick warehouse at Free Trade Wharf (which has since been demolished), the picture cuts to photos of the warehouse from the late 30s, barges hauled up on the foreshore at low tide, and children playing cricket beside them. Eliot's voice enters, pronouncing the famous lines about present, past and future:

> Time present and time past
> Are both perhaps present in time future,
> And time future contained in the time past

as the picture cuts to the present-day view of disused jetties and abandoned warehouses behind them, before cutting back to a clip from a 1930s' public service documentary called *The City of Ships*, and dockers unloading sacks.

A sequence on the Prime Meridian (a reference surprisingly absent from *The City of Ships*): engravings from Pennant's manuscript. The soundtrack explains succinctly: 'Set at the Azores by Spain and Portugal; lost to France and moved to Paris. Taken by England and set at Greenwich.' The river runs on anyway, and Raban's camera continues downstream; here there are container ships in what are now called 'deep water terminals'. The voice adds: 'The Prime Meridian, symbol of power and changing fortune', and then we hear Eliot again:

> Whatever we inherit from the fortunate
> We have taken from the defeated
> What they had to leave us – a symbol:
> A symbol perfected in death.

Further references to death abound, in picture and commentary. An engraving from the old days: 'Gallows raised on the low water mud at Execution Dock. The hanging body left there to be covered by three full tides before sentence was complete.' And the fate of convicts in prison ships, taken ashore to labour then locked up at night below decks with the hatches closed: 'The living next morning often find their comrades dead by their side.' The whole film is thus permeated by the sense of death, which comes in many ways, overtakes every generation and undoes empires. While the river runs on. And when the empire is finally undone, then the port itself dies. What *Thames Film* shows us is the river returned to a placid existence, because the port has gone and the trade moved elsewhere, but still flowing between its banks as a sign of the city's history. Towards the end of the film, a piece of commentary sums up:

> The river journey unwinds a distant memory, each moment has a particular meaning and relation to the past . . . On this journey time is exposed: the past and present form one continuous pattern of unfolding experience.

The words crystallise both the method of the film's exposition and the quality of the chronotope of which this film is an exemplar.

Notes

1. Christian Metz, *Film Language: A Semiotics of Cinema* (Oxford: Oxford University Press, 1974), p. 194.
2. Metz, *Film Language*, p. 94.
3. The most sustained are those of Nichols, *Representing Reality* (Bloomington: Indiana University Press, 1991), and Carl Plantinga's *Rhetoric and Representation in Nonfiction Film* (Cambridge: Cambridge University Press, 1997)
4. Dai Vaughan, 'Aesthetics of Ambiguity', in Dai Vaughan, *For Documentary* (Berkeley and London: University of California Press, 1999), p. 64.
5. See Richard Abel (ed.), *French Film Theory and Criticism, I, 1907–1939* (Princeton, NJ: Princeton University Press, 1988).
6. Epstein in Abel, *French Film Theory and Criticism*, p. 317.

7. Abel, *French Film Theory and Criticism*.

8. Abel, *French Film Theory and Criticism*, p. 293.

9. William Guynn, 'The Art of National Projection: Basil Wright's *Song of Ceylon*', in Barry Keith Grant and Jeannette Sloniowski (eds), *Documenting the Documentary: Close Readings of Documentary Film and Video* (Detroit, MI: Wayne State University Press, 1998), p. 87.

10. Dziga Vertov quoted in Masha Enzensberger, 'Dziga Vertov', in *Screen Reader 1, Cinema/Ideology/ Politics* (London: SEFT, 1977), p. 395.

11. Leif Furhammer and Folke Isaksson, *Politics and Film* (London: November Books, 1971), p. 13

12. Nichols, *Representing Reality*, p. 131.

13. P. E. Salles Gomes, *Jean Vigo* (London: Faber and Faber, 1998), p. 58.

14. Salles Gomes, *Jean Vigo*, p. 63.

15. Salles Gomes, *Jean Vigo*, p. 63.

16. Quoted in Salles Gomes, *Jean Vigo*, p. 68.

17. Quoted in Salles Gomes, *Jean Vigo*, p. 72.

18. Plantinga, *Rhetoric and Representation in Nonfiction Film*, p. 156.

19. Nichols, *Representing Reality*, p. 131.

20. Nils Lindahl Elliot, 'Signs of Anthropomorphism', *Social Semiotics* vol. 11 no. 3, 2001, p. 293.

21. Brian Winston, *Claiming the Real* (London: BFI, 1995), p. 134.

22. Richard Barsam, *Non-Fiction Film: A Critical History* (Bloomington: Indiana University Press, 1992), p. 185.

23. Gavin Lambert, 'Jennings' Britain', *Sight and Sound* vol. 20 no. 3, May 1951, p. 25.

24. Nichols, *Representing Reality*, p. 179.

25. Jim Leach, 'The Poetics of Propaganda, Humphrey Jennings and 'Listen to Britain', in Grant and Sloniowski, *Documenting the Documentary, Close Readings of Documentary Film & Video*, p. 157.

26. Leach, p. 159.

27. Cited in Leach, p. 164.

28. Winston, *Claiming the Real*, p. 104.

29. Henri Lefebvre, *Rhythmanalysis* (London and New York: Continuum, 2004), p. 30.

30. Mikhail Bakhtin, *The Dialogical Imagination* (Austin, TX: University of Texas Press, 1981), pp. 140, 250. The term, which means 'time-space', is borrowed by Bakhtin from Einstein's Theory of Relativity, and functions, he says, 'almost as a metaphor (almost, but not entirely). What counts for us is the fact that it expresses the inseparability of space and time (time as the fourth dimension of space).'

31. See for example Stephen Bottomore, 'Shots in the Dark, The Real Origins of Film Editing', in Thomas Elsaesser (ed.), *Early Cinema: Space, Frame, Narrative* (London: BFI, 1990), pp. 104–13.

32. 'On the road . . . the spatial and temporal paths of the most varied people — representatives of all social classes, estates, religions, nationalities, ages — intersect at one spatial and temporal point. People who are normally kept separate by social and spatial distance can accidentally meet; any contrast may crop up, the most various fates may collide and interweave with one another. On the road the spatial and temporal series defining human fates and lives combine with one another in distinctive ways, even as they become more complex and more concrete by the collapse of *social distances*'. Bakhtin, *The Dialogical Imagination*, p. 243.

33. See Michael Chanan, 'Talking Film with Fredric Jameson: A Conversation', in Douglas Kellner and Sean Homer (eds), *Fredric Jameson: A Reader* (Basingstoke and New York: Palgrave Macmillan, 2004), p. 133.

34. Charles Musser, 'The Travel Genre in 1903–1904', in Elsaesser, *Early Cinema*, p. 123.

35. Roland Barthes, 'The Rhetoric of the Image', in *Image, Music, Text* (London: Fontana/Collins, 1977), p. 45.

36. Mary Anne Doane, *The Emergence of Cinematic Time* (London and Cambridge, MA.: Harvard University Press, 2002), p. 103.

37. W. G. Sebald, *The Rings of Saturn* (London: Vintage Books, 2002), p. 154.

38. Pier Paolo Pasolini, 'Observations of the Long Take', *October . . . /Filmwaves* no. 9, Autumn 1999, p. 35. Italics in the original.

39. See Simon Campbell-Jones, *Horizon at the Frontiers of Medicine* (London: Ariel Books, BBC, 1983), for a transcript of the film; however, note that this is a prose version which differs in certain ways from the film as broadcast.

40. Personal communication.

7 Soundscapes

The challenge of sound

I

The coming of sound did much more than turn the moving pictures into the talkies. By adding a new sonic dimension to the screen, it radically altered its nature as a representational space, in the process rendering 'silent' cinema rapidly extinct. For documentary, however, this evolutionary break was initially a mixed blessing, because sound was introduced to serve the purposes of shooting fiction in the studio, and for many years it remained deficient for location recording. There is a familiar pattern here of corporate battles over rival systems using different technologies, until one of them wins out; it would happen again with analogue video and is now going on with new kinds of digital video discs. The optical system that emerged as standard in the 1930s used a photoelectric cell to turn the signal from the microphone into a light beam which could be photographed, but the earliest versions, being technically not much more than prototypes, could only record live with the picture; the sound could not be re-mixed and re-recorded until post-production techniques were introduced around 1932. The frequency range was very limited. Location recording remained difficult because the microphones were unselective and omnidirectional, fragile, sensitive to wind and other ambient noises, resulting in excessive background noise and lack of detail. Not least, the gear was bulky and heavy and needed a truck of its own. Just about usable for conventional newsreel work, it was hardly practical for most documentary, and certainly not in far-flung locations.

The soundtrack was more than a technical accomplishment – it changed the relationship of film and viewer. The silent days, of course, were not actually silent, since even in the absence of the film lecturer of the early years, there was generally a musical accompaniment as an ever-present supplement to the projection, lending it the quality of live performance and allowing local variations in the style of presentation. The soundtrack replaced this immediacy with its automation. Music became acousmatic – a word (derived from classical Greek) adopted in the 1940s by the pioneer of *musique concrète*, Pierre Schaeffer, for sound that is heard without seeing its source. In the process, many thousands of musicians around the world were thrown out of work, their jobs transferred to a much smaller number of élite musicians in the studios under direct control of the film's producer. At the same time, the film lecturer of early days returned in the disembodied voice on the soundtrack, like the Greek acousmatics giving their lectures from behind a screen so that they couldn't be seen. But in adding a new dimension to the screen, the loudspeakers, which in the new cinemas were hidden behind it, not only bodied forth the unheard sounds which silent cinema frequently invoked through its visual imagery, they also created different planes of sounds in and around the image, different acoustic zones, both on and off screen. Speech, music and noises (or 'sound effects') could each occur in view of the camera; or in the off-screen space contiguous with the profilmic scene; or in a disconnected acousmatic soundspace with no direct link to profilmic events. They could also slide between these different positions almost imperceptibly. In a word, the soundscapes first explored in fiction cinema by directors like Rouben Mamoulian, King Vidor and Ernst Lubitsch, and in documentary by Joris Ivens, the visionary cinema of Dziga Vertov, and more modestly in England, the GPO film-makers under Grierson.

The introduction of sound led to what one film historian has called the return of the silent cinema's repressed – the voice.[1] As sound became obligatory, it had the paradoxical effect of depriving documentary of what it never previously possessed, namely, the instrument of direct speech. While the fiction film reverted to the primacy of dialogue, which for many critics represented a regression to theatricality, documentary was largely condemned (with some notable exceptions) to the oratorical speech of the commentary which could be added to the edited film, the invisible voice that inflects the film's whole mode of address. Documentarists chafed against the effects of this semantic domination, which all too easily limited and reduced the power of the image; Paul Rotha called the commentary's authoritarian impression of omniscience, as it boomed out from an unidentifiable off-screen location, the 'voice of god'. Films like this end up being alienated from both their own better intentions and the perspective of the viewer.

It turns out that this is partly a question of enunciation. Like radio, documentary followed the imperative to deliver a standardised and uniform mode of pronunciation in order to reach the widest possible audience. Given the limited quality of early sound recording – the narrow frequency range, high signal-to-noise ratio and liability to acoustic distortion – clarity was all. The problem is that this is inseparable from the question of pronunciation and accent. In many languages, variety of accent is a matter of regional diversity, and the mass media play a crucial role by favouring one or other to create a national tongue. But accent is also always, to greater or lesser degree, a marker of class and education – infamously so in the case of Britain in those pre-multicultural years, where god spoke in the tones of a university-educated grammar-school-master. The GPO film-makers tried experiments like using poetry instead of prose, and experiment is what they often remained: the famous final sequence of *Night Mail*, with Benjamin Britten's music and the verse of W. H. Auden (himself a one-time schoolmaster) is brilliantly done in itself, but sits at the end of the film somewhat like an afterthought, which is what the production history tells us it was. Joris Ivens took a more direct approach with *The Spanish Earth*, working with Ernest Hemingway to turn the commentary into the voice of the camera as witness, at once functional and terse, informative and partisan.

The development of the technology was driven by what is nowadays called a corporate agenda. It accelerated the consolidation of relations between different sectors of capital at the very moment of crisis, the years of the Wall Street Crash and the Great Depression, bringing cinema and entertainments (including the other new medium of radio, and of course the record industry) into a new alignment with the electrical industry. One commentator who saw this clearly enough at the time was Walter Benjamin, who wrote in a footnote to his essay on 'The Work of Art in the Age of Mechanical Reproduction':

In 1927 it was calculated that a major film, in order to pay its way, had to reach an audience of nine million. With the sound film, to be sure, a setback in the international distribution occurred at first:

audiences became limited by language barriers. This coincided with the Fascist emphasis on national interests. [. . .] The simultaneity of both phenomena is attributable to the depression. The same disturbances which, on a larger scale, led to an attempt to maintain the existing property structure by sheer force led the endangered film capital to speed up the development of the sound film. The introduction of the sound film brought a temporary relief [to capital], not only because it again brought the masses into the theatres but because it merged new capital from the electrical industry with that of the film industry. Thus, viewed from the outside, the sound film promoted national interests, but seen from the inside it helped to internationalize film production even more than previously.[2]

Or as Laura Mulvey puts it, 'not only did the human voice arrive on the screen at a time of political and economic tension, but within the sphere of cinema, it arrived to exacerbate already existing competition between Hollywood and its would be European competitors.'[3] The presence of speech brought questions of language, which silent cinema had sidestepped, into the centre of the film industry: national cinemas could now respond, through language, more closely to the nuances of national cultures. Music also played a significant role here; it was one of the main factors, for example, to promote the emergence of new film industries in the three largest countries of Latin America, Mexico, Argentina and Brazil. (However, this doesn't include the tango singer Carlos Gardel, a big enough star internationally that his films were made by Paramount, first in Paris and then in the US.) Documentary, however, was disadvantaged, caught between the practical limitations of the early equipment, which was plainly deficient for location sound recording, and a technical agenda which was set by the studios. Not only was its radical modernism paradoxically threatened by the introduction of speech, but music was also problematic, precisely because it isn't factual or neutral or even limited to the descriptive, but also emotive, expressive and associative. It therefore inevitably functions as a form of implicit commentary, sometimes all the more insidious for not declaring itself as such.

The bulk of documentary production all too readily succumbed to the overuse of both music and commentary, and far from fulfilling its cinematic vocation, descended towards a form of illustrated radio. Buñuel parodied the commentary-and-music documentary to devastating and deeply disturbing effect in *Land without Bread*. Ivens, on the other hand, driven by a sense of experiment to seek the radical integration of the whole soundtrack, approached his first sound film by shooting *Philips Radio* (1931) silent and then turning to the composer Lou Lichtveld to compose a soundtrack which would combine music and noise in the spirit of the musical avant-garde. Lichtveld used a small band, playing somewhat fragmentary music in a modernist style, combined with a whole range of noise effects – grinding stone, windlass, oxygen tank and what-have-you – recorded live to projection. Hollywood developed a comparable technique, which later came to be known by the name of its progenitor, Jack Foley, but there's a critical difference: the Foley artist became a specialist within an elaborate division of labour, in which sound effects were separated from both dialogue and music, rather than all elements in the soundtrack being treated as a musical ensemble. Ivens succumbed to the American method when he came to make *The Spanish Earth* with post-production in the United States. The results were professional but bland, and here another problem set in. The music was selected by the composer Marc Blitzstein, assisted by Virgil Thomson, from records Ivens brought back from Spain. However, when I showed the film a few years ago to a class of Masters students in Barcelona, who had never seen it before, they were impressed with its portrayal of the Civil War, but criticised the music, because it came from a different region of the country from the places portrayed in the film, which to them felt inauthentic.

II

It should hardly come as a surprise that it was the Soviet Union where the prospect of sound stimulated the first extended critical debate on its uses, which started even before the first Soviet sound systems were deployed. In the capitalist West, the transition to sound was not accomplished overnight; it was an extended affair which began seriously in 1926 and took several years to sort itself out; there were corporate battles over patents and markets, involving confrontation between the US and Europe, where the struggling film industry showed little interest in the various prototypes until American sound films began to arrive in 1928. This, however, quickly provoked the reaction of European electronics companies, who as Karel Dibbets puts it, 'immediately began to organise resistance'.[4] Beyond the reach of the cartels, in the Soviet Union, where sound technology was not included in the first Five Year Plan, the prototypes were only demonstrated in 1928–9. The enforced delay gave time for a series of polemics on the challenges of sound, including a short and famous 'Statement on Sound' signed by Eisenstein, Pudovkin and Alexandrov (which Vertov criticised as too schematic). The debate did not ostensibly involve the differentiation or opposition of fiction and documentary, but began as a response to a situation which threatened to leave Russian cinema stranded just at the moment it had established itself internationally. The film-makers found themselves in a no-win situation: they would lose out by being unable to make films with sound; and if they could, there would be an immediate language problem. As Douglas Kahn wittily puts it, 'With the advent of sound Stalin's doctrine of socialism in one country would enjoy its cinematic counterpart.'[5] Indeed, before their little group headed to the United States to investigate, Stalin told them, as reported by Alexandrov, 'Study the sound film in detail. This is very important for us. When our heroes discover speech, the influential power of films will increase enormously.'[6]

The Hollywood model was exactly what Eisenstein and others were worried about, not for political but artistic reasons – except that certain kinds of aesthetic often imply a certain politics. Eisenstein feared that sound would proceed on a naturalistic level, doubling the action on the screen, compacting an illusion of people talking, audible objects and the rest. This would destroy montage, so he argued for sound to be taken up as a new element of montage and be treated separately from the image. While Hollywood was falling back into a logocentric form of filmed theatre, the 'Statement' argued that

> Only the contrapuntal use of sound *vis-à-vis* the visual fragment of montage will open up new possibilities for the development and perfection of montage. The first experiments in sound must aim at a sharp discord with the visual images. Only such a 'hammer and tongs' approach will produce the necessary sensation that will result consequently in the creation of a new orchestral counterpoint of visual and sound images.[7]

In this way, the 'Statement' concluded, the sound film would not be imprisoned within national markets, but would preserve its global viability. In short, Eisenstein was a true internationalist.

Ironically it was Vertov, in his first sound documentary, *Enthusiasm* (1930), subtitled 'Symphony of the Donbas', who took a hammer-and-tongs approach. To counterpoint the images of this portrait of the coalminers of the Don Basin four years into the first Five Year Plan, Vertov builds a soundtrack out of 'the clash of hammers, of train whistles, and the songs of workers at rest', recorded on location in the mines and villages visited by the camera, and as Sadoul put it, from the distance of France after World War II, 'edited as freely as he cut visuals, creating a kind of *musique concrète*'.[8] This contrapuntal asynchronism resulted in the abstraction of both soundtrack and image, which he employed for its graphic qualities and iconic power. One of those whose ears were captured by the film, at a screening in London in 1931, was Charles Chaplin, who wrote that he would 'never have believed it possible to assemble mechanical noises to create such beauty. One of the most superb symphonies I have known. Dziga Vertov is a musician.'[9] Indeed he was: before he became a film-maker, Vertov had studied at the Bialystok Conservatory and then carried out experiments with sound recorders at Petrograd's Psychoneurological Institute. He also mixed with the artistic avant-garde in wartime Petrograd, among them Vladimir Mayakovsky. Mayakovsky wrote a poem entitled 'Little Noises, Noises, Booms' for the Russian futurist almanac of 1914 that also included a translation of the manifesto 'The Art of Noises' by the Italian futurist Russolo. For applying these ideas to the cinema, Vertov was inevitably attacked for formalism. Today, of course, the musicalisation of noise is grist to the mill. A fine example is the Cuban documentary *Suite Habana* (2003) by Fernando Pérez, a visual tapestry of the city with practically no dialogue nor any commentary, but an extraordinary soundtrack composed both of music and a huge range of urban sounds, which captures a melancholy mood in present-day Havana through wordless portraits of a cross-section of characters. Reports said that many Cubans were surprised that such a bleak film was allowed to be shown, but the newspaper *Trabajadores* said that Pérez's images 'speak of the daily feat of existence, of how one can live in poverty without losing dignity or renouncing one's dreams'.[10]

What Pérez and Vertov both do is, in Dibbets' phrase, stick 'to the principle of speechlessness as the essence of film art'.[11] Pérez's film includes small snatches of dialogue but he refuses the hierarchical relations between voices, music, noises and silence that governs the soundscape of narrative cinema, treating all sounds as having equal aural weight. Ivens took a similar approach for *Philips Radio*, writing in his autobiography that he was determined from the outset 'to avoid the clichés that were already forming around the industrial advertising film', but he was constrained by the terms of the commission; prohibited, for example, from filming the workers anywhere but in the factory, or showing their private lives.[12] Nonetheless, he succeeded in projecting an image of the modern industrial enterprise that was not only, as the company wanted, highly photogenic, but also widely perceived as critical of the system it portrayed. According to a contemporary review by Léon Moussinac in *L'Humanité*,

it raises the spectre of the physical and moral ruin which threatens those workers who are the victims of capitalist rationalisation . . . To a certain extent, as well as being an accomplished piece of cinema, [it] is an act of accusation against the present economic system. That is why we can remain indifferent to the advertising cause it serves (although not very effectively).[13]

This is highly ironic. Philips wanted to project a clean modern image, and they got it, but the effect was the opposite of what they intended.

Bill Nichols considers how this reversal of meaning takes place. Even 'without actually naming the capitalist or capitalism as such', the assembly line comes to be read as a synecdoche for the capitalist mode of production by means of the contrast with the old-fashioned artisanal methods of the glass-blowers.[14] Ivens had worked hard to make this work. He was worried at the potentially comic sight of the blowers' cheeks puffing out 'further than you could ever imagine cheeks could puff',

> so I deliberately repeated the glass-blower's puffed-out cheeks in an even bolder close-up to obtain a more grotesque effect, and then came even closer to the flesh of his cheeks and intercut this close-up with the slow, careful, backward steps that he took throughout the process. This deliberate repetition tends to silence the audience and make them aware of the inhuman aspect of the work.[15]

A contemporary newspaper report on the production (Philips' public relations ensured extensive coverage of the film) describes the sound recording for these shots, in which the following dialogue occurred:

> Mr Startz, will you stand near the microphone? Attention – we will project the glass-blowing one more time. When the picture of the blower is shown you start to breathe heavily – slowly and with difficulty, as if you are doing a heavy job. But do not forget – we are not concerned with a naturalistic clarification . . . we only want a strengthening of the sensation: laborious work. You absolutely need not breathe completely in synch with the labourer on the screen.[16]

Every newspaper, says Dibbets, praised the scene of the glass-blowers, which, on the other hand, troubled Philips, who wanted to cut it out.

Noises were a key element in the soundtrack. Ivens pointed out the sound of the place to a reporter when they were filming in the glassworks: 'Inhuman symphonies of tinkling glass combined in all kinds of strange, chime-like chords. Low, dull, explosive sounds like faraway timpanic beats, and in between, the voice of a warehouse manager, who bellows through the loudspeaker.'[17] The only problem was not being able to record these sounds on location. It was impossible to isolate the sounds they needed. Philips wouldn't let them interrupt the work to make a clean recording, so they had to recreate them in the studio. Because the studios were equipped for mixing but not re-recording, everything had to be recorded simultaneously. All they could do was break the film up into sections, and turn the recording session into a performance. This needed careful rehearsal by both performers and recording engineers, above all the mixer who had to adjust the levels of the different microphones. If anyone made a mistake, the section had be recorded again from the start. Another journalist reported, 'volunteers assist with the grinding stone, the windlass, the oxygen tank, or on any other noise-making device that can be dragged in'.[18]

If some of these difficulties were alleviated by the development of mixing and re-recording techniques over the next few years, serious limitations remained until the development of magnetic recording after World War II. Tape recording introduced new possibilities of pre-editing, on the one hand, and a new range of mixing and dubbing techniques on the other. All these things can nowadays of course be achieved with great ease by a single person with suitable skills on a laptop computer.

III

Esfir Shub demonstrated the quality of Soviet sound technology in a forgotten film of 1932, *K.Sh.E.* ('Komsomol, Patron of Electrification'), which contains extensive location filming with synchronised sound, including both speech and musical performance; this is three years earlier than the GPO Film Unit's *Housing Problems*, the film usually cited as the earliest example of the new filmic trope of the interview. The claim is misleading; the preceding years saw several experiments in shooting speech on location. Jean Renoir had managed to shoot a feature film called *Toni* with synchronous dialogue on location in the South of France, an extraordinary example of neorealism *avant la lettre*, and in the same neck of the woods Marcel Pagnol was making features using location sound to bring the regional speech to the screen. In Germany, Leni Riefenstahl had all the resources she needed to shoot location sync at the Nuremberg Rally in 1934, although the technology wasn't quite up to it and she had to reshoot speeches by Rudolf Hess and others back in Berlin. For regular documentary work, the technological limitations were indeed too restrictive. While hankering after location sound, many documentarists preferred the agility and immediacy of the clockwork camera, for which film-makers like Ivens, or the Russian news cameraman Roman Karmen, developed a formidable hand-held shooting technique. *K.Sh.E.* is remarkable because it points in quite a different direction.

The opening sequence establishes the film's experimental spirit, following the self-reflexive mode of the Vertov of *Man with a Movie Camera*, but unlike the asynchronous soundtrack of *Enthusiasm* where sound is counterpointed against image, this soundtrack is synchronous. We are taken, without commentary and only a brief explanatory title, into a studio where a musical performance is being filmed – we see the filming apparatus, including the sound recorder being turned on and off, and we see and hear what it's recording: a concerto for orchestra and a strange new electronic instrument, the theremin, named after its Russian inventor (and whose eerie ethereal tones were later introduced into Hollywood by Bernard Herrmann). Propelling us musically into modernity, the scene immediately announces the film's theme: synchronous sound = the advance of electricity = the construction of the new society and a new culture. The metaphor is then expanded to take in, always in sync, a telephone exchange and a radio station, exemplary sites of modern communications, where different languages are spoken – the internationalism of the modern world is another of the film's themes – before reaching a factory full of women workers making light bulbs and valves, one of whom now talks to the camera about the meaning of their work. This lucid exposition is accomplished without resort to commentary, and as it proceeds through different locations of industrial production, the film uses a form of indirect narration divided dialogically between a variety of speakers in front of us – individuals speaking to camera, others addressing political meetings – in short, not the conventional 'official spokesperson' type, but working people, both men and women, involved in the activities portrayed.

There is no other documentary of the time I'm aware of that works in quite this way. The speakers are supplemented by a few informative intertitles, but also complemented by extensive use of a variety of music which has more than an illustrative role. We not only have montage sequences set to an orchestral score, but several scenes with live music and dance. These have all been recorded *in situ*, at a slightly low level doubtless in order to minimise distortion. A revolutionary ballet is performed for the workers on the factory floor by three energetic male dancers accompanied by a single accordion. At a ceremony at the foot of the new dam, a boy dances gracefully to drum and pipes. A band of traditional brass instruments performs revolutionary marches. This varied musical discourse seems to promise that the new society will be inclusive, but there is also another element – relaxing on the banks below the new dam before the opening ceremony, a group of Americans are playing jazz on a wind-up gramophone. A forgotten item of history: the electrification of the USSR was accomplished with the help of the first US corporation to sign a contract with the revolutionary government, some years before the Soviet Union was officially recognised in Washington – none other than General Electric. These are GE's employees and their families.

It's true that the interviews in the film are not exactly interviews, but they aren't in *Housing Problems* either. The subjects in the English film are speaking for themselves and using their own words, but the statements are clearly rehearsed, there are no off-screen questions, and they show a certain awkwardness, thus indicating that speaking to a camera is not yet felt as a natural thing to do, as it has since become. The same effect can also be seen in *K.Sh.E.*, where sometimes a subject isolated in the frame in close-up attempts to speak directly to the camera lens but seems embarrassed at doing so, averting their eyes and talking instead as if they were addressing the film crew. But there are also scenes of political meetings at various workplaces where speakers are addressing a group, and here they clearly and proudly belong to a new political culture which the film celebrates along with electrification and progress. In fine, a film in which propaganda and artistic experiment are still combined in a constructivist spirit, pointing way beyond the norms of documentary narrative in the 30s.

IV

The arrival of sound also had the effect of inhibiting documentary's adoption of 16mm, which had been promoted as an amateur format since the mid-20s. Hindsight suggests this should be seen as a puzzle, since it seems obvious that agile, lightweight cameras are exactly what documentary needed (not to mention newsreel). But although 16mm sound projectors were introduced in 1933, soundtrack production was only possible on 35mm. Winston speaks of a failure on the part of both newsreel and documentary producers in the 1930s to press for the development of 16mm sound camera systems, which he argues were technically feasible and only needed the right stimulus. This neglect he attributes in part precisely to the disparagement of 16mm as an amateur format, and in part to the sclerotic attitude of producers and exhibitors who regarded non-fiction films as a minor branch of show business rather than a matter of public interest and information. Nevertheless, following the dictates of show business, newsreels offered the first use of sound in non-fiction cinema, although the change-over was gradual, and several companies issued both sound and silent versions for several years. However, the newsreels' 'curious version of topicality', as Winston puts it, 'was never abandoned in favour of a more responsive news agenda'. Since dictators, the Depression and breaking news were not what newsreels were about, 'there was not much impetus coming from the editorial side to produce cameras that would allow for a more investigative and thorough approach' – and sound did not induce them to think any differently.[19]

The construction of the newsreel soundtrack was entirely prescriptive: the liberal use of formulaic music as backing to a commentary. Location sound remained exceptional, even when the introduction of the first sound-on-film cameras (where the sound was recorded down the side of the picture) made such things easier. The obvious limitations of sound were dealt with by simply ignoring the challenge, says Winston, 'except for the stultifyingly deferential interviews with authorities of all kinds that became a feature of the [news]reels in the later 30s'.[20] This mould would be broken in the US by the monthly *The March of Time*, launched by the news magazine *Time* in 1935, where the format was livened up, when evidential footage was not available, by introducing dramatised segments shot by actors in the studio to illustrate a more urgent news agenda. Henry Luce, the magazine's publisher, called it 'fakery in allegiance to the truth'. The truth was delivered in the stentorian tones of America's version of the voice of god, Westbrook Van Voorhis – Barnouw calls him apocalyptic, Waugh says oily and authoritarian, Jack Ellis describes him as 'deep and commanding, ominous and reassuring at the same time'.[21] I would just say unctuous. The effect of its practised fakery is that *The March of Time* is completely unreliable as archive footage of the events portrayed.

The professional disparagement of 16mm was also the result of a divided industrial scenario. For the manufacturers of cameras and film stock, amateur cine might represent a sizeable market, but with the big producers resistant to 16mm, this market required a special strategy of its own, in which it was treated separately from professional cinema and labelled substandard. Film inherited the concept of the amateur from photography, but as Patricia Zimmermann observes in her social history of amateur film, without at first the means to cater for a mass market, largely because lack of standardisation prevented economies of scale.[22] The substandard 16mm format was the result of a concerted effort by three American manufacturers (Bell and Howell, Eastman-Kodak and Victor Animatograph) to overcome the fragmentation of the market by a proliferation of film gauges (from 9mm all the way up to 28mm). It also required cameras to be reduced in size and simplified to allow for easy loading and unloading without exposure to light, and the development of appropriate non-flammable safety film. Eastman-Kodak came up with an integrated solution when their research laboratory devised an acetate-base reversal stock, which produces a positive image when processed, thus eliminating the costly negative-to-positive process (and its advantages for editing). The 16mm gauge was chosen to prevent people using 35mm split down the middle (whereas later on, when 8mm was devised, it was more economic to split 16mm). The launch of the Cine-Kodak in 1923, says Zimmermann, marked a significant change in the definition of amateur film, which was now colonised by the big manufacturers and promoted as a new consumer market.

The reversal process offered the advantage that this market could be ring-fenced and kept entirely separate from cinema as such, contained within its own separate sphere: it denied the amateur the easy means of making copies of their films. As Zimmermann puts it

The construction of amateur technology excised any possibilities of competition with the 35mm professional format; it thus became firmly embedded in the domain of individual hobbyists or families . . . The 16mm amateur gauge formed a filmmaking caste system: 35mm for professionals and 16mm for families.[23]

A whole consumer industry would be constructed around it, replete with magazines full of 'how to' advice and tips and tricks, annual competitions judged by worthies, and a market for accessories. But for Bell and Howell, 16mm was also 'a source of innovation and improvement for the development of professional equipment', or in other words, part of their research-and-development programme.[24] Two years after launching their first amateur camera, the 16mm Filmo, in 1921, came the 35mm Eyemo. Similarly spring-driven and relatively easy to hand-hold, the Eyemo was quickly taken up for newsreel shooting, employed by Hollywood cinematographers for shooting difficult angles, and would become the preferred camera of documentarists like Ivens. And there's the rub, because with this most agile of 35mm cameras, you couldn't shoot sync sound.

Sixteen mm would only become the standard documentary production format much later, through the exigencies of wartime use by the military and then its adoption for television news after the war. When Grierson started out, it was still in its infancy, and in lacking the sound systems which pronounced the death sentence on the silent movie, not yet a viable format for either production or distribution of documentary. Contrariwise, the addition of sound initially impeded the development of non-theatrical distribution, since few non-commercial outlets could afford the necessary equipment, until reliable and inexpensive 16mm sound projectors first became available in 1933 and non-theatrical distribution switched to the new format. Even then the take-up was slow; according to an estimate two years later by a lecturer at the Institute of Education, there were only around 1,000 projectors in use in the country's schools and colleges, compared with 9,000 in France and 20,000 in Germany.[25] At the beginning of the decade the problem was circular, as in any instance of technical linkage between commodities where the market for one is interdependent with that of the other; as with record player and record, camera and photographic film, or in the language of the computer age, hardware and software. Since you can't have one without the other, lack of appropriate projectors, the hardware, meant that the educational film market was initially considered too small to warrant pursuing, while prospective users held back for lack of appropriate software, the films. Here the Empire Marketing Board (EMB) made a real difference, and when Western Electric began selling their 16mm sound projectors in the UK, they found that the EMB was the schools' biggest supplier of films.

V

The first films Grierson produced to get cinema distribution had their soundtracks added by the distributors, who simply applied the conventional formula of decorous music and instructive commentary, in the inevitable plummy accent and with an occasional touch of whimsy. The move to the GPO brought improved facilities and allowed a bolder approach, although still constrained by the limitations of early mixing systems. The practice adopted at the GPO and exemplified in films like *Night Mail* was to shoot sound in the studio and match the results carefully with inserted silent location shooting – or the other way round: studio shots inserted into location scenes – to which music, commentary and effects were judiciously added.

In composing for *Coal Face* (1935) and *Night Mail*, Benjamin Britten took a similar approach to Lichtveld for Ivens' Philips film. The steam engine gathering energy, for example, its pistons beginning to drive the wheels, is scored for a very unorthodox seven-piece percussion group consisting of compressed air, sandpaper on slate, a small trolley, clank, drill, hammers, siren, etc. As the musicologist Donald Mitchell remarks, this is more like the sound-world of the outlandish Varèse, but it comprises, in the name of documentary realism, 'a kind of a musical factuality' – which again he calls a kind of *musique concrète*.[26] In short, films like *Enthusiasm* (1981), *Philips Radio* and *Night Mail* are not only signal experiments in the construction of the sound documentary, but in the process they also show a strong affinity with the modernist musical avant-garde. From this perspective, they belong in the line of experimentation that leads from the noise machines of the Italian futurists to the concrete sound art of Pierre Schaeffer and the postwar musical avant-garde associated with the Darmstadt Summer School (especially Stockhausen, Berio and Nono). This is a link that seems to have been lost, a connection that quickly became difficult to sustain in the face of the cultural populism of cinema as a social institution. Even in the 1930s it was exceptional. Jean Rouch would later complain of the old-fashioned music, along with its 'colonial exposition' style of commentary, in early films of African ethnography like *Sous les masques noirs* of 1938 by Marcel Griaule (who would become his professor and thesis supervisor). His own first efforts, shot in silent 16mm, suffered the same fate. Released in the cinema in 1947 under what Rouch called the 'abominable' title of *Au pays des mages noirs* (In the Land of the Black Seers), the film had been bought by a commercial producer who blew it up to 35mm, reduced it from thirty minutes to ten, and put it out along with Rossellini's *Stromboli* (1949).

> In the absence of real sound, it was accompanied by idiotic music and a narration spoken by the commentator of the Tour de France bicycle race, in his characteristic voice . . . My reaction after this film is to say, 'No! It's not possible!' The music is worthless; the tone of the commentary is insufferable. It's really an exotic film, a film that should not have been made. I've never shown it in Africa. I'd be ashamed.[27]

Another celebrated example was Basil Wright's *Song of Ceylon* of 1934, a film lauded for its poetic lyricism but, as Stuart Hood remarked, devoid of the slightest reference to the question of colonial labour and the economic exploitation of the colonies.[28] The score for this film, by Walter Leigh, was an example of the kind of musical orientalism that Pierre Boulez would later describe as 'the clumsy appropriation of a "colonial" musical vocabulary' to be found in the numerous *rhapsodies malgaches* or *cambodgiennes* of the early years of the century.[29] If this kind of music nevertheless fits the film's political naivety, then this tells us something about one of T. W. Adorno's favourite subjects, music and ideology, because it points towards the ideological functions that music introduces to the soundtrack for the simple reason that music is never neutral, but always implies attitude; and thus the choice of music betrays the film's ideological stance by signalling too much about the film-maker's habitus.

Flaherty, in *Man of Aran*, managed to sidestep the problems of documentary sound with great panache by adopting a more organic approach. The setting, the Aran Isles off the west coast of Ireland, is almost outside history, the subject is a nuclear family in a small community battling against nature, hunting for shark (a tradition Flaherty had them resuscitate because it was no longer practised). There is no plot, but much of the action is dramatised. That is, Flaherty has constructed his characters using non-actors to act the parts, and has directed their acting (which it must be said is very natural). If the dominant thematic remains that of the perennial struggle of man against nature, the film also has three non-human protagonists – the sea, the sharks and the wind – who are also present on the soundtrack. The extremity of the conditions meant that the film had to be shot mute and sound added afterwards; it also required lengthy periods of shooting and editing which are fully justified by the results: the film is extraordinarily photogenic – no one has ever filmed the sea raging at the coast to better effect – and the editing has been worked at to match, achieving an exceptional degree of fluidity. But the soundtrack is just as remarkable, comprising wild track location sound, a few sound effects, a great deal of music and a good deal of speech. Flaherty has spared us a voice-over commentary – there are a few intertitles – instead employing the natural dialogue of the actors recorded separately and carefully edited to hide the lack of true lip-sync. The soundtrack thus represents the adaptation of fiction film techniques. The dialogue has been recorded with close microphones, which produces a flat signal with no acoustic envelope (similarly the sound effect used for the splashing of the sharks' fins, although the clifftop shouting near the end seems to have been recorded at a distance). As if to compensate, Flaherty has achieved a very natural delivery of speech by his actors, and the film he ends up with as a result is probably the first time that something approaching authentic regional speech from anywhere within the British Isles or Eire was heard on the cinema screen.

The music, by John Greenwood, is designed to support the integration of the soundtrack elements into an organic whole through conventional orchestral programme music with occasional 'mickey-mousing' (where music is precisely matched to actions in the picture, like the hammering in the seaweed sequence). The style is comparable to Virgil Thomson's scores of the 1930s in the US for *The Plough That Broke the Plains* and *The River* (and later, Flaherty's *Louisiana Story*), but here modelled on the pastoralism of the English composers of the folk-sing revival movement (Vaughan Williams, Gustav Holst etc.); at one moment, as the storm begins to gather, it becomes a pastiche of Claude Debussy's *La Mer*. But unlike the avant-garde practice of composing noises into the musical score, or films like *The Plough* . . . where noise drops out and music fills the entire soundspace, here the music is craftily mixed with location sound – the sea, seabirds and the wind. The recording of the wind is the most remarkable – every variety of wind without any trace of distortion (surely a major landmark in the history of sound recording, and testimony to the technical expertise of the whole sound crew, including the laboratory that processed the film). In short, *Man of Aran* is a film with very advanced sound design, especially but not only for a documentary.

VI

Hemingway's narration for *The Spanish Earth* introduced a new tone of colloquial speech. It also used the commentary to represent various different voices within the film, without dramatisation, but simply, as journalism does, by quoting. In the opening sequence the words are those of the villagers of Fuentedueña in front of us, spoken in the first-person plural: 'For fifty years we've wanted to irrigate, but they held us back' (now they will do so in the teeth of war in order to help provision the capital). Later the commentary will represent the voice of refugees fleeing the bombs: 'Where can we go? Where can we live? What can we do for a living?' In between, it switches into the first-person plural of the film crew themselves: 'The bearded man is Commander Martínez de Aragón . . . he died in the attack on the Casa del Campo on the day we filmed the battle there.' If this informal style provided an elegant solution to the problem of the impersonality of the conventional commentary, the film's production history reveals a hard-earned result which raises certain theoretical problems.

Ivens wrote in his autobiography that Hemingway was in Spain as a reporter for NANA (the North American News Alliance); on meeting Ivens he offered his assistance, and eager to extend his writerly skills in a new direction, simply became part of the crew.[30] The two agreed to the principle that commentary should be kept to a minimum, just a few words at the beginnings of sequences 'as a sort of springboard', and should avoid overstatement or tendentious material 'to forestall any of the expected accusations of purveying red propaganda'.[31] Ivens also worked hard to get Hemingway not to duplicate the images in words unnecessarily. The result was the quiet resonance, which continues long after the words have been uttered, of a sentence like 'Men cannot act before the camera in the presence of death'.

Hemingway's commentary insists on its paradoxical function as what Derrida called a supplement: an added element which is nonetheless integral to the whole, of which the simplest examples are the preface or afterword to a book, or the newspaper, say, which is not complete without its supplement. The soundtrack as a whole is a supplement to the image, a novelty when it was first introduced but soon to become a taken-for-granted part of the whole, with a role that shifts between that of a supplement in the sense of something extra which is included, and a substitute, which provides something that is missing. (This is the way music is often used in fiction cinema – much less so in documentary – supposedly to tell us what a character is feeling.) Ivens wanted to be sure that the necessary addition of the commentary would not create redundancies, but Hemingway goes further. Establishing a gap between image and voice, a distance between the image and the commentary's reflection on the image, it draws attention to the fact of representation itself.

Ivens originally had the commentary recorded by Orson Welles, but after a trial screening in Hollywood decided to replace Welles with Hemingway himself. Ivens' biographer Hans Schoots says that Welles' voice was criticised for being too detached.[32] According to Ivens, 'there was something in the quality of his voice that separated it from the film, from Spain, from the actuality of the film'. Perhaps his rounded Shakespearian delivery, he says, 'hadn't made the necessary adaptation to the "stripped" sentences of Hemingway'. But Hemingway, when it came to it, sounded like 'a sensitive reporter who has been on the spot and wants to tell you about it – a feeling that no other voice could communicate'. His very 'lack of a professional commentator's smoothness helped you to believe intensely in the experiences on the screen'.[33] This can be understood as a question of the actor's performance versus the performativity of the author reading out loud. With Hemingway reading his own words, the 'we' of the commentary includes himself, whereas it didn't when it was read by someone else. To (mis)appropriate the terms familiar from Barthes, one might say that whereas Welles gave a readerly (or actorly) reading, Hemingway's reading of his own text is a writerly reading.

But this still leaves certain conceptual problems. The first is authorship. Ivens says that Hemingway participated during the filming in conversations with himself and his cameraman, John Ferno, about the what and how of the filming, like the best way to film a battle, and 'he helped us with what you might call the general strategy'.[34] If this is what Ivens means when he speaks of working with a writer, who, then, is the author of such a film? More generally – and even if we're careful not to confuse the writing of a documentary with the job of writing a fictional screenplay – what does it mean when a documentary has a writer's credit? Is it only the commentary they've written? Nor should we forget the other crucial member of the team, the editor, in this case Helen van Dongen, who joined in from a distance by sending her comments on the rushes as they reached her back in New York. (Such forgetfulness is easy – hence the ironic title of Dai Vaughan's study of Humphrey Jennings' editor, Stewart McAllister, whom he called 'The Invisible Man'.) Whatever theoretical answer is found for this conundrum, it needs to respect the facts of aesthetic teamwork: on the one hand, a space where suggestions suggest suggestions which suggest more suggestions; on the other, the gap between the collective identity of the crew and the division of labour indicated in the credits.

Another gap: the disembodied voice that stands out on the soundtrack, even if it has a famous name, is still a voice detached from its owner. (I am tempted to say that we shouldn't speak here of Ernest Hemingway but the-name-of-Ernest-Hemingway.) The result, once the Hemingway effect has entered the repertoire of commentary-speak, is to turn the first-person plural into a kind of fiction, but a peculiar kind, because the viewer doesn't identify it as fiction and it doesn't make the film as such into fiction. (I am thinking here, for example, of my own experience of the conventions of current affairs television. For a film I directed on human rights in Cuba, I myself wrote the first-person plural reportage-style commentary and, following standard editing practice, recorded a working version. But, of course, the channel required it to be re-recorded by their own voice for transmission. I have always found it disconcerting that the voice which says 'we' in the finished film was not with us when we were shooting it, but no one else has this response.)

Even more crucial is the disappearance of the gap between image and discourse which is entailed by any supplementary commentary on the soundtrack, simply because any such voice-over necessarily comes after the event, is joined to it in editing, and fuses with it on projection. The problem is famously exposed by Chris Marker in *Lettre de Sibérie* (Letter from Siberia, 1957), when he shows the same brief set of images four times with different commentaries: on the streets of a city, a bus passes a luxury car, followed by road-levellers at work and a pedestrian with a squinting eye. As we first see these images, the commentary becomes self-reflexive: 'While recording these images [of Yakutsk] as objectively as possible, I frankly wondered whom they would satisfy. Because of course you can't describe the Soviet Union as anything but the workers' paradise, or as hell on earth.'

Then the images are repeated three times, with three different versions of possible commentary:

For example: 'Yakutsk: capital of the Yakutsk autonomous Soviet socialistic republic is a modern city, in which comfortable buses made available to the population share the streets with powerful ZIMs, the pride of the Soviet automobile industry. In the joyful spirit of socialist emulation, happy Soviet workers, among them this picturesque denizen of the Arctic reaches, apply themselves to making Yakutsk an even better place to live.'

Or else: 'Yakutsk is a dark city with an evil reputation. The population is crammed into blood-coloured buses, while the members of the privileged caste brazenly display the luxury of their ZIMs, a costly and

uncomfortable car at best. Bending to the task like slaves, the miserable Soviet workers, among them this sinister-looking Asiatic, apply themselves to the primitive labour of grading with a drag beam.'
Or simply: 'In Yakutsk, where modern houses are gradually replacing the dark older sections, a bus less crowded than its London or New York equivalent at rush hour passes a ZIM, an excellent car, reserved for public utilities departments on account of its scarcity. With courage and tenacity under extremely difficult conditions, Soviet workers, among them this Yakut, afflicted with an eye disorder, apply themselves to improving the appearance of their city, which could certainly use it.'

What Marker demonstrates here is that the gap between image and voice breeds ideology, as the semantic domination of the voice imposes itself on the image, slanting it this way and that. Is the third version objective just because it avoids political interpretation and judgment? But objectivity, the commentary continues, isn't the answer either.

It isn't the answer, I would say, because although the gap may disappear from view, it cannot be eliminated; it remains inevitable. This is demonstrated by unfortunate moments which force it back into view; for example, when something looms up in the image which contradicts the linguistic discourse. I remember an ethnographic documentary on television, which claimed that the Andean tribe under investigation had no contact with civilisation, just as the camera panned across the inside of an adobe hut lit by oil-lamps made out of coca-cola cans. Lazy film-making. A marvellous parody of this slippery relationship is found in John Smith's short *Girl Chewing Gum* (1976) in which a peremptory voice-over appears to be directing the action on a bustling London street, ordering people and cars about as well as issuing camera instructions, and then does the same in a field at the edge of the city. As these directions grow more absurd, including commands for a clock to move its hands or flocks of birds to fly through the frame, we realise, of course, that the voice-over has been recorded after the event, and what we see is observed reality, which could be any place whatever. In short, the director and not the shot is fictional – a fiction maintained to the end as the gap looms larger and the magical control exercised by the voice at the start dissolves into a forlorn attempt to keep hold of its authority. There is little point arguing whether or not this very funny film counts as a documentary. What is true is that there are many documentaries which leave the impression of the same loss of authority in the face of reality.

The gap appears to be closed up again, or sidestepped, in a new style of reportage which made its first tentative appearance on television in the 1950s, and then developed apace in the 1960s, when the new sync sound systems allowed the commentary to become the speech of the reporter in front of the camera, no longer purely disembodied but attached to a visible personality; now we can see the body that is the source of the voice. This also represents a shift in the register of authorship. The supplement takes its revenge, as the reporter displaces the director, and the camera itself is turned into the reporter's inevitable appendage, and now serves merely to illustrate the verbal discourse. Later still, another act of revenge will bring back the director, but this time in the first-person singular and often on screen, with the name of Marcel Ophuls or Nick Broomfield or Michael Moore, reasserting a form of authorship that folds back into the primacy of the camera itself as both witness and *agent provocateur*.

The puzzle of authorship refuses to go away. Consider the selection of clips shown at the session on documentary authorship at the Sheffield Documentary Festival in 1996. There was *Death of Nation*, dealing with the genocide in East Timor, by the journalist John Pilger. Then, a visually stylish piece called *The Lido* by Lucy Blakstad, about the suspension of ego and identity that comes with going swimming. Third was *League of Gentlemen*, written and directed by Adam Curtis in the BBC series 'Pandora's Box', an examination of some of the myths of modern economics. Last came Molly Dineen's *In the Company of Men*, filmed in a British army barracks. The selection was intended to illustrate the diversity of types of approach which might be considered under the rubric of authored documentary, although no one thought it necessary to observe that they each involve a different division, distribution and combination of the roles assumed to constitute the conventional division of labour in the film crew which contributes to the collective author. Pilger, for example, is a writer-reporter, supported by a director-led crew, whereas Blakstad is herself the director, supported by a cinematographer-led crew. Curtis is a director who writes and narrates his own films (supported by the crew), while Dineen folds the roles of director, cinematographer and interviewer into one. There was consequently no recognition here that 'authorship' is hardly a simple and transparent concept, still less any consideration of the post-structuralist argument that the author is not a person but a property of the text. But then the habitus in these gatherings is resolutely anti-academic, even anti-intellectual. Curiously, film-makers who are nonetheless conscious of the problematic articulated in the theoretical debates, spoke of the suspension of authorship – although they sometimes confused this with the suspension of ego – in favour of the film as, let us say, a multiply coded construct.

The nearest we got to a definition was the formula of one of the panellists that 'authorship is the aesthetic and intellectual coherence of a particular voice'. This conceptualisation, however, remains as vague here as in an essay of 1983 by Bill Nichols called 'The Voice of Documentary'. Voice in this sense is not restricted to, nor to be identified with, any particular element such as dialogue or spoken commentary. On the other hand, says Nichols, it is 'narrower than style'. It conveys 'a sense of a text's social point of view, of how it is speaking to us and how it is organizing the materials it is presenting to us'. It is the pattern formed by the interaction of the film's various codes, and it therefore applies to all modes of documentary.[35]

But this leaves us with the same problem of the identity of the voice that we already stumbled across. Does this voice have a name? Does it have an owner? Or is it only a virtual quality, an effect of the text? The same speaker who proposed the definition just mentioned – a commissioning editor for a cable television channel – went on to give it a twist. There is no reason, he continued, why it shouldn't be the voice of a broadcaster rather than the film-makers on the credits. This is undoubtedly correct, just as the effective author of many a Hollywood film is the studio that produced it. Many film-makers in the audience saw this as an attack on their rights of authorship, although it is also a proposition about the very possibility of authorship in the individualist sense they aspire to. Others, of an older generation, formed in the 60s and 70s, in the traditional ethos of public service, took a significantly different position. One of them declared 'We are all authors. We pick the shots that do the job, and that's the slippery slope to authorship.' Another put it in three words: 'Authorship is responsibility', meaning, in the particular context of the debate, that in the end it cannot be evaded.

Notes

1. Rick Altman, 'The Evolution of Sound Technology', in Weis & Belton, 1985, p. 51.

2. Walter Benjamin, 'The Work of Art in the Age of Mechanical Reproduction' in Arendt (ed.), *Illuminations* (New York: Shocken Books, 1969), p. 244.

3. Laura Mulvey, 'Cinema, Sync Sound and Europe 1929: Reflections on Coincidence', in Larry Sider *et al.* (eds), *Soundscape: The School of Sound Lectures 1998–2001* (London: Wallflower Press, 2003), p. 16.

4. Karel Dibbets, 'The Introduction of Sound', in Geoffrey Nowell-Smith (ed.), *The Oxford History of World Cinema* (Oxford: Oxford University Press, 1996), p. 212.

5. Douglas Kahn, *Noise Water Meat: A History of Sound in the Arts* (Cambridge, MA, and London: MIT Press, 1999), p. 146.

6. Quoted in Kahn, *Noise Water Meat*, p. 146.

7. Sergei Eisenstein, Vsevolod Pudovkin and Grigori Alexandrov, 'Statement on Sound', in Richard Taylor (ed.), *The Film Factory: Russian and Soviet Cinema in Documents 1896–1939* (London and New York: Routledge, 1988), p. 234.

8. Georges Sadoul, *Dictionary of Films* (Berkeley: University of California Press, 1972), p. 104.

9. Sadoul, *Dictionary of Films*.

10. Quoted in Anthony Boadle (Reuter's), 'Cuban Film Shows Raw Side of Life in Havana', 29 July 2003, <washingtonpost.com>.

11. Dibbets, 'The Introduction of Sound', pp. 215–17.

12. Joris Ivens, *The Camera and I* (Berlin: Seven Seas, 1969), pp. 61–2.

13. Reprinted in Rosalind Delmar, *Joris Ivens: 50 Years of Film-making* (London: BFI, 1979), p. 23.

14. Bill Nichols, 'The Documentary and the Turn from Modernism', in Kees Bakker (ed.), *Joris Ivens and the Documentary Context* (Amsterdam University Press, 1999), p. 148.

15. Ivens, *The Camera and I*, p. 60.

16. Karel Dibbets, 'High-tech Avant-garde: *Philips Radio*', in Bakker, *Joris Ivens and the Documentary Context*, p. 80.

17. Quoted in Dibbets, 'High-tech Avant-garde', p. 77.

18. Quoted in Hans Schoots, *Living Dangerously: A Biography of Joris Ivens* (Amsterdam: Amsterdam University Press, 2000), p. 67.

19. Brian Winston, *Technologies of Seeing* (London: BFI, 1996), pp. 64–5.

20. Winston, *Technologies of Seeing*, p. 65.

21. Barnouw, *Documentary*, p. 121; Thomas Waugh, 'Men Cannot Act before the Camera in the Presence of Death', in Barry Keith Grant and Jeannette Sloniowski (eds), *Documenting the Documentary* (Detroit, MI: Wayne State University Press, 1998), p. 148; Jack Ellis and Betsy McLane, *A New History of Documentary Film* (New York: Continuum, 2005), p. 80.

22. Patricia Zimmermann, *Reel Families: A Social History of Amateur Film* (Bloomington and Indianapolis: Indiana University Press, 1995).

23. Zimmermann, *Reel Families*, pp. 22, 27.

24. Zimmermann, *Reel Families*, p. 61.

25. J. A. Lauwerys, *The Film in the School*, 1935, cited in Rachael Low, *Documentary and Educational Films of the 1930s* (London: Allen and Unwin, 1976), p. 40.

26. Donald Mitchell, *Britten and Auden in the Thirties* (Woodbridge and Rochester, NY: Boydell Press, 2000), p. 83.

27. 'Cine-Anthropology', interview with Enrico Fulghignoni, in Jean Rouch, *Ciné-Ethnography* (Minneapolis: University of Minnesota Press, 2003), p. 161.

28. Stuart Hood, 'John Grierson and the Documentary Film Movement', in James Curran and Vincent Porter (eds), *British Cinema History* (London: Weidenfeld & Nicolson, 1983), p. 102.

29. Pierre Boulez, *Orientations* (London: Faber and Faber, 1986), p. 341.

30. Ivens, *The Camera and I*, pp. 103ff.

31. Schoots, *Living Dangerously*, p. 129.

32. Ibid.

33. Ivens, *The Camera and I*, pp. 128–9.

34. Ivens, *The Camera and I*, p. 113.

35. Bill Nichols, 'The Voice of Documentary', in Alan Rosenthal (ed.), *New Challenges for Documentary* (Berkeley: University of California Press, 1988), p. 50.

8 Public Address

The Grierson Model and its alternatives

I

When John Grierson, architect of the British documentary movement of the 1930s, argued for the production of documentaries in the public interest, he spoke of the function of documentary in terms of 'sociological rather than aesthetic aims'.[1] Echoing the words of his American mentor Walter Lippmann, he argued that 'democracy was in danger of collapse, because its citizens did not know how to make it work'.[2] Indeed on the continent of Europe democratic states were struggling to survive. As Eric Hobsbawm has reminded us, the twenty years between Mussolini's so-called 'March on Rome' in 1922 and the height of the Fascist powers' success in World War II 'saw an accelerating, increasingly catastrophic, retreat of liberal political institutions', and the only European countries which functioned continuously with democratic institutions during the entire interwar period were Britain, Finland, the Irish Free State, Sweden and Switzerland.[3] In other words, Grierson conceived his documentary project against the background of rising Fascism, as a means to help strengthen the democratic system through civic education. In short, he maintained that the weakness of the system could be addressed by using the mass media in the interests of education for citizenship, and that documentary, which he proceeded to define accordingly, was an ideal tool for the job.

Since it was plain that such a project would find no support from commercial interests, his solution was to see the State itself as the necessary patron for the social role of the documentary. If it needed his considerable powers of persuasion to bring this off, it was not such a far-fetched idea in a country that had accepted the argument for a state monopoly of broadcasting but in order to keep it separate from the state apparatus itself, invented a new form of public ownership to run it. According to Armand Mattelart in a study of the relations between communication, war and culture, the country among the democracies that drew the most intelligent lessons from its experience of 'information' during 'the first modern propaganda war' of 1914–18, was Britain.[4] Thus we find a subcommittee of functionaries reporting to an Imperial Conference in the 1920s advancing the idea that cinema was not merely a form of entertainment but a powerful instrument of education in the widest sense of the term, which indirectly exercised 'a great influence in shaping the ideas of the very large numbers to whom it appeals' even when it wasn't used for instruction, advertisement or propaganda.[5] The Conservative Party acted accordingly, and established its own Film Department, which became a pioneer in non-theatrical film distribution using mobile film units. Mattelart cites the example of the Empire Marketing Board (EMB), created to promote international trade. With a brief to include all forms of media to publicise the products of the Empire, the EMB would become Grierson's first patron. In short, the moment must have seemed timely.

Nor was Grierson inventing something out of nothing. The production of actualities, factual or so-called 'interest' films, and scientific shorts like the cine-biology series, *The Secrets of Nature*, was one of the few successful parts of the British film industry at the time. This not being what Grierson wanted to emulate, the documentary unit which he set up at the EMB in 1930, thanks to the patronage of a progressive civil servant, Stephen Tallents, was a contradictory animal. On the one hand, it was out-side the commercial film industry, who viewed it with suspicion from the start (even while doing busi-ness with the unit). On the other, it meant drawing government departments into quasi-commercial activities of a kind which were not at all normal for government agencies.[6] The tensions this produced are recorded in the history of the movement written by one its participants, Paul Rotha, who worked under Grierson for some months in 1932 and then as an independent documentarist.[7] In Rotha's ver-sion, documentary production started out as the smallest of the agency's forty-five departments, 'junior even to poster advertising and leaflet distribution',[8] and the movement created by Grierson in the inter-stices of the civil service aroused the hostility of the political establishment as soon as they found out what was going on from their confrères in the film business. The latter objected that film production by government departments was unfair competition. Evidence taken by a Select Committee, Rotha writes, studiously ignored 'the fact that the films had gained an international reputation for their qual-ity and outlook, a reputation secretly envied by the Trade'.[9] But before the government moved to close the film unit down, Tallents managed to save it by arranging to take it with him when he moved from the EMB to the Post Office (GPO). The pretty argument which won the day was that the Post Office made a natural home for the documentarists because they were both about communication – as the unit proceeded to demonstrate with films like *Night Mail*, a publicity film for the Post Office and its overnight postal train from London to Edinburgh which became one of the emblematic films of 1930s' documentary.

II

In the ethos of the time, the new concept of the documentary film came under the general rubric of publicity, which also included propaganda, public relations and advertising – all were seen in the con-ventional wisdom as forms of public persuasion, devoted to shaping, managing, if possible controlling public opinion; and it was to satisfy this doxa that Grierson framed his idea of documentary in the way that he did, contradictions included. As Jürgen Habermas has taught, the changing concepts of publicity and propaganda rehearse the transformation of the public sphere in the passage from its eighteenth-century bourgeois origins to the corporate capitalist state of the late twentieth.[10] The argument goes that democracy depends on the participation of an informed and rational electorate, which in turn requires that politics be pursued in a public arena where knowledge, information and discussion circu-late freely, guaranteed by freedom of speech; and thus authority and power can be monitored, criticised and moderated by public opinion. Many critics consider this an idealisation – Stanley Aronowitz some-where called it 'the mythic town square in the sky' – and indeed the concept theorised by Habermas has never, in historical reality, been found anywhere in untrammelled form. Not only has it always varied according to the different national and political histories in which it took shape, but the rise of the mass media would seriously distort the public world, tending to turn the public commons into what Habermas himself calls a pseudo-public sphere, where the exchange of ideas is replaced by one-way messages with only the semblance of dialogue, and the practice of communicative action is deformed. Indeed, as Derrida saw it, the 'topological structure of the *res publica*, of public space, and of public opinion' was already upset by the technical, scientific and economic transformations which came about after World War I. The new media created new forms and rhythms of communication and information – the documentary is an example – which altered the very concepts of communication and information, but in the process, rendered problematic the presumption that there was an identifiable place, a stable location 'for public speech, the public thing, or the public cause', thus throwing liberal, parliamentary and capitalist democracy into crisis and opening the way for totalitarianism and Fascism.[11] In a word, the stakes were high, and Grierson understood this very well.

Grierson devised his documentary project after going to America as a Rockefeller student in 1924 to study the new practice of public relations, where he discovered the problem writ large. The emergent mass media (the press, films and the phonograph were now joined by radio) began to be seen, especially after the experience of the great propaganda war, as both part of the problem and part of the solution. This is indeed when 'mass communications' first began to take shape as both a dominant social phenomenon and a field of enquiry, and when the young Grierson arrived in the United States, Lippmann had just brought out an influential book on *Public Opinion*, where he held that ordinary citizens were in no position to make rational judgments on public issues: there was too much to know and the mass media didn't help. Lippmann was well placed to make such a judgment, a Harvard graduate who served as Assistant Secretary of War during World War I, who then returned whence he came, to journalism, as an editor and essayist. Soon after, and to use an appropriate Americanism, he spilled the beans: our thinking, he wrote in 1920, is 'shrivelled with panic'. The argument (if you make allowances for words like 'civilisation' and 'man') still applies today: 'civilization', he wrote, was too extensive for personal observation. 'The world about which each man is supposed to have opinions has become so complicated as to defy his powers of understanding.' Honest journalism becomes guerrilla warfare against misunderstanding and intolerance. But 'there can be no liberty for a community which lacks the information by which to detect lies'.[12] He added that the speed and condensation of information required by the media tended to produce slogans and degrade the content (what is known in today's sloganistic language as dumbing down). The notion of public opinion was vague and something of a mystery, he said, but there were skilled organisers of opinion (today they're called spin-doctors) who understood it well enough to create majorities on election day. There was clearly plenty of room in this debate for mystification. Approaching the same issues from another angle, in a book called *Crystallizing Public Opinion* of 1923, was Edward Bernays, who defined his calling as 'the engineering of consent'. The Viennese-born Bernays, who set up a public relations business in New York in 1919, and as a good self-publicist, made much of being the nephew of Sigmund Freud, conceived of public opinion in terms of the group mind and argued that to understand its mechanisms and motives made it possible to control and regiment the masses without their knowing it. (Bernays himself later said he was shocked when he learned that one of his readers was Goebbels, but his uncle would have known how to analyse the incipient megalomania in these theories.)

Back in Britain, these issues were linked to questions of democracy by social thinkers of the left like the moral philosopher A. D. Lindsay, the first confessed socialist to head a college in Oxford and one of the leading public intellectuals of his generation. When Lindsay crossed the Atlantic in 1929 to lecture on 'The Essentials of Democracy', he appealed to his religious roots, which were the same Scottish Presbyterian as both Grierson and a third figure of the moment, the founder of the BBC, John Reith. (This is one of those coincidences which is not so coincidental, since it says something about where the British establishment of the day found its progressive thinkers and doers.) Lindsay's ideal democracy was not the polis of ancient Greece but certain post-Reformation Christian sects – Independents, Anabaptists, Quakers – which made the small congregation the unit of government of the community of believers; except that this cannot translate into the political democracy of the state because here direct democracy is no longer possible. The problem with direct democracy is that it is limited in the Aristotelian model to the range of an orator's voice, or else to government by public meeting according to the Levellers, so the modern democratic state has to develop representative machineries instead. This is where broadcasting enters. 'Thanks to broadcasting, the whole world might become in some sense a public meeting.'[13] (Both Vertov and Brecht, as we saw, had a similar dream.) Lindsay was sensitive to history, adding that

> long before radio was invented, skilful reporting and a cheap press had done something of the same thing. They had transformed the representative assembly into the platform of a public meeting. On it men talked only partially to one another and increasingly to the invisible public behind.[14]

Here, we can add, is the space where 'public opinion' takes shape, an amorphous zone somewhere between the newspaper page (loudspeaker, screen) and the places where people actually meet and discuss, be it assembly, political meeting or pub. Since Lindsay was speaking in the US, where there was no publicly owned broadcasting, he spelled it out for them (again in very modern-sounding terms): 'What we have done is to let into this public meeting a private transmitting medium, which controls what the public hear', and which lies in danger of coming under the control of fewer and fewer people.[15] But it could be different, and the 'application of broadcasting to politics', if regulated so as to ensure fair discussion, could make a remarkable contribution to political education 'as against the production of mass consciousness'.[16]

Reith harboured a similar vision from a more rightwing position, defending his patrician ideas in a 1924 book called *Broadcast over Britain*, in which he held out high hopes of broadcasting. Its extension would mean a more intelligent and enlightened electorate, it could be 'an integrator for democracy', as long it was not used for the pursuit of entertainment alone. This position he defended on the grounds that few people know what the public really want, and it is better to overestimate the mentality of the public than to underestimate it; one Reithian principle which it would have been worth preserving. Grierson's politics were closer to Lindsay than to Reith, but what he intended for the documentary was of a Reithian mould: the interpretation of social reality for the benefit of the populace who urgently needed a better conception of their relation to the State.

III

Grierson's project was inherently fragile. The EMB, as a recent study puts it, proved to be a transient institution, and 'anything but a secure foundation' for the purpose, especially after the introduction of major tariff reform in 1932–3 rendered it irrelevant.[17] The very claims that Grierson made for documentary in order to gain official support in the first place, aroused political suspicions. When Grierson first started to work with Tallents in 1927, Rotha tells us that he mounted a series of screenings for the EMB Film Committee and their guests of anything he thought would serve his purpose. These films included *Nanook*, *Moana*, *Berlin*, *Grass* and, from the Soviet Union, *The Battleship Potemkin*, *Storm over Asia* and *Turksib*, for which he prepared the English version himself. Nor was he afraid to make the link with the Russians publicly, arranging for his own film, *Drifters*, to be premièred in the same London Film Society programme, on 10 November 1929, as Eisenstein's *Battleship Potemkin* – in the presence of Eisenstein himself as guest of honour.[18] A few years later, however, when Rotha asked him to read the manuscript of his new history of documentary, Grierson came back with 'Why the hell do you have to include Marx in the thing, it'll only make it more difficult for me with the Treasury.'[19]

In other words, first, you have to educate your sponsors, by showing them what the film is in the process of becoming, even frightening them a little with what foreigners and revolutionaries are doing with the medium. But as Rotha puts it, the 'background and training' of the people you are trying to persuade, 'engender fear and mistrust of anything to do with "art" and "aesthetics"'.[20] Grierson therefore dissociated documentary from 'art', and substituted a discourse of 'public service' and 'public education'. But you're tarred with your own brush, and your association with outlandish European avant-garde artists, and even worse with Communists, makes you suspicious. The State provides support but takes appropriate precautions, and Barnouw, in his history of the non-fiction film, is only repeating what was well known in the movement's oral history when he reports that for a time Grierson's unit was observed 'by a secret-service operative in the guise of a trainee film-editor'.[21] Rotha records an incident in which a Conservative Party apparatchik and one-time director of the British Film Institute told the press 'that it was common knowledge that senior members of the British documentary group were in receipt of funds from the Soviet Union', but the charge was considered so ridiculous that no slander action was taken against the man.[22] Tallents was a liberal who understood all this very well, and protected them 'from the inevitable slurs that began to be bruited round Whitehall that we were "a gang of Bolsheviks"'. According to Harry Watt, co-director of *Night Mail*, 'Not many of us were communists, but we were all socialists and I'm sure we had dossiers.' Like Meyerhold, he said, they believed that 'Art cannot be non-political'. But they knew from seeing the 'monotony' of Fascist and Communist propaganda, that overt political rhetoric was 'a kiss of death'.[23] The position they took was described by Rotha, in a phrase repeated by Watt, as 'neither henchmen nor mercenaries'. As Barnouw sees it, the situation they were in 'kept them sharply aware of the political limits inherent in government sponsorship',[24] while, according to Rotha, the movement was entangled in a 'skein of intrigue and manoeuvre which most documentary film-makers themselves, intent on their creative work on production, were unaware of'.[25] Both things are true; the habitus is a place of contradictions.

This band of well-educated oddballs inherited the main aesthetic tendencies of the preceding decade – Russian montage, European experimentalism and American narrativisation – more or less equally, but Grierson's guiding hand gave them a particular slant. The unit went to work with huge energy, producing 100 short films in three years. A large number, known as Poster films, were assembled out of available footage, not only because this was cheap but also because of Grierson's conviction, learned from Soviet montage, that editing was the key to film structure and therefore offered valuable schooling. The Poster films were film loops shown on daylight projectors at EMB exhibitions and in shop windows, on subjects like Scottish tomatoes, Empire timber, Australian wine, wool and butter; Rotha, who considered that they demanded both imagination and economy and indeed made 'a wonderful discipline for beginners', called them forerunners of the TV commercial.[26]

To inspire his team of new film-makers, Grierson grabbed the chance of bringing in Flaherty and Cavalcanti to teach them about cinematography and sound respectively. Flaherty's working practices were at odds with the unit's limited resources, and he stayed only long enough to impress them with beautifully photographed footage of industrial landscapes and craftsmen at work. The film for which this footage was intended, *Industrial Britain* (1932), was edited by Grierson and Edgar Anstey after Flaherty departed to begin work on *Man of Aran* for Gaumont-British. Rotha reports the account of Flaherty's production manager, one J. P. R. Golightly, who said that

> Flaherty would watch a process, such as glass-blowing or pottery-making, for a long time and with deep concentration. He would observe every movement of the workers on the job so that when he came to use his camera, he could anticipate their every action. Such a method was . . . to make a deep impression on the documentary makers at the EMB.[27]

Cavalcanti, on the other hand, found the environment of the unit highly congenial, and remained with it for several years, before making the move to Michael Balcon's Ealing Studios and directing several distinguished features during the 1940s. Under Grierson, he says in his reminiscences,

> We worked in conditions that were similar to those of craftsmen in the Middle Ages. The work was collective, and each person's films were discussed by everyone else. If the film of a companion required some assistance, it was offered. However, each team retained their own profile, within a spirit of healthy competition.[28]

Even at the GPO, when the unit acquired a sound studio of its own, conditions remained artisanal in comparison with commercial production, and they enjoyed a licence to experiment impossible under conditions in profit-making studios. Here we find another characteristic of the Griersonian documentarist's habitus. The ambience of collectivity and collaboration, to which Cavalcanti and others attribute a certain carelessness about credits, corresponded perfectly to the disposition of those whom Grierson attracted to his team. Their temperament combined a predilection for what Rotha called the 'realist' aesthetic of the new art of documentary with an aversion to commercial cinema, not just on aesthetic grounds but as Annette Kuhn observes, because the industrial system of production, the 'scientific management' of studio film, was readily understood as an 'inevitable and alienating concomitant of the profit motive'.[29] This is very much like the atmosphere at the Cuban Film Institute (ICAIC), created by the revolutionary government in 1959. In 1930s Britain, the result was to create the only group of film-makers outside the Soviet Union at the time with a collective experience and discourse of documentary as an alternative mode of cinema to the dream palace (and as Flaherty said when he came to join them, nor was there anything like it in the US).[30] On this reading, what Grierson created was a school of documentary, which became a movement as its example spread and stimulated the production of sponsored films by a new generation of small independent producers.

IV

With the move to the GPO and Cavalcanti's arrival came the new emphasis on sound which always features in accounts of the Grierson documentary. *Night Mail* became one of the emblematic films of the movement largely on account of its closing sequence combining the verse of W. H. Auden and the music of Benjamin Britten. Sadoul called it a 'film-poem' in which 'images, natural sounds . . . music and . . . verse are edited together to create a rhythmic unity'.[31] This unity revolves around the projection of a vision of national integration: as Ian Aitken has it, '*Night Mail* mobilises a metaphor of the speeding train, disseminating communication, and uniting the regional and the national, the technological and the rural.'[32] If this social conception clearly makes it more than a mundane postal promo, not everyone was satisfied by its photogenic pleasures. Rotha recalled how critics at the time complained that there was nothing in the film about post-office wage rates and working hours, and the hero was the train, not the people working in it. Auden himself, reviewing Rotha's book on documentary in 1936, expressed the view that film was not a good medium for factual information, that the film-makers worked too quickly to understand their subjects, they were too middle class to relate to workers, and sponsorship by government departments and industrial companies would never permit a truthful account of working people anyway. He was duly was ticked off by the movement's journal, *World Film News*. But if certain elements of this critique nevertheless go to the heart of the movement's institutional setting and the susceptibilities of its young tyros, at the same time, the involvement of Auden himself, together with Britten and others who worked with the unit at one time or another, attests to the centrality of the aspirations which could be mobilised around the documentary idea – and in Britain, it should be said, this was the first generation of artists and intellectuals to be actively drawn into film-making.

Night Mail followed one of the key formulas of the Grierson documentary: the people seen in the film are social actors portraying themselves. This is not 'portraying themselves' as in purely observational filming, where they are not bidden to do anything special, because here they are acting their social roles at the camera's behest – and not always in the actual location. Because of the huge difficulty at that time of shooting sound on location, especially in a moving train carriage, these are real mail-sorters sorting mail in a mock-up of a rail carriage in a studio in London, intercut with the montage of location shooting of the train traversing its route. (Ivens also practised judicious re-enactment by social actors. In *Borinage*, in the sequence where the miners resist the bailiffs, he not only has them playing themselves, but also, perforce, the bailiffs' roles.) Later, the susceptibility of the Grierson school to the practice of enactment, which the success of *Night Mail* contributed to authorising, will lead to various experiments in documentary dramatisation, culminating in two wartime films by Humphrey Jennings – one well-known and one forgotten, *"Fires Were Started –"* and *The Silent Village* (1943) – remarkable for their anticipation, as acted films played by non-professional social actors, of neorealism. The former, which re-creates a night in the Blitz as experienced by London's firemen, combining studio-shot reconstruction with location shooting and library footage, is already a remarkable foretaste of neorealist technique. The second goes even further, to re-enact the brutal Nazi occupation of the Czech mining town of Lidice in a Welsh mining village, with the villagers as actors.

By contrast, another key film of the first years of the GPO unit pointed documentary firmly towards reportage. *Housing Problems* (Edgar Anstey and Arthur Elton, 1935) is famous as the first British film where working men and women spoke on camera in their own homes about their lives and living conditions. Not by accident, it is also a film which rejects the photogenic and the picturesque, as if heeding Benjamin's complaint against photographers who 'can no longer record a tenement block or a refuse heap without transfiguring it';[33] or Ivens' warning, talking about filming *Borinage*, against 'the error of exotic dirt': becoming fascinated by dirt and making it look 'interesting and strange, not something repellent to the cinema audience'.[34] As Anstey explained years later, they deliberately shot in the plainest fashion and edited without any music or other aesthetic devices, because they felt that the film they were making wasn't their own but belonged to the subjects:

> Rotha often criticised *Housing Problems* because he thought there wasn't enough directorial inter-vention and guidance and shaping of the material. Well, Arthur [Elton] and I talked a lot about this, and we felt that the camera must remain sort of four feet above the ground and dead on, because it wasn't our film.[35]

We can read this as telling us something about the habitus of the Griersonian documentarist and their disposition in the face of certain subjects. Anstey is reporting something about the shock of encounter with reality which they felt with all the force of its novelty because no one (in Britain, that is) had done what they were doing here before. But we can also see in these remarks the beginnings of a certain notion about documentary truthfulness that will later surface repeatedly, the idea that the documentarist must curb the temptation to aestheticise their subject matter because this is to interpret instead of record. Or as Dai Vaughan puts it, discussing the susceptibilities of ethnographic film-makers: 'What may seem to be at stake, from the filmmakers' viewpoint, is to prevent their own perceptions from intervening between the viewer and the profilmic.'[36] If this idea retains its force, even while aesthetics has its way and summons up creative judgment, not only at the editing table but even while filming, it is part of the conundrum of Grierson's 'creative treatment of actuality'.

John Corner calls *Housing Problems* 'a work of radical ethnography . . . giving previously margin-alised or unheard voices a chance to express their grievances publicly'.[37] This was more radical than the radio documentary, which was hemmed in by tight editorial procedures, and Graham Greene, writing in 1936, found the film's treatment of its subjects superior to the radio: 'Compare the characters in *Housing Problems* with the frightened, ironed-out personalities with censored scripts whom the BBC presents as documentary.'[38] Yet nowadays, says Corner, many viewers of *Housing Problems* 'register uneasiness at what they believe is the uneasiness of the speakers', who look and sound 'a little awk-ward'. Is this the Solidarity syndrome at work, the altered import of a film seen from a different histori-cal perspective? Was it something that the film's first viewers overlooked in their surprise at what they saw and heard – these stories of vermin and rats?

Stuart Hood, remembering these films forty years later, attests to their power. Despite the omissions – talk of the dignity of labour while avoiding mention of wages and conditions and trades unions – 'the images of workers in such films had an extraordinary effect'. It is difficult, says Hood, to convey to view-ers accustomed to the routine images of television documentaries, the impact of such pictures in the 30s: 'their appearance on the screen caused spontaneous applause from spectators used to the rep-resentation of workers in British feature films', where their typical roles were comic relief, buffoons, idiots or servants.[39] This supports Rotha's claim that 'from a sociological point of view', the Griersonian docu-mentary represented.

> the first attempt to portray the working class of Britain as a human, vital factor in present-day exist-ence, to throw on the screen the rough labour of the industrial worker, the skill of the trained craftsman and the toil of the agricultural labourer.[40]

But these appreciations do not quite apply to *Housing Problems*, which according to Winston was the film that introduced 'the voice of the victim', the impoverished and uneducated individual who was effectively excluded from both participation and representation in the public sphere; and 'given that the victim was to become a staple of the realist documentary, especially on television, the significance of *Housing Problems* cannot be overstated'.[41] This significance includes its reformist character. As Swann puts it in his study of the movement, films sponsored by government and quasi-official bodies suffer from a reluctance to contradict the philosophies and interests of their sponsors, and therefore tend to concentrate on alleviating the symptoms of an ailing economy rather than demanding fundamental structural changes.[42] Or as Ivens remarks, who of all people was entitled to make such a criticism, 'If the British films had been sponsored directly by social organisations fighting the bad housing conditions instead of by a gas company, they would have closed in on such dramatic reality as rent strikes and protest movements.'[43]

Critics varied in their vehemence, but many public intellectuals of the day were not persuaded, like J. B. Priestley, chronicler of working-class Britain and screenplay writer for Gracie Fields musicals, who wrote and delivered the narration for a short by Cavalcanti about modern communications in 1937, *We Live in Two Worlds* (an interesting film because, with Switzerland as an example, the two worlds are the old rhythms of rural production and the modern rhythms of the new technologies of communication). Priest-ley complained that the film-makers seemed to imagine they could come nearer the truth than any other medium, like printed word or stage, yet the films produced 'a very romantic heightening of ordinary life' closer to 'the picturesque and highly coloured fictions of the romancer' than the realist novel or drama.[44]

The most sustained critique, however, came from another writer, Arthur Calder-Marshall, who called the documentarists 'grimly obsequious, like boys toadying to masters or clerks smarming to the boss'. In sheer technique, he said, the GPO Film Unit are the most progressive unit working in England. But they are paid for by the Government to publicize Government services. The scandalous working conditions in the GPO are not mentioned in their films. All we hear is of the wonderful efficiency, the huge expansion of business handled. We are told nothing of the way the staff is limited so that the GPO can make bigger and bigger profits . . ..

Progressive tendencies are muzzled not by complete suppression but by semi-expression. We go as far as we can, say the documentarists, 'in expressing discontent, in criticizing faults in the system. But of course we're working for an official organization, and we don't have very much rope.' Were it completely suppressed, says Calder-Marshall, this desire for reform would become revolutionary. As it is, it is kept tame, and officialdom even thanks them for their propaganda.[45]

V

In advancing a claim for documentary on the grounds of its civic functions, as a prompt contribution to public knowledge of social issues, Grierson can be seen as advocating an aesthetic version of what Habermas has called communicative action: namely, the practice of communication aimed at common understanding and agreement, conducted through the informed exchange of arguments and ideas, which is posited as the proper basis for the democratic social contract and governance by consent. Grierson's concept of documentary occupies a similar terrain. Its aims are shared by communicative action: to inform, enlighten, instruct, persuade or bring up some public issue or aspect of social reality. This is an instrumental conception, intended to influence public attitudes, which mobilised the poetic and photogenic qualities that the 1920s discovered in documentary, but asked them to fulfil a public and social, rather than a private and affective function. As Grierson would retrospectively describe the movement:

> Documentary was from the beginning — when we first separated our public purpose theories from those of Flaherty — an 'anti-aesthetic' movement. We have all, I suppose, sacrificed some personal capacity in 'art' and the pleasant vanity that goes with it. What confuses the history is that we always had the good sense to use the aesthetes. We did so because we liked them and because we needed them. It was, paradoxically, with the first-rate aesthetic help of people like Flaherty and Cavalcanti — our 'fellow-travellers' so to speak — that we mastered the techniques necessary for our quite unaesthetic purpose.[46]

Grierson's use of the expression 'fellow-travellers' is indicative of a man whose way of thinking was deeply political (Cavalcanti called him 'half Presbyterian and half Marxist').[47] At the same time, if he already speaks in 1942 of 'the history' of the movement that is linked to his name, only five years after he gave up the position described by Priestley as that of 'the great white chief of British documentary films', then it is not just because the movement had been swallowed up by the war effort.[48] Priestley's suggestive description of Grierson, which dates from 1939, attests to the fact that the movement had already, before the war, acquired the status of myth; and it was this myth, rather than the films themselves, which has resonated down the decades, and therefore needs unravelling.

And the myth was a powerful one. Grierson once described his own politics as 'an inch to the left of whichever party is in office'.[49] Evidently this was enough for the movement he created to leave a strongly progressive example which had a radical impact beyond the reach of the films themselves. Fernando Birri who, as a film student at the Centro Sperimentale in Rome in the early 1950s, learned about Grierson along with the principles of Italian neorealism, carried back with him to Argentina the idea, as he later put it, of documentary as 'a tool with which to mould reality'.[50] In 1958, Grierson was guest of honour at a film festival in Montevideo where Birri showed his first film, *Tire die* (Throw us a dime), a collaborative social enquiry into the shanty towns around the city of Santa Fe, which later came to be celebrated as the founding social documentary of a new film movement, *el nuevo cine latinoamericano*. Grierson, a leftist social democrat, thus becomes one of the intellectual patrons of a cinema which in the 1960s aligned itself with Marxist revolutionaries and guerrillas across the continent. Yet here we have affirmed what several recent writers have argued, that the aesthetics of the Griersonian documentary are intimately linked to the institutional context in which it developed, and the need to manoeuvre between conflicting political interests and ideas. As William Gwynn puts it, 'the British documentarists identified themselves as socialists with a "progressive outlook" [but] they worked within a conservative state bureaucracy that demanded restraint and self-censorship'.[51] Thus the habitus of the Griersonian documentarist. It doesn't mean the Latin American trail is false, but that the habitus and dispositions of the Latin American documentarists allowed them to take Griersonian ideas in another direction.

Ironically, something similar had already happened in Britain in the 1930s, but outside Grierson's immediate domain. Largely forgotten by orthodox film history, the Grierson school was part of a broader 'independent' film network, mainly operating on 16mm because it was cheaper and exempt from censorship regulations, which extended through the labour movement, exhibiting films in trades union and Labour Party branches, the halls of the cooperative and workers' film society movements – in short, the parallel public commons of leftwing socialism contested by the Communist Party and other groups like the Left Book Club.[52] This parallel network, whose apologists were liable to criticise the Grierson camp for political conformism, produced its own films, through associations like Kino Films and the Worker's Film and Photo League. From the first Workers' Newsreels of 1930 to Ivor Montagu's *Peace and Plenty* of 1939, these films embraced what the official documentary necessarily shunned – the politics of class confrontation; the groups which produced and exhibited them were aligned with the anti-Fascist movement and the Popular Front policy adopted by the Communist movement in the middle of the decade. If most of the workers' movement films were hardly more sophisticated than home movies, and could be said to represent the political wing of the amateur cine movement, there were several that followed the example of the Soviet experimental agitprop of ten years earlier, often made by middle-class professionals working in an independent capacity precisely because it was impossible to make such films officially – sometimes people who also worked for Grierson. This group included both fellow-travellers and fully fledged Communists. Montagu, for example, co-founder of the London Film Society, was a Party member active in the workers' film movement but also Hitchcock's producer; while another exemplary figure is that of Benjamin Britten, the politically unaligned but pacifist composer of scores for several Grierson films, who also wrote music for a peace movement film of 1936, *Peace of Britain* and *Advance Democracy* for the cooperative movement two years later.

Rotha also mentions 'the steady flow of writing and lecturing about the documentary idea' which helped establish the movement's reputation at home and abroad.[53] Here too Grierson's project belongs to a wider movement, interconnected through a range of publications and activities in a manner similar to the independent film movement of the 1970s. Publications like *Close Up*, *Film Art*, *Cinema Quarterly*, *World Film News* and *Documentary Newsletter* covered experimental, documentary and fiction film, while simultaneously promoting 'independent' production and the serious use of amateur cine. There was even – again like the 70s – an Independent Film Makers' Association, with its own newsletter and summer school. There were other links with the wider left-oriented public sphere. Two members of the GPO Film Unit, Humphrey Jennings and Stuart Legg, were also members of Mass Observation, a project launched in 1936 with the object of applying the methods of anthropology to the participant observation of everyday life at home on a mass scale: 'the observation of everyone by everyone, including themselves'.[54] In the understanding of a writer on Mass Observation like Ben Highmore, the movement was a complex amalgam of a number of influences, including surrealism and psychoanalysis, which took the task of a popular ethnography as uncovering the mythologies of daily life which normally remained hidden, unremarked and unexamined.[55] A kind of parallel domain to the interests of the documentary.

Meanwhile, 16mm sound projectors stimulated a growing supply of suitable films. In 1938 the two-year-old British Film Institute estimated the number of educational films in distribution at 2,250 – but as Rachael Low describes it in her study of the decade's documentaries, this figure consisted in a 'rag-bag' of 'informational' titles of which only a 'very small proportion . . . could usefully be connected with the school syllabus'.[56] On the other hand, they included 'a few more sophisticated and advanced teaching films' usually made 'as a result of individual effort'[57] and sometimes shot on 16mm; her foremost example is *An Outline of the Working of Money*, a twenty-one-minute silent diagrammatic film about the monetary system made by the scientist Michael Polanyi. What she unwittingly identifies here is another potential habitus for the documentarist, that of the educated amateur (generally male) who took up cinematography in the same stride as fifty years earlier he would have taken up photography. In general terms, there is the world of the serious 'hobbyist' described by Patricia Zimmermann in her history of amateur film, who bought magazines devoted to amateur photography and popular technical journals like *Technical World*, *Science*, *Illustrated World*, magazines that were themselves symptomatic of an expanding 'technical' public sphere.[58] But the figure of Polanyi points to the particular habitus of the scholar and public intellectual who sees the pedagogic potential for documentary's contribution to the dissemination of knowledge. The main examples from the 30s are anthropologists, including Frank Boas and Margaret Mead, who saw the film camera as a means of collecting field data and presenting it for scholarly consideration, rather than making films as such.

The visual aesthetics associated with 16mm were far from simple. On the one hand, an established current categorised amateur as spontaneous, professional as disciplined; on the other, the amateur was promised 'professional results with amateur ease', as the Filmo advertising slogan put it. The dominant discourse of pictorialism, which Zimmermann finds in the journals and magazines, 'directed amateurs toward creating a narrative spectacle of idealized family life', and discouraged them from the awkward subjects of modern industrialism. There was also lots of advice for foreign travel filming, and a collection at the Human Studies Film Archive of the Smithsonian Institution reveals the class character of these pioneers of the holiday movie: in Zimmermann's words,

> wealthy hunters on safaris in Africa, explorers searching for minerals and precious metals, wealthy people touring Egypt, archaeologists on digs in China, military men stationed in the Philippines, teachers in India, missionaries in Iraq and India, and adventurers in Tahiti.[59]

Their technical and aesthetic competency, she says, varies enormously, but remains free from the proclivities of the professional – many are not even edited, but were deposited in the form of what professionals call rushes, the film as it comes out of the camera. Zimmermann reports that their representation of the foreign and exotic varies according to the film-maker's positioning. Tourists preserve a distance from their subjects; those who stay longer in the same location get closer to the daily life of the indigenous people they portray, and this progression, she says, from distanced records of culture and terrain to more intimate images of private life, 'suggests that the social relations of the [film-] makers with the culture impacted the style and content of shooting with more force than did aesthetic discourse'.[60] Here we find the amateur unwittingly rehearsing the same situation, the relation to the Other, that would also challenge the special genre of the ethnographic documentary.

Notes

1. John Grierson, 'The Course of Realism', in Forsyth Hardy (ed.), *Grierson on Documentary* (London: Collins, 1946), p. 140.
2. John Grierson, Grierson Archive, University of Sterling, G5:16:1, p. 1, quoted in Jacquie L'Etang, 'Grierson and the Public Relations Industry in Britain', in John Izod, Richard Kilborn and Matthew Hibberd (eds), *From Grierson to the Docu-Soap: Breaking the Boundaries* (Luton: University of Luton Press, 2000), p. 83.
3. Eric Hobsbawm, *Age of Extremes: The Short Twentieth Century 1914–1991* (London: Michael Joseph, 1994), p. 111.
4. Armand Mattelart, *Mapping World Communication: War, Progress, Culture* (Minneapolis: University of Minnesota Press, 1994), p. 61.
5. Quoted in Paul Swann, *The British Documentary Film Movement, 1926–1946* (Cambridge: Cambridge University Press, 1989), p. 12.
6. Cf. Swann, *The British Documentary Film Movement*, p. 98.
7. Since Rotha was also a historian of documentary, his retrospective *Documentary Diary* of the 1930s, published in the year of Grierson's death, has the rare quality of an autobiographical memoir written with a certain historical rigour, even if Rotha subscribes to an unreconstructed understanding of history in which opinions and deductions can be separated from facts. Paul Rotha, *Documentary Diary* (New York: Hill and Wang, 1973); cf. p. xiii.
8. Paul Rotha, *Documentary Film* (London: Faber and Faber, 1952), p. 96.
9. Rotha, *Documentary Diary*, p. 117.

10. See Jürgen Habermas, *The Transformation of the Public Sphere*, and 'The Public Sphere' in Armand Mattelart and Seth Siegelaub, *Communication and Class Struggle, Vol. 1, Capitalism, Imperialism* (New York: International General/Bagnolet: IMMRC, 1979), pp. 198–201.

11. Jacques Derrida, *Spectres of Marx* (London: Routledge, 1994), p. 79.

12. Walter Lippmann, *Liberty and the News* (New York: Harcourt, Brace & Howe, 1920), pp. 37, 64.

13. A. D. Lindsay, *The Essentials of Democracy* (London: Humphrey Mitford, 1929), p. 26.

14. Lindsay, *The Essentials of Democracy*, p. 26.

15. Lindsay, *The Essentials of Democracy*, pp. 28–9.

16. Lindsay, *The Essentials of Democracy*, p. 39.

17. Ian Aitken (ed.), *The Documentary Film Movement: An Anthology* (Edinburgh: Edinburgh University Press, 1998), p. 3.

18. Don MacPherson (ed.), *Traditions of Independence: British Cinema in the Thirties* (London: BFI, 1980), p. 105.

19. Rotha, *Documentary Diary*, p. xvii, footnote 2.

20. Rotha, *Documentary Diary*, p. 269.

21. Erik Barnouw, *Documentary* (Oxford: Oxford University Press, 1974).

22. Rotha, *Documentary Diary*, p. 116.

23. Harry Watt, *Don't Look at the Camera* (London: Elek Books, 1974), p. 47.

24. Barnouw, *Documentary*, p. 91.

25. Rotha, *Documentary Diary*, p. 122.

26. Rotha, *Documentary Diary*, p. 49.

27. Rotha, *Documentary Diary*, p. 55.

28. Cavalcanti in Aitken, *The Documentary Film Movement*, p. 212.

29. Annette Kuhn, 'British Documentary in the 1930s and "Independence": Recontextualising a Film Movement', in McPherson, *Traditions of Independence,* p. 27.

30. Swann, *The British Documentary Film Movement*, p. 47.

31. Georges Sadoul, *Dictionary of Films*, ed. Peter Morris (Berkeley: University of California Press, 1972).

32. Aitken, *The Documentary Film Movement*, p. 20.

33. Walter Benjamin, 'The Author as Producer', *Selected Writings, Volume 2, 1927–1934*, (Cambridge, MA, and London: Harvard University Press, 1999), p. 775.

34. Joris Ivens, *The Camera and I* (Berlin: Seven Seas, 1969), p. 88.

35. Elizabeth Sussex, *The Rise and Fall of British Documentary* (Berkeley: University of California Press, 1975), p. 62.

36. Dai Vaughan, *For Documentary* (Berkeley and London: University of California Press, 1999), p. 57.

37. John Corner, *The Art of Record: A Critical Introduction to Documentary* (Manchester: Manchester University Press, 1996), p. 64.

38. Graham Greene, *The Spectator*, 19 October 1936; quoted in Corner, *The Art of Record*, p. 66.

39. Stuart Hood, 'John Grierson and the Documentary Film Movement', in James Curran and Vincent Porter (eds), *British Cinema History* (London: Weidenfeld & Nicolson, 1983), p. 108. The list of typical working-

class characters is drawn from Ralph Bond, Communist film-maker and one of the founders of the Association of Cinematograph Technicians, the British film trade union, in the 1930s.

40. Rotha, *Documentary Film*, p. 97.
41. Brian Winston, *Claiming the Real* (London: BFI, 1995), p. 45.
42. Swann, *The British Documentary Film Movement*, p. 113.
43. Quoted in Hood, in Curran and Porter, *British Cinema History*, p. 102, quoting Rotha, *Documentary Diary* (Secker & Warburg, 1973), p. 157.
44. Swann, *The British Documentary Film Movement*, p. 67.
45. Rotha, *Documentary Diary*, p. 139.
46. Letter to Basil Wright, in 'Grierson and Film Aesthetics', *Journal of the Society of Film and Television Arts*, June 1972, quoted in Rotha, *Documentary Diary*, pp. 273–4.
47. Alberto Cavalcanti, 'The British Contribution (1952)', in Aitken, *The Documentary Film Movement*, p. 205.
48. J. B. Priestley, *Rain upon Godshill*, quoted in Rotha, *Documentary Diary*, p. 135.
49. Forsyth Hardy, *John Grierson: A Documentary Biography* (London: Faber and Faber, 1979), p. 80.
50. Fernando Birri speaking in *Cinema of the Humble*, New Cinema of Latin America, Part One, dir. Michael Chanan, 1983.
51. William Guynn, 'The Art of National Projection: Basil Wright's *Song of Ceylon*', in Barry Keith Grant and Jeannette Sloniowski (eds), *Documenting the Documentary* (Detroit, MI: Wayne State University Press, 1998), p. 84.
52. See MacPherson *Traditions of Independence*; Bert Hogenkamp, *Deadly Parallels, Film and the Left in Britain 1929–39* (London: Lawrence and Wishart, 1986); and Trevor Ryan, '"The New Road to Progress": The Use and Production of Films by the Labour Movement 1929–1939', in Curran and Porter, *British Cinema History*.
53. Rotha, *Documentary Diary*, p. 45.
54. Quoted in Ben Highmore, *Everyday Life and Cultural Theory* (London: Routledge, 2002), p. 83.
55. See Highmore, *Everyday Life and Cultural Theory*.
56. Rachael Low, *Documentary and Educational Films of the 1930s, The History of the British Film, 1929–1939* (London: Allen & Unwin, 1979), p. 39.
57. Low, *Documentary and Educational Films of the 1930s*, p. 36.
58. Patricia Zimmermann, *Reel Families: A Social History of Amateur Film* (Bloomington: Indiana University Press, 1994), p. 17.
59. Zimmermann, *Reel Families*, p. 74.
60. Ibid.

9 Essays and Endeavours

From the postbellum to Free Cinema

I

In certain ways World War II was good to documentary. With an audience avid to see its compelling image, and distributors and exhibitors eager to prove their patriotic credentials by showing them, documentaries were an accepted part of the cinematic institution. Snippets from this extensive output regularly return to us from the archives in the shape of new made-for-television historical documentaries on the war. Too often, however, the method in these historical compilations is to plunder the archive to illustrate a narration seemingly written independently of the images. The images are then assembled from a whole variety of sources, sometimes without even questioning the significance their source may have for what they show (or don't show). Occasionally a film stands out by approaching matters differently, like Marcel Ophuls' *Le Chagrin et la pitié* (The Sorrow and the Pity, 1969), which counterposes wartime newsreels and documentaries with oral testimony in a dialectical form of montage that exposes the contradictions and aporias of official memory – the myth of a France united against Nazi Germany and the collaborationist government through which de Gaulle unified a demoralised country after the war.

An unusually controversial film which French television failed to show until many years later, but which ran in the cinemas in Paris for over eighteen months, the story is an epic one (and the two-part film extends to more than four hours). Ophuls takes the town of Clermont-Ferrand in the Auvergne as the geographical focus for an investigation of the occupation, through interviews with some three dozen witnesses who lived through the events. He casts his net wide to take in all sides – both collaborators and resistance fighters, townsfolk and former German occupiers, along with political figures like Pierre Mendès-France and Anthony Eden – with the result that the accounts we hear, extending from valour to perfidy, heroism to inhumanity, are often conflicting and contradictory. Which of course is precisely the point. As Ian Buruma has written, this is much more than a history lesson but a film about memories and the tricks they play.[1] Or better, it's a lesson in historiography which uses the propensities of the documentary to teach that history is not as coherent as it otherwise appears in public discourse. The documentary recombination of individual recollection reveals inconsistencies, contradictions and disavowals that crowd into the gap between public history and private memory. Here, the archive clips do not simply illustrate the times recounted by the witnesses remembering on screen, but become slippery and ambiguous screen memories that deal a decisive blow to the Gaullist version.

The Nazis themselves filmed incessantly, not just propaganda for public consumption but also for the record. Barnouw remarks that Allied research teams at the end of the war 'were astonished at the care with which the Germans had documented their crimes' – a four-hour compilation was presented in evidence at the start of the Nuremberg trials.[2] In Britain, the GPO Film Unit was turned into the Crown Film Unit in 1940, under the Ministry of Information, and continued producing meanwhile, while in France, something like 400 documentaries were made during the occupation; and then a huge amount of wartime propaganda documentary was also produced by the US after Pearl Harbor. Among those drafted in to the war effort were Hollywood directors like William Wyler and John Ford; Frank Capra directed the series *Why We Fight* (1942–5), and John Huston made two films which proved deeply problematic, *The Battle of San Pietro* and *Let There Be Light* (both 1945), both of them censored for not conforming to the obligatory positive message of the propaganda film.

Of the former, Scott Hamen has written:

> The War Department had commissioned the film to explain to the public at home why the American forces had advanced through Italy so much more slowly than had been predicted. Huston's response to the assignment not only makes it amply clear why the Italian campaign hadn't gone smoothly, it inspires a good deal of amazement as to how Allied forces had managed to prevail at all . . ..[3]

The second is a report on the psychological traumas suffered by many soldiers who survived such slaughter, which, according to Huston himself, was intended by the Army to persuade employers 'that nervous and emotional casualties were not lunatics; because at that time these men weren't getting jobs'.[4] Huston spent three months filming at a psychiatric hospital, a substantial length of time for a documentary. But if this was the time scale needed to match the cycle of treatment, enabling the film to follow a cohort of patients from arrival to release back into civvy street, at the same time the controlled conditions allowed Huston to treat the location as a studio set in which a collective drama was unfolding. This meant he could use lights, shoot synchronous sound, even film with two cameras simultaneously, and because everyone was under military discipline, not have to worry too much about upsetting his subjects (or should that be characters?). There is nevertheless a self-reflexive moment near the beginning of the film where the plan is laid out, when the welcoming officer tells the assembled ranks, 'There's no need to be alarmed at the presence of these cameras, as they are making a photographic record of your progress at this hospital from the date of admission to the date of discharge' – a reassurance that is thus relayed to the viewer, who has already been told in the opening caption, that 'no scenes were staged. The cameras merely recorded what took place in an army hospital.' This 'merely' licenses Huston to treat his subject as a drama with a collective hero, but because it's documentary, that is to say, it isn't scripted, the result is seriously discombobulating. While the disorders manifest by these soldiers are routine and quite susceptible to appropriate therapy, the harrowing accounts they give of their traumatic experiences sound, as Hamen puts it, like descriptions of scenes from *The Battle of San Pietro*, and the result was a film that left the Army deeply unhappy, to the point where they insisted on an optimistic ending and then still held the film back from public exhibition.

Viewing it nowadays, there is something a little disconcerting in the film's precise and careful *mise en scène*, the two-camera set-ups which allow shot/reverse shot cutting without 'cheating', the occasional short tracking shots, above all, the way the film is lit for dramatic effect in classic key-and-filler Hollywood style. It almost seems as if we're watching a cast of characters played by actors who have studied this very film in order to portray in Hollywood movies ever since the parts of characters with psychological disturbances, like the pathological criminal, amnesiacs or mental patients in general. A further irony is the film's stylistic affinity to the paradigm of Soviet socialist realism (although this begs the question whether it would have been treated any better under Stalin). It employs exactly the right formula: a representative cast of social actors, a narrative which observes the unities of time and space, a voice-of-god narration (beautifully delivered by Walter Huston) and liberal use of a music score not only behind the narration but also at dramatic moments during the patients' individual therapy sessions. There is even, towards the end of the film, a scene of music therapy where the recovering patients affirm their sense of community by playing in a band together – in a Russian version it would have been balalaikas, here it's guitars. Yet the film has a rare power to communicate the virtually uncommunicable, the internal trauma of the private soldier. And it does this without recourse to illustration by library footage inserted like flashbacks, but through the soldiers' enactment of symptomatic behaviour. This is the same territory as a medical documentary called *War Neuroses* (1918) made in Britain at the end of World War I, which Elizabeth Cowie has written about, where the display of hysterical symptoms produced by post-traumatic stress confronts us, she says, with what Lacan meant by the Real.[5] Lacan's Real is not the external physical reality but a psychic space which escapes incorporation or translation into either the illusions of the Imaginary, or regulation by the Symbolic Order, the domain of social law embodied by language and social authority. On this reading, the soldiers' symptoms represent the unrepresentable, this inner space of the invisible wound we call the experience of trauma. Both films are narratives of cure, which demonstrate the conceptual categories of psychiatry by which the symptoms are classified – the Symbolic Order – only to be interrupted by the soldiers' involuntary enactment of these symptoms in front of the camera, producing signifiers of what cannot be signified – the psychic Real – because it lies beyond or behind the word by which psychiatry names it, and paradoxically, the appearance of the image which pictures it.

Doubtless this contradictory representation contributed to the discomfort of the military officials who decided to keep Huston's film under wraps, but a further problematic element is the sequence at the end of the film of the final large group therapy session, where the men are encouraged to discuss their fears and apprehensions as they're about to re-enter society, and what emerges above all is not individual unease but the threat felt by the black soldier-patients of meeting with racism. If the military could not allow such sentiments to escape into the public sphere, then censorship is a form of denial in the psychological as well as the legal sense. And, if this is true, then the common factor that would be shared by such two different films as Ophuls' in 1969 and Huston's in 1945 is the documentary vocation for collecting testimony which in the face of ideologically vested interests turns into critique.

If the official and unofficial bans on the two films suggests the paranoia of authority towards the avowals collected by the camera, then it hardly comes as a surprise that the first documentaries directly revealing the Nazi atrocities were kept back. *Memory of the Camps* is the title allocated by the Imperial War Museum to an unfinished documentary in its archives on the concentration camps. Filmed by cameramen accompanying the troops who liberated them in 1945, and primarily intended for German audiences as part of the de-Nazification programme, it was never completed, because, according to one account, due to its 'disturbing pictures of mass graves being excavated and filled with emaciated corpses by captured S.S. guards, [it] was considered so inflammatory to the newly forged postwar alliances that the British government suppressed it', and it languished in the archives until it was rediscovered in the mid-1980s.[6] This film suffered minor notoriety because at one point Hitchcock was engaged to direct it, although he didn't stay on the project very long. According to the Museum's viewing notes for the film, his

> chief interventions, according to the testimony of the editor Peter Tanner, were concerned with the need to avoid any tricky editing that might lay the film open to later accusations that it was in any way contrived or faked. He suggested the use of long shots and of uncut panning shots . . ..[7]

There is no evidence, according to these notes, of a conspiracy behind the failure to complete the film, which was overtaken by the difficulties of the circumstances, but these difficulties included 'the evolution of occupation policy as far as the question of "war guilt" was concerned to the point where the authorities no longer considered a one-hour compilation of atrocity material appropriate'. A similar fate befell an American film called *Nuremberg*, which has an equally murky production history. The version that has come quietly back into limited circulation is credited to Pare Lorentz, but it's not the film which Lorentz intended, which the US government called in before it was finished. It appears to be an English-language version, transmitted once on US television in 1949, of the first version which was shown for two years in Germany, combining scenes from the Nuremberg Trials with some of the Nazi footage shown in evidence. According to Barnouw, Lorentz's American edition was withdrawn 'apparently in deference to pleas' by the West German Chancellor Konrad Adenauer, for fear it would arouse anti-German sentiments. So it was buried, says Barnouw, and became a non-film, until it was unearthed in 1996 by a team of Holocaust researchers.[8] Something similar happened in US-occupied Japan at the end of the war, where a few controversial documentaries encountered censorship problems, and the first films about the atom bomb were delayed for a number of years.[9]

For the most part, however, as Margarita Ledo has observed, war's end brought a return to the thematics of the ordinary,[10] and the shift rendered some of the more traumatic aspects of the war beyond reach and susceptible only to metaphorical allusion. This applies above all to the Holocaust, a horror so incomprehensible and difficult to grasp that on the one hand Theodor Adorno asked if it was possible still to write poetry after Auschwitz and, on the other, writers like the Auschwitz survivor Primo Levi or the historian Raul Hilberg at first found it difficult to get their work published. In the cinema, it took ten years before the first documentary devoted to the concentration camps appeared in 1955, Resnais' *Nuit et brouillard* (*Night and Fog*, 1955). We shall come back to it shortly; here we should note that even this film was censored, with the removal of a shot of a gendarme at a transit camp because it alluded to French collaborationism – an exclusion of precisely the kind that Ophuls exposed in *Le Chagrin et la pitié*.

The horrific images of the Holocaust – so frequently described as 'unspeakable' – bring us sharply back to the question of Lacan's Real, of which they constitute the most extreme visual figuration. At the risk of oversimplifying, what the Lacanian scheme might mean for the documentary endeavour has to do with the resistance of the image to interpretation, an image that is not of the Imaginary, and defying incorporation into the Symbolic Order, refusing the semantic domination of the commentary, on or off screen, direct or implied. The problem here is the slippage, or rather the gap, between the reality in the picture and the Real as the psychic domain of the subject's experience. Certain types of imagery intensify this gap, to produce an uncanny feeling in the image of refusing to give up its meaning.

II

Most of the wartime output sank into oblivion as either reportage or propaganda, so that a major strand of documentary over several years is reduced to a library resource. But then the same is also true after-wards, and the known history of documentary over the following fifteen years has fared little better. The period is too often treated as if documentary form was only marking time, until the means of renova-tion came along at the end of the 1950s – when a new generation of film gear at last allowed synchro-nous sound shooting with agile cameras on location almost anywhere, and this immediately produced the movements of cinéma vérité and Direct Cinema.

In one of the books to accompany the return of documentary to the cinema screens in the 1990s, an anthology aimed at the general reader called *Imagining Reality*, the 50s are reduced to 'the essayists' – a bunch of film-makers in Britain and France who rejected 'the restrictive notion that documentary was merely a medium for mass communication and "social betterment"', and instead looked at documen-tary 'as a means to express strong personal opinions and points of view'.[11] In Britain this was the pos-ition of a group of young iconoclasts – Lindsay Anderson, Tony Richardson, Karel Reisz and a few others – who launched themselves in 1956 under the banner Free Cinema, and went on to create British new wave cinema in the 1960s; in France there was a loose-knit group that included Georges Franju, Alain Resnais and Chris Marker. But this is a seriously denuded version of the history, which neglects signifi-cant currents like independent production in the US, as well as the growing practice of ethnographic film-making by figures such as Jean Rouch and John Marshall, where the most critical questions were raised about the nature of documentary representation. It is also problematic to disregard the develop-ment of documentary in other countries, like Poland or India or Japan, as if that were merely a second-ary phenomenon. And it also ignores the documentary's continuing political role, especially in the critique of colonialism, to which the postwar European state still responded with censorship. First to suffer was Joris Ivens, whom the Dutch deprived of his passport for making *Indonesia Calling!* in 1946. In France, the limits were crossed in 1950 by René Vautier in *Afrique 50* and by Resnais and Marker in 1953 in *Les statues meurent aussi*, both of which were banned by the French censors for many years. Marker would suffer censorship again in 1961 for *Cuba Si!*

In the US, where the euphoria of victory rapidly gave way to the ideological embattlement of the Cold War, and dissident and radical voices were suppressed by the hysteria of anti-Communism, docu-mentaries nevertheless appeared which contested the so-called American Dream, films like Leo Hurwitz's *Strange Victory* and *The Quiet One* by Sidney Meyers (both 1948), Lionel Rogosin's *On the Bowery* (1955) and *The Savage Eye* (Meyers *et al.*, 1959), all of them made on the margins and dealing with sub-jects that Hollywood at that time would barely have considered: racism, delinquent youth, alcoholism and the social alienation of a young divorced woman in the modern city. These films provide lessons about the politics of documentary which remain entirely pertinent. Highly diverse in style and approach, with various experimental currents running through them, they represent the first stirrings of an inde-pendent cinema that fully emerged only twenty years later to challenge Hollywood's inflated budgets and lack of artistic integrity, the loose-knit movement that will then bring a turn towards new and highly playful forms of documentary in the 90s. Such films in the 50s paid the price of denial of access to commercial distribution at home, while enjoying a measure of success abroad. *The Savage Eye* won awards at the Edinburgh and Venice film festivals.

Strange Victory is a work of montage, selected from thousands of feet of assorted shots by nameless military cameramen combined with specially shot scenes both staged and unstaged, on the disquieting theme that the victory over Fascism did not alleviate continuing racism back home. According to a contemporary account,

> It should surprise no one that every company from MGM down to Film Classics has refused to release this film in the United States. It will have to play at those houses not owned or controlled by the major companies. Meanwhile, it is playing to large audiences in England, France, Czechoslovakia. In Italy, in towns where theaters are not available, it is shown on street corners and town squares by those who recognize the film's value and importance.[12]

The Quiet One, made for all of $30,000, was scripted by the critic James Agee, who also narrates, and filmed at a progressive school for delinquent children with a non-professional cast, centring on an emotionally disturbed boy from Harlem under the compassionate ministrations of a psychiatric counsellor. A contemporary account by Walter Rosenblum commends the film especially for its soundtrack:

> The use of dubbed-in sound, which was a financial necessity because of the small film budget, is itself turned into a virtue. Sound is used to highlight the visual image, and the emotional impact of its use is always overpowering. There is one scene where Donald, while walking through Central Park, comes upon a crying child who is being comforted by an anxious mother. In his own frustration, he mimics the child, crying mama, mama, mama. And as he walks away from the mother and child, he enters a tunnel. The reverberation of those sorrowful words bouncing off the tunnel walls multiplies his anguish a thousandfold.[13]

On the Bowery avoids such expressionism. Shot on the streets in New York's skid row by a small and flexible crew of just four people, the film's writer Mark Sufrin explained that their 'actors' were 'taken from the street and would speak in their own argot, with guides of what to say only for story purposes'. They looked for men 'who would not only *be* what they were supposed to be *acting*', but capable of performing before a camera. In any other milieu this would not be too difficult a task; but here, among derelicts wasted by alcoholism, trapped by loneliness and the futility of their lives, was 'the added problem of the psychologically unstable character of their subjects'.[14] The result was widely praised for its sense of veracity and its low-key compassion.

III

In Britain, the politics of Free Cinema were leftist but relatively subdued, despite their association with the *Universities and Left Review* (forerunner of *New Left Review*), which published articles by Anderson and Reisz and organised screenings of the films around the country. They first came together, like their French counterparts, the directors of the *nouvelle vague*, through film criticism; in the English case, in the shape of a little magazine called *Sequence* which originated in postwar Oxford. *Imagining Reality* describes the group as 'outspoken in its criticism of conventional, class-bound British cinema'; they derided 'glossy stylistic perfection' and 'insisted on shooting real people in real locations, frequently with a hand-held camera, foreshadowing many of the techniques of cinéma vérité'[15] – although this only repeats an old pronouncement which begs the question of what cinéma vérité consists of.

As a habitus, Free Cinema was not so much a movement as an umbrella for a restless postwar generation which had no consistent or coherent aesthetic programme but only general tendencies. The group had strong ties with the theatre and a new generation of writers who emerged in the late 50s to find themselves marketed as the 'Angry Young Men' (after John Osborne's play, *Look Back in Anger*) – a generation whose plays and novels they later put on screen (beginning with Richardson's version of Osborne's play in 1959). They were also institutionally linked to the British Film Institute, which formed an essential part of their framework of operation through its magazine, its experimental film fund and the National Film Theatre, where Reisz worked for a period as the programmer and the Free Cinema screenings were held. The fund and the theatre were new features of the Institute's operations introduced in the early 50s, part of the halting postwar growth of the cultural welfare state advocated by the economist Keynes, founder of the Arts Council. Free Cinema exploited the ambiguous space which emerged in this way, which allowed them to take dribbles of state funds in order to challenge orthodoxy.

They knew how to play the game: they were later ready to admit that they invented the group's name in order to attract publicity. As Anderson told the film critic Alexander Walker, it was 'nothing more than a label of convenience . . . It was pragmatic and opportunist . . . a successful piece of cultural packaging'.[16] But it was a well-chosen slogan to express their individualistic dissent. 'THESE FILMS ARE FREE in the sense that their statements are entirely personal', said of one of their handouts, adding that

> Most of them . . . have been produced outside the framework of the film industry. This has meant that their directors have been able to express their own viewpoints, sometimes unusual, without obligation to subscribe to the technical or social conventions imposed on work under commercial conditions.[17]

Walker correctly concludes that as long as their films were film essays rather than revolutionary pamphlets, then their challenge to orthodoxy was not a political danger. On the other hand, in chafing against the industry, they knew what they were talking about. Anderson had been making industrial and sponsored documentaries since 1948. The complaint against industry convention was a crucial element in the face of the rigid attitudes of professional conservatism which dominated the industry, 'from an unwillingness to consider a hand-held track to the inability to conceive of a woman gaffer', as Margaret Dickinson puts it; but she adds that this critique of industry methods was attached to quite traditional ideas about individual artistic expression.[18] In fact, whatever else it was, Free Cinema was the ploy of a group of aspiring film-makers looking for a way into an industry which had become highly sclerotic as well as reactionary.

One of the most remarkable aspects of the group was that they were unusually open towards Europe – far more so than would later be the case, as if joining Europe has had the paradoxical effect of widening, not narrowing, the English Channel. Two of the six Free Cinema programmes at the National Film Theatre between 1956 and 1959 consisted of films from France and Poland. The group were staking their claim to being part of a continent-wide renovation of cinema in which, alongside the impulse of Italian neorealism, the documentary return to immediate reality was widely considered a first small but necessary step. If this implied a critique of crass American-style commercialism – an attitude which also characterised the magazine *Sequence* – the group declared their brotherhood with similar stirrings in America itself with the inclusion in the second Free Cinema programme of *On the Bowery*, which was shown alongside Norman McLaren's *Neighbours* (1952), and the earliest of the French films included, Franju's *Le Sang des bêtes* (The Blood of Beasts) from 1949.

McLaren and Franju both represent links between pre- and postwar susceptibilities. McLaren was one of the foremost animators of his generation, a Communist who had made political films in the 30s but had also worked at the GPO under Grierson, who brought him to Canada in 1941 to join the National Film Board where he founded the animation department. *Neighbours* is a short parable, combining pixilated live action and stop-motion animation, about a destructive feud between two neighbours over a flower that straddles the boundary between their two properties. Franju made his first short in 1934 with Henri Langlois, with whom he subsequently founded the *Cinémathèque française*. Sadoul describes him as 'a film maker with a mocking sense of anarchic black humour and a feeling for unusual atmospheres'.[19] Here he presents his subject, the everyday life of a Parisian abattoir, with 'dreadful directness',[20] aided by a commentary written by Jean Painlevé and a score by Joseph Kosma – two of the leading figures of prewar French cinema.

Le Sang des bêtes can be described formally as an essay in photogenic montage with a counter-pointed soundtrack of music and commentary. To follow an account by Jeannette Sloniowski, 'the slaughterhouse sequences are shockingly graphic, and have often been regarded as among the cruellest in the history of documentary'.[21] But they are shot with a great deal of artistry, and the film is also given to distinct touches of surrealism, like the image in the opening sequence of the waste-ground along a railway line, with apartment blocks in the distance, and in the foreground an armless unclothed mannequin and the horn of an old gramophone. Then a pair of lovers kissing cuts to electric wires and railway yards, before we arrive at the gates of the abattoir 'which are disturbingly similar to the gates of Auschwitz'.[22] Towards the end of the film, unflinching but always artful images of slaughterers and slaughtered – blood flowing away, close-ups of cows being hacked apart, a dead foetus, calves having their throats cut (here the narrator explains that the blood must be drained in order for the meat to be called veal); and then, decapitated, the carcasses continuing to twitch (the narrator explains the twitching is just a reflex) – after all this, as a herd of sheep is being led down an alley to the abattoir, the narrator talks of the 'Judas goat' that leads them to the slaughter while being spared itself and, after another image of twitching headless carcasses, quotes a line from Baudelaire: 'I shall strike you down, without anger or hate, like a butcher.'

As Sloniowski emphasises, this is a film that makes very uncomfortable viewing not only because of the cruelty of the images but also their aestheticisation, in a manner she associates with the 'Theatre of

Cruelty' conceived by another surrealist, Antonin Artaud. The result is a film that strains the conventions of documentary, especially the Griersonian model with its stance of objectivity, low-key approach and pretence of imparting useful knowledge. Here the beauty becomes unsettling but the film resists direct interpretation

> as a moral statement about cruelty to animals, or humankind's survival at the price of the deaths of its fellow creatures, or even as an allegory about the Holocaust; the film may be all these things, but it is not obviously any of them.[23]

There is less ambivalence in *Hôtel des invalides* three years later, of which Sadoul gives the most beautifully succinct account:

> The Army intended this film as a prestige documentary but Franju turned it into a sustained attack on war and its effects, juxtaposing banal scenes of a guided tour of the War Museum with shots of the effects of war. 'Legend has its heroes, war its victims,' says the commentary as the camera moves from a statue of Napoleon to a cripple in a wheelchair.[24]

Perhaps what also makes this mode of documentary seem 'intellectual' is the literary style of the commentary, but that is exactly the strength of the French essayists. Here we should include two French-language films by Ivens which revisit the theme of the city, *La Seine a rencontré Paris* (1957) and *À Valparaiso* (1962), although the former, more accurately, is not an essay-film but a film-poem, since the narration by Jacques Prévert is in verse. For the latter, the text is a vivid prose-poem by Chris Marker, and the combination of the two turns a modest travelogue about the Chilean port city into the finest of all Ivens' city films. This is not just to say that the practice in French documentary was to regard the spoken text as a province of writerliness, but also to perceive it as a source of dialogue with the image.

In Resnais' *Toute la mémoire du monde* (All the World's Memory, 1956), a film about the national library which was number five in a series called 'Encyclopaedia of Paris', the commentary is both sparse and metaphorical. Near the beginning, the camera prowling through basement storerooms settles on a microphone which mysteriously drops into the frame in front of it, and a voice calmly speaks: 'Confronted with these bulging repositories, man is assailed by a fear of being engulfed by this mass of words. To assure his liberty, he builds fortresses . . . In Paris, words are imprisoned in the Bibliothèque Nationale.' This metaphor pervades the whole film, as the camera continually glides around the library, between the stacks, along the aisles, up lift shafts, pausing only when Resnais wants to show us a page or an object among the millions of manuscripts, periodicals, etchings, lithographs, photographs and maps, and the commentary explains that no item that enters the library ever leaves it again. A review by Nöel Burch was fulsome in its praise. From beginning to end the film is one long 'dolly-shot', which he compares with 'the rather primitive' ten-minute takes in Hitchcock's film *Rope* (1948):

> . . . whereas the over-all impression created by Hitchcock's camera as it doggedly followed his characters around the set was an absolutely static one (as a matter of fact, this was the most interesting

feature of that film), Resnais produces an effect of absolute dynamism by juxtaposing dozens of highly stylized dolly-shots designed to 'describe' the various halls, reading rooms, and stacks of the edifice on the Rue Richelieu.[25]

He also praised the photography of Ghislain Cloquet for lighting the cramped quarters of the library 'as though he were working on the best-equipped set in Hollywood', and the intelligent score by Maurice Jarre, which indeed is probably one of the best he wrote.

In the case of *Nuit et brouillard*, Resnais said that he didn't dare make it by himself: 'I accepted only on the condition that the commentary would be written by Jean Cayrol, because he was himself a survivor.'[26] Cayrol had been a political prisoner in Matthausen and published a volume of poetry after the war from which the film takes its title, *Poèmes de la nuit et du brouillard* (Poems of Night and Fog). The phrase is originally a German one, which the Nazis adopted for the decree of 1941 which initiated one of their rules of terror, turning the common idiom, *bei Nacht und Nebel davon gehen* – to get away under cover of darkness or fog – into an order to have people vanish without trace. Cayrol and Resnais re-appropriate it for the purpose of bearing witness.

There is much more to this than ensuring the narration would possess the requisite tact. *Nuit et brouillard* is composed from ground up in the form of double perspectives. On the level of technique, for example, there is the alternation between the monochrome archive footage and the colour of the long tracking shots in which we see the austere landscapes of the deserted camps as they appeared ten years after the war; this translates on the thematic level into a counterpoint between past and present which is mediated by the commentary – as in the very opening, which begins with a verdant landscape, blue sky and fluffy clouds, and the voice on the soundtrack: 'Even a peaceful landscape . . . an open field . . . an ordinary road . . . a resort town with a steeple and a marketplace . . . can lead all too easily to a concentration camp.'[27] As the film unfolds, the viewer is transformed from passive spectator into active interlocutor by a commentary that drops the pretence of impersonal historical narration and adopts the less formal tones of conversational address, a relationship that allows the use of an inclusive 'we'. Moreover, eschewing the pretence of imparting impartial facts, the commentary starts asking awkward questions of the image which the camera cannot answer. Over another tracking shot along an abandoned railway line: 'Today, along the same tracks, the sun shines. Go slowly along it, looking for what? For a trace of the corpses that fell out of the cars when the doors were opened?' A few moments later, over another tracking shot: 'And who knows anything? Is it in vain that we try to remember?' The shifting mode of address is analysed in a thoughtful account of the film by Sandy Flitterman-Lewis.[28] The wartime footage is narrated in the historical present ('The deportation extends throughout the whole of Europe') while the present-day interludes employ the past tense ('Goethe's oak tree at Buchenwald. They built the camp around it, because they respected the oak tree'). The film thus works by inscribing the present within the past and the past within the present.

Twenty years later, when Claude Lanzmann makes *Shoah* (1985), he will rely entirely on the paradoxical power of evocation in those same images of railway lines traversing peaceful landscapes and dispense entirely with archive footage, on the grounds that the visual traces of the events themselves are entirely inadequate to represent their horrific enormity. Just as Cayrol already says in *Nuit et brouillard* as the camera moves along the tiers of beds in an empty barracks:

> No description, no pictures can restore their true dimension . . . We would need the very mattress where scraps of food were hidden, the blanket that was fought over, the shouts and curses . . . Of this brick dormitory . . . we can only show you the shell, the shadow.

But Lanzmann's method was not an option for Resnais, the first to tackle this impossible subject. Indeed the resonance of the railway shots in *Shoah* comes in part from Resnais making use of them previously (but also other sources, especially Hilberg's study of the role of the railways in making possible the huge organisation of the extermination, which Hilberg himself discusses in the last part of Lanzmann's film). Accordingly, in *Nuit et brouillard* the historical imagery is composed of varied materials: newsreel and archive from various sources, photographs, personal footage shot by Allied soldiers, other documentaries (including Riefenstahl's *Triumph of the Will*) – in short, found footage; which means, as another account puts it, that the camera mostly belongs not to Resnais but to the builders and operators of the camps, and sometimes to the Allied 'liberators'.[29] But this is not a compilation film, like the unfinished films of the camps ten years earlier. By means of the complex narrative scheme of the film, with its double perspective, Resnais contrives to use the Nazi footage to undo itself: time and again we are induced by the montage or the commentary to ask ourselves who took these images, and what is it they show. We are able to grasp neither the suffering, nor the ideology that caused it. These are the traumatic wounds of history, the Real, which, as Lacan has it, escapes being named and represented but remains in the (collective) psyche. We feel we are confronted with iconic images whose significance is that they are *not* like the object they signify; like the scratches in the concrete of the gas chamber of which the commentary observes, 'The only sign – but you have to know it – is this ceiling, dug into by fingernails.' At the end, over one last vista of fields, the voice finally says 'I-You-Us': 'At the moment I speak to you, the icy waters of the ponds and ruins is filling up the hollows of the charnel house. A water as cold and murky as our own bad memories . . .'. By means of this grammatical operation, 'I am speaking to you about us', the film brings three different moments to coalesce in a single instant: the historic time of the depicted events, the film-time of the narration, and the present time of the viewing – whenever that is: 1956, when the film was first shown, 2004 when I write this, the future when you read it. This is one documentary that doesn't date, ever.

IV

In an essay of 1948 called 'The Birth of a New Avant-Garde: The *Caméra-Stylo*', the French critic and film-maker Astruc argued, rather impressionistically, that since cinema had left behind the stages of fairground attraction and boulevard theatre, it had become a means of artistic expression like any other, and the camera might therefore be seen as an artistic instrument like the writer's pen; hence *le caméra-stylo*.[30] The very vagueness of the metaphor invited divergent interpretations. It could be taken, for example, to license the kind of highly individual style of a Franju, an oblique poetic realism which speaks through montage, where the image-narrative is deflected by unexpected cuts, strange juxtapositions and recurrences, comprising what Nichols, citing Franju's *Le Sang des bêtes* as an example, calls the elements of a 'stylistic reflexivity' which calls attention to the constructed nature of the illusion.[31] On the other hand, Rouch would associate the idea with the agility of 16mm, which makes the film camera as easy to use as a Leica 'or a pen, to recall the model of the "prophet" Alexandre Astruc'.[32] This has particular implications for the kind of ethnographic documentary practised by Rouch where director and cinematographer are the same person, and the film is made without a script and is therefore 'written' by the camera in the moment of shooting, an approach that was more widely taken up in the 60s.

If this penchant for reflexivity was absent in the British example of Free Cinema, nonetheless Lindsay Anderson, for one, identified with the avant-garde tradition of the 30s, which he interpreted broadly to include both Vigo and British documentary, and valued as a model of an alternative way of working to the orthodoxy of industry structures. As he'd written in *Sequence*, the limitations of such films were obvious:

> they lack polish, film stock is often bad, lighting variable, sets (where used) unconvincing. Yet they date less, or less damagingly than more elaborate productions because they have not compromised with the fashions and prejudices of their time; execution has followed from conception, not from the demands of box office. They remain fresh, spontaneous, individual.[33]

There is indeed a certain affinity with *À propos de Nice* in Anderson's *O Dreamland* of 1953, a wordless portrait of an English seaside funfair, a rough-and-ready film, little more than a sketch book but full of strong images and a noisy soundtrack in strange counterpoint with each other (Frankie Laine's raucous 'I Believe' over a lion pacing his cage, Muriel Smith's sultry 'Kill me-thrill me' over model spaceships in frenzied flight and, to top it all, the sound of mechanical laughter). Here are the crowds on their daytrips, determined to have a good time at any cost, including exposure to the lens of a film-maker intent on harsh satire. Except that Margate isn't Nice, and where Vigo's film feeds off his political anger with the French bourgeoisie, Anderson's target is narrower and the source of his sour impatience much more ambivalent (a displacement, perhaps, of his anger at the inanities of commercialised popular culture including the episodes of *Robin Hood* which he himself directed for television).

Since Free Cinema was a highly successful publicity ploy, *O Dreamland* has entered the canon of significant titles while a gentler film of the same year on the same theme, Anthony Simmons' *Sunday by the Sea*, is forgotten, even though it won an international award at Venice and, unlike Anderson's film, actually achieved a cinema release. (That, however, was something of a lottery: Anderson himself won an Oscar but failed to obtain a circuit release for *Thursday's Children* [1954], a touching film about a school for deaf children in the same seaside town where he shot *O Dreamland*.) It may be that the cinema release for Simmons' film, which enabled him to follow it up with another even more delightful film in the same vein, *Bow Bells* (1954), was due to its frank appeal to the sentiments of working-class audiences. The two films – the second a portrait of London's East End – use the same means of candid location images filmed with a mute camera and cut to music, but instead of the usual, Simmons uses the repertoire of the music hall and the tone of these films is therefore peculiarly affectionate. His cinematography, on the other hand, was essentially no different from Anderson's, or rather, his cinematographer, since the two films by Simmons were shot by Walter Lassally who also shot *Thursday's Children* and several other Free Cinema films, and then went on to become the leading cinematographer of the new wave in the 60s. The difference, then, is more a matter of cultural politics than aesthetic form, and even comes down partly to class – Anderson, who was born in Bangalore in 1923, was the rebellious scion of the British colonial classes, who became an anarchistic leftist and CND activist. Simmons, two years his junior, was the son of Jewish immigrants and himself an East Ender, who joined the Communist Party and got his start in films through a workers' film society which devoted itself to filming Party activities.[34] *Sunday by the Sea* and *Bow Bells* were not explicitly political films, but then nor was *O Dreamland*. On the other hand, Anderson's eye is that of an outsider, alienated from what he films, while Simmons offers an insider's vision of working-class conviviality which is only a step away from political solidarity. The former might strike us as more modernist, the latter as more nostalgic, but in terms of the documentary habitus, and in spite of their political difference, their images occupied the same iconic space, bringing to the screen excluded images of working-class life, implicitly critiquing the repressive conservative culture of the decade in which the Tories had returned to power.

Lassally also shot another film in the first Free Cinema programme, *Momma Don't Allow*, directed by Karel Reisz and Tony Richardson in 1955, a portrait of a jazz club in North London with the music of the Chris Barber band. This film exemplifies the characteristics of the group in its 'personal' treatment of unfamiliar subject matter representing the candid portrayal of the contemporary world, shot with a hand-held camera and proffered without the mediation of a commentary. However, on this occasion the segment of the world portrayed is not one to which the film-makers were social outsiders, but one in which, as young tyros of the artistic community of the capital city, they might expectably participate. The Chris Barber band was at the centre of the traditional jazz revival of the 50s, which was one of the defining features of taste for the whole generation: you were either 'trad' or 'mod'.[35] (A few years later, Richardson included Barber's trumpet-playing in his debut feature film, *Look Back in Anger*.) The structure adopts the well-tried formula, beginning with introductions to a range of characters, here discovered in the process of finishing their day's work and setting out for the club: a woman railway cleaner, a butcher's boy, a dentist's nurse, all cross-cut with the band setting up in the room at the pub which serves as the club's venue. The shooting is agile (though not as daring as Richard Leacock filming a similar subject in New York a year or two earlier), and the editing expertly disguises the fact that the film is shot without synchronous sound. A late arrival is a bunch of poncy types in a swish car going slumming (who unscrew their car-mascot from the bonnet before entering) and who join the jiving rather awkwardly. It is all beautifully done, including hesitant slow motion for the awkward slummers, and a delicate moment when a couple who've had a tiff make it up in a corridor. It is here that the film betrays its transitional status between the old style of constructed documentary and a new free form to which Free Cinema aspired but which was not yet always within its grasp. But this can also be read another way: if these episodes are necessarily set up for the camera, they also hint at ambitions towards a new tone for realist fiction which both directors went on to realise in their early feature films.

While *Momma Don't Allow* was one of several Free Cinema films funded by the BFI's new Experimental Film Fund, the funding for the two most ambitious films came from the Ford Motor Company, in a final fling of disinterested sponsorship of the kind advocated by Grierson, though as a concession to the

sponsor, both films add a spoken commentary – of a very different kind from the French. Exchanging the
cynicism of *O Dreamland* for a celebration of the virtues and dignity of the same ordinary people at work,
Anderson's *Every Day Except Christmas* (1957) presents a day in the life of London's primary fruit-and-
vegetable market at Covent Garden. Or rather, a night and morning, a temporal segment that allows the
film its metaphorical level, because these are the night-workers on whom the rest of us depend, and
Anderson's market, a microcosm of a self-regulating society, is a symbol of the social coherence of the
nation. It is not quite as bad, says Roy Armes, as the rhetoric suggests, but it subtly patronises its subjects
– the dedicatees 'Alice and George and Bill and Sid and Alan and George and Derek and Bill and all the
others'.[36] Reisz's *We Are the Lambeth Boys* (1959) is a group portrait of working-class teenagers belonging to an inner-city youth club in South London, which was praised by the sociologist Richard Hoggart for
capturing the teenagers' vitality, and 'their lively, tolerant and complex sense of community'.[37] It is also
a film that made a particular impact on the present writer, when it was shown at the school film society.
I was about sixteen at the time, and the lads in the film were my contemporaries, and for me the most
remarkable thing about the film was that it showed things that were going on on the other side of my
own city which I knew nothing about, in a part of London which was like a wilderness to me. In short, it
had the effect on a grammar-schoolboy in a leafy well-off suburb of substantiating the abstract knowledge that you had of living in a class society – knowledge partly acquired from reading Hoggart's signal
study of working-class culture, *The Uses of Literacy*, which came out two or three years earlier.

 Hoggart makes an unusually astute critic. He contrasts the film with

> the stream of well-meaning television documentaries on 'The Colour Problem', or 'The Problem of
> Youth' or 'Human Relations in Industry', all desperately anxious to be comprehensive ('the whole
> picture'), objective ('unbiased') and balanced ('a fair cross-section') – and all disjointed and dead.

Such programmes, he says, 'may be well-meaning but they are also drained of meaning'. What is lost is
the sense of life itself, the pattern of emotional pressures which is different from the pattern made by
statistics. Reisz's film has

> no plot, no invented characters or dialogue and no imposed dramatic pattern . . . it does not seek to
> be objective, balanced or comprehensive. It says nothing about juvenile delinquency, home relation-
> ships, personal problems or private sex-life . . . It sets out to show, not the whole truth, but some
> aspects of the truth, wholly.

In short, it is imaginatively committed and communicates a felt emotional depth. And I agree, this is what
I also somehow sensed in the film, in which I could recognise that there was nothing staged. However,
when I look at it again today, it entirely lacks the power to excite that I felt at the time.

 This is not simply because I am no longer the same person, but also because of the shift in perception with the alteration of the time and space in which the film is viewed which I've called the Solidarity syndrome. This applies especially to the film's commentary, entirely shallow and wholly
paternalistic, which for Hoggart was the only thing to strike a false note, and which inevitably grows

more dissonant with the distance of time. A central sequence in the film compares the lives of those who are still at school and those already working for their living. The image cuts from hymn-singing at school assembly to one of the lads in a Post Office sorting room, apparently whistling the hymn tune; then one of the girls in a dressmakers, another of the lads, a butcher's apprentice, another girl at the bench of a food factory. The bland middle-class voice of the commentary tells us there are plenty of jobs available, at least at the moment, especially for the girls, though there isn't much to choose between them, except that an office is cleaner than a factory. 'Being a butcher, like everything else, needs learning,' says the commentary, 'Woody's getting good at it. With luck he thinks he may be in the meat trade for life.' As for the Post Office, 'Life can be dull for an internal messenger with odd jobs to do between errands. But Bobby's keen on cars. He'll be driving a post-office van soon, and his days will liven up.' In the food factory: 'Beryl sits at a bench making food in a factory. She has done for three years. Probably will do until she gets married.' When viewing the film again to write this account of it I watched this sequence with mounting incredulity. Then I turned the sound down and looked again. The picture told a different story. A slow, frightening sequence of almost expressionless faces and meaningless actions, repetitive and dislocated. Occasionally a face twitched, an eyelid blinked. Bobby sighed through clenched teeth. Nothing could better illustrate the power of a commentary to distract attention from the concrete representation of the picture. The import of the pictures is negated by the flow of words, and the patronising banter eradicates the film's 'subjective' dimensions.

There is no overall organising metaphor to the film, but there are certain potent icons. The film opens with the boys playing cricket in the nets at the club. Later they pay a visit to a minor public school to play a match. 'Old boys from the school,' the commentary tells us, 'have long been connected with the club.' It does not expand the point, leaving us to realise for ourselves that the club must be one of those flowers of upper-middle-class charity towards the deprived working classes. Such knowledge only underlines the resonance of the cricket symbol: as long as there is unity on the games field we can assume that society is stable and unruffled. Perhaps this is intended to be ironic; if so, it fails. At the end of the sequence the camera lingers on the faces of some of the Lambeth boys. Hoggart asks about this moment, 'Were those faces sad, slightly pathetic? What was going on behind each one?'. There isn't only the question of the boys' inaccessible inner life. One of those faces stares at the camera. It looks resentful. Another shot near the end of the film has a similar effect. 'When the club make for Tony's fish-bar after a Saturday dance, you can hear the shouting all the way down the road,' goes the commentary, over shots of the crowd outside the fish-and-chip shop.

> There's more of it probably than there used to be when the people who complain about the young were young themselves, but then there's more traffic in the streets now too, and more lights, and more people in the district since the flats were built all around. Just the same, a good evening for young people is much as it has always been – it's for being together with friends, and shouting when you feel like it, things we all like to do.

As this absurd smooth-tongued piece of pretence ends, the camera settles on a sullen girl biting her fingernails.

V

Probably the most astute critique of Free Cinema as a whole comes from a very different quarter. Writing in *Cine Cubano* in 1960, Tomás Gutiérrez Alea wondered how much relevance it had to the new situation created in Cuba by the Revolution, where film-makers no longer found themselves opposing an unfree cinema compromised by its economic and political connections.[38] Free Cinema was obviously appealing, he said, because it was by definition anti-conformist. Its origins lay with a group of young film-makers faced with obstacles to their freedom of expression erected by the commercial institution of cinema: the demand for scripts, actors, lights, make-up, planned camera movements, special effects and all the other ingredients of the 'proper' movie. As a style, it was characterised by great mobility and agility, in which the film-maker took up position as a spectator and filmed fragments of reality spontaneously, as they unfolded. The Free Cinema group had thus offered up, in a spirit of opposition, simple fragments of daily reality, modest film-essays on things close to common experience, where film was used as a witness of this reality, a testimonial that brought a living document to the screen. Its strength was in the way the film thus 'liberated itself not only from various economic and political obstacles, but also largely from the dead weight which the normal processes of film production have to suffer'. If, he said, a certain degree of technical perfection has to be sacrificed to achieve this, what is returned to the audience by way of the invitation to engage with what is on the screen, is more important.

Here the future director of *Memorias del subdesarrollo* (Memories of Underdevelopment, 1968) is among the first to express one of the foremost concerns of Cuba's revolutionary cinema, the conviction that technical perfection – the well-crafted aesthetic surface – is less important than being attuned to the sensibilities of the audience. This is clearly a different habitus from that of the Free Cinema directors themselves, who were more concerned with the personal artistic aspirations of the individual director. Alea placed a high value on spontaneity and creative freedom, because the reality the Cubans were faced with filming was changing very fast, under their noses, but when cultural predilections are translated from the great metropolis to the artists' cafés of peripheral capitals, their character changes, especially in the middle of a revolution. As Alea saw it, the imperative in Havana at that moment was to acknowledge that artistic creation presupposed an attitude in the face of reality which was not impartial. Artistic creation involves judgment, and 'all attempts to portray reality while avoiding judgment on it, are dud. Sometimes this leads to half-truths, which can be more immoral than a complete lie.' Hence his conclusion that 'one shouldn't think that Free Cinema is the new cinema . . . [it] is only a new step in a particular direction, of great value but with great dangers'.

The sense of a transitional moment was not at all limited to the inside of a revolutionary movement. Writing in *France Observateur* in January 1960, the French sociologist Edgar Morin, who had published a study of cinema four years earlier, surveyed the state of documentary as he saw it on screen in Florence the previous month as a member of the jury at the first international festival of ethnographic film. Under the title 'For a New Cinéma-Vérité', Morin speaks of *We Are the Lambeth Boys*, *On the Bowery*, *The Hunters* (1958) – a film by John Marshall and Robert Gardner on the Bushmen of the Kalahari which made it into the theatres and university film libraries – 'and, of course, the already well-known films of Jean Rouch'.[39] These films, he said, give the impression of 'a new movement to re-interrogate man by means of cinema'. *We Are the Lambeth Boys* 'tries to show us what young people are really like at play'; *On the Bowery* 'penetrates the real society of drunkards'; *The Hunters*, instead of showing the 'exotic foreignness' of the Bushmen, 'revealed to us our inconceivable yet certain kinship' with these tough and tenacious people. These films all pointed, he thought, in a certain direction: 'we have the feeling that the documentary wants . . . to leave the world of the bizarre or the picturesque in order to research the world of intimacy in human relations'.[40]

Notes

1. Ian Buruma, 'Marcel Ophuls', in Kevin Macdonald and Mark Cousins (eds), *Imagining Reality: The Faber Book of Documentary* (London: Faber and Faber, 1996), p. 227.

2. Erik Barnouw, *Documentary: A History of the Non-fiction Film* (Oxford: Oxford University Press, 1974), p. 173; and Clifford Rothman, 'Ending the Silence over "Nuremberg"', *Los Angeles Times*, 2 June 1997.

3. Macdonald and Cousins, *Imagining Reality*, pp. 146–7.

4. 'The Courage of the Men, An Interview with John Huston', in Robert Hughes (ed.), *Film: Book 2, Films of Peace and War* (New York: Grove Press, 1962), p. 30.

5. Elizabeth Cowie, 'The Spectacle of Actuality', in Jane Gaines and Michael Renov (eds), *Collecting Visible Evidence* (Minneapolis and London: University of Minnesota Press, 1999), p. 21.

6. Paula Rabinowitz, 'Wreckage upon Wreckage', *History and Theory* vol. 32 no. 2, May 1993, p. 120. There is a small error in this account. Rabinowitz refers to Sydney Bernstein, credited as Executive Producer, as the Minister of Information; in fact he was Films Advisor to the Ministry.

7. 'Memory of the Camps' Film Viewing Notes, Imperial War Museum Film and Video Archive.

8. See Barnouw, *Documentary*, p. 175; <www.nurembergthemovie.com/indexmedia2.htm>; Clifford Rothman, 'Ending the Silence over "Nuremberg"'.

9. Charles Musser, 'Documentary' (Sound Cinema 1930–1960), in Geoffrey Nowell-Smith (ed.), *The Oxford History of World Cinema* (Oxford: Oxford University Press, 1996), p. 330.

10. Margarita Ledo, *Del cine-ojo a Dogma95, Paseo por el amor y la muerte del cinematógrafo documental* (Barcelona: Paidos, 2004), p. 86.

11. Macdonald and Cousins, *Imagining Reality*, p. 211.

12. Warren Miller, 'Progress in Documentary' (1949), in Lewis Jacobs (ed.), *The Documentary Tradition*, 2nd edn (New York: W. W. Norton, 1979), p. 248.

13. Walter Rosenblum, 'The Quiet One – A Milestone (1949)', in Jacobs, *The Documentary Tradition*, p. 245.

14. Mark Sufrin, 'Filming Skid Row', in Jacobs, *The Documentary Tradition*, p. 308.

15. Macdonald and Cousins, *Imagining Reality,* p. 212.

16. Quoted by Alexander Walker, *Hollywood England: The British Film Industry in the Sixties* (London: Michael Joseph, 1974), pp. 26–7.

17. Quoted in Alan Lovell and Jim Hillier, *Studies in Documentary* (London: Secker and Warburg, 1972), p. 136.

18. Margaret Dickinson, *Rogue Reels: Oppositional Film in Britain, 1945–90* (London: BFI, 1999), p. 28.

19. Georges Sadoul, *Dictionary of Film Makers*, ed. Peter Morris (Berkeley: University of California Press, 1972), p. 91.

20. Sadoul, *Dictionary of Films*, p. 245.

21. Jeannette Sloniowski, '"It Was an Atrocious Film": Georges Franju's *Blood of the Beasts*', in Barry Keith Grant and Jeannette Sloniowski (eds), *Documenting the Documentary: Close Readings of Documentary Film and Video* (Detroit, MI: Wayne State University Press, 1998), p. 171.

22. Sloniowski, "It Was an Atrocious Film", p. 177.

23. Sloniowski, "It Was an Atrocious Film", p. 172.

24. Sadoul, *Dictionary of Films*, pp. 151–2.

25. Nöel Burch, 'Four French Documentaries', in Jacobs, *The Documentary Tradition*, pp. 321–2.

26. Quoted by Annette Insdorf, *Indelible Shadows: Film and the Holocaust* (Cambridge: Cambridge University Press, 1989), p. 213.

27. Quotations from the commentary taken from the version published in Hughes, (ed.), 1962.

28. Sandy Flitterman-Lewis, 'Documenting the Ineffable: Terror and Memory in Alan Resnais's *Night and Fog*', in Grant and Sloniowski, *Documenting the Documentary*, pp. 204–22.

29. William Rothman, *Documentary Film Classics* (Cambridge: Cambridge University Press, 1997), p. 52.

30. See Alexandre Astruc, 'The Birth of a New Avant-Garde: Le *Caméra-Stylo*', in Peter Graham (ed.), *The New Wave,* trans. from *Écran Français* 144, 30 March 1948.

31. Nichols, *Representing Reality* (Bloomington: Indiana University Press), p. 70.

32. Jean Rouch, *Ciné-Ethnography* (Minneapolis: University of Minnesota Press, 2003), p. 269.

33. Quoted in Alan Lovell and Jim Hillier, *Studies in Documentary* (Minneapolis: University of Minnesota Press, 2003), p. 149.

34. Personal communication.

35. See Michael Chanan, 'Television's Problem with (Classical) Music', *Popular Music* vol. 21 no. 3, October 2002.

36. Roy Armes, *A Critical History of British Cinema* (London: Secker and Warburg, 1978), pp. 266–7.

37. Richard Hoggart, 'We Are the Lambeth Boys', *Sight and Sound* vol. 28 nos 3/4, pp. 164–5.

38. T. G. Alea, 'Free Cinema', *Cine Cubano* no. 4, 1960. This paragraph is borrowed from my 'Cuban Cinema'.

39. Edgar Morin, 'Chronicle of a Film', in Rouch, *Ciné-Ethnography*, p. 252.

40. Ibid.

10 Truth Games

Cinéma vérité and Direct Cinema

I

There is one thing in the history of documentary everyone seems to agree on. No one doubts that documentary changed radically at the start of the 1960s, apparently as the result of a technical breakthrough: a new generation of 16mm cameras light enough to rest on the operator's shoulder, fitted with lenses and film stock which allowed filming in available light, and capable of shooting in synchronisation with portable tape recorders. The result, in the felicitous phrase of Mario Ruspoli, one of a new breed of film-makers who first filmed this way, was that for the first time 'sound and picture stroll along arm-in-arm with the characters in motion'.[1] This innovation produced one of those distinctive moments of remediation when the quality of filmic representation shifted gear and a new paradigm of observed reality was installed, to be known by epithets like cinéma vérité, Direct Cinema or fly-on-the-wall.

Ten years after it began, Lewis Jacobs described the transformation of documentary in language not yet inflected by the problematics of the new film theory gestating in Europe in the same period. Before the breakthrough, documentary was restricted by the inconveniences of cumbersome apparatus and the crew needed to operate it. Conventional cameras and sound-recording gear were bulky, inflexible, awkward and totally unsuited 'to capture the emotional truth of unstaged human situations quickly, candidly, and with a sense of immediacy or directness'. By the end of the 50s,

> technological advances produced a lightweight, handheld reflex motion picture camera and compact, miniaturized tape recorders, both powered by small battery units that enabled synchronized pictures and dialogue to be recorded quickly, easily, and at low cost. What's more, the new equipment required only a crew of two – and, if necessary, could be handled by one person. The gain in mobility and flexibility allowed the filmmaker for the first time to enter directly – but without intruding – into the very heart of the situation he was documenting. Instead of staging or directing the subject, the subject was allowed to lead the camera and shape its own coherence at the very time of shooting, with action following action naturally. The result was a strong feeling of immediacy and involvement that transmitted to an audience a keen sense of participation.[2]

In other words, the documentary camera is now able to follow its subjects across social boundaries and borders which previously served to keep it from intruding, whose portrayal was previously the privileged province of fiction – to wander into the semi-private spaces and exclusive places of everyday social life, in short, to cross from the public sphere into the private domain. Just as important, it could now overhear what was being uttered, because this is a camera with ears. Edgar Morin, co-director of the key film *Chronique d'un été* (1961), spoke of 'an authentic talking cinema' where 'there are no fistfights, no revolver shots, not even any kisses, or hardly any', in which 'the action is the word', conveyed by 'dialogues, disputes, conversations'.[3] Henceforth, the development of documentary is in crucial respects the discovery of varied forms of speech and dialogue – including the invention of new modes of address made possible by the medium itself.

For a number of commentators, the new focus of speech was the central feature of the new documentary, even more than the fluid cinematography elicited by the hand-held camera. For thirty years, said Barnouw, writing in 1974, documentary had featured people talking only in brief and static scenes; mostly their movements, looks and gestures were freely subjected to the designs of montage. 'But talking human beings with their own, spontaneous speech [are] not puppets', and they begin 'to take control away from the director'.[4] In other words the film-maker is forced into a more responsive mode. D. A. Pennebaker, writing about filming Bob Dylan and his entourage in *Don't Look Back* (1965), calls it 'a sort of complicated game':

> Neither side quite knows the rules. The cameraman (myself) can only film what happens. There are no retakes. I never attempted to direct or control the action. People said whatever they wanted and did whatever. The choice of action lay always with the person being filmed.[5]

Of course, as Pennebaker immediately goes on to admit, the film-maker retains their full prerogatives over the editing. Nevertheless, in order to be more responsive to what they've filmed, the editing also must become more dialectical, breaking with the conventional linear exposition usually furnished by the commentary. An early example of the dialectical pull is found in *Primary* (1960), where two camera crews follow John F. Kennedy and Hubert Humphrey through the Wisconsin primary for the Democratic presidential nomination, and the film is constructed accordingly through the alternation of sequences between the two of them. But this is only a simple version of the kinds of complex structures that documentary will subsequently learn to elaborate.

The initial moves towards the new style happened simultaneously on both sides of the Atlantic, in France, Canada and the United States, and within a few years a league of film-makers emerged doing similar things in similar ways but using different terms to describe what they were up to. One account lists more than a dozen such terms: not only cinéma vérité, but living camera, Direct Cinema, mobile camera, realistic cinema, film enquiry, synchronous cinema, cinema of common sense, cinema of behaviour, personal documentary, tele-vérité, truth film, direct shooting and candid-eye. Sometimes these terms implied important differences of emphasis, but at least one writer of the day blamed the confusion on journalists avid for new catchphrases.[6] This confusion would be compounded by some of the first books on the new movement appearing in the 70s, which tended to use such terms interchangeably despite the differences. (This is a usage repeated by two documentary films about the movement, made in the 1990s, which both used cinéma vérité in their titles.)[7]

Historically speaking the most interesting of these books is the first of them, *Living Cinema* by the French film critic Louis Marcorelles, whose survey is the shortest but the broadest, for he not only includes Canada but also developments further afield in places like Brazil, where in both cases he connects the importance of the movement with the crucial role of speech in bringing to the screen a new sense of lived experience.[8]

II

Two things are missing in the common version of the story: the gestation of the technology, with the main demand for 16mm sound shooting coming from the nascent television industry, and the institutional context, which is different in each country. Television turned to 16mm for its own newsreel usage because it was cheaper and easier to handle than 35mm, while the smaller size of the frame was nonetheless perfectly adequate for the limited resolution of early transmission standards; various systems were tried out during the 50s using a magnetic stripe along the length of the film in the camera, with limited success. Magnetic sound recording had first been perfected in Nazi Germany but was only more widely developed after the war when German patents became available as part of the war spoils.[9] According to Brian Winston, the first such systems came into use in West Germany itself in 1953, building on the technology they pioneered in the 30s; the first similar American system was introduced by Auricon two years later.[10] But having sound recorded on a magnetic stripe along the side of the film made for difficulties in editing, because the sound head in the camera was separated by a number frames from the picture gate; you either had to cut for sound or for picture – or dub the sound off onto a separate magnetic band. Moreover, cameras like the Auricon were too heavy and unergonomic to allow them to be taken off the tripod, which their manufacturers never intended but which meant they were frustrating for documentarists who always wanted to move around. As Winston observes, television saw the matter primarily as a more convenient way of doing what they were already doing (while the film industry regarded it as nothing more than 'candid photography').[11]

Institutionally, the most favourable environment for a new style of 16mm sound documentary was Canada's National Film Board (NFB), officially charged with 'interpreting Canada to the Canadians' (especially in the face of the growing media influence from south of the border). Some of the first direct sound documentaries came out of the NFB's experimental Unit B and were screened on television in a slot called Candid Eye. Last and best known of the Candid Eye series was *Lonely Boy* (Wolf Koening and Roman Kroiter, 1961), a study of the idolatry of the pop idol as personified by the Canadian pop singer Paul Anka, and thus the prototype of one of the most popular documentary genres ever since. There was also a group of French-Canadian film-makers based in Quebec with ideas of their own. Where *Lonely Boy* used a variety of techniques available to the sync camera, including unscripted observational filming and spontaneous interviews, this equipment was not yet available to Gilles Groulx and Michel Brault in 1958 when they made *Les Raquetteurs* (Snow Shoes). Shooting hand-held on 35mm, the key to the soundtrack was the use of a portable magnetic tape recorder which used perforated tape to provide synchronisation. A vivid, joyful and poetic portrayal of winter sports in Quebec, *Les Raquetteurs* announces the vocation of the new documentary for a new cultural politics. This is not a dialogue film, with neither commentary nor interviews, and it makes no explicit political claims. But as a depiction of *les Québécois* through their social rituals and their music, it was one of a number of documentaries that made a key contribution to Quebec's 'quiet revolution' of the 1960s, when a national linguistic minority under Anglo-Saxon hegemony asserted its cultural and political identity. As Groulx expressed this, 'When we try to find out what the problems of our culture mean, we become aware that our uneasiness is not artistic but social: we might call it the attempt to express the man born in this country.'[12] Four years later, this time collaborating with Claude Jutra, Brault made *Québec-USA ou l'invasion pacifique* (Quebec-USA or the Peaceful Invasion), where the advances in sync sound filming allowed them to take language itself as the subject of enquiry, in a humorous portrait of tourists from across the border who come to Quebec to learn French, which in the film becomes an ironic reflection on Québécois identity.

This is also the central theme of Pierre Perrault's *Pour la suite du monde* (co-directed by Michel Brault) which in 1964 became the first Canadian feature ever shown at Cannes, and its sequel, *La règne du jour* (1966). (For some reason the first of these films has acquired three different English titles: 'The Moontrap', 'Of Whales, the Moon, and Men' and, nearest to the French, 'For Those Who Follow'. The latter is known as both 'Reign of the Day' and 'The Times That Are'.) In the former, a community of fishermen on the Ile-aux-Coudres in the St Lawrence River undertake a traditional whale hunt last practised in the 1920s. Unlike Flaherty, who hid the fact that his walrus and shark hunts were re-enactments, here the hunt is openly revived at the film-makers' instigation as a symbolic act (the whale ends up being sold to an aquarium in New York). Flaherty's scenarios lie outside history; here the hunt is an explicit act of historical recovery, a ceremony of cultural celebration. In the latter film, Perrault takes one of these fishermen, Alexis Tremblay, and his wife Marie, on a trip to France, land of their ancestors, where their reactions are decidedly mixed. Both films represent an application of the methodology of cinéma vérité as a form of instigation of the action and speech captured by the camera. Especially speech. Deleuze sees this as a kind of transcendence of fiction through storytelling. When Perrault, he says, 'is addressing his real characters in Quebec', his idea is not simply to eliminate fiction but to free it from a certain model of truth, and 'to rediscover the pure and simple storytelling function which is opposed to this model'. What is opposed to fiction, says Deleuze, is not the real, it is not 'the truth', which is always that of the masters and the colonisers, it is the storytelling function of the poor. In the process, the storyteller becomes another person, 'when he begins to tell stories without ever being fictional' – those kinds of stories that are not just individual but which talk of the speaker's culture.

Marcorelles, who remarks on the space that the new documentary grabbed for cultural minorities precisely like these fishermen, also commented on Perrault's predilection for filmed speech, and the way it brings about a sharpening of aural apperception. According to Perrault,

> When you listen to someone talking for ten minutes, you hear a certain number of things. If you've taped what he said and play it back the next day, you hear ten times as much. This is particularly so when you're talking to ordinary people, and there are all sorts of words you don't follow at once ·because of accents and intonations and because they're talking fast: but if you've got it down on tape you can listen to it slowly until you know it, reproduce it, assimilate it.[13]

Perrault is here ascribing to the analysis of filmed speech the same dynamic that Walter Benjamin ascribed in the 1930s to the moving image, when he compared the camera's capacity to isolate unnoticed features of behaviour to the discoveries of psychoanalysis. But Perrault also sees it in terms of overcoming death and thus preserving cultural truth. Speaking about him years later, he muses that

Alexis is dead, and yet he talks to me again. Does that mean he's still alive? Now, there's a mystery. Because as he wasn't an actor, as he wasn't someone playing someone else, it's really him who's there in the words I'm listening to . . . You know, people have been talking since the world began. They talked before they wrote, but all we know about the people who talked is what was written down, and here suddenly you can possess their words just as they are, and examine them.[14]

There is a double movement here that goes beyond the simple displacement of historical time that I earlier called the Solidarity syndrome, or rather, lies implicit within it. On the one hand, the impact of these films in their own day – their role in asserting the presence of a marginalised culture – has receded into our historical (and political) unconscious; and this original impact can never be recovered, since we are now fully accustomed to the unscripted speech of all sorts of marginalised people (who despite the efforts of the film-makers unfortunately often remain marginalised). On the other hand, when we bring these films up out of the archives and watch them today, seeing Alexis talk is to be plugged back into the past, not only returning us to history, but also returning history to us.

Derrida, in a filmed conversation with Bernard Stiegler about television, speaks of the death implicit in the recorded image from the point of view of the subject: 'because we know that, once it has been taken, captured, this image will be reproducible in our absence, because we know this already, we are already haunted by this future, which brings our death. Our disappearance is already here.'[15] One of the most dramatic examples of this effect I am aware of occurs in the Mexican documentary *Los últimos Zapatistas* (The Last Zapatistas, Francesco Taboada Tabone, 2005), where a dozen veterans of the revolutionary army led by Emilio Zapata, all now aged around 100, offer their testimony of the Mexican Revolution and its failure, one of whom, having spoken his piece, gives out his final breath and dies in front of the camera.

III

The new documentary came in different shapes, sizes and styles; we can agree that its common basis was technical without falling into technological determinism. Nor shall we allow that technological developments have 'a life of their own', but rather, as Winston puts it, that 'technology is always responsive to forces outside itself'.[16] These forces, however, are mediated by markets, and the market for sound cameras was dominated by television stations, not documentary film-makers. What new documentarists wanted – a lightweight sound camera designed to fit on the shoulder, which Winston remarks was something for which nobody in the sixty-five years of cinema's history had ever asked before – would have to come about through a creative collaboration between engineers and practitioners, as occurred in Canada at the NFB. On the independent film scene in New York, practitioners like Richard Leacock were often technically creative themselves, and given to a bit of bricolage where necessary in order to get something to work in a certain way. With funding from *Time-Life* to develop the necessary gear, Drew Associates photographed *Primary* (1960) with a modified 16mm Auricon fitted with a zoom lens (a relatively heavy camera compared to the German Arriflex used by the Canadians), using a tape recorder running off a separate power supply and synchronised by means of an electronic watch, a device developed for use in the space programme. Meanwhile in France, André Coutant introduced Jean Rouch to the prototype of a new lightweight camera employing a small film mechanism developed for a military surveillance device by the Paris company Éclair where Coutant worked; Coutant knew that Rouch would find more liberating uses for it. The new camera was practically silent, and ergonomically designed to rest on the shoulder; the magazine, holding a 400-foot roll of film – more than ten minutes – could be changed very rapidly, and the camera could be used in conjunction with a portable tape recorder which could be swung on the sound recordist's shoulder. This was the gear Rouch used to film *Chronique d'un été*.

These systems were conducive to steady hand-holding for lengthy periods of time without the camera causing excessive fatigue by its weight. They allowed the film-maker to hang around, camera at the ready to shoot whatever might transpire. Add in a number of improvements elicited by the camera's mode of use, including a flexible reflex viewfinder which could be turned in different directions, making it easier to film from difficult angles, and combined with the zoom lens, whose design had only recently been brought to perfection, which avoided the interruption caused by changing lenses on cameras with turrets. Just as important was the new freedom from the need for special lighting. Film lights not only restrict the movement of the camera but alter the character of the location, bathing it in an artificial hue which makes it impossible for people to forget they're being filmed. The problem was solved by the introduction of faster film stocks, and often by the practice of 'cooking' or 'pushing' the stock, that is, processing it in the laboratory as if it were even faster. This produces a more grainy image, but allows the film-maker to shoot spontaneously under available light. Where the use of lighting was unavoidable, new, more subtle lights and techniques were developed, including portable lights which could be 'bounced' or reflected off surfaces like walls and ceilings. It also became possible to film in 16mm and enlarge the result to 35mm for theatrical distribution. *Chronique d'un été*, *Pour la suite du monde*, Ruspoli's *Les Inconnus de la terre* (The Unknown of the World, 1961) and Marker's *Le Joli mai* (1962) were all enlarged to 35mm for this purpose.[17]

The camera's mobility was critical. In some of the first systems, the movement of the camera operator was restricted by the need to link the camera to the tape recorder by means of a cable carrying the synchronisation pulse. The introduction of the method known as 'crystal sync' allowed the pulse to be supplied to camera and recorder independently, abolishing the 'umbilical cord' between them. The recordist could now concentrate on finding the best positions for a clear soundtrack. To assist in the job came a range of new microphones with different sensitivities and pick-up envelopes, including directional mics allowing the selection of individual speech across a distance that would previously have yielded only an acoustic mush; these, because they took the form of rods which were pointed at the target, became known as 'gun mics'. Not all cameras were quiet enough in all situations, and not all situations were quiet enough to film in. To overcome some of the difficulties, the Canadians adapted the principle of the walkie-talkie (another military device developed in World War II) to devise the radio microphone, which allowed the camera to remain at a distance using a telephoto lens, while the subject wears a neck mic attached to a miniature radio transmitter which sends its signal to the tape recorder. This also had the benefit that the subject was unaware when the camera was rolling, thus reducing, perhaps, the effect of the camera's presence. (Nowadays it has given rise to other uses, including the very opposite: allowing someone at a distance from the camera to talk to it knowingly – one of the favoured tropes of television documentaries narrated by a travelling presenter.)

'Perhaps', because caution is needed in evaluating the effects of these improvements, which do not always support the early advocates of observational filming so easily. Not just for theoretical reasons but also practical ones. In certain situations the camera may take a hand in directing activity without seeming to do so, simply by pointing this way or that; and not because the film-makers intend to, but because, for example, they're following a particular subject. Something similar goes for the sound recordist, who is no more invisible than the camera operator, easily identifiable from their headphones. A recordist using a gun mic can affect the flow of conversation in a group also just by pointing this way or that. Moreover, sound recording is in certain respects an art of deception. As Marcorelles pointed out (and this remains true): 'The difficulty is to keep the main sound uncluttered by secondary sounds, and yet preserve the rich amount of sound which the normally formed ear is able to take in.'[18] The problem is that the microphone is no more like the ear than the camera is like the eye. The ear is naturally able to pick out certain sounds within a noisy aural field (the famous cocktail party effect), but not the microphone. If location sound easily degenerates into unintelligible cacophony, microphones must not be designed for fidelity only but also for selection, and these may be less conspicuous than a camera.

Since the footage has to be edited, synchronous sound also entailed the adaptation of editing machines and the introduction of new ones. As the editor learned to keep the growing footage under control, new flatbed editing tables allowed the development of new editing techniques, especially in the handling of sound against picture, which further extended the choices to be made in turning the rushes into a finished film. Most of these sound techniques remained, as always, 'invisible' to the viewer. If this is inevitable, it is also, by the same token, part of the necessary and normal process of artistic shaping and construction. But since this includes the ability to inflect what someone says, for example by leaving some things out or changing the context, the editing table would consequently become a site of intense debate over the collisions of ethics and aesthetics, and film-makers became divided over how the secrets of their craft affected their claims to be presenting a cinema of truth.

IV

These techniques contributed to new styles of reportage which began to be seen on television in programmes like the BBC's *Tonight*, launched in 1959, or *CBS Reports* in the US two years later. These programmes did not escape the journalistic codes of the departments that made them – an institutional concept of objectivity, and the logic of a spoken commentary adorned with pictures – and television's adoption of the newest technology and techniques was gradual. Nevertheless, programmes like these attracted a new breed of television journalist who went around collecting visible evidence, like the young Caribbean writer George Lamming investigating the extent to which landlords in London were operating an illegal colour bar; and they encouraged new working practices, like the two-man team of Slim Hewitt and Trevor Philpot, cameraman and reporter, venturing into the field with nothing more than a motorised Bolex linked to a Uher tape recorder hitched to Hewitt's other shoulder. If the story is now no longer told by an anonymous voice on the soundtrack, then figures like Philpot (or Fyffe Robertson, another *Tonight* favourite) who projected a lively presence on screen within the same space as the subject they were filming, are the grand-daddies of every on-screen reporter since. They are also practitioners of a direct mode of address which on a grander scale has come to dominate television documentary to the present day, the illustrated discourse delivered by its author – reporter or intellectual expert, John Pilger or Simon Schama – in ever-changing locations, partly to camera and partly voice-over, manoeuvred by a director whose essential function is the technical one of devising the visual treatment.

Those like Hewitt, who came from photojournalism, were easily frustrated by conventional television, and in New York, then the headquarters of US broadcasting, it fell to Robert Drew to put together a team and get the backing from *Time-Life* to try something different. He aimed at a new kind of mobile reportage, first attempted in *Primary*, which would discover what he called a dramatic logic in the chosen subject. He would later describe this as 'theatre without actors, plays without playwrights, reporting without summary and opinion'.[19] The odd thing about this formulation is that it makes Drew's aspirations sound strangely like those of Rouch, with whom he is usually contrasted, who had been experimenting for several years with something rather different, which might be called improvised documentary fictions. While Drew set up his production house specifically to make films for television, in France, Rouch had an institutional base in an academic institution, the Musée de l'Homme, which allowed him total freedom to experiment. Over the course of the 50s he made three films which the anthropologist Paul Stoller calls 'ethnofictions', because they are based in his field work but involve their subjects playing roles which they invent together.[20] Not only that, but he takes the experiment further by showing them the film and getting them to improvise their own commentary and dialogue.

Rouch devised this method to overcome the limitations of trying to shoot sync in the field, but it yielded extraordinarily interesting results. A veteran of more than a decade filming among the Songhay and Dogon peoples of West Africa, Rouch had begun making films in 1946. Legend has it that he abandoned the tripod in 1948 when he was shooting a hippopotamus hunt (*Chasse à l'hippopotame*) in order to follow the hunt in a canoe, and never used it again. As an inquisitive student in prewar Paris, he would have seen many documentaries where the hand-held camera was used intelligently, but abandoning the tripod altogether raised the stakes. Because the entire film was now to be composed of the flow of hand-held images, Rouch developed his own style of highly mobile shooting with a spring-wound camera, moving around while winding the camera and continuing to shoot from a slightly different angle. Because he was free of the fixed-distance tripod, he could also move in for close-ups of significant details in a manner quite novel for the ethnographic film.[21] All this made for fluid editing, which was then accompanied by a sober, factual commentary, together with authentic music and sound recorded on location with a magnetic tape recorder, not recorded in sync, but allowing continuous location sound to be used to bind the sequences together. Rouch's most sustained application of the technique comes in his most famous film of this period, *Les Maîtres fous* (1955), where the narrative is carried by a commentary running through the length of the film. Doubtless without it, these strange and bizarre proceedings, with their unique and syncretistic symbolism, would make no sense at all, but the commentary also allows Rouch to have his cake and eat it, by dipping the level of the location soundtrack the better to hide its non-synchronicity; a problem that would soon be superseded by a technological breakthrough, so that Rouch's style in his later ethnographic films would turn on the use of long takes with proper synchronous sound.

First, however, came the three experimental ethnofictions, which point in a different direction, towards a kind of cinema that fuses documentary and fiction to create a new kind of representational space which is both and neither. *Jaguar*, the first of them, was filmed in the mid-50s but not completed till the mid-60s; it recounts the adventures of a group of young Nigerians who migrate to the Gold Coast. Rouch explained:

> It is very difficult to do a documentary on migrations, so we decided to make a fictional film, improvised as we went along. At the beginning we had simply decided who the characters would be – Illo, the fisherman; Lam, the shepherd; Damouré, the gallant – and then we took off for a year, filming a sort of improvised travelogue, shot mostly without sound.[22]

The soundtrack is thus post-recorded. The first to be seen, however, was *Moi, un noir* (1959), which follows another bunch of young migrants from Niger, in the Ivory Coast port of Abidjan over the course of a week. We not only see where they live, what they eat, what jobs they do and how they spend their free time, but hear about these things in their own words, which also speak of their dreams and aspirations – matters hardly considered in the anthropology of the period. The soundtrack reveals a completely unexpected dimension, which is not only beyond the ken of orthodox anthropology but also the scope of conventional documentary, when it turns out that these dreams include projective identification with film stars. Rouch explains the set-up in his opening piece of commentary:

> For six months I went around with a small group of young immigrants to Treichville, a suburb of Abidjan. I suggested to them making a film in which they would play their own roles, where they would have the right to do and say anything. That is how we came to improvise this film. One of the two, 'Eddy Constantine', was so faithful to his character as Lemmy Caution, an American Federal Agent, that during the shooting he was sentenced to three months in prison. For the other man, 'Edward G. Robinson', the film became the mirror in which he discovered himself: a veteran of the Indo-China war, harassed by his father because he had lost the war. He is the hero of the film, and I'm turning the story over to him . . .

La Pyramide humaine, the last of the trilogy, was shot in Abidjan in 1958–9, but in a very different social milieu – the country's young elite, in the shape of the senior class at the city's top high school. It begins with Rouch inviting two separate groups of students, one white and one black, to participate in a film about black–white relations, but warning them that 'some of you will have to be the racists'. Rouch again:

> I was using a camera with an electric motor, which permitted me to make longer shots. I started filming scenes that took place outside the school during vacation. And before my very eyes, incredible things appeared: young blacks and whites discovering, all of a sudden, South Africa's apartheid, racism. They began to ask themselves questions about what they were, about their own relationships in class, about their identity; the film was a veritable provocation.[23]

Perhaps what Rouch achieved in all three films, by inventing for them a novel participatory form, was a dynamic representation of the habitus of West African urban youth which was not only beyond the grasp of the orthodox anthropology of the day, but also outside the purview of the realist documentary, both of which represented only the view of the outsider. Deleuze likened the effect to the storytelling in Perrault. The character must first of all be real if he is to affirm the power of storytelling: 'he has to start to tell stories in order to affirm himself all the more as real and not fictional'. But what is true of the character is also valid, says Deleuze, for the film-maker: 'he too becomes another, in so far as he takes real characters as intercessors and replaces his fictions by their own storytelling'. In this way, 'Rouch makes his own free indirect discourse at the same time as his characters make that of Africa. Perrault makes his own free indirect discourse at the same time as his characters make that of Quebec.' Their situations of course are different.

> For Perrault, the concern is to belong to his dominated people, and to rediscover a lost and repressed collective identity. For Rouch, it is a matter of getting out of his dominant civilization and reaching the premises of another identity . . . Nevertheless each one as a film-maker sets off with the same slender material, camera on the shoulder and synchronized tape-recorder; they must become others, with their characters, at the same time as their characters must become others themselves.[24]

V

The opening of the film that gave the French wing of the movement its name, *Chronique d'un été* by Rouch and sociologist Edgar Morin, with Michel Brault from Canada as cameraman, has Rouch's voice on the soundtrack over shots of Paris announcing 'This film was not played by actors, but lived by men and women who have given a few moments of their lives to a new experiment in cinéma vérité.' Whereupon the picture cuts to Rouch and Morin sitting at a table with a young woman called Marceline discussing with her the film they are about to make; and then we are out on the streets with Marceline approaching people, microphone in hand, asking them if they're happy, in a parody of the technique of street interviewing known in the trade as the vox pop (*voces populi*, 'voice of the people'). Indeed the BBC had carried out just such an opinion poll in 1957, when 'Are you happy?' was the very question that they posed.

Shot in sync and building on the experience of the preceding psychodramas, the film that now unfolds focuses on a small group of characters selected by the film-makers to represent 'the strange tribe that lives in Paris'. Starting out as a type of reverse ethnography, it turns into a kind of group therapy, its characters entering into its unconventional experiment in the name of a special kind of truth, with the self-consciousness of a very particular cultural and intellectual world. Who were they, then? Of the six main participants, three were students, two were women, one African, one Italian, and one a car worker and union militant. A few years later one of the students, who in the film is just called 'Régis', became deeply involved in the Cuban Revolution and Latin American liberation struggles. In 1967, imprisoned in Bolivia as an associate of Che Guevara, Régis Debray recorded his memory of those days: 'With the academic year measuring out our seasons and weeks,' he wrote in his *Prison Writings*:

we could stroll around the streets of the Latin Quarter with nothing to worry about except ourselves and our salvation . . . we roamed about the Sorbonne in groups, as we met to found a magazine, or work out a manifesto, or drink a beer . . . we were the hopeless prey of eroticism, little in-groups, literary journalism and the *cinémathèque* . . . We also learnt, for we were good pupils, that the sirens of ideological error are always singing, on the cinema screen, in novels and in the street, and that few scholars are wise enough to close their ears fully to them.[25]

What emerges is different both from Drew and from Vertov's *Kino Pravda*, but a kind of unscripted psychodrama enacted by real persons which is called into play by the camera itself. The film proceeds in this way to create a strange reality which only exists because it is the result of the film-makers' activity, the reality of a situation which the camera provokes but that isn't fiction, because the subjects are not invented characters but people expressing their own selves, where everything is unrehearsed and nothing is repeatable.

There are very few films that so completely break the rules and invent new ones. Throwing out the conventions that suppress the traces of the cinematic apparatus, there are shots where a microphone boom can be seen in frame or the camera can be glimpsed, reflected in a mirror or a window. Whether or not these moments occurred by accident, they acquire a kind of studied nonchalance which serves constantly to remind the viewer of the filmic set-up, like Brechtian 'alienation' effects in the theatre; they are the seeds of self-reflexivity. By including and indeed eliciting them, a documentary signals its own processes of production, the manipulation which goes into the construction of meaning, precisely in order to counter the illusion of verisimilitude in the traditional mode of the documentary. (But of course this can also become an affectation, and even an object of parody in the fake documentary.)

Rouch and Morin repeatedly put themselves in the picture, questioning and even goading their subjects. In one particularly disturbing scene, where Marceline meets a group of African students and they discuss racism, Rouch points out the number tattooed on her arm and asks them what they think it is. Perhaps because African traditions of bodily decoration look nothing like this, the question leaves them flummoxed – a moment of engineered, perhaps unkind, but real (not realist) drama which reveals a cultural chasm of existential dimensions; at which point the film cuts to Marceline by herself, in a scene which was filmed at her own suggestion, the camera tracking her at a distance from a car as she walks through an almost deserted Place de la Concorde, speaking of her deportation to Auschwitz and the loss of her father. But here it turns out that because of the way it was shot, the raw emotional power of the scene was completely unexpected. Marceline is talking into a lapel-mic clipped to her dress (they were still experimenting with its use), the camera mounted in the back of a Citroën 2CV which receded very slowly in front of her. Later Rouch explained that they

did not know that she was telling of her despair when, coming back from the concentration camps, she rejoined her mother and her brother at the Gare de l'Est. This is, for me, the creation of something that goes beyond the tragic: an intolerable *mise en scène*, like some spontaneous sacrilege that pushed us to do what we had never done before.[26]

The film's conclusion is another piece of manipulation or invention. As Winston puts it, 'They have invited all the participants to see a rough cut (this courtesy, by the way, being no part of [New York-style] direct-cinema practice).' Their reactions are followed by Morin and Rouch pacing the halls of the Musée de l'Homme, questioning themselves about the rights and wrongs of probing someone's emotional crisis, or whether Marceline's account of wartime deportation was not perhaps self-dramatised for the camera. 'At the door of the museum Rouch asks Morin what he thinks. He replies, "I think we are in trouble".'[27] *Nous sommes dans le bain*.

The American practitioners of Direct Cinema never had any such doubts, or if they did, they repressed them, as good pragmatists. Drew and his team, which included Richard Leacock, D. A. Pennebaker and the Maysles brothers, came up with a string of films for television, beginning with *Primary* and *Yanki No!* in 1960, which established a new form of unscripted documentary reportage. According to Drew, '*Primary* was the first place where I was able to get the new camera equipment, the new editing equipment, and the new ideas all working at the same time'; and Leacock: 'For the first time we were able to walk in and out of buildings, up and down stairs, film in taxi cabs, all over the place, and get synchronous sound.'[28] In other words, *Primary*, which was shown on four *Time-Life* television stations but not on national network television, was not a sudden breakthrough, but the result of long deliberation which brought together technical innovation and critical thinking about the conventions of representation.

Here too the film-makers announce their novel intentions at the beginning of the film, in the opening piece of commentary, two-and-a-half minutes in, after shots of both Humphrey and Kennedy on the trail:

> Now travelling along with them, you are about to see a candidate's view of this frantic process, and an intimate view of the candidates themselves, in their cars and buses, behind the scenes in TV studios and hotel rooms, excited, exhausted . . .

As Leacock put it, 'We made a film that captured the flavour, the guts of what was happening. No interviews, no re-enactments. No staged scenes and very little narration.'[29] The result could be summed up as vicarious participation, but of quite a different order from the French version. In Charles Musser's account, the viewer is given glimpses behind the scenes, the candidates are seen 'posing or being posed for the media'. Particularly notable is the scene where we observe Kennedy having his portrait taken in a photographer's studio, with the implication that the documentary film camera gives us the 'real' Kennedy instead of the photographer's carefully constructed image.[30] The scene presents an impossible conundrum – are we seeing Kennedy posing for the photographer, or are we watching him posing at posing? An ambiguous metaphor for the film as a whole, perhaps.

In the New York version of Direct Cinema, which was deeply implicated in the establishment discourse of journalistic objectivity, this quality of observation-without-intervention became one of the key claims of its truth-value. Maysles maintained they were just 'trying to find out what's going on', Drew asserted that 'The film-maker's personality is no way directly involved in directing the action', Leacock and Pennebaker made similar statements.[31] According to the American film historians Robert Allen and

Douglas Gomery, the style was tailor-made for the ideological susceptibilities of American liberalism and the idea of the press as a social watchdog. Not only did these films succeed in portraying stuff that was normally hidden from public view, but they also allowed the subjects of the films to speak for themselves. The tacit assumption was that 'if right-thinking people become aware of the way things "really are", they will take steps to correct injustices and inequities'. On this reading, the film-maker's task was not political advocacy, 'it is enough to reveal the "truth" of a social situation to the viewer'.[32] But this involves a curious sleight of hand for, as Winston has pointed out, we learn nothing in *Primary* about the election issues or of what divides the candidates: 'The politics of the situation – *Primary*'s subject matter, after all – remain hidden.'[33] Here perhaps we can see the beginnings of an unhappy tendency in television's treatment of politicians ever since, even if this was not exactly the film-makers' intention. But the relationship becomes a cat-and-mouse game, and what looked like the opening of previously closed doors, says Winston, turned out to be no such thing, because politicians and their advisors soon became as adept at controlling this new form of access as previously.

On a broader level, the political implications of New York Direct Cinema are perhaps most clearly revealed in the contrast between *Yanki No!* and Chris Marker's *Cuba Si*. The former, shot by Leacock and Albert Maysles in 1960, is a film on Latin American attitudes towards the US for ABC television which presented itself as 'a film editorial' and concluded with an open plea for increased aid to Latin America. The project comes undone in the face of a subject that is too dispersed for their observational method to show more than the surface. It allowed people in the US to hear Fidel Castro speaking for the first time but, bowing to the demands of television for which it was made, it overlaid a tendentious commentary which (not unlike *We Are the Lambeth Boys*) undid much of what the film-makers may have intended: over shots of people on their way to a rally, the narrator intones 'Now the Revolution is going to stage a show'; and about Fidel: 'Fidel Castro, who looks like a raving madman to North Americans, is seen by Latin Americans as a sort of messiah. Now you will see him at his messianic best.' Marker's title alone, taking the other half of the revolutionary slogan – ¡Cuba Si! ¡Yanqui No! – already tells us to expect something very different, a film which identifies with the Cubans' revolutionary spirit and aims to counter the misinformation about Cuba in the French media. In fairness, Leacock was both an old Communist and a member of the Fair Play for Cuba movement that sprang up in 1959 within the New Left in the United States. (The journalist K. S. Karol shared a table with him at the 'Fair Play for Cuba' meeting on the eve of Castro's UN address in 1960, where they met Fidel and the rest of the Cuban delegation; Cartier-Bresson was there and took photographs.) But *Yanki No!* is caught up by the limitations of the liberal ideology that dominated the solidarity movement and led the film-makers to compromise in the interests of getting the film made and seen.

Marker comes at the subject from an angle that repudiates the liberalism of the New Yorkers, but also comprises a very different kind of truth-telling to cinéma vérité à la Rouch and Morin. For one thing, he is not yet shooting with synchronous sound, and his style is that of the personally narrated travelogue which thinks in terms of montage; a choice which expresses his distrust of the institutional documentary stance of objective reportage which he'd already exploded with brilliant irony in several films, above all *Letter from Siberia*. Turning to Cuba, he again employs a whole range of materials, largely in function of what became available to him (the same approach to found material that Santiago Alvarez would develop in the newsreel department of the new Cuban film institute, ICAIC, and in the same spirit of politically committed irony). To the scenes he shot himself in January 1961, Marker adds photographic montages, collage animations and found footage from ICAIC's library, and two interviews, one with a revolutionary priest and one with Fidel Castro himself, supplied to him by the television reporters who had shot it for French television. Eschewing the conventional po-faced kind of solidarity film, he uses montage and commentary to question the way the events he chronicles are represented. His method is interrogative, inclusive and gently ironic, a point of view drawn out by the commentary, which teases us about Castro:

> Perhaps he is Robin Hood . . . Only that in this century taking from the rich to give to the poor does not necessarily mean attacking stage-coaches. And when Robin Hood has read Marx, when up in the mountains he is preparing the laws and reforms of the future republic . . .

– and here we get a snatch of a song about agrarian reform – 'the myth of Robin Hood is shattered. In its place a Revolution.' The film became a cause célèbre when the French censors banned it, the reasons given by the Minister of Information being three: it was not a documentary but 'an apologia for the Castro regime'; no film 'which is ideological propaganda can be authorised if only because of the risks this type of production entails for public order'; and the Cuban press frequently attacked the French administrations of Martinique and Guadeloupe, and it therefore 'does not seem suitable to offer a cinematographic hearing to Cuba's leaders'.[34] If the ban tells us of French government nervousness about its Caribbean territories in the year that Paris finally acceded to Algerian independence, the repetition of the television interview with Castro must have been particularly galling. For sixty years, says Castro, Cuba had to put up with the farce of a pseudo-democracy, and 'the French ought to be the first to understand: the French have an election almost every year . . . they can perfectly understand that political factions [and] electoralism have not solved a single one of France's fundamental problems'. Marker got round the ban by providing a new commentary full of the touristic clichés of an innocent travelogue, which enabled him to get an export visa, then sent the film to Belgium where the original commentary was restored.[35]

VI

French television took the plunge and invited leading practitioners of the new documentary to come together at a conference in Lyon in 1963, including Jean Rouch from France; Robert Drew, Richard Leacock and the Maysles brothers from the United States; and Michel Brault from Canada. The event was part of an international market of television programmes and equipment, arranged in collaboration with the research team of the French state broadcaster ORTF, headed by Pierre Schaeffer (the pioneer of *musique concrète*). Also present were two technicians: the Frenchman André Coutant, camera designer, and, from Switzerland, Stefan Kudelski, who designed the Nagra tape recorder. The line-up points to the variety of interests involved, but the event focused down to a fierce disagreement between two rival practices, personified by two contrasting practitioners, Rouch and Leacock, widely understood to be two camps with irreconcilable views. In certain measure, it was a clash of cultures and the philosophies informing them, the pragmatic empiricism of the North Americans against the dialectical subtlety of the French, but it also represented two opposed modes of relationship to the profilmic scene in front of the camera. The Americans argued, according to one report, that 'because they could now record actual events and sounds, they believed that anything else, including any sort of rehearsal or post-synchronisation, was immoral . . . If the material was not spontaneous, they said, how could it be true?'[36] The French position was that there was also truth in what the camera elicited by provocation. To show this interaction instead of hiding it produces a new form of documentary reflexivity, already fully present in *Chronique d'un été*. The markers of this reflexivity were intervention from behind the camera in earshot of the microphone, and the film-maker coming into view: 'we are speaking to you about this'. Direct Cinema, the Anglo-American, non-interventionist observational style defended by Leacock, is marked by the self-effacement of the camera and an attentive ear: 'Listen, this is telling you about itself.'

Rouch, for his part, believed they were all practising cinéma vérité, because not intervening, he said, is a way of intervening, adding that 'it is the very presence of the camera, when it is doing its mysterious work, that constitutes the kind of "provocation" that most interests us'.[37] Nevertheless, there seemed to be a difference, and Barnouw summed it up: Direct Cinema aspired to the camera's invisibility, cinéma vérité considered it a participant; in Direct Cinema, the film-maker played the role of uninvolved bystander, in vérité, that of *provocateur*. 'Direct Cinema found its truth in events available to the camera. Cinéma vérité was committed to a paradox: that artificial circumstances could bring hidden truths to the surface.'[38] But this is a little too neat, because Rouch is right, and the activity of filming is already an artificial circumstance. Indeed evidence for this can already be found in a number of mildly self-reflexive moments in *Lonely Boy*, the result of keeping in what the traditionally illusionist film would leave, as one used to say, on the cutting room floor. There is the scene, for example, where Anka enters his dressing room to find the film crew lurking there, stares hard at the camera for a moment, then tells his entourage to 'just forget they're even there', which is clearly addressed to himself as much as them. The signal this sends to the viewer is ambiguous. It not only draws attention to the invisible lens, but accentuates the ensuing scene, to impress on us, as Anka strips to his underpants in order to don his stage costume, the intimacy of backstage space – as if to say, 'Look, a little voyeurism – this is what you see when the camera takes you into private spaces.'

Moments like these reveal different facets of the profilmic situation, sometimes serving to draw attention to the camera and sometimes to the subject. They are often revealing because they catch the instant of transition in which a subject steps in and out of character, so to speak, crosses a boundary between different personae. In *Lonely Boy*, the nightclub owner asks the cameraman 'You want the waiters to move around a little bit?' and a little later, 'Is it alright if I light the cigar?'. The eagerness he displays to please the image-makers allows them later to give him a nudge when, at the end of Anka's engagement, he kisses the star on the cheek and a voice from behind the camera asks him to do it again. This is a piece of direct intervention which seems to break the rules of 'pure' observation, but the earlier moments are the kind of instances that occur spontaneously, and which often show in the smallest ways. (Like anyone who has filmed this way, I know from my own experience that, for example, someone being followed by a camera as they pass through a door will hold it open. And sometimes they address the situation directly. The choice is then whether to cut them out or keep them in, and why. On one occasion, we were stationed inside a car, waiting to take the conductor Pierre Boulez to a concert. He got in and dropped the scores cradled in his arms. As he bent down to retrieve them, he said 'Whoops, that was absolutely live, you know.' Of course I kept the shot in, because it was not just a self-reflexive marker but also communicated Boulez's sense of ease in front of the camera.)

The one thing that both positions agreed about was the active role of the cameraperson. In order to freely follow unfolding action, the director had to stop directing the camera – or become their own camera operator. There was, of course, a long tradition of the director-cameraman going back to early Flaherty and Ivens. This was also Rouch's practice until *Chronique d'un été*, when he chose to work with Brault. Flaherty and Ivens also worked with separate cinematographers in their later films, the cinematographer on Flaherty's *Louisiana Story* being none other than the young Leacock, fresh from serving his apprenticeship as an army newsreel cameraman during the war. What struck him, he later said, was the disparity between the two methods of filming: 'when we were using small cameras, we had tremendous flexibility, we could do anything we wanted, and get a wonderful sense of cinema'. The moment they had to shoot dialogue, everything had to be locked down, and the whole nature of the film changed. 'We could no longer watch things as they developed; we had to impose ourselves to such an extent upon everything that happened before us, that everything sort of died.' [39] And it made him furious. For years – the way he tells it in various interviews – he hankered after spontaneity and involvement. Hand-held 16mm sync finally eliminated the problem. It also upset the division of labour in studio camera departments between the camera operator and the director of photography, who is primarily concerned with the lighting. In documentary shooting, especially in available light, the elements of framing, composition, exposure and focus are all subject to the judgement of the eye at the viewfinder moving unrehearsed through the profilmic space. Several early directors of vérité films heaped praise on their cameramen. Chris Marker named his photographer Pierre Lhomme as co-director of *Le Joli mai*, of whom Mario Ruspoli wrote that

> it is completely staggering to see what he can extract from a take, the way in which he continually sculpts his characters, moving from one to another, drawing near and shifting away, forever selecting different angles, following each gesture, 'spotting' an expression here and there . . ..[40]

If this was the closest yet to Astruc's caméra-stylo, of writing with the camera, Leacock went further, arguing 'there will be no such thing as a cameraman; there'll be film-makers. There'll be no such thing as editors, there'll be film-makers. It'll become an integrated process.'[41] A prophecy that reached fruition around the end of the century in the form of digital video.

Here we also see the crucial difference between documentary space and the orchidean reality of the fiction film described by Benjamin. The camera operator in fiction shooting concentrates entirely on the space within the frame – nothing else is relevant precisely because the action is already designed to fit. The roaming documentary operator has to be aware of what is beyond the frame, the non-orchidean space that contains both the subject and the film crew in which they both move. The good documentary cameraperson shoots with both eyes open, and develop a technique for switching their attention from one to the other, so that they can always see where someone's looking, where they're moving towards, what they're pointing at, or who's approaching (which is also why they like mirrors, because they help them to see what's on their blind side). This is the style that is mimicked by any number of fiction films shot to simulate documentary, but here it risks turning into mannerism, because when the action is rehearsed and prepared, the result is that the camera movements are no longer in spontaneous dialogue with the activity in front of it. (To create the same spontaneity, you need a technique like that of Ken Loach, for example, who encourages his actors to improvise in the take, not just beforehand.)

Digital video produces a new relationship to space not only by being small and light and unobtrusive but also by using a small LCD screen for viewing as an alternative to the viewfinder. The image lacks the clarity and brightness of the viewfinder, but it means that the camera no longer has to be held up in front of the face. It is possible to see more of what's going on around about. The body with the camera is no longer cut off at the edge of the subject's space but becomes a person within it. The eye of the lens is replaced by the I of the documentarist, and both 'vérité' and 'direct' are subsumed in the new mode of first-person documentary cinema, investigative, essayistic, or autobiographical, which characterises our postmodern times.

Notes

1. Quoted in M. Ali Issari and Doris A. Paul, *What Is Cinéma Vérité?* (Metuchen, NJ: Scarecrow Press, 1979), pp. 7–8.
2. Lewis Jacobs, 'Documentary Becomes Engaged and Vérité' in Jacobs, ed., 1979, p. 376.
3. Edgar Morin, 'Chronicle of a Film', in Jean Rouch, *Ciné-Ethnography* (Minneapolis: University of Minnesota Press, 2003), p. 252.
4. Erik Barnouw, *Documentary* (Oxford: Oxford University Press, 1974).
5. D. A. Pennebaker's introduction to the book of his film *Don't Look Back* (New York: Ballantine Books, 1968); quoted in Louis Marcorelles, *Living Cinema: New Directions in Contemporary Film-Making* (London: Allen and Unwin, 1973), p. 25.
6. Issari and Paul, *What is Cinéma Vérité?*, pp. 6–7.
7. The first was a BBC2 Late Show Special (Tim Kirby, 1993), the second is *Cinéma Vérité: Defining the Moment* (Peter Wintonick, 1999).
8. Marcorelles, *Living Cinema*; Stephen Mamber, *Cinéma Vérité in America: Studies in Uncontrolled Documentary* (Cambridge, MA: MIT Press, 1974); Issari and Paul, *What is Cinéma Vérité?*.
9. See Michael Chanan, *Repeated Takes* (London and New York: Verso, 1995).
10. Brian Winston, *Technologies of Seeing* (London: BFI, 1996), pp. 78–9.
11. Brian Winston, *Claiming the Real* (London: BFI, 1995), p. 147.
12. Quoted in Marcorelles, *Living Cinema*, p. 19.
13. Pierre Perrault speaking to J.-L. Comolli and André Labarthe on the television programme *Pierre Perrault ou l'action parlée*, quoted in Marcorelles, *Living Cinema*, p. 26.
14. Ibid.
15. Jacques Derrida and Bernard Stiegler, *Echographies of Television* (Cambridge: Polity, 2002), p. 117.
16. Winston, *Technologies of Seeing*, p. 86.
17. Issari and Paul, *What is Cinéma Vérité?*, pp. 164–5.

18. Marcorelles, *Living Cinema*, p. 29.

19. In extras on the DVD release of the film from Docurama, 2003 <www.docurama.com>.

20. Paul Stoller, *The Cinematic Griot: The Ethnography of Jean Rouch* (Chicago, IL: University of Chicago Press, 1992).

21. Cf. Issari and Paul, *What is Cinéma Vérité?*, p. 68.

22. Rouch, *Ciné-Ethnography*, p. 164.

23. Rouch, *Ciné-Ethnography*, p. 166.

24. Gilles Deleuze, *Cinema 2: The Time-Image*, trans. Hugh Tomlinson and Robert Galeta (London: Athlone Press, 1989), pp. 152–3.

25. Régis Debray, *Prison Writings* (London: Penguin, 1975), pp. 176–9.

26. Rouch, *Ciné-Ethnography*; Issari and Paul, *What is Cinéma Vérité?*, pp. 153–4.

27. Brian Winston, 'Documentary: I Think We Are in Trouble', in Alan Rosenthal (ed.), *New Challenges for Documentary* (Berkeley, Los Angeles and London: University of California Press, 1988), p. 24.

28. Mamber, *Cinéma Vérité in America*, p. 30.

29. Macdonald and Cousins, *Imagining Reality* (Faber and Faber, 1996), p. 253.

30. Charles Musser, 'Extending the Boundaries, Cinéma-Vérité and the New Documentary', in Geoffrey Nowell-Smith (ed.), *The Oxford History of World Cinema* (Oxford: Oxford University Press, 1996), p. 528.

31. Quoted in Winston, *Claiming the Real,* p. 149.

32. Robert C. Allen and Douglas Gomery, *Film History: Theory and Practice* (New York: Knopf, 1985), p. 239.

33. Winston, *Claiming the Real*, p. 152.

34. 'Cuba Si!, Censor No!', trans. Garry Broughton, *Movie* no. 3 (October 1962), pp. 15–21.

35. Personal communication.

36. Mark Shivas, 'New Approach', *Movie* no. 8, April 1963, p. 13.

37. Quoted in Rothman, p. 87.

38. Barnouw, *Documentary*, p. 254.

39. Quoted in Issari and Paul, *What is Cinéma Vérité?*, p. 84, from Gideon Bachmann, 'The Frontiers of Realist Cinema: The Work of Ricky Leacock', *Film Culture* vols 19–23, Summer 1962, pp. 13–14.

40. Mario Ruspoli, *The Light-weight Synchronised Cinematograph Unit* (Paris: UNESCO, 1964), mimeograph, p. 24 (BFI Library).

41. Ian A. Cameron and Mark Shivas, Interviews, *Movie* no. 8, April 1963, p. 17.

1958: Karel Reisz (right) shooting *We Are the Lambeth Boys*

1960: Shooting *Primary* (Drew holding the microphone on the left)

1968: Shooting *Salesman* (Albert Maysles on camera, David Maysles as sound recordist)

LATIN AMERICA

1956: Cuba, filming *El Mégano*

1982: Nicaragua, INCINE
newsreel crew

1983: Mexico City, projector arriving for a screening in a shanty town

1985: Cuba, editing the
newsreel at ICAIC

1986: London, William Raban filming *Thames Film*. Raban still shoots on film twenty years later

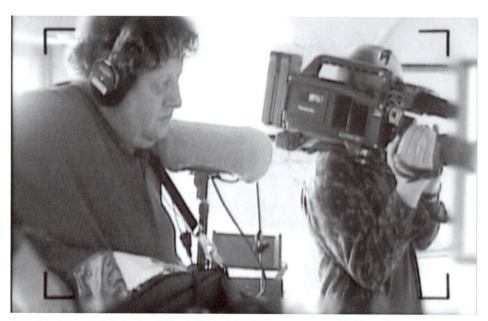

1999: Peter Wintonick (left) shooting *Cinéma Vérité: Defining the Moment*

2000: Washington DC, PBS cameramen at human rights event (left and middle)

2000: Washington DC, delegate at the same human rights event

Part III Contemporary Themes

11 Different Histories

Japan, Iran and Latin America

I

The impression given by the most common accounts is that up until the 1960s, and with one major exception, the art of documentary belonged in the West. It was found alongside the main centres of the film industry in Europe and North America (Canada as well as the US) – the heartlands of the First World. The exception was the Soviet Union, where pioneering films were made in the 1920s, but the creative quality of the form supposedly declined after the rise of Stalinism and the regimentation of public discourse (the same thing supposedly happened in Eastern Europe after World War II). This reading is seriously flawed. It is problematic because it represents an occidental perspective, similar to the way that the history of cinema as a whole is seen in terms of the Hollywood–Europe axis with everywhere else as the periphery. In this picture, documentary is dispersed across the Western heartlands, where it offers a marginal alternative to the narrative economy of the dominant industrial cinema. But while it's largely true that the West has historical primacy, the occidental view still reinforces a binary division of the world between centre and periphery which devalues documentary production growing up beyond these heartlands and diminishes the power of other perspectives to provide a more appropriate and decentred vision of the modern world. It is easy to see how this unbalanced purview comes about, because most documentary never circulated abroad, or only did so within the restricted sphere of the art film or political movements. But what is lost as a result is an aspect that underpins the documentary endeavour whatever the subject matter and wherever it is made and seen, namely, documentary as a form of negotiation of modernity and modernisation, of which the practice of documentary is itself an instance, at the same time as an indirect discourse on the process that produces it and the effects it brings.

Consider the case of Japan, which takes us back in film history because it already had one of the world's major film industries between the two world wars, with a lively amateur sector and a radical, anti-establishment documentary movement going back to the 1920s. Indeed, just as in the West, the documentary instinct in Japan goes back to the earliest days, since factual educational films began to appear in 1901, while the Russo-Japanese War of 1905 stimulated a wave of war reportage, and newsreels began around 1908 (although for some years their production was sporadic). But these roots developed unusual branches after World War I when the Ministry of Education entered the field of factual film production in the 1920s – perhaps the first peacetime, government-sponsored film production anywhere in the world bar the Soviet Union. By the time of the China wars in the 30s, a number of government ministries had film production units, a complex system of censorship was in place aimed mainly at documentary, and there was legislation requiring the screening, before the feature, of what were now called 'Culture films', after the German term *Kulturfilme*. The response from the left to this growing state propaganda was not long in coming, with the formation of the Proletarian Film League, known as Prokino, in 1929, a year before the Worker's Film and Photo League in the US. In short, the early documentary was firmly installed in the public sphere, where it played a highly ideological role, but in just the same way as Europe or the US, in a very unequal relationship between major sponsors and small independents, or in other words, the established rule of the State and political opposition.

This early history is unusual – and problematic – for a number of reasons. Outside the birthlands of cinema – the industrialised countries of Western capitalism – Japan was exceptional in its early creation of a domestic film industry, perhaps because it was the only other country apart from Russia where industrialisation had developed before 1914 to the point where it generated both the capital and the urban mass audience needed for a film industry to flourish. But if the question is why the Japanese government concerned itself with documentary film production so early, a parallel might be found in another forgotten episode recorded earlier in these pages, namely, the creation of an in-house production unit by the Ford Motor Company, which by the early 20s had become the largest producer of factual and educational films in the United States (which they practically gave away free). These (as we saw) were not just advertising films or patriotic tub-thumping, but also useful educational films about geography and agriculture and road safety. In other words, they answered to the perceived need of modern society for public information across a whole range of concerns, and from the point of view of a state or a corporation preoccupied with the modernisation of civil society – the Soviet Union is another example – the emergent documentary was regarded as a utilitarian form which mobilised the spectacle of the actual in favour of social conformity.

However, the early history of Japanese documentary also tells us about the susceptibilities of a militaristic government with imperialist ambitions and a deepening Fascist ideology, and how the very same forces of modernisation that encouraged this wave of production, proceeded to control and eventually destroy it. Government encouraged the industry, as did imperial expansion. Studios and production companies collaborated in running studios in Taiwan, Korea, the Philippines, Java, Shanghai and Manchuria, but as war dragged on, the government found it expedient to control scarce resources and potentially damaging content by consolidating and centralising this activity. Before the 1939 Film Law, says one account – a law which was modelled on Nazi legislation – there were between 200 and 300 documentary production companies in Japan; by the end of the war there were only four. 'This new, monolithic bureaucracy could easily control the flow of chemicals and raw film stock, enforce complicated and stifling censorship laws, and regulate the workplace to a startling degree.'[1]

Nonetheless, films would occasionally emerge that authority found troublesome, including more than one by Kamei Fumio, a prolific documentarist who had studied in the Soviet Union in the early 1930s and for whom Soviet cinema was indeed a model. Barnouw describes Fumio's feature-length *Shanghai* of 1937 – the first Japanese documentary with synchronous sound – as 'a film of fascinating ambiguity' in which, although it is not explicitly an anti-war film, Japanese officers describing their victory are intercut with scenes of devastation, the camera travelling 'over city ruins teeming with uprooted humanity', and graveyards of Japanese soldiers suggesting a higher price than news reports had been claiming.[2] Two years later he came out with *Fighting Soldiers* (*Tatakao heitai*, 1939), which instead of celebrating their bravery in combat showed the soldiers' physical exhaustion. Equally disconcerting, the film eschewed a narration but used intertitles to create what one writer calls 'a dissonance between the rhetoric of wartime ideals and the reality of devastation' in war-torn China.[3] The film was banned as a result, and Fumio was imprisoned as a Communist agitator, although not before he'd made a non-military film which nevertheless seemed to compound the offence. *Kobayashi Issa* (1941) was a commissioned film intended to promote local tourism which would later be acclaimed as a pioneering example of poetic documentary in Japan. Fumio turned it into a tribute to the nineteenth-century haiku poet Kobayashi by the simple device of using Kobayashi's poems on the soundtrack. The poetic images of the Nagano mountains and their farmers caught between nature and poverty are thus rendered into words, with evidently subversive effect, as 'Spring has come / but my happiness / is moderate', or 'Three things are important / here: the moon, Buddha, /and noodles', etc.[4]

The resurgence of Japanese documentary at the end of the war was both stimulated and hindered by the US occupation. On the one hand, the occupation poured money into the production of films intended to re-educate the population; they also supplied the 16mm projectors which would subsequently provide an infrastructure for the distribution of independent cinema. On the other hand, they interfered, and two major films were banned, the first being a project, under Prokino veteran Akira Iwasaki (who had also been imprisoned during the war), to document the effects of the atom bombs on Hiroshima and Nagasaki, which ran into trouble when one of its cameramen was arrested by US troops; the filming was allowed to continue under American supervision but the finished film was confiscated. When a copy of the negative that Iwasaki had hidden away subsequently came into the possession of the studio which legally owned it, he was refused permission to turn it back into a film (although a few feet were released to Alain Resnais for *Hiroshima mon amour* in 1959 and the studio itself issued an expurgated version). It would only properly reappear many years later when the Pentagon released the footage to a group of academics at Columbia University, including Erik Barnouw, who put it together in 1970 as *Hiroshima-Nagasaki, August 1945*.[5] The second case was Fumio's first postwar effort, *The Japanese Tragedy* (1946, produced by Iwasaki), which one account describes as a collage drawing on newsreels not only to expose the lies of the war-mongering government but also to demonstrate through analytic editing the manner in which Japanese newsreel and documentary makers had collaborated with the government in waging total war.[6] Apparently the film had so enraged the Prime Minister on duty, Shigeru Yoshida, that the Americans had obliged by withdrawing it from distribution (it reappeared many years later when a copy turned up at the US Library of Congress). Fumio would nevertheless continue to tackle problematic and political subjects, thus constituting a bridge to the new social and political documentary of the 1960s and 70s.

That little is known about this tradition in the West is a consequence of documentary's exclusion from international distribution, its marginalisation from both mainstream and, until recently, academic film culture, and the supposition, which accompanies and justifies this situation, that documentary somehow thrives best on local subjects and domestic issues which don't travel well. If this is patently untrue in a case like that of Fumio, it is also anyway only half the story. There are also practical and economic reasons, like the language barrier and the cost of versioning or subtitling, which could well be prohibitive for the independent distributors who might otherwise have taken the risk, but normally restricted themselves to festival winners. In postwar Britain, for example, the only foreign documentaries with any kind of circulation apart from rare birds like *The Picasso Mystery* (1956) or the underwater adventures of Jacques Cousteau, came from Russia and Eastern Europe, supplied through the cultural agencies and friendship societies which provided subtitled versions to independent distributors. In Britain, for example, there was Plato Films, an operation set up by the Communist Party precisely for this purpose which sent their films round schools, colleges and political groups. In this way, a couple of houses in North London ended up holding an extraordinary collection of historical film material from around the world, not only from the USSR and Eastern Europe but as far afield as China, Vietnam and Cuba, covering – always from a socialist point of view – events like the Spanish Civil War, the Nazi Holocaust, the Chinese Revolution, the Korean War, the Algerian War of Independence, the Cuban Revolution, the Chilean coup of 1973. Over the years, what started as a distribution library turned into an archive (which was also the repository for the films of the prewar British labour movement) to act as a source for television documentarists engaged in producing massive and sometimes revisionist television histories of the twentieth century, looking for different versions of history to incorporate into their own.

There are also other histories hidden in these film cans, which not only represent the global reach of the Communist movement, its scale and continuities, but also contain evidence of the movement's divisions and fissures. Searching the index cards you could find two films of the events in Czechoslovakia in 1968, one Russian, one Czech; the card for the latter has been marked 'this one not to be shown'. In fact there is a postwar history of documentary in Eastern Europe which is largely ignored, and goes counter to the general picture, namely, the rise of what were known as 'black films', a term that, according to Barnouw, originated in Poland in the mid-50s and then spread to Hungary, Czechoslovakia and Yugoslavia.[7] Black here is not pejorative (as in 'black propaganda') but simply the opposite of the 'rosy-hued booster films' of socialist realism; they were films, as another source puts it, 'which attacked problems that were not supposed to exist',[8] like juvenile delinquency, or housing problems, or prostitution – the subjects, respectively of three Polish documentaries, Jerzy Hoffman and Edward Skozewski's *Watch Out! Thugs!* (1955), Jerzy Bossak's *Warsaw 56* (1956) and W. I. Borowik's *Paragraph Zero* (1957). One notes that these developments took place not at the centre but on the periphery of the Soviet empire, where local cultural policies and imperatives had room to assert themselves, but it would be too easy to say that these films represent opposition to the system just because they push at the boundaries of permitted discourse: the same subjects were beyond the pale for television in the US in the same decade. In other words, on both sides of the Iron Curtain, documentary played a crucial role in forcing authority to publicly admit to social phenomena they would rather not acknowledge. It still does.

The 'black films' movement represents the revival of documentary as the investigation of social reality in peacetime in a similar but more politicised way to the impulse, for example, behind Free Cinema in England. It seeks the documentary subject that calls to it from social reality, not the office of the bureaucrat. Its appearance was facilitated by a combination of factors: the new and expanding postwar film industries of Eastern Europe with their film schools producing a new generation of film-makers, combined with degrees of post-Stalinist liberalisation of cultural policies. In Czechoslovakia the black documentary became part of the movement for a more democratic socialism that produced the Prague Spring. Barnouw mentions another film about juvenile delinquency, Kurt Goldberger's *Children without Love* (1964), because it produced a controversy that led to a shift in government policy. In Yugoslavia, an early exponent was Dušan Makavejev. Assigned to cover the May Day parade of 1963, he turned it into a satire on bureaucracy by filming the preparations rather than the event. Barnouw explains that 'Makavejev saw cinema as a "guerrilla operation . . . against everything that is fixed, defined, established, dogmatic, eternal" – which meant, for him, Stalinism and the Pentagon alike.'[9]

II

Implicit in the common picture I'm criticising, notwithstanding, is the wholly justifiable claim that documentary is associated with freedom of speech in the mass media of the modern public sphere (however imperfect the operation of the public sphere in the countries that proclaim themselves bastions of such freedoms). But in that case, what should interest us is precisely the expansion of documentary into new territories, especially after World War II where its appearance would signal new conditions for public speech. The film histories tell us little about these far-flung initiatives, but the erratic spread of documentary beyond the main centres of the film industry always reveals a process of struggle for the exercise of this right, everywhere contingent on local circumstances but part of the unequal process of modernisation around the globe. What happens is that the forms and strategies of modernisation adopted in different countries are placed in question by one of the primary and most potent instruments of communication introduced by the very process of modernisation itself.

Take the case of Iran, where the first films, dating from before the ill-fated Constitutional Revolution of 1906, were shorts made under the Shah's personal patronage by the court photographer, a pattern familiar in many other countries. Likewise the paradox noted by Hamid Naficy, that 'until 1930, when the first Iranian fiction feature film was made, Iranian cinema was entirely dominated by the production of nonfiction films'.[10] These films, sponsored and viewed by the royal family and the upper classes, created a model of a kind of 'private' cinema which remained aesthetically 'primitive', with no place in it for creative documentary vision. Nor were these conditions conducive to developing the economic and technical infrastructures (such as labs, technical training schools and regulations) necessary to support an indigenous film industry. The film pioneers, says Naficy, were educated abroad and connected to the ruling elite (though not always their supporters), and despite the appearance of commercial venues, cinema largely remained a diversion of the upper classes. Moreover, religious prejudice against cinema as a source of moral corruption of youth and women, along with other unwelcome Westernisations like novels, plays and popular music, played a constricting role (and continues to do so).

If these are signs of a society struggling to come to terms with what modernisation might mean (a struggle that has continued into the present century), Persia attracted foreign adventurers in search of the exotic like the North Americans Merriam C. Cooper and Ernest Schoedsack, who went there in 1925 to film *Grass*, a quasi-ethnographic travelogue of the annual migration of the nomadic Bakhtiari tribe from their winter grazing to their summer camps across the Zardeh Kuh mountains. That this seemingly innocent portrait of a primitive way of life – an example of an imaginary geography of the un-modern set against the civilisation from which the film-explorers set out – that this film was then banned from screening in Iran itself was not owing to discomfort about the way the nomadic people were represented, but the fact that they were represented at all: their presence on the screen was an offence to an authoritarian government engaged in a military campaign against the country's nomadic tribes in order to end the threat they represented to centralising state power, which was still at that stage the primary aim of the modernising regime. There is of course nothing about this within the film, which nevertheless becomes the locus of a set of contradictions pointing beyond itself to the historical world where its subject is located. In the film, the nomads struggle nobly against nature to sustain themselves. In reality, many tribes were being forcibly settled by government troops, and became impoverished as a result, while tribal uprisings against this policy were cruelly suppressed.[11] The image which simultaneously shows and hides the conditions of nomadic life is trace and mask at the same time, and perhaps this is precisely the measure of its documentary quality.

Early 1930s' German- and French-made documentaries about Iran were similarly displeasing to the regime, who responded by adopting a censorship law against the negative portrayal of the country. This refusal of the documentary image broke down with the coming of war, and the arrival of the cameramen accompanying the American, British and Russian troops who overran the country and forced the abdication of the Germanophile Shah. Their shorts, on political as well as military subjects, were shown in Iranian cinemas; the regime responded by setting up an Iranian Army film studio to produce their own propaganda. But while the postbellum saw the country's political radicalisation, there was still no proper infrastructure that would allow the emergence of a documentary film movement. To the state propagandists of the newly influential US, at a moment when they still had a naive belief in the power of film propaganda and were flush with funding, the conditions were not dissimilar to those of postwar Japan, and USIS, the United States Information Service, working with the local government, brought in forty mobile film units to take films to the villages and towns. However, since the object was to stimulate the production of suitable local propaganda, there was a difference. Japan had a reservoir of skill and tradition which Iran was lacking, for which the USIS came up with a novel solution: import a team of filmmakers recruited by a suitable US university (Syracuse) to set up a production facility, make films on subjects like Iranian geography, nutrition, sanitation and agriculture, and provide training for the locals. The results were far from spectacular, but at least opened up a space into which a new generation of film-makers would emerge in the 60s and 70s.

The new wave began to appear sporadically only after the overthrow of the secular nationalist Mossadeq in 1953, when the political circumstances were hardly the most favourable. Mossadeq's offence had been to challenge Western hegemony by nationalising the oil industry; his overthrow, and the return of the Shah, was engineered in Westminster and Washington, but while the Shah pursued a Westernising policy, it did not include the democratisation of the public sphere. On the other hand, it provided a space of operation for the country's public charitable institutions, who began to commission their own documentaries, sometimes battling with the censors to get them shown. Documentarists, says Naficy, were subject to a more incessant and direct form of censorship than their counterparts in the feature industry, which operated at all stages of production and limited the subject matter and its presentation.[12] The resulting films concerned themselves with Iran's past glories, traditional arts and crafts, and safe treatments of new institutions and modernisation. There are what Reza Poudeh calls the poetic documentaries by Ibrahim Golestan of the late 50s about the interaction of the oil industry and the environment, and a range of ethnographic films devoted to subjects like Islamic religious ceremonies, including the coexistence of different religions, and then the first signs of something more risky when Forough Farrokhzad, working with the Society for Assistance to Lepers, made The Home Is Dark in 1961, which Poudeh calls 'a sensitive and riveting work on the life of people with leprosy'.[13] Naficy explains that

Farrokhzad draws an analogy between the leper colony and Iranian society, a point not lost on the Iranian public, which rose up briefly in the early sixties to fight the malaise and corruption of the shah's regime. For its part, the government felt that Farrokhzad had presented a false and unnecessarily cruel picture and suppressed the film.[14]

The same fate befell a trilogy by Kamran Shirdel, returning from studies in Italy to make documentaries on the underprivileged and producing *Tehran Is the Capital of Iran*, *Women's Prison* and *Women's Quarter* for a women's organisation in 1965. There is no political or any other kind of rhetoric in these films, which combine a sociological sensibility with a quiet sense of compassion, and are anything but strident. With their black-and-white hand-held images and non-synchronous sound, they perform the task of making visible the downtrodden and giving them, if only briefly, a voice, like similar films in Latin America in the same period.

Two years later, Shirdel ran into trouble again for *Story of a Boy from Gorgan, or, The Night It Rained*. a film which is not only a completely unexpected departure for Iranian cinema but has very few precedents anywhere else – unless perhaps you go back to Buñuel's parody documentary *Las Hurdes*. Of all the films I've discovered in the course of writing this study, this one – which arrived by happy accident with Shirdel's 1965 trilogy in the form of a subtitled DVD from one of my students – is one of the most surprising and delightful of finds, a playful documentary satire on the condition of documentary. The film enacts the expedition of a film crew to investigate an incident which has hit the news, in which a teenage boy is said to have averted a catastrophic rail crash near the town of Gorgan, only to discover that the 'heroic' act may be in question. A conventional pretitle sequence sets up the story, ending with a mysterious shot of a voice declaring 'It's all a pack of lies, sir', over a close-up of a pairs of hands playing with prayer beads. The entry of the commentary introduces an oddity: instead of addressing the audience in the cinema, this voice addresses the head of the studio back in Tehran for whom the film is being made, by way of explanation for the confusing material they've come up with. They have filmed interviews with everyone involved they could find and present them in the order in which they found them (of which one result is that the boy himself comes late in the process). Several times Shirdel repeats the denial shot of the hands with the prayer beads, until finally the speaker and his companion are revealed as the fireman and engine driver of the alleged train, but it's too late to squelch the confusion. He also includes occasional shots of the film crew. Naficy sums up:

> Shirdel skilfully juxtaposes contradictory interviews with numerous people involved in the event. The viewer is faced with a bewildering range of accounts of what was done by whom and when. A salient comment on reality and perception, this film was banned for years before winning the 1974 Tehran International Film Festival as best short film.[15]

And then it was suppressed again. What is going on here is that the film plays into an ideological quagmire in which one ambiguity compounds the next, and of course this is maddening to authority. But the result is a deconstruction of the representation of truth.

Persheng Vaziri considers the film an antecedent of the playful tradition of docu-fiction later developed by Kiarostami and Makmalbaf, and draws out its sociological aspect:

Each person involved in the incident tells the version befitting his position in the hierarchy of power in Iran in the time of the Shah, when pomp and self-aggrandizement were the norm. In the end, the contradictions make us doubt if the boy ever saved the train, or even if there was a train at all, thus holding up a mirror to the absurdity of official 'truth'.[16]

In short, a relentlessly teasing film, which makes you suspect that reality cannot be grasped. It's too elusive, and not to be got at by such blunt instruments as the mass media, documentary included. But the problem isn't just the intractability of reality, so much as the character of the official regime of truth. Vaziri holds that 'Iran's long history of repression has blurred the line in artistic production between reality and fiction: true and made-up stories, fact and myth are easily interchangeable to fit circumstances and appease authorities.' *Story of the Boy from Gorgan* is at the beginning of this discovery, which feeds into the playful ambiguities of later Iranian cinema, especially the work of Kiarostami. But this isn't just what happens in Iran, and what *the Boy from Gorgan* shows is that the most local of subjects has resonance for all of us.

III

In Latin America, the early flowering of the documentary instinct that we noted earlier in the case of Mexico during the Revolution, was exceptional, the result of opportunity, initiative and a brief absence of repressive authority. Cinema spread through Latin America quite rapidly, and the earliest films were mostly taken by European immigrants or residents (the gringos tended not to penetrate very far south, where European immigration was at its height, and in Argentina and Brazil the pioneers were French and Belgian, Austrian and Italian.) The varying dates of these first films – 1896 in Mexico, 1897 in Cuba, Argentina and Venezuela, 1898 in Brazil and Uruguay, 1902 in Chile, 1905 in Colombia, 1906 in Bolivia, 1911 in Peru – reflect the geography of underdevelopment in a period when urban development was concentrated on the coasts and ready access petered out as you went inland. Film followed the routes of commerce. In the novel by Gabriel García Marquez, *One Hundred Years of Solitude*, it arrives in the town of Macondo with the same trains that bring the United Fruit Company. Early films were the usual actualities: they picture official ceremonies and presidents, with their families and entourages; military parades and naval manoeuvres; traditional festivities and tourist scenes, including views of city architecture, picturesque landscapes and pre-Colombian ruins. The Brazilian film historian Paulo Emilio Salles Gomes reckoned that the work of the first Latin American *cineastas* was roughly divided between depicting 'the splendid cradle of nature' and 'the ritual of power'.[17] He also affirms the intimate connection between cinema and modernisation when he remarks that if cinema didn't take root in Brazil for about a decade after its introduction, 'it was due to our underdevelopment in electricity. Once energy was industrialised in Rio de Janeiro, exhibition halls proliferated like mushrooms' and production soon reached 100 films a year.

The subsequent evolution of cinema as a commercial institution under the aggressive tutelage of Hollywood, which was not auspicious for documentary anywhere, was compounded in Latin America by the terms and conditions of underdevelopment, which stunted growth and resulted in the development of domestic film industries in the three largest countries only, Mexico, Brazil and Argentina, and even these were plagued by structural weakness and weak access to their own markets. Early documentary in Europe was succoured by the first art houses and the film society movement, both emerging in the 1920s; these did not appear in Latin America (apart from Brazil) until somewhat later (the 1940s in Uruguay and Argentina, the 50s in countries like Chile, Bolivia and Cuba). The Soviet or Japanese models were out of the question, nor were there any agencies, para-governmental or corporate, interested in developing 16mm distribution of sponsored or educational documentary, as happened, for example, in Britain, where a strong documentary movement grew up in the 1930s as a result. Throughout the silent period and beyond – until the rise of a new film movement in the 1950s – Latin American documentary was confined to minor examples of conventional subgenres like the travelogue or the scientific documentary.

A singular example from 1930s' Mexico points in another direction. *Redes* (Nets, aka The Wave, 1934), which Sadoul calls a semi-documentary, was shot on location in a fishing village on the Gulf of Mexico with non-professional actors enacting a story taken from contemporary life – the struggle of the fishermen against poverty and exploitation. A film commissioned by government to demonstrate the potential for Mexican sound cinema, it carries an impressive score by Silvestre Revueltas which sometimes turns up in the concert hall. The script was written by a progressive politician of the day called Velásquez Chávez, who was in charge of public education under President Cardenas, and who invited an international team to make it, including the cinematographer Paul Strand and, as co-director, Fred Zinnemann, a refugee from Nazi Germany working his way to Hollywood. Zinnemann brought his experience as assistant director on the landmark German film *Menschen am Sonntag* (1930). In swapping the Berlin petit bourgeoisie for Mexican fishermen, *Redes* articulates a radical political critique which may have been just a little much even for a progressive government; at any rate the initiative was never followed up. The script provides a highly intelligent synthesis of popular political discourse and cultural symbolism. In an idiosyncratically Mexican way, the narrative is enclosed between two deaths – that of a child at the beginning, and his father at the end. But the drama is also unified by a metaphor about the fishermen and the fish which is visually articulated in the montage, and then comes up in verbal form, translated into the dialogue: '*El tiburón siempre le pega el róbalo*' – 'the shark always gets the fish', a very Brechtian message. Strand, in order to represent the reality of the location with documentary accuracy, first undertook a photographic study of the village, which he used to construct a visual elaboration of the script. The cinematography discovers an epic quality in its visual discourse which resonates with echoes of Eisenstein's cinematographer Edouard Tissé, and chimes with other films that celebrated the dignity of labour, like Grierson's much less political *Drifters*. It also presents us with a paradox – a film which at the same time is both experimental in its iconoclasm, and in its visual idiom, a classical narrative. In sum, an extraordinary piece of neorealism *avant la lettre*, and precursor of what will later become a major tendency of politically committed film-making in every corner of Latin America.

The work of the Brazilian Humberto Mauro is also exceptional – first of all in its extent: after a number of features in the early part of his career, he made over 200 documentary shorts as the director of INCE, the National Institute of Educational Cinema. Here he developed a lyrical, plastic and poetic visual discourse to depict various aspects of Brazilian geography and popular culture, like the landscape series *Brasilianas*, made between 1945 and 1956, in a style that gives the feel of something both slightly idealised and highly authentic. According to Paulo Antonio Paranagua, Mauro was an advocate of documentary as a serious aesthetic and ethical alternative to commercial cinema, speaking of it already in the 1940s as a more viable form for an authentic national cinema than the industrial model of the studios.[18] The studios were highly imitative of foreign models, documentary was a low-cost means of producing authentic films with nothing more than a camera, a tripod and a light-meter. But INCE remained unique, and the emergence of the Latin American social documentary twenty years later marks the appearance of a new generation of film-makers, who benefited from the new economic and political conjuncture following World War II. In a new wave of modernisation, the US now extended its presence in the expanding domains of radio and television, and embarked on a drive to open up markets among the Latin American bourgeoisie for the appurtenances of the 'American way of life'; these naturally included amateur cine, for which official Washington publications like *World Trade in Commodities* recorded increasing sales in several countries. The spread of film clubs and magazines, art houses and festivals was part of this process of cultural modernisation, but produced a sting: the new generation rejected both what they saw as the cultural imperialism of the gringos and the crass commercialism of local film industries, where they existed, which together prevented the emergence of authentic autochthonous voices. Some looked to new film movements in Europe for inspiration. Several of the pioneers – Fernando Birri, Tomas Gutiérrez Alea, Julio García Espinosa among them – had taken themselves to Italy to study cinema in Rome, returning with the ideals of both neorealism and the social documentary, which they would adapt to the state of affairs they found back home, the social, economic and political undertow in the sight of immediate reality. Concrete results were few and far between, but they were often highly original. In Mexico, Carlos Velo made *¡Torero!* (1956), a partly dramatised account of the career of the matador Luís Procuña, in which Procuña plays himself, and from Venezuela came an extraordinary film of poetic realism, depicting everyday life in the feudal salt marshes, called *Araya*, by Margot Benacerraf (1959).

Other initiatives turned on the autochthonous. Another singular example is *Kukuli*, the first film to be spoken in Quechua, dating from 1961 – a film from the margins of the margins, the ancient Inca city of Cuzco in the interior of Peru, where a film club was set up in 1955 by the photographer Manuel Chambi, whose members had already made a number of short documentaries on ethnographic and sociocultural themes before this more ambitious piece – Sadoul called them the Cuzco School. Directed by Luis Figueroa, who studied film in Paris, the background influence here is the French tradition of *photogénie*, applied to an indigenous legend which is enacted for the camera by non-professional actors in a naturalistic style and setting. The legend tells of a confrontation between a *campesino* and an *ukulu* – a mythological bear – over their love for the same woman, which in this version reaches its tragic climax at a boisterous fiesta, where the bear is one of the masked dancers. The film is remarkable for both its visuals and its soundtrack; the beauty of its colour cinematography makes the most of the spectacular Andean landscape and then takes us right into the music and dance of the fiesta. Since it was filmed mute, a few snatches of dialogue in Quechua have been post-synchronised, together with intermittent commentary in Spanish, delivered in the style of an ethnographic documentary, and a feast of music, consisting of both an orchestral score and location recording of the fiesta music, matched to the image by brilliant editing. The result is a film that indeed has the values of the ethnographic document (the fiesta is the genuine article, filmed in the town of Paucartambo) which nevertheless is not exactly a documentary, but since the legend is not a fiction invented by the film-makers, but a living tissue in the documented ethnographic world, not simply fictive either.

The Cuzco School were not unique, but represented a growing desire found throughout the continent for cultural self-expression beyond the bounds that were sanctioned by the ruling creole elites. Several such groups were linked to social movements which espoused leftist and Marxist principles, like the cultural club Nuestro Tiempo run by the Young Communists in Havana in the 50s, which harboured several future Cuban film-makers. The first international meeting place for the young film-makers was a film festival in Montevideo, set up in 1954 by the SODRE, Uruguay's national radio station and a progressive cultural promoter. Among the film-makers attending in 1958, when John Grierson was the guest of honour, were Chambi from Peru and Birri from Argentina. The film exhibited by Birri and his students, *Tire Die* (Throw us a dime), a collaborative social enquiry into the shanty towns around the city of Santa Fe, later came to be celebrated as the founding social documentary of the new film movement. The title echoes the refrain called out by the shanty-town kids at their favourite sport, running alongside the train which crawls slowly across the nearby bridge, as they beg for a coin.

The designation of this movement as *el nuevo cine latinoamericano* (the New Latin American Cinema) dates from a meeting of film-makers from across the continent in the Chilean seaside town of Viña del Mar in 1967, hosted by a Catholic film club which started a small film festival for aficionados in 1963. Documentary, for this movement, leftwing but non-sectarian from the outset, was far from marginal, because it embodied the imperative to turn the cameras on the actuality of the social world, to escape the distorted imagery of the dominant cinema's imaginary. But now, fiction cinema became inflected by the same impulse, and there is a long list of dramatic films, from Nelson Pereira dos Santos in Brazil in the 1950s, by way of Jorge Sanjinés working in Bolivia, Peru and Ecuador in the 60s and after, to the recent work of Víctor Gaviria in Colombia, which represent the persistent pull that the documentary instinct and its disciplines have exercised on the Latin American fiction film. As for documentary proper, among the films shown at Viña in 1967 were no less than seventeen from Brazil, where film-makers had been stimulated by the arrival of Birri and several of his associates, who had been forced to flee Argentina. Benefiting from more up-to-date equipment, Brazilian documentary established a particularly strong line in political reportage, exemplified by films like Leon Hirszman's *Maioria Absoluta* (1963) and Geraldo Sarno's *Viramundo* (1964), on illiteracy and internal migration in Brazil respectively. A distinctive feature of these films is the dissolution of the authoritative monologue of voice-over narration in favour of the dialogical juxtaposition of different speakers, which allows the film-maker to apply a dialectical, and hence highly politicised, interpretation of the subject matter. *Viramundo*, for example, constructs a montage of multiple voices that contrasts the aspirations of peasants from the drought-ridden North-East who migrate to São Paulo in search of work with what they find when they arrive there.

Elsewhere, however, sync cameras were still relatively rare, and the documentarist had to find other means to construct a soundtrack which displaces the voice of authority. Here an exemplary film is the Uruguayan Mario Handler's *Carlos: Cine-retrato de un caminante* (Carlos: Cine-Portrait of a Walker, 1965), which combines patiently filmed images of a vagabond's everyday life with his own account of his life which Handler recorded after the filming. Through the exemplary aesthetic construction of the subjectivity of an individual discarded by society, the film demonstrates another fundamental impulse of the new documentary, that of giving voice and image to those who have been condemned to silence and invisibility. In this way, Latin American documentary shared the aim defined by the radical Christian educationalist Paulo Freire as breaking 'the culture of silence' to which underdevelopment condemned the subaltern classes – Freire's term for the condition of ignorance, political powerlessness, backwardness, misery, dehumanisation and lack of means of expression of the popular masses.

Freire argued that human self-knowledge is only possible because human beings are capable of objective distance from the world they live in, and 'only beings who can reflect upon the fact that they are determined are capable of freeing themselves'.[19] Documentary, in this perspective, is not the simple reflection of reality, but an act of reflection upon it, first by the film-maker and then by the audience. As long as it remains dialogically oriented, it thereby contributes to the burgeoning of political self-awareness which Freire calls *concientización*, a term roughly equivalent to consciousness-raising in English, which comes about 'because human consciousness, although conditioned, can recognise that it is conditioned'. The result can even be a double unveiling, because '[j]ust as there is a moment of surprise among the masses when they begin to see what they did not see before, there is a corresponding surprise among the elites in power when they find themselves unmasked'. The urgent task of documentary is this act of unmasking.

IV

Among the films on show at Viña in 1967 were several from Cuba. If the politicisation of the 60s received a strong fillip from the Cuban Revolution, Cuban documentary contributed powerfully to the tendency to combine explicit political content with an experimental aesthetic, above all in the work of Santiago Alvarez, who reinvented the newsreel, the compilation film, the travelogue and every other documentary genre he laid hands upon in an irrepressible frenzy of filmic bricolage licensed by that supreme act of bricolage, the Cuban Revolution. Unique in Latin America in the status it awarded to its own cinema, Cuba was the one country in the subcontinent where local documentaries were widely seen in the cinemas, since distribution was run by a state film institute (ICAIC, or Cuban Institute of Film Art and Industry) created within months of the Revolution taking power in 1959. The Institute set out to supply its own documentaries and a weekly newsreel along with every feature film, foreign or domestic, which it distributed. Newsreel and documentary became the requisite form of apprenticeship for new directors, a crucial schooling in direct encounter with a rapidly changing reality which fed into their subsequent fiction films.

The Institute was the brainchild of Alfredo Guevara, a close political friend of Fidel Castro from student days and a kind of Cuban Grierson, who had worked for a time in Mexico in the 1950s as an associate producer with Buñuel. I have written in detail elsewhere about the political battles he fought in these early years against both old Communists and young liberals to defend the autonomy of the ICAIC.[20] When matters came to a head in 1961, the trigger was a short independent documentary called *P.M.*, which the Institute, to the ire of the liberals, refused to distribute, even though it had been shown on television already. The director, Sabá Cabrera Infante (brother of the novelist) had been making short films for television for several years and was now a television news editor. According to the film's photographer, Orlando Jiménez Leal, *P.M.* was intended to show a different Havana from the bellicose city preparing to resist an invasion,[21] and the film they turned out is a wordless Free Cinema-style depiction of nocturnal Havana, its bars and boleros, which unfortunately also meant, as Guevara put it, 'the drunks, the small cabarets where prostitution was still going on, where there was still drug trafficking', and which he likened to the world of *On the Bowery* – except that here the lumpenproletariat in the film were mostly black.[22] In the meantime, of course, the invasion took place, not in Havana but the Bay of Pigs, only to be thwarted in three days flat, after Castro, on the eve of the attack, had for the first time declared the socialist character of the Cuban Revolution. In these heady circumstances, when the ICAIC turned *P.M.* down for the cinemas because they saw as it racist, everyone overreacted, and the resulting commotion led to a meeting where Fidel Castro, after listening to the arguments, gave the speech of his known as 'Words to the Intellectuals', where he encapsulated the cultural position of the Revolution in the phrase, 'Within the Revolution, everything, against it, nothing'.[23]

If rarely has a short documentary enjoyed such an enormous impact on the public sphere, *P.M.* nonetheless disappeared. (It would resurface only many years later, in the year 2000, under the closing credits of *Before Night Falls*, Julian Schnabel's film about the émigré Cuban writer Reinaldo Arenas.) All the benefit was reaped by the ICAIC, which was henceforth protected by Castro's formula from the discomfort of the hardliners of the left as the euphoria of revolution imbued the Institute's films with an experimentalist aesthetic. No one was more audacious than Alvarez, who headed the newsreel section, which he turned by his own example into a school of militant documentary and a training ground in how to make films quickly and cheaply. Alvarez was not only the man who put Cuban documentary on the world map, but also one of the most innovative and prolific documentarists in the history of cinema. Plunging into production in a small underdeveloped country meant employing whatever means and resources were available, and Alvarez, who once called himself a product of 'accelerated underdevelopment', became a master in the use of found material. Newsreel footage, photographs, cuttings from newspapers and magazines, clips from Hollywood movies and cartoons, in short, an eclectic mix of every kind of visual imagery, is typically combined in an Alvarez film of the 60s into a fast-paced montage, wherein, guided by a dynamic graphic sensibility, Alvarez amalgamates revolutionary politics and artistic kleptomania to reinvent Soviet montage in a Caribbean setting. The effect is completed by eschewing the verbosity of commentary in favour of short animated texts, and emblematic musicalisation. Alvarez had worked before the Revolution as a record librarian in a television station, and he now developed a keen sense of the possibilities of matching – and mismatching – music and images. In *Cerro Pelado* (1966) – the name of the ship taking Cuban athletes to the Pan-American Games in Puerto Rico in 1966 – shots of a training camp for Cuban counter-revolutionaries are juxtaposed with a band arrangement of Rossini's 'William Tell Overture', which naturally recalls the use of the same piece as the title music of the television series *The Lone Ranger* (1949–57), perfectly familiar to Cuban audiences; thus Alvarez presents the counter-revolutionaries as imitation cowboys, in an image which the music renders both satiric and deflating.

When Alvarez's films began to circulate abroad, and film critics began to compare them to the work of Vertov, it emerged that Alvarez hadn't seen any. When he finally did so, and of course recognised the similarities, he could only explain them as a consequence of an historical parallel: the discovery of cinema in both countries in and through the revolutionary process.[24] Politically speaking an orthodox Fidelista – he has been described as Fidel Castro's poet laureate for his loving film portrayals of the Cuban leader – his filmic style was anything but conventional. Perhaps it was the anarchist susceptibilities in his political background that gave his aesthetics their particular slant – a healthy disapproval of schools, conventions and orthodoxy, together with a penchant for the deployment of pithy, intelligent and often didactic montage. These susceptibilities rapidly induced him to discard the conventional piecemeal language of the newsreel, and turn the format inside out. Instead of an arbitrary sequence of disconnected items, Alvarez joined them up into a single political argument, or turned them into single-topic documentaries. He used this technique in the first of his films to win international awards, *Ciclón* (Hurricane, 1963) and *Now* (1965). *Ciclón* was an extended newsreel about a hurricane and the subsequent clear-up operations (personally directed in the field by Fidel) which dispenses with the usual commentary to present a fluid visual narrative that speaks for itself. In *Now*, the commentary is replaced by a song, while the visuals consist entirely of found materials. This is Lena Horne singing a militant call for black liberation, written by the lyricist Adolph Green (rather oddly to the tune of 'Hava Nagila'), which was banned by many US radio stations. Alvarez pins the song onto a powerful collage of racial discrimination in the United States, and thus invents the music video several years ahead of its time.

In 1967 came *Hanoi Martes 13* (Hanoi, Tuesday 13th), a lyrical portrayal, sans commentary, of what daily life was like in war-torn North Vietnam (here the music was an original score in a modern idiom by Leo Brouwer, who was emerging as Cuba's most original film composer). Then comes *LBJ* (1968), a stunning satire on political assassination in the US (the Kennedy brothers and Martin Luther King) with a *mélange* of music from Carl Orff to Miriam Makeba, where Alvarez's penchant for the montage of found material unqualified by commentary reaches entirely beyond the normal premises of the documentary as a veridical report on some aspect of reality. Accusations by unsympathetic critics that the film is nothing but the expression of Marxist hysteria about conspiracy entirely miss the point of a film that wants to show the contradiction of a country which claims allegiance to democracy but is gripped by gun law. A year later there is *79 Primaveras* (79 Springs, 1969), a deeply poetic tribute to the Vietnamese leader Ho Chi Minh, where Alvarez uses techniques more associated with experimental film than with documentary. The climax is a split-screen, multi-image sequence of war footage, freeze frames, scratches, loose sprocket holes, flashes, guns, planes, bombs, sounds of battle with electronic synthesiser noises on the soundtrack, in which brutal reality bursts through the limits of its portrayal on celluloid in an unrelenting and terrifying assault that ends in the annihilation of a freeze frame, which burns up before our eyes leaving a blank white screen. These are the films by which Alvarez became known abroad, but he applied the same aesthetic bravado to those which dealt with domestic topics, which were sometimes even bolder in their aesthetic strategies; like *Despegue a las 18:00* (Take off at 18:00, 1969), which confronted the failures of the Cuban economy – the queues at the foodshops and the despondency of 'No hay!' – 'There isn't any!' – with images of a kind that we were always told were never publicly shown in Communist countries, and without any preachy commentary to take their sting away.

Alvarez's films were hugely popular. Researchers from the ICAIC would find that people sometimes went to the movies because they wanted to see the new Alvarez, and would then stay and watch whatever feature was put on after it – a complete inversion of normal cinemagoing behaviour. And it wasn't only Alvarez. A stream of inventive, intelligent documentary shorts came from a bevy of young directors, like Pastor Vega, Sara Gómez and Sergio Giral. A few examples, almost at random: Vega's *Hombres del cañaveral* (Men of Sugar, 1965) is an observational study of a brigade of voluntary workers from the city at work in the sugar harvest, with a meticulous camera and no commentary. *La muerte de J. J. Jones* (The Death of J. J. Jones, 1966), Giral's satirical portrait of a GI in Vietnam, is a found material montage with a highly inventive soundtrack which dissects and dismembers the imagery of consumer society, the mass media, the movies, comics, he-men of the Mr Universe type, a patriotic army commercial. Like *LBJ*, it skirts the edges of the conventional documentary. Gómez's *Ire a Santiago* (I'm Going to Santiago, 1964) is a fond and gentle portrait of her home city, Santiago de Cuba, shot in Free-Cinema style with the addition of music and an informal first-person commentary (and in fact an early example of a kind of first-person essay style which would later become common everywhere). She followed it with shorts on music and sociopolitical themes, including reform schools for delinquent youth, where she always foregrounds the experience of women and black people. If Gómez is ready to mobilise her own unusual personality as a black woman with a camera, one of her great talents as a documentarist is the informal interview technique which enables her to gain the trust of her subjects, drawing out of them stories and reflections which go far beyond the usual, and often raise social issues from unusual angles. In her film about the people of the Isle of Pines, *En la otra isla* (On the Other Island, 1967), a young man speaks of his experience of racism as a black singer in Havana eager to sing in opera. A two-shot of the both of them, sitting very relaxed in the open air, ends with him voicing his inmost desire, asking his interviewer, 'Sara, do you think one day I'll sing *Traviata*?'. Her first feature, *De cierta manera* (One Way or Another, 1977), sadly also her last film because of her early death, is a striking experiment in the cross-fertilisation of fiction and documentary, where fictional characters are combined with social actors in a popular Havana neighbourhood, with the interpolation of conventional documentary sequences with commentary, to portray the challenges of the revolutionary process.[25]

The result was a paradox: Cuba, where supposedly the public sphere had been replaced by the totalitarian control of the Communists, nonetheless maintained a space on the cinema screen for a vivid documentary encounter with social reality which was not so easily found on the principal screens of the democracies, where commercial criteria drove them out. Indeed, with the growing control exercised by the ruling Communist Party over the press and broadcasting, the film institute's autonomy allowed it to take a position not unlike that of Grierson, 'a little to the left of whoever is in power', or in this case, a little to the left of what anyone else was allowed to say. Doubtless because of its privileged relation to the source of power and authority, Cuban cinema became a unique cultural space as a major site of public discourse within the Communist state, a kind of surrogate public sphere, in which documentary occupied a key position. Occasionally someone went too far, and a few films, including documentaries, were either not approved for production or else withheld from exhibition. This happened to Sara Gómez, but the most unfortunate case, which I mention here to make amends for omitting it in my book on Cuban cinema, was that of Nicolás Guillén Landrián, who had already made ten films before he came undone with *Café Arábica* in 1968 and, sad to say, subsequently fell prey to mental illness. Landrián took his cue from Alvarez's montage style but gave it a more personal inflection, both lyrical and quirky.

Café Arábica uses highly inventive montage and a vertiginous narrative rhythm to celebrate a government coffee-growing campaign with pricks of gentle satire; it was withdrawn because of the offence
caused by the juxtaposition of the image of Fidel Castro and The Beatles' song, 'The Fool on the Hill' –
at a time when The Beatles were briefly banned in Cuba.

The paradox remains, and both documentary and the 'documentarised newsreel' continued to
occupy a privileged position within Cuban cinema until the economic collapse at the start of the 1990s.
It is possible to see the ICAIC as occupying the same relationship to the state as the BBC in Britain – a
major part of the cultural apparatus which is allowed to operate at arm's length from power, trusted to
run itself except in moments of crisis when the state intervenes, but generally free to experiment in the
full glare of its public (which the BBC also once used to do). But the conditions in Cuba were always
fluid. As Ambrosio Fornet, a literary historian and a scriptwriter of both fiction and documentary,
summed up in the late 1990s: 'the "everything" permitted is not a permanent right but an arena of conflict that must be renegotiated every day, with no quarter granted to the bureaucracy and with the temptation of irresponsible whimsy firmly resisted'.[26]

Notes

1. Abé Mark Nornes, 'Japan', in Ian Aitken (ed.), *Encyclopedia of the Documentary Film* (Abingdon and
    New York: Routledge, 2006), p. 672; see also Abé Mark Nornes, *Japanese Documentary Film*
    (Minneapolis: University of Minnesota Press, 2003).
2. Erik Barnouw, *Documentary* (Oxford: Oxford University Press, 1974), p. 129.
3. Michael Arnold, 'Fighting Soldiers', <www.midnighteye.com/reviews/fightsol.shtml>.
4. Quoted in Barnouw, *Documentary*, pp. 129–30.
5. See Erik Barnouw, 'Iwasaki and the Occupied Screen', in Kevin Macdonald and Mark Cousins (eds),
    Imagining Reality (London and Boston, MA: Faber and Faber, 1996), pp. 182–98.
6. Nornes in Aitken, *Encyclopedia of the Documentary Film*, pp. 672–3.
7. Barnouw, *Documentary*, pp. 262–3.
8. Frank Bren, *World Cinema I: Poland* (London: Flicks Books, 1986), p. 48.
9. Barnouw, *Documentary*, p. 266.
10. Hamid Naficy, 'Iranian Cinema', in G. Nowell-Smith (ed.), *The Oxford History of World Cinema* (Oxford:
    Oxford University Press, 1996), p. 672.
11. Nikki R. Keddie, *Modern Iran: Roots and Results of a Revolution* (New Haven, CT: Yale University Press,
    2003), p. 91.
12. Hamid Naficy, 'Iranian Documentary', *Jump Cut* no. 26, December 1981, pp. 41–6,
    <www.ejumpcut.org/archive/onlinessays/JC26folder/IranDocy.html>.
13. Reza Poudeh, 'Iran', in Aitken, *Encyclopedia of the Documentary Film*, p. 633.
14. Naficy, 'Iranian Documentary'.
15. Naficy, 'Iranian Documentary'.
16. Persheng Vaziri, 'Between Reality and Fiction: Iranian Documentary Cinema', *The Iranian*, 27 August
    2003, <www.Iranian.com/Arts/2003/August/Vaziri/>.

17. Paulo Emilio, Salles Gomes, *Cinema: trajetória no subdesenvolvimento*, in *Cinema: trajetória no subdesenvolvimento* (Rio de Janeiro: Editorial Paz e Terra/Embrafilme, 1980). An incomplete translation is included in Randal Johnson and Robert Stam (eds), *Brazilian Cinema* (Toronto: Associated University Presses, 1982).

18. Paulo Antonio Paranagua, 'Orígenes, evolución y problemas', in P. A. Paranagua (ed.), *Cine Documental en América Latina* (Madrid: Cátedra, 2003), pp. 30–1.

19. Paulo Freire, *Cultural Action for Freedom* (Harmondsworth: Penguin, 1972), pp. 52ff.

20. Michael Chanan, *Cuban Cinema* (Minneapolis: University of Minnesota Press, 2004).

21. Obituary for Sabá Cabrera Infante, Miami, *El Nuevo Herald*, 30 May 2002, <www.cubanet.org/Cnews/y02/may02/30o1.htm>.

22. Chanan, *Cuban Cinema*, p. 133.

23. Fidel Castro, 'Words to the Intellectuals', in Lee Baxandall (ed.), *Radical Perspectives in the Arts* (Harmondsworth: Penguin, 1972), pp. 267–99.

24. Quoted in Miguel Orodea, 'Alvarez and Vertov', in Michael Chanan (ed.), *Santiago Alvarez*, BFI Dossier no. 2, 1980.

25. A full account of this and other Cuban documentaries can be found in Chanan, *Cuban Cinema*.

26. Ambrosio Fornet, 'Introduction' A. Fornet (ed.), *Bridging Enigma: Cubans on Cuba*, Special Issue of *South Atlantic Quarterly* vol. 96 no. 1, Winter 1997, pp. 11–12.

12 Living History

Latin America in the 1970s

I

The rightwing authoritarianism of established rule in much of Latin America during much of the Cold War, reaching from Mexico's frozen revolution to the neofascist military dictatorships Brazil, Argentina and Chile, often had the counter-intentional effect of stimulating autonomous activity among those it held down. Across the continent, under regimes of different types, popular organisations grew up at community level, especially in the shanty towns, to deal with the problems of inadequate housing, water and electricity supplies, food distribution and health care, encouraging popular democracy among those neglected by the state, and sometimes becoming the locus for resistance to military repression. Film-makers, seeing these organisations as the natural audience for their work, created alternative exhibition circuits using portable 16mm equipment, on the rural model established in the 60s in Bolivia by the Ukamau collective, or the urban form of independent distribution collectives like Zafra in Mexico. In the early 80s, when I made a documentary for Channel 4 about cinema in Latin America, we filmed screenings of this type in three different countries. In Mexico City, we accompanied the Zafra people to a shanty town for a Sunday afternoon screening of a Chilean film from 1968 (*El chacal de Nahueltoro*, The Jackal of Nahueltoro, by Miguel Littín), followed by a discussion led by one of the local organisers which focused on the film's theme of alcoholism and its social causes. In Colombia, we went with the documentarists Marta Rodríguez and Jorge Silva to a screening of one of their films in a local hall in a popular district of Bogotá. In Nicaragua, where soon after the Sandinista Revolution the new film institute, INCINE, set up mobile projection units to take films to the countryside, we joined one of them in a rural community centre, for a screening of a Canadian documentary about Nicaragua. The *campesinos* who attended spoke in the discussion afterwards with full awareness of our camera's presence and the power of film in shaping the impressions it carried to people in distant countries. They were ordinary country folk but not quite naive realists: it was clear from the tenor of their remarks that they saw the film screen as a constructed reality, and a site of ideological battle.

Where independent documentary remains outside the world and discourse of television, and alternative distribution constructs a parallel public sphere for its circulation, the documentarist has the advantage of a closer relationship with small but particular sectors of the public. In Latin America, this was reflected in the elaboration of a distinct vocabulary for the discussion of documentary in the journals and publications of the film movement they belonged to: terms like *cine didáctico, cine testimonio, cine denuncia, cine encuesta, cine rescate* and, not least, *cine militante*. This list is not exhaustive or definitive and there is no single source from which it is drawn. These are only the most frequently used of a series of terms that occurs across the whole range of radical Latin American film writings which express its preoccupations and objectives. They are found in film journals from several countries, with titles like *Hablemos de Cine*, *Cine al Día*, *Primer Plano*, *Octubre* and *Cine Cubano* (from Peru, Venezuela, Chile, Mexico and Cuba respectively). The distinctive feature of all the terms listed is precisely their intentional character. They indicate a variety of purposes which can all be construed in political terms: *cine didáctico* is to teach, *testimonio* to offer testimony, *denuncia* to denounce, *encuesta* to investigate. *Cine rescate* is to bring history alive, *celebrativo* to celebrate revolutionary achievement. *Cine ensayo* is the essay film, to provide space for reflection. *Cine militante* or *cine combate*, militant cinema or cinema of combat, is the most explicit expression of the revolutionary imperative of those years.

In short, Latin American documentary became involved in the creation of an alternative audiovisual public sphere at the level of the community and its popular organisations, and sharing the same preoccupation to give voice to people normally excluded from public speech and outside the political power structures. In some cases, films were made and exhibited within the orbit of particular political forces, sometimes banned ones. The most famous example is that mammoth three-part, four-hour political testimony called *La hora de los hornos* (1968), a product of the Peronist movement in Argentina, and the film that prompted two of its makers, Fernando Solanas and Oc Getino, to write their manifesto 'Towards a Third Cinema'. A blueprint for militant film-making which was widely translated and reprinted around the world, the manifesto would be much more widely diffused than the film, which was made and released under the most difficult conditions. Not only filmed clandestinely, but also shown clandestinely, it was designed for an audience of the politically engaged, using a heavily rhetorical but analytic commentary counterposing a rich and fluid montage of images and imagery taken from numerous different sources to analyse the state of the country and the conditions of struggle. Yet the film is less dogmatic and authoritarian than its origins, scale and scope might suggest. Intertitles placed at strategic moments invite the projectionist to pause the film to allow for debate among the audience, a gesture which exemplifies another essential characteristic of the movement to which it belongs, the direct mode of address and the invitation to dialogue. This reaching out to engage the audience in dialogue about a social process to which film and viewer both belonged was a very different stance to the orthodox documentary, replete with its impersonal and supposedly objective commentary, where the film is removed from direct engagement with the world it pictures.

If the surge of Latin American documentary went together with social ferment in countries where political upheaval was on the agenda, and from which the film-makers took their cues, this was nowhere more true than in Chile in the late 60s, where a small tribe of young film-makers formed a committee of support for the leftwing coalition of Popular Unity and its Marxist presidential candidate Salvador Allende.[1] Both before and after his electoral victory in 1970, film-makers engaged in a cinema of urgency and produced a stream of highly inventive films, ranging from campaign propaganda and agitational shorts to investigations of the political process and full-scale dramatisations (like *El chacal de Nahueltoro* [1969]) denouncing the ills of underdevelopment. This was the milieu in which Raúl Ruiz, who would later make his career among the French avant-garde, first discovered his talent for improvisation – the improvised fiction of *Tres tristes tigres* (Three Sad Tigers, 1968) and the improvised documentary in the case of *La Expropiación* (Expropriation, 1972). The most extraordinary film to emerge from this period, however, was Patricio Guzmán's three-part chronicle *La batalla de Chile* (The Battle of Chile), a record of the tumultuous months leading up to the brutal military coup of 1973, backed by the CIA, in which Allende was overthrown. A fertile mixture of Direct Cinema observation, investigative reportage and political analysis, the footage was smuggled out immediately after the coup and edited in Cuba at the ICAIC, the first part appearing in 1976 and the last in 1979.

The story has been told many times on the screen (including the factually based political drama *Missing* by Costa Gavras in 1981), and provides a lesson in the intricacies of the Solidarity syndrome – the shifting perspectives induced by the passing of time on the reading of the images in which events are recorded. But here we discover that this shift occurs in more than one temporal dimension. First there is the growing distance of the film-makers from the moment of the event, and only second the distance of the viewer from the moment of the film. The first images of the Chilean events that entered the global public sphere were of course those of television news, which had emerged by the 1970s as the hegemonic form of news transmission, though still very unequally distributed across the globe; Guzmán's film begins with television news footage of the bombing of the Moneda Palace on 11 September 1973. The first sustained pieces of reportage about the immediate aftermath began to appear soon afterwards; these included an extraordinary edition of *World in Action* from Granada Television, entitled 'Chile: The Reckoning',[2] much of it filmed clandestinely on Super-8, including interviews with victims of the repression speaking of torture and brutality, and ending with an extraordinary scene inside the French Embassy, crammed full of people seeking refuge and safe passage out of the country, holding their tears back and defiantly singing the 'Marseillaise' at the top of their voices. If I remember rightly, it also included shots of the funeral of Chile's great poet, Pablo Neruda, who died a week after the coup; but this was a massive public demonstration, and these images were widely seen. They are also found in the first independent documentary dealing with the coup that reached Europe, *Chilean September* (1973) by the French team of Bruno Muel and Théo Robichet, where huge numbers march under soldiers' bayonets singing the 'International' (Neruda was a Communist) and proclaiming their grief with cries of 'Compañero Pablo Neruda, Presente' and 'Compañero Salvador Allende, Presente'. This was soon followed by several films made by the East German team of Walter Heynowski and Gerhard Scheumann in their familiar style, a combination of investigative film journalism, extensive off-screen narration and strongly agitational message. *I Was, I Am and I Shall Be* (1974) (a title taken from Rosa Luxembourg) is an exposé of the neofascist concentration camps, which includes footage shot clandestinely in the National Stadium in the days following the coup, which the *golpistas* turned into a prison camp and where many people perished. Then came a heavy-duty film from France, *La Spirale* (The Spiral [1976]), which went back and told the whole story, the work of a collective led by the sociologist Armand Mattelart, who had been expelled from Chile after serving as an adviser to Allende on the mass media, and guided by Chris Marker, who wrote the commentary (the voice for the English-language version was done by Donald Sutherland). An analysis of how the rightwing reaction, with the backing of the US, sabotaged Popular Unity and brought it down, *La Spirale* is a compilation film which draws on the abundant wealth of material produced by Chilean and foreign film-makers and news teams over the whole period.[3] In short, by the time that *La batalla de Chile* appeared, the novelty was not in telling an unknown story but in the way it was told, through a present-tense visual narrative, structured retrospectively by what every viewer already knew – the tragic outcome.

Taken together, the three-part *La batalla de Chile* comprises a work of historical testimony unique in the annals of documentary for its scope, density and poignancy. Guzmán and his group had been filming the political process in Chile since Allende's Popular Unity government took office in 1970, producing *El primer año* (The First Year) in 1971 and the following year *La respuesta de octubre* (The Answer of October), about the massive workers' response to a CIA-backed truck-drivers' strike against the government. Their intention, when they started shooting *La batalla de Chile* early in 1973 (supported by Chris Marker sending them film stock from France to shoot on) was to go beyond the chronicle of events in those two films and try to analyse the intensifying process of class struggle which was being played out increasingly on the streets. They positioned themselves as Marxists but without alignment with any particular party or group, the aim being to present the debates between them. Since no script can be written for unfolding events which cannot be predicted, they decided that the best approach was observational filming of representative points of conflict and the simultaneous collection of testimony by those involved, which would add up to a map of the key battlegrounds within the larger conflict. (And then, of course, the analysis had to be repeated when they started editing, in the light of what they'd succeeded in filming and what had actually happened; hence the time it took to complete.) The analysis in the finished film is not presented by political pundits or commentators, but provided through the dialectical structuring of the events portrayed and the words of those participating in them, filmed throughout with a highly agile hand-held camera and narrated intermittently by a judicious commentary which avoids the agitational or denunciatory manner of *cine militante*. In the first part, for example, we move through street demonstrations of the left and the right, political rallies and meetings, with vox-pop interviews in the midst of the throng. In the mid-term elections, we are on the streets at night as the results come through, when violence breaks out. Then the camera is inside Parliament as the results are confirmed and new deputies sworn in. When we find ourselves there again a few weeks later, the film-makers already know the space, and move around with an enormous agility right there on the floor of the chamber, catching the nuances of factional in-fighting and listening to Allende speaking.

The impact of the film comes very largely from the exceptional camerawork of Jorge Müller (the only member of the team who failed to make it into exile and disappeared after being detained by the security forces). First of all, he is always there in the middle of it, generally at eye level. Second, he's always on the move, shooting continuously. The camera is rarely still for more than a few seconds before it pans off to take in the surroundings, listeners, goings-on, zooming in and out with great fluidity, before going back to its original subject. The editing tends to favour these long takes for the demonstration they provide of the places where these things are happening; the effect is strengthened by the fact that the soundtrack is entirely location sync and the commentary is not allowed to punctuate the long takes which thereby emerge as the film's 'set pieces' (this is the reason why the film isn't dominated by its commentary, which is generally kept to bridging sequences composed of a series of shorter shots). All this required flexible shooting techniques. When Guzmán is conducting vox pops, he is leading the camera among the crowd; we often hear his instructions to the camera to turn on or to follow him, and it gives a tremendous sense of being there (or in Spanish, *presenciar*, to be a witnessing presence). In other situations, Guzmán would act as a second pair of eyes for Müller, 'surveying the action and trying to anticipate what was to come'. For example, in a street demonstration where the police were about to intervene in clashes between workers and fascist groups, he might be telling him

> Now you need to climb up on this box here . . . I'll steady you while you climb up. Now you have the best possible angle on the whole thing. Stay there until I tell you, because to the left a troop of police whom you can't see yet are about to come into view. As soon as they come into range, close in on them.[4]

In short he could direct him 'to make certain movements that are much more readily identified with fictional than with documentary filmmaking', a feature that gives the visual discourse of the film an unusual kind of dramaturgy for this type of film. The manner of shooting in the Chamber of Deputies is an example. This is such an unusual way for a camera to behave in a formal space like a parliamentary chamber, where if the camera is admitted at all it is generally required to occupy a fixed position, that we only expect to see this kind of shot in fiction films. Yet the effect of it here is not to fictionalise the scene in any way, but the very opposite, to intensify the sense of historical reality unfolding before the camera. This is very close to Pasolini's idealisation of the long take as 'the reproduction of the language of reality' which 'coincides with human action'.[5]

To fulfil their plan, they sometimes had to dissemble: 'one day we claimed to be filming for Chilean television, the next day for French or Swiss TV'.[6] In one of the scenes filmed this way, which has drawn the attention of several commentators, the film crew visits a well-appointed apartment block on the pretext of being a television crew looking for a good view of the city. While Guzmán engages a middle-aged woman and her foppish son in a polite interview, the camera pans around to show the fixtures and furnishings of the room, and then gazes down from the balcony on the streets below. For Ana López, this is an example of the way the camera emulates the independent gaze of the lens in a fiction film.[7] For Jorge Ruffinelli, the gesture turns the viewer into an accomplice, spying on the way these people live, spotting the social signs in the furnishings and objects on display, eloquent in what they say of their owners.[8]

Perhaps the most extraordinary example of the long take is the first shot in the sequence of the funeral for the worker killed by a sniper during a demonstration, where a grim-faced Allende is one of the mourners. The camera's starting position is walking through the crowds gathering for the funeral towards a steward calling instructions, close to the highly decorated coffin, then zooming in over people's shoulders to catch a glimpse of Allende standing in the portico of the state building where they've assembled, then back out to the throng as a steward calls the name of the dead man, 'Comrade José Ricardo Ahumada!', the crowds answering with 'Presente!' – then walking backwards as the procession moves off, circling around, and when it stops again, circling even closer, panning closely along the side of the coffin and up to the faces of the mourning family, and then walking backwards again along the workers' guard of honour. This is all a single take. Not the least remarkable aspect of this mesmerising shot is how close the camera gets to the protagonists in the scene, impinging on their personal space, without the slightest sign of them flinching. This is because we are in a space transformed by events into a very public zone indeed, where the camera's presence is witness to the truth of the moment – a moment in which the individual belongs most fully to the collective. *La batalla de Chile* is perhaps above all a film about crowds and power and the streets of the city as the stage of history. But the sheer number of people we see on the screen playing their historical role in the historical drama – the commentary tells us there were 300,000 of them at the funeral – makes it a city film with a difference, because this is a city that is living its public sphere on the streets, in direct confrontation with itself. The result, as the cumulative effect of the dramaturgy of the long take unfolds, is the vivid impression of something that is usually forbidden to the documentary, because it's usually always going on somewhere else, namely, the feel that the subject in the frame is history itself.

II

A different picture of the Latin American city is found in Ciro Durán's *Gamín* (1978), where the same basic techniques of observational cinema employed by Guzmán, the long take included, are used to reveal what is under everybody's nose but is never seen: the private life of the Bogotá street urchin. In one of the most memorable and disturbing sequences, a small boy is playing not merely in the street but in the very roadway, with a plastic toy vehicle on a string, which he rolls in the pathway of approaching cars and then pulls back just in time to prevent the toy being run over. Sometimes he even rolls it between the front and back wheels of a vehicle as it tries to edge its way forward in the busy street and honks its horn in fear of running over not the toy but the child. No doubt the child is performing for the camera, but he's playing a daredevil game at which he is patently an expert. The sequence is a rich metaphor of the child's life, the gamin of the film's title. Here are children from marginal communities whom circumstances – the break-up of families in the face of urban poverty – have driven out of house and home, who join up in gangs and manage to survive through petty dishonesty, thieving and prostitution, but who still have a desperate need to play. Indeed the game defines the relationship of the children's world to that of the city in which, in playing the toy-car game, the child gets in the way of the real cars. The city gives them no place of their own – another sequence shows a gang sleeping on the grass of the central divide in the middle of a dual carriageway – and therefore they have to steal their space, just as they have to steal for their wherewithal.

Scenes like this are doubly disturbing because Durán is prepared to violate the institutional codes of observational filming in order to film them, and it turns out that some of them are set-ups. Several shots, for example, show street robberies where a kid swipes a piece of jewellery from round a woman's neck, or a chicken someone has just bought from a take-away foodstore, or a radio from a car parked in a suburban driveway. These shots were achieved by choosing someone to play the victim, but without knowing who the culprits were to be or how they would strike. The police were informed, to protect the children, but the passersby in the street knew nothing.[9] The shots are deceptive, and according to the institutional codes of practice in British television, for example, might well be considered unethical unless labelled as 'reconstruction' – which would impede their force. Yet the end result is strangely Brechtian: a theatre of the streets, the children playing themselves, and the viewer caught wondering at the veracity of the image.

Although the 70s sees a growing mastery of observational filming in Latin American documentary, there is no particular stylistic current that predominates, but rather a spirit of iconoclasm with diverse results. In several instances the film-makers turn to anthropology in order to bridge the gap between their own habitus as well-educated intellectuals and that of their marginalised subjects. Indeed, the Colombian film-maker Marta Rodríguez had been a student of Jean Rouch in Paris, as well as of the radical sociologist-priest Camilo Torres in Bogotá, before she teamed up with Jorge Silva, who came to documentary through journalism, photography and the film club movement. *Chircales* (Brickworkers, 1972), their first film together, is a study of a family working in the brickyards on the outskirts of Bogotá, a denunciation of the conditions of indentured labour among millions of landless peasants living on the fringes of the cities. In accordance with a careful methodology, it took five years to make: fieldwork first, using stills photography and tape recordings; then the elaboration of a script, followed by filming, and then editing, all the while allowing time for the subjects of the film to participate in the process at every stage. The outcome is a film that moves from the explicitly political and sociological register of the opening towards the subjective and introspective, drawing the viewer into the subjects' own subjectivity without losing a sociopolitical perspective. Since the film was made without the benefit of sync sound, the soundtrack is constructed as a counterpoint to the visual narrative, through the subjects' voices, passages of commentary, music and sound effects. The man's voice speaks of their terrible living conditions while the image shows us, step by step, the labour process required for the artisanal production of clay bricks. In another particularly poignant sequence, one of the women of the family is engaged in the back-breaking labour of laying out the finished bricks to dry, while we listen to the inanities of a radio soap opera. Later, the girl's first communion is elided with scenes of widowhood and mourning. Poised between observation and interiority, *Chircales* is a quite exceptional fusion of politics, visual poetry and ethnographic documentary.

The Mexican director Paul Leduc also drew on fieldwork by anthropologists in making *Etnocidio: Notas sobre el Mezquital* (Ethnocide: Notes on the Mezquital, 1976), an ABC of indictments against the modern Mexican state which uses a simple idea to break completely with the conventions of documentary exposition. A portrait of the Otomí of the Mezquital Valley, north of Mexico City, the film is organised by chapters in which successive letters of the alphabet name the theme to be treated – A for Antecedents, B for Bourgeoisie, C for Class, D for Democracy, etc. There is no commentary, but a variety of music on the soundtrack, from indigenous pipe-and-drum to dance bands. The voice is given predominantly to the Otomí, to provide their own account of their miserable conditions, their exploitation by the rich landowners, their own history; with additional contributions by a boss, a shady priest and, near the end, an intellectual speaking about the US.

The film is steeped in death. The pretitle sequence quietly shows the simple burial of an infant in the countryside (we catch sight of more funerals later). 'Antecedents' is a wordless portrayal of the poverty of the Indians' way of life, seamlessly giving way to 'Bourgeoisie', where a man is first seen out shooting in the fields, and then in his role as the boss of a modern milking plant with herds of cattle and the agricultural machinery which the peasants lack, who speaks of the Indians as a manipulable workforce. This is answered by the next chapter, 'Class', where a large group of Otomí are lined up in a field (long shot), and speak one by one (close-ups) about the expropriation of their communal lands by the rich and the conditions of exploitation (the set-up recurs at intervals in the film, constantly bringing us back to this voicing of the collective experience). 'Democracy' then arrives in the form of a presidential election campaign (the candidate this time round is López Portillo); and so on. The chapters have different dura-tions and are treated in different ways; a couple of times, captions are superimposed giving the social statistics. In short, the film is structured as a series of dialectical juxtapositions which, starting with the funeral of a child in the countryside, opens out progressively to take in a wider world, moving with the migrants to Mexico City, and in the end reaching north to Washington. Like *La batalla de Chile*, then, a film of sociopolitical analysis.

The alphabetic chapter headings function as a framing device, and as one account sees it, have the effect of creating a disconcerting distance from the very people who are the film's subjects.[10] In other words, the opposite of Rodriguez and Silva taking us into their subjects' interior world. But this is of a piece with the stylisation of the cinematography. Here Leduc is quite unlike Guzmán, using a mobile observational camera only for sequences like the election campaign. Mostly the camera is on a tripod, with slow and deliberate panning and zooming and even tracking. This stylisation lifts the image from merely illustrating what is said, by giving visible form to a whole complex of relations which lie behind the visible surface. H for History, for example, has the camera tracking slowly among pre-Hispanic ruins; then it cuts to church altarpieces with skulls, rusting machinery 'made in the USA' inscribed '1891', and cupboards in the State Archive stuffed full of deeds; here the camera tilts down to the figure of an old peasant sitting on a bench presumably waiting for someone to find some papers; last comes the recon-struction in Mexico's famous Anthropology Museum of an indigenous hut with its figurines, going to a shot of coffins laid out in an undertakers, before cutting to a young peasant woman holding a baby. The sequence is unified by a single piece of music on the soundtrack (with no other sounds): a move-ment from a late-period Beethoven string quartet. The great disparity with the image produces a strange sensation, a sense of distance both cool and intense, in which history is seen as another world, cold and unmoving, where the Indian is relegated to a museum display while she stands unnoticed on the pave-ment outside.

III .

If Guzmán's Santiago is a city of living history, then Leduc's Mexico is a country where (in the familiar metaphor of the Mexican Revolution) history has been frozen, where the future exists only in the shape of people's apprehensions and hopes, and the past merely as memory. In contrast, Durán's Bogotá has neither past nor future but only the narrow day-to-day present of the urchins' lives; while the Bogotá of Rodríguez and Silva is a kind of suspended present, hung between the fantasy promises of the church and the radio soap opera. Taken together, these are all different ways of feeling the bewildering quali-ties of temporal experience which seem to characterise everyday life across the whole of Latin America, in contradistinction to the uniform, rationalised, utilitarian experience of quotidian time in the North. For example, as Nestor García Canclini sees it (from a Mexican perspective), Latin American culture is shaped by contradictions between cultural traditions with different forms of rationality (the indigenous, Catholic colonial Hispanicism, modernising liberalism) which end up, through uneven development, as different historical temporalities that coexist in the same present (Fredric Jameson has a similar reading of magic realism). How this syncretic sense of time can be reconstructed through the temporality of the screen is taken on in these films in full awareness of its elusive quality. Guzmán, for example, said that in approaching the filming of what became *La batalla de Chile*, they rejected a chronological approach because they realised that

> many events occur only as the result of a long process – a process that . . . often seems invisible. What you are able to film is the culmination of the process, the final, visible event: the workers taking over a factory, for example.

In Brazil, however, Eduardo Coutinho found himself in a different relation to these unfolding historical processes when he came to make *Cabra marcado para morer: vinte anos depois* (Man Marked To Die: Twenty Years Later) in 1984, which offers a testimony to the political history of the preceding twenty-five years, at the moment when the first signs of liberalisation appeared in the Brazilian regime. The beginning of a new thematic in Latin American cinema which is still unfolding, it remains the most thoughtful of film testaments of this history of repressions and aporias.

Cabra marcado, as Julianne Burton remarks, defies easy summary.[11] Opening with a long shot of a silhouetted hill at dusk, a burst of light illuminates the foreground, and we see two figures threading a film projector while a small group look on expectantly. This is Eduardo Coutinho and his assistants, holding an open-air screening of the footage he shot for an unfinished film, seventeen years after production was halted by troops on the day of the military coup in 1964. What unfolds begins as an investigation into the assassination of a peasant leader in the North-East of Brazil twenty years earlier to become a film about its own history, and about the inscription of history in the form of film. The earliest footage in the film, in black-and-white, dates from 1962 and 1964. The earlier pictures a small demonstration in the provincial town of Sapé, State of Paraíba, called to protest the brutal murder of João Pedro Texeira. This scene, which Coutinho filmed almost by accident as he was travelling around the country, became the catalyst for the1964 footage, in which Coutinho set out, in neorealist fashion, to reconstruct the events leading up to the assassination with the participation of the man's wife, family and comrades. The project proved abortive. They were stopped from filming in the original location of the events and forced to move elsewhere, losing almost all their cast, then after a few weeks filming around the town of Galilea, the military coup obliged them to give up and flee the scene. Luckily the film negative was hidden away where the military couldn't find it and, nearly two decades later, Coutinho set out again, this time to find out what happened to the Texeira family and the community of Galilea.

The investigation uncovers its own enigma – the whereabouts of the former cast, above all Texeira's widow Elizabeth and her dispersed offspring. Each time he meets up with someone again, he shows them the footage from 1964 to prompt their memories of the events and what happened to them afterwards. He is thus constantly cutting back and forth between footage from different time planes showing the same social actors at different ages and in different roles, and in this way the fictionalised version of 1964 stands in for the mediations of memory; the images become screen memories of the best kind, which activate the memory instead of hiding it. This includes the film-maker himself. Coutinho's role in the film is one more social actor among others, with his own memory of the events under investigation to put alongside the film record and the other participants; the result is a consistently self-reflexive aesthetic. But like any of the others, he only knows part of the story, which he amplifies by including several kinds of historical evidence: newspaper articles and other period documents; still photographs; archival footage; production stills from 1964.

The impact of historical events is traced in a composite combining disparate kinds of images bridging the gap from 'truncated past' to 'uncertain present', as Burton puts it. The result is an intricate palimpsest of documentary and fictional images, and historical and contemporary modes of representation, which in the end is less concerned with the man marked to die, or the film his death inspired, than with Elizabeth Texeira, a woman marked by life, and with Coutinho himself, a film-maker marked by being silenced. The deterioration of Elizabeth's haunting beauty in the twenty-year lapse between historical and contemporary images is a locus of visual fascination, one more tragic and irrevocable loss in this lament for a stolen past.[12]

Let the last word go to the Brazilian film-maker Walter Lima, Jr, whose comments on the film bring together a number of themes which have concerned us in these pages. He starts with Coutinho's hybrid aesthetics: 'Without concealing the adventure of its realization, it transforms that adventure into a filmic style using devices from television journalism, Direct Cinema, traditional documentary and montage.' But

> to walk amidst reality with tape recorder and camera turned on can signify a gesture of power that will certainly subvert or contradict the real unless the film-makers renounce the ease of domination which their tools confer upon them.

In front of a camera, he continues, a person is much more than simply a person; they are the awareness of their own image, a more acceptable 'hypothesis' of themselves. This is natural, because cinema carries with it a strong dose of idealisation of the real, independent of the film-makers' good intentions. Here the argument turns on a question of ethics which runs through the history of documentary: to achieve the proper aesthetic form, it is essential, he says, to observe and listen, and submit oneself to the rhythms of the people whom one wants to film.[13]

This is exactly the approach Coutinho applied when he moved onto video in the 90s, in a series of films which turn away from big subjects like history, to contemporary everyday life, including *Boca de Lixo* (Scavengers, 1993), *Babilónia 2000* (2001) and *Edificio Master* (2002). What Coutinho does in these films is fix on a location and portray the people to be found there: a rubbish dump on the outskirts of the city, a shanty town overlooking the bay of Rio de Janeiro, an apartment house a block away from the beach. At first sight these films don't look unlike many television 'talking heads' documentaries, but there are certain critical differences, to do with place, people and the film-maker's procedure. (You could even say that what these films do is take the idea of reality TV, and by turning it upside down, put it back on its feet.)

The choice of location is crucial, because it allows the film to portray a social microcosm without losing contact with the macrocosm outside and beyond the frame. Take the opening of *Boca de Lixo*. The film crew arrives at a huge rubbish tip overrun by scavengers. The scavengers don't exactly like it, but the camera attracts a few of the bolder children, who immediately challenge it as an interloper – 'What do you get outta holding this thing in our faces?' – which comes from a place which to us is the public sphere but from which they've been banished. The principle of the 'unique location', as Coutinho

calls it, is a geographical choice to focus on a place which, first, is defined by and through a certain population and, second, allows him to establish a relationship to his subjects on the basis of their lived space.
In each case, this is a delimited space which evokes certain generalisable characteristics while remaining
quite concrete and specific. It is also constantly connected with the wider world through the people in
each location, who often speak of other places they've been or come from. The dialectic at work here
is that the location itself establishes determinate limits and boundaries, which define a certain place in
the world, which then becomes a kind of extended or expanded metaphor for the lives of its population.
The rubbish dump becomes a metaphor of social rejection, the apartment block of the internal life of
the city dweller; and in the case of *Babilónia 2000*, since the film is shot in a shanty town overlooking
the bay of Rio de Janeiro on 31 December 1999, the metaphor is simply the hopes of the people at the
turn of the millennium.

Because each location is socially different, so each of these films works a little differently. Coutinho
doesn't apply his method rigidly but adapts it to the circumstances. *Edificio Master*, for example, is interesting because it leaves behind the domain of the disinherited to enter the domicile of the petit bourgeoisie, where it discovers the internal worlds of the atomised individual of modern urban living,
expressed especially in private acts of creativity – writing poems, painting and, since this is Rio de Janeiro,
after all, in music and singing. The other films are not devoid of music either, but here it acquires special
resonance as a very personal form of spiritual sustenance.

The result is that, taken together, these films represent the way people live in various environments
typical of a modern Third World city called Rio de Janeiro. But if the places are typical – every such city
has its scavengers, its shanty towns, its petit bourgeoisie – the people we discover in them disabuse us
of ready-made assumptions about what the typical consists of. This is because of the extraordinary range
of characters he finds in each place – who are exemplary in not being exemplary, not being stereotypes
– and the way he approaches them. Coutinho's questions are all about *them*, not about their opinions.
He doesn't ask people what they think about politics or current affairs or social issues, but just about
their lives – where they were born, went to school, how they met their partner, if they have children,
about their jobs, how they got where they are – in short, the unique and personal stories of their life
experiences. He's never judgmental. He asks them to talk about themselves, and lends them an inquisitive and sympathetic ear. He isn't trying to prove an argument or demonstrate a thesis. (Nor do these
films analyse anything in terms of cause and effect, nor offer solutions.)

What Coutinho gives us is a gentle but arresting re-visioning of everyday life – its difficulties, small
pleasures, fears, frustrations, spiritual beliefs, consolations, loves, encounters, friends, education, rewards
– in the telling of which people reveal both the symptoms of social and personal misfortune and those
of health and sanity. Their stories are all the more engaging because they have a strong tendency to
escape the categories of social stereotyping which dominate the cinema of fiction. The people we see
are not presented as examples of anything, the personification of some kind of category – the shanty-
town dweller, the scavenger, the religious believer, the petit bourgeois man or woman. Moreover, the
various testimonies sometimes contradict each other, revealing a diverse and heterogeneous world of
lived experiences which point in different directions, a series of small disconnected tales with a fragile
relation to each other, lacking any obvious forms of causal linkage but with a cumulative effect. In short,

echoes arise between different speakers, but what the viewer perceives is a mix of talk, sounds and images, which are not put in place by a controlling voice, with its generalisations and classifications, for there is no commentary to centre the narrative, in fact there's no overarching narrative at all, only lots of little ones.

If all this implies a certain concept of documentary, Coutinho, says Consuelo Lins, one of his collaborators on *Babilónia 2000* and *Edifício Master*, is an inveterate critic of theories that foreground cinema as image, thereby reducing the soundtrack to mere accompaniment of the picture, rather than a fully audiovisual medium which encompasses the richness and complexity of speech, including its silences, rhythms, inflections, slippages and resumptions of discourse, its looks and gestures, fleeting wrinkles of lips and eyebrows, shrugging of shoulders and so forth.[14] Coutinho himself speaks of this as a 'conversational cinema', which draws on the spontaneity of oral expression, the impromptu and ad-lib, without imposing a predefined scheme of investigation. This, in Coutinho's words, doesn't exclude a central idea prior to the film which guides its construction, but this idea is not in the form of a working hypothesis which the film tries to demonstrate through the succession of encounters with flesh-and-blood people. It also doesn't mean there is no preparation, which is described by Lins as a phase of research intended to get a clear idea of who and what is to be found in the chosen location: the researchers interview and film those people who are prepared to participate and the director uses this information to select his cast of characters. The research completed, the film is then shot rapidly over a short period of time and centres on the moments of encounter between the director and the characters. Coutinho even counts on this, he counts on his characters feeling the sense of occasion which the camera produces when it comes to visit them, and therefore giving of their best. They might have told the researchers the same things already, but they will be eager to tell them anew, to a new interlocutor, a new guest.

To explain what is going on here, Lins refers to a passage by Deleuze that we've already noted, speaking of the cinema of Perrault and Rouch, where the character 'becomes another, when he begins to tell stories without ever being fictional'.[15] Something is created here, in the space between the word and the ear, a kind of storytelling where the character reinvents themself, creates themself anew in the act of speaking; a form of utterance that transcends the relationship of interviewer–interviewee, but which constitutes a novel speech genre created by the act of filming. The most poignant example is the stammerer in *Edifício Master*, who begins by saying the interview will be terrible because he stammers so much, and then speaks fluently for several minutes, and when Coutinho asks him how come he didn't stammer, breaks into a broad smile and says it must have been God's doing. In fact, of course, it was the camera's doing.

These moments, when the character in front of the camera becomes other, have a corresponding effect, according to Deleuze, on the film-maker: 'they must become others, with their characters, at the same time as their characters become others themselves'. In other words, '[the director] too becomes another, in so far as he takes real characters as intercessors and replaces his fictions by their own storytelling'. The paradox, then, is that Coutinho continually makes his presence felt as the director, only in order to be self-effacing.

Deleuze pointed out a certain difference between the two pioneers. For Rouch, the concern was to escape his own dominant civilisation and reach for the premises of another kind of identity. For Perrault, it was to identify with his own dominated people, to rediscover a lost and repressed collective identity to which he himself also belonged. Coutinho is closer to Perrault than Rouch. When Perrault, says Deleuze, is addressing his real characters in Quebec, it is not simply to eliminate fiction but to free it from the dominant models that penetrate it, in other words, to use one kind of storytelling against another. What is opposed to fiction is not the real, says Deleuze, not even 'the truth', which in the public sphere is generally truth according to the masters or the colonisers, but the simple capacity for another kind of storytelling which is found among those who have the least part in the public sphere, the poor. Or as Coutinho puts it, he is driven by something very simple: 'to look and listen to people. Mostly, the rural and urban poor, the social and cultural Other. To try and understand the country, the people, history, life and myself, but always connected to the concrete, the microcosm.' Richard Leacock once spoke of documentary as gathering data to try to figure out what was going on – Coutinho might well say the same.

Notes

1. See Michael Chanan, *Chilean Cinema*, 1976.

2. Producer, Mike Beckham, transmitted 3 December 1973.

3. Cf. Catherine Lupton, *Chris Marker: Memories of the Future* (London: Reaktion Books, 2005), pp. 136–7.

4. Julianne Burton, *Cinema and Social Change in Latin America: Conversations with Filmmakers* (Austin: University of Texas Press, 1986), p. 57.

5. Pier Paolo Pasolini, 'Observations on the Long Take', *October* no. 134 (1980), p. 5.

6. Burton, *Cinema and Social Change in Latin America*, p. 52.

7. Ana López, '*The Battle of Chile*: Documentary, Political Process and Representation', in Julianne Burton (ed.), *The Social Documentary in Latin America* (Pennsylvania: University of Pittsburgh Press, 1990), pp. 279–80.

8. Jorge Ruffinelli, *Patricio Guzmán* (Madrid: Cátedra/Filmoteca Española, 2001), p. 138.

9. Conversation with Ciro Durán, Havana, 1979, reported in Michael Chanan, 'Festivals: Havana', *Framework* no. 12, 1980.

10. Julia Tuñón, 'Etnocidio: Notas sobre el Mezquital', in Paulo Antonio Paranagua (ed.), *Cine Documental en América Latina* (Madrid: Cátedra, 2003), p. 351.

11. Julianne Burton, 'Transitional Status: Creative Complicities with the Real in *Man Marked to Die: Twenty Years Later* and *Patriamada*', in Burton, *The Social Documentary in Latin America*, p. 373.

12. Burton, *The Social Documentary in Latin America*, p. 385.

13. Burton, *The Social Documentary in Latin America*, p. 381.

14. Consuelo Lins, 'Eduardo Coutinho', in Paranagua, *Cine Documental en América Latina*, p. 228.

15. Gilles Deleuze, *Cinema 2, The Time-Image*, trans. Hugh Tomlinson and Robert Galeta (London: Athlone Press, 1989), p. 150.

13 The Space of the Subject

The projection of personality

I

Dai Vaughan recalls a television programme about George Bernard Shaw he saw back in the early 1950s,

> doubtless shot with the full panoply of 35mm equipment and its attendant hordes of technicians. A mid-shot of Shaw sitting down at his typewriter was followed, in classic fashion, by an over-the-shoulder shot as he began to type. What he typed was, 'I don't normally behave like this at all.'[1]

An equivalent moment occurs in *Derrida* (2002), a portrait of the French philosopher by Kirby Dick and Amy Ziering Kofman. Derrida is seen at home in his study, in shirtsleeves, surrounded by books, talking to camera:

> This is what you call cinéma vérité? Everything is false. Almost everything. I'm not really like this. First of all, I don't usually dress like this. No, when I stay at home alone in the daytime, I don't get dressed. I stay in my pyjamas and a bathrobe.

It's a trivial scene and a trivial remark, but what Derrida fears is real enough – that even though he's a willing subject (he has agreed to the film and invited the camera into his home) he will somehow be forced to misrepresent himself, and even if he doesn't, being filmed is to give up your own authorship of yourself; because it's in the nature of documentary, and of what happens afterwards in the process of editing, that as Vaughan puts it, 'people are having scripts written for them out of their own words, and performances drawn from the repository of their unguarded gestures'.[2]

   This is not to say that the result is fiction. Writing about *Chronique d'un été*, Edgar Morin suggested that the 'truth' in the idea of cinéma vérité was akin to 'psychoanalytic truth', because of the way the camera brings to the surface what is normally hidden or repressed in the subject's social personality.[3] Recent decades have seen a great deal of writing in the quest for a psychoanalytic understanding of the nature of film, but almost all of it is about fiction cinema, not documentary. A rare exception cropped up at a symposium on 'The Couch and the Silver Screen' in 2001, where the psychologist Emanuel Berman agreed in effect with Morin that the introduction of the agile camera and direct sound produced a new relationship to the subject which bears comparison with psychotherapy. Documentaries, said Berman, are not about fictional figures invented by the scriptwriter or the director, but about flesh-and-blood individuals, who – although the two activities are very different from each other – tend to become invested in their relationship with the film-maker in a way that evokes what goes on in psychoanalysis: 'the process of transference and counter-transference, therapeutic alliance, resistance and so forth'.[4] In other words, the film-maker's need of the subject invokes a complementary need in the subject for the film-maker. This relationship is not symmetrical, however. Berman observes that the topic of the documentary is 'almost universally' chosen by the film-maker, and the point of entry is often a certain attraction by the film-maker to the topic or the figure of the subject, which is sometimes related to deep personal identification. Then the other question, as in any relationship, is 'What is the motivation of the other side, the protagonist?'. It turns out that there are common interests which lead to a kind of alliance: 'the need to be heard, a need to be seen, a wish for mirroring, a wish for a sympathetic ear, for an admiring eye, for an interested eye, for an empathic eye/ear combined'.[5] In short, at least in the kind of portrait film of which *Derrida* is an example, on the film-maker's side there is scopophilia and even voyeurism, while on the side of the subject there is narcissism and often exhibitionism. (And even more so, of course, in genres like the docusoap, which is designed to bring this on.)

One of the things that makes *Derrida* the film such a playful documentary is that Derrida the man is completely aware of these processes, which he holds up and turns around in front of the camera. At the start, we find him at home preparing to go out, he's lost his keys, and greets the camera with a playful negation: 'Forgive me for not even saying hello. It's a bit difficult.' A moment later, he addresses the camera again, 'So you're going to come with me'. On a sidewalk in New York, the conversation is about being filmed, and Derrida warns the cameraperson not to trip on the pavement. At a seminar in Paris, he begins by pointing out the camera:

> I want to explain the presence of and ask your permission for this film crew on my left. They'll be recording some images and I hope this occurs as imperceptibly as all the other recording devices we've become accustomed to. Recording devices, notably video or filmic ones, have been a topic of our seminar. On several occasions, we examined them in light of the example posed by the Rodney King verdict. This is a Californian film crew, by the way. In that case we posed the question: What happens to the testimonial archive when one takes into account that the classic definition of testimony excludes the intervention of recording devices? So as an experiment we'll see what it's like to work for a moment in the presence of these archiving machines.

When he visits an art gallery for an exhibition which includes his own portrait, it gets more personal. He admits the portrait makes him anxious – 'We've already spoken a great deal about the difficult rapport I have with my image' – and he finds it uncanny and bizarre,

> but I don't have the desire to destroy it as I often have with other photos or images. It's a very nice gift she [the artist, Dominique Renson] has given me. That she's given to a little narcissist. (Pause) An old narcissist.

Later on he speaks about the paradox of eyes and hands, which are the parts of our selves, our bodies, that we see the least easily:

We can look in a mirror and see ourselves and have a reasonably accurate sense of what we look like. But it's very difficult to have an image of our own act of looking or to have a true image of our own hands as they move. It's the Other who knows what our hands and eyes are like . . . These gestures of the hands are seen better by the Other than myself.

Or by the camera, of course, which thereby offers us the chance of seeing ourselves from outside (which is what makes it uncanny).

It's not just what he says that strikes us but the way it's filmed. Watching him in close-up, when he mentions hands, the camera zooms out just far enough for us to see his own hand gestures; there is a cut as he speaks and then as he rounds off his point, the lens swings round to reveal that we've been looking at his image in a mirror, and we see that he's also being filmed by a second camera. This is nowadays a common stylistic marker of video documentary – in the days of 16mm, interviews were never shot with two cameras, it was too expensive – but rarely has it been used with as much metaphorical effect. (By comparison, Oliver Stone's multi-camera interview with Fidel Castro in *Comandante* is pure mannerism, where none of the cuts makes any particular point.)

Shot over a period of several years, Derrida is seen at home in Paris with his wife, and in a couple of scenes with family and friends, while his public persona is portrayed in seminars and lectures in France and trips abroad, always surrounded by an entourage of admirers. In South Africa, he visits Robben Island to see Mandela's prison cell, and then lectures at the University of Cape Town, where he addresses the subject of forgiveness. In California, he visits the Derrida Archive at UC Irvine, opened in 1995. In Australia he tells a television interviewer that deconstruction is not a sitcom. These moments are interwoven with several different interview sessions, with the questions asked off camera by one or other of the film's directors. The structural elements of the film are thus little different from the conventions of the television-style celebrity portrait, but with a couple of crucial differences. For one thing, apart from a recitation of biographical facts near the beginning there is no commentary, but we get Kofman's voice reading excerpts from Derrida's writing on the soundtrack – this is much more intellectually demanding than the genre normally admits. Also, the period of time over which the film was shot implies a certain claim about the personality that emerges: the portrait will be more measured, discovering constancy of character rather than its passing moods.

However, Derrida does his best to undermine things, taking nothing at face value, becoming an active participant in the deconstruction of his own documentary, and on several occasions challenging his interviewer, complaining, always with good humour, that this question is too general, and that one too complicated, to be able to give a reply. Asked by Kofman to discuss the origins of deconstruction, he looks around him and (as if echoing Shaw) begins, 'Before responding to this question I want to make a preliminary remark on the completely artificial character of this situation.' He wants to underline rather than efface the technical conditions, not allow it to appear that this is a natural thing to do. And then he immediately adds,

I've already in a way started to respond to your question about deconstruction because one of the gestures of deconstruction is to not naturalize what isn't natural – to not assume that what is conditioned by history, technology, institutions, or society is natural.

Sitting down for an interview with his wife Marguerite, a psychoanalyst, there is a false start, and he complains 'How can I start to think about responding to your question when you interrupt me to adjust the lights?'. The picture cuts to the same image of Marguerite on a television monitor with Derrida watching. Later, we see him watching the image of himself watching the image of Marguerite, and in a snatch of interview he professes that it's difficult to speak of certain personal things in front of a camera, but it was a scene he liked because they didn't say anything. Late in the film, asked what he'd like to see in a documentary about a philosopher, he responds, 'Their sex lives . . . you want a quick answer, no?' Why? 'Because it's something they don't talk about', but then he turns it into a serious point: 'Why do philosophers present themselves as asexual beings?' And then, near the end, his remark to the film-makers that now 'you're going to edit this down to an hour . . . it'll be yours, your signature and your biography, in a way'.

For all the banter, the camera repeatedly catches him doing what he does best: deconstructing. The film-makers enter into the spirit, playfully deconstructing their own process in cahoots with their subject, and Derrida's philosophical wariness about becoming a 'subject' for the camera serves them as a springboard to investigate the limits of the biographical film portrait. *Derrida* is thus an exemplary film, not for reasons of originality or impressive cinematography – the camerawork is rather rough and ready – but as a postmodernist text which constantly questions itself about what it is able to represent. There is hardly a sequence in the film without reflexive signs of the film-making process, but as in Vaughan's description of *Lorang's Way* by David and Judith MacDougall, not only is the presence of the camera acknowledged in every sequence, but 'it is acknowledged by successive sequences in contrast-ing ways – as companion during a walking track, as interlocutor during a formal interview, as casual nuis-ance in an occasional verbal jibe' and so on. Here the documentary idiom stakes a claim on reality that has nothing to do with 'realism' in a literary or fictional sense. The juxtaposition of these various modes of acknowledgment sustains a constant interrogation of the status of the filming 'which inhibits the semantic closure to which realism constantly tends'.[6] But precisely in remaining open and at the same time asserting these constant gaps in communication, the film insists on the documentary quality, the spontaneity of the unrepeatable, of the profilmic scene, and in *Derrida* the film, the result, in spite of everything, is a true and real portrait of Derrida the man.

II

It's worth reviewing how we got here. 'Paradoxically,' says Winston, 'because the new equipment made filming so much less intrusive than it had been, the finished films were far more so.'[7] There are two things going on in these films which are directly or indirectly related to each other, one of them con-cerning the representation of space, and the other the personality of the subject who is found within that space. Because people behave differently in different social spaces, then as the documentary camera enters spaces that were previously inaccessible to it, it encounters the subject in situations where they are not used to being under scrutiny, like Paul Anka in his underpants in *Lonely Boy*, or Derrida not wear-ing his pyjamas. If as Pennebaker said, neither side quite knew the rules, the results had the effect of raising new questions about the performance of the subject. Apologists for Direct Cinema were wont to argue that if the crew were sufficiently self-effacing, then the effect of the camera's presence could be largely eliminated or at least minimised; whereas cinéma vérité deliberately probed with the camera, and worked with the assumption that people are always adopting roles, corresponding to the different situations of everyday life, and therefore the way they behave in the eye of the camera is another role. Either way, however, the situation created by the observational camera has very interesting properties, because even though no one is fully in control either in front of it or behind, it allows the subject to project something of themselves that is normally kept at bay.

Prior to the 1960s, there are very few examples of sustained direct sound filming in private or even semi-private locations, but several highly striking moments, like the camera's entry into the homes of slum-dwellers in *Housing Problems*. These scenes are the proverbial exceptions that prove the rule – those slum-dwellers remain social ciphers; they are there to personalise the film, but they have no personality of their own. The social actors in Jennings' *"Fires Were Started –"* have much more personality, but this was only achieved through studio re-enactment and the strong communal spirit of the war effort. *On the Bowery* is rare among films before the 60s for the portrayal of the personality of its characters, perhaps because they are down-and-outs and drunkards who no longer have anything to lose. But in the new mode of sync sound filming which began in the 60s, the subjects have increasing space to become individuals who reveal their personality through the situations in which the camera finds them. Because the potential for the documentary camera to draw a living portrait of the human subject on the move has now been expanded, the projection of personality is enlarged and extended. This is a moment of historical significance in both the political and the cultural domain. *Primary*, despite its lack of political content, is celebrated as the first time Jack Kennedy's impact and charisma were captured on film, 'marking a cultural shift in the United States to a political system dominated by media influence'.[8] And more generally too, documentary from now on centres increasingly on individual people as subjects, rather than on impersonal subject matter in the matter-of-fact world; one of the results is the re-invention of celebrity as the photogenic object of the roaming camera.

Kennedy himself, whose father after all was an erstwhile movie tycoon, was a willing accomplice, at least to begin with, and *Primary* came about in part because he was well prepared to take on the rapidly evolving media as a condition of political success. According to one account, Kennedy was somewhat uncertain about what he was letting himself in for, but *Primary* was a critical success. Nevertheless, when Drew went back to Kennedy in 1961 to persuade him to let himself be filmed in the White House going about his business, Kennedy wasn't certain the experiment would work. 'If I can actually lose consciousness of the camera and it doesn't intrude, we might be able to do something. If the camera is bothersome then we can't. But we could try it.'[9] The modest results were seen on ABC television under the awkward title *Adventures in Reporting: Adventures on the New Frontier*. Drew decided he wanted to try again. He had come to the conclusion that mere observation wasn't enough, and reasoned that in order to avoid a string of uneventful scenes, your subjects needed to be caught up in testing circumstances which would allow them to forget the presence of the camera and at the same time provide the film with narrative drive – the dramaturgy of what came to be called the 'crisis' scenario, after the title of this third film with Kennedy (*Crisis*, 1963). But this time, after seeing it shortly before his assassination, it seems that Kennedy had changed his attitude, and Pierre Salinger recalled that he was quite upset about it: 'He thought he'd gone too far . . . He said he had forgotten the cameras were

there. He was not sure that the image he gave was the right image.'[10] Kennedy is an exceptional subject, his ambivalence is not. It is not only the ambivalence of the subject, however, but also of the
viewer, who often cannot believe that the subject is not in some way acting themselves for the camera,
that is, acting up, putting on a performance. (And if they are? We remember Pennebaker's answer
about Bob Dylan in *Don't Look Back* that of course Dylan was acting, he was playing himself, and he
was doing it very well.)

What the camera captures is the subject's self-presentation in the situation that confronts them,
which includes the presence of the camera. The situation inevitably produces a filmic version of the
Heisenberg principle, which says not that the presence of the observer changes the behaviour of the
observed, but that it introduces uncertainty. It is certainly not a question of special access to a hidden
truth, except insofar as the camera, as in Benjamin's thinking, is an instrument of the perceptual unconscious: it allows us to see fleeting gestures and looks – and hear vocal inflections and intonations – that
usually flit by in the flow of the present moment but which the camera foregrounds by its framing and
composition, and the microphone by its selectivity, and which the editor then works up through montage into the finished film. In short, the wager of Direct is its ability to record, always subject to the judgment of the eye behind the viewfinder, the dynamics and nuances of what Erving Goffman called 'the
presentation of self in everyday life'.[11] *Whose* everyday life, however, was determined by the susceptibilities of the television channels who were the main outlet, and it is no accident that most of these films
dealt with celebrities leading highly public lives, and therefore used to projecting themselves. Moreover,
since the film-makers were after 'revelation through situation', the more dynamic the situation the
better. The crisis scenario that Drew added in to the attraction of celebrity offered several benefits, which
were analysed by Stephen Mamber back in the 70s. Not only would the intensity of the situation help
to give the camera team its desired cloak of invisibility, it also brought reportage and storytelling together
into 'a paradigmatic structure' where the narrative of the film could 'correspond to the chronology of
the filming'. As long as you picked the right situation, then, as Drew put it, 'Whatever happens, [you]'ll
have a story.'[12]

Whatever happens, you'll have a story. The problem hidden in this assumption is ironically illustrated
by a pair of films, unexpected in this context, about the same subject – the end of Communism – made
ten years apart in two different European countries. First comes Roger Graef's story of what happened
when he made *Decision: British Communism*, screened by Granada Television in 1979. The background
was the growing debate about Eurocommunism and the independence of the Party from Moscow, a
notable political shift, but after months of shooting, there was no 'story', he felt, which bound it all
together, and he was running out of film stock. The film was only 'rescued' when he discovered at the
last minute that a resolution to send fraternal greetings to the Kremlin on the sixtieth anniversary of the
Russian Revolution, to be presented at the congress on Party Democracy in September 1977, was going
to be opposed by the Eurocommunists. This, of course, was the crisis moment that the film needed to
give it some kind of narrative shape, and by feverishly shooting both sides over the conference weekend, the film was in the can.[13] Twelve years later, in the same months as the fall of the Berlin Wall, Nanni
Moretti filmed the fierce debate within the Italian Communist Party about its post-Eurocommunist identity. *La cosa* (The Thing, 1991) takes its title from the term people used for what was coming into being

– 'this thing' – to replace the old Communist Party, but turning resolutely away from narrative cinema, Moretti deals with the problem of closure, or rather its lack, by running his scenes of passionate speech-making, shot in eight party sections scattered around the country, in reverse order – like Benjamin's angel of history, irresistibly propelled into the future to which his back is turned – and ending in a cacophony of voices as history slips away.

    Back in the 60s, various types of situation were found to fit Drew's crisis formula, including public contests (a car race, a bullfight, a football match, a musical competition) and activities which tested the protagonist (a Broadway opening, the performer on tour, a test flight). These scenarios also created a documentary version of the all-American hero, active and positive – success in a Drew film, as in a film by Howard Hawks, says Mamber, 'is measured by the way you handle yourself in a tough situation'.[14] Indeed, the play in *Jane* (1962) was a flop, but it didn't do Jane Fonda any harm to have made the film. In the figure of the performer, however, the American hero also takes the form of the anti-hero, which if anything only accentuates the question of the subject's performativity. There are very few moments in *Don't Look Back* when Dylan doesn't seem to be performing a role, whether on stage or off, as if the film wants to say, without explicit editorialising, that this is what happens to the celebrity performer on tour, a round of concerts and fans, travelling, hotels, press and radio interviews and the rest, where it's difficult to find private moments to relax. If the 'central conceit' of the film, as Jeanne Hall puts it, is the presumed contradiction between Dylan's on-stage and off-stage personae, then in picturing this off-stage world – where the singer is obliged to continue performing himself – it reveals the constructed nature of celebrity and, with Dylan's connivance, 'mounts a critique of the dominant media'.[15] Indeed one of things that makes Dylan such a magnetic subject is his refusal of the roles that the media try to impose on him, his impatience with the labels and simplifications they seem inevitably to trade upon, and the film gives him plenty of time to articulate his critique in these encounters with the media. One of its lasting pleasures (apart from the music, of course) is his astute attack on the interviewer from *Time* (a sequence of fully seven minutes): 'There's no ideas in *Time* magazine, there's just these facts' and 'I mean, it's a certain class of people that take the magazine seriously' and

> I don't take it seriously. If I want to find out anything, I'm not going to read *Time* magazine, I'm not going to read *Newsweek*. I'm not going to read any of these magazines. I mean, because they've just got too much to lose by printing the truth.

(The response of the press was bemused superiority. *Variety* reported that 'There is Dylan, faintly hostile, "putting on" the press', while the *New York Times* noted that 'Mr. Dylan parries and thrusts with inter-viewers (some of them impossibly square, of course, and therefore perfect targets for the put-on)'.[16]) Much more discomfiting is another long sequence, in a dressing room before a concert, where in front of his entourage, Dylan metes out the same treatment to a student journalist, who is presumably much closer to his fanbase, whom he nevertheless enjoys baiting and goading, turning the interview round and interrogating the interviewer, who sums up the encounter in the exasperated comment that 'the whole thing that gets me about you is you're knocking me from the moment I come in'. The inevitable question: is Dylan not being egged on by the camera? The worrying contradiction emerges that precisely in moments like this the film appears to be claiming a special status for itself, as if Pennebaker's camera is excluded from Dylan's strictures about the media, and there is nothing here to get other than what you see. But perhaps the most extreme example is Madonna in *Madonna: Truth or Dare* (aka *In Bed with Madonna*, Alek Keshishian, 1991) which purports to show the queen of artifice and the makeover 'as she really is', but as Warren Beatty remarks, 'everything she does is for the camera'. Paula Rabinowitz sums up, 'Madonna never lets down her guard. When the camera rolls, she acts.'[17]

These portrait films are an exception to the general rule that the topic of the documentary is usually chosen by the film-maker, since they were made at the invitation of their subjects. William Rothman points out several moments in *Don't Look Back* where Dylan throws fleeting glances of acknowledgment at the camera.[18] But there are also numerous scenes where it can be said that Dylan is not acting for the camera at all because he's making music, performing in concert for the audience, or else for himself and his companions. And since his companions include other musicians (notably Joan Baez, Alan Price and Donovan), they also contribute moments of music-making for each other. These scenes, which show how musicians share their music away from the audience, are among the most satisfying. They are also when Dylan appears to be most completely himself, doubtless aware of the camera's presence, not performing for it, however, but happy for it to do its job. The musician making music is already performing a role which the camera can observe without affecting it – and this is true whether or not there's an audience at whom the performance is projected, or the camera is part of a private gathering where musicians play for each other – because making music already involves the whole person in an act of communication which the film-maker can shape, but which is given by the performer as a gift. In this sense, music-making serves as a model for all those other situations where the film-maker hopes for the subject to be so engrossed in what they're doing that the presence of the camera makes no effective difference.

Here we should really go on to speak of a long lineage of music documentaries for both cinema and television, built around musical performance and covering every musical genre, which although comprising one of the most consistent strands of documentary film-making, are among the least discussed. They come, of course, in many shapes and sizes, and some belong more to the history of celebrity while others belong more to the history of music, but either way they are slices of social history. The paradigms of the rock documentary date from 1969, when the Maysles brothers filmed the infamous Altamont Speedway concert by the Rolling Stones which broke up in chaos and death, as portrayed in *Gimme Shelter* (1970), and Mike Wadleigh shot the music festival at Woodstock. The same observational techniques were also applied more intimately to portrait films of classical musicians, like Leacock's *A Stravinsky Portrait* of 1966, or *Arthur Rubinstein: L'amour de la vie* (François Reichenbach and S. G. Patris, 1968), both of them about patriarchal figures in their eighties. The former finds the eighty-four-year-old composer at home in California, conducting an orchestra rehearsal in Hamburg, holding a press conference in London and talking in a multiplicity of languages – holding it together, Leacock goes beyond the tenets of Direct Cinema by whispering in the viewer's ear, thus anticipating a mode of documentary narration that was yet to come. The latter, according to *Time* film critic Jay Cocks, had 'the same makeshift style, the same kind of groupie's reverence' as a rock documentary – one of those films that rely not on their own quality but the musical magnetism of their subject.[19] But the same approach could be used for decidedly non-patriarchal purposes. The subject of Jill Godmilow's film of 1974, *Antonia: Portrait of a Woman*, is Antonia Brico, who in 1930 at the age of twenty-eight became the first woman to conduct the Berlin Philharmonic Orchestra, and now, in her early 70s, conducts a semi-professional orchestra in Denver just a few times a year. The film, in which Brico is interviewed by the singer Judy Collins, traces her struggle to survive in a male profession which Adorno once called 'the imago of power'. The result, said one New York critic, was 'a film that is both a testament and a tribute' and 'much the best example so far of a new feminist consciousness' on the screen,[20] while another called it a 'truly subversive and revolutionary' film about 'one woman's resistance against public prejudice'.[21]

The attractions of the music documentary were (and are) several, not only that of capturing the electricity of live performance or the personal magnetism of the performer off stage, but the capacity of the camera to enter the space of rehearsal and capture the musical process in the making. This kind of filming can often sustain long observational shots with no need of commentary and because the subjects are fully invested in their music-making, without the presence of the camera having any substantial effect on their behaviour. There is an exemplary sequence of this kind in *Miriam Makeba* (1973), a Cuban film of the African singer's visit of 1973 by Juan Carlos Tabío, where Makeba and her band meet a group of Cuban musicians to learn about each other's music; the language gap between them proves no obstacle, and what we witness is a spontaneous exchange of musical communication. As in other Cuban documentaries about visiting musicians – especially Americans like Harry Belafonte and Dizzy Gillespie – there is a political subtext here about international solidarity, which rests on the utopian character of music as a universal language. Something similar occurs when Isaac Stern visits China in *From Mao to Mozart* (Murray Lerner, 1980), which again suggests the possibility of an encounter of cultures through the non-verbal language of music, but here the political subtext is ambiguous: as China was opening up after Nixon's famous visit of 1972, here is the Western patrician teaching teenage violinists emerging from the Cultural Revolution, when everything Western was vilified, how to play Mozart. But why not? Shouldn't Mozart's beauties be everybody's heritage?

The ambiguities of music have a habit of inveigling the music documentary into political subtexts beyond the control of the film-maker. Take the case of *Buena Vista Social Club* (1999), when Wim Wenders scored a worldwide success with a film of music by a band of old-time acoustic musicians who had been rescued from obscure old age by the American guitarist-producer Ry Cooder. With Buena Vista Social Club, Cooder enjoyed the biggest success of his career as an animator of so-called world music, but in Cuba the results of his efforts touched on a domestic politics of music which its foreign popularity hardly registered. I learned from a friend that there were different shades of opinion about the international take-off of the '*vieja guardia sonera*' – 'the rearguard of *son*' – and the consequent resuscitation of their music in the mass media. Many people were surprised and pleased, but the youth tended to think of them as 'antediluvian monsters', albeit genial ones, while musicians and a few music critics were ambivalent. 'They ask whom this praise is directed *against*, and how many people extol the "music of yesteryear" in bad faith, in order indirectly to attack the music of today.'[22] The other place where this old-time music raised political pitches was of course Miami, where Wenders' film had its US première, and where concerts by musicians from over the water were usually subjected to vilification and bomb threats. According to an account published on the internet, 'the warm response to Wenders' stirring film represents progress of sorts for a community still shaped by the feverish right-wing exile politics that have turned Miami into the nation's most repressive city for artistic free expression'. But now, the writer continues, the climate has begun to soften, and 'pulled along by the seductive, irresistible lure of both newer and older forms of Cuban music, a younger generation of Cuban-Americans is eager to rediscover its roots and seeks out the music without fear'.[23]

III

What observational documentary proposed is difficult, perhaps impossible, and depends on both the film-maker's competence and the subject's assent and cooperation. Subjects must feel the film-maker can be trusted and the documentarist must work to create conditions of acceptance. Indeed, in ethnographic film-making, a substantial period of fieldwork prior to introducing the camera became part of orthodox methodology, where it was intended to give the ethnographer an apprenticeship in the culture to be filmed and at the same time accustom the subjects to being observed. It did not take long for the observational documentarist to learn the benefits of allowing people time to become used to the camera's presence, because cameras tend to make people feel self-conscious, and they need to feel that this is something other than reportage, where cameras merely rush around grabbing stuff.

When Allan King made *Warrendale* in 1966, a grim study of a centre for disturbed children in Ontario famous for its special 'holding' therapy, he began by spending a month in one of the houses getting to know the children, then brought in his cameraman and sound recordist for another fortnight of similar visits before shooting over five weeks. Not a lot of time in terms of academic fieldwork, but enough to make a difference. The result is a gruelling observational record of extreme behaviour, succinctly described by the US film critic Stanley Kaufman: 'These children act out, in exaggerated and baroque ways, many feelings that other children, other people, feel and suppress or understand objectively and can control.'[24] Faced with a film both raw and disturbing, both the BBC and the Canadian Broadcasting Company, which commissioned the film, refused to show it, using the excuse of its scatological language, with the result that it was first seen on the cinema screen. Reactions from the critics were mixed. Kaufman praised it to the skies for its compassion, preferring it to Wiseman's *Titicut Follies* the year before, which exposed the terrible conditions in a Massachusetts mental hospital. For Kaufman, who thought that documentary subjects pass from self-consciousness to seeming forgetfulness of the lens by several stages, the film-makers have 'empathy, communion, [and] credibility'. For Jan Dawson in *Sight and Sound*, however, they intrude, and she found the film an extreme case of invasion of privacy, plunging the spectator into a disturbing spectacle 'whose therapeutic effects are neither demonstrated nor described', and which thus encourages voyeurism.[25]

The question is not, of course, which of them is right, but how it can be possible, if we are not to suppose that their disagreement is just a matter of personal taste, for the film to sustain both readings. The film itself sends ambiguous signals. There is a scene where the boys are outside playing Grandma's Footsteps (the playground game also known as Red Light). The camera is facing the children from a distance, as the boy out front (whom we know quite well from earlier scenes) stops and turns, claiming of course to see one of the boys behind him still moving. When the culprit naturally denies it, he gestures towards the camera, calling out 'Yes you did, and there's the proof . . .'. The boy who has not let the camera inhibit his behaviour suddenly reveals his ready awareness of its presence. But this is more than simple acknowledgment; it seems to confirm that even in moments of absorption and seeming forgetfulness, the subject remains conscious of the camera's presence without showing it. Or at least it's always there in the periphery of awareness, like the presence of an audience to the musician engrossed in performing. And in that case, the image we see of them is one they have themselves contributed to creating.

For her part, Dawson singles out the scene where one of the staff telephones the centre's director for advice when the cook in the house where the film is being shot dies unexpectedly during the night. (Kaufman remarks about this event that, although it occurred early in the shoot, King understandably shifts it to a point near the end, because strict chronology was not important, and if he'd left it in its proper place, the film would then have run downhill.) The man doesn't know whether to allow the crew to film the children's reactions to the announcement of her death: 'Is it intruding too much? . . . Is it going too far? . . . Would it be more natural to have them film it or not film it?' This is the only moment in the film when the idea of the individual's right to privacy is even considered, says Dawson, who is astonished that he could even imagine the presence of the camera being 'natural'. But she traces the problem astutely to the very setting of the film: since Warrendale is a community that presupposes the desirability of 'acting out' emotions, since it succours a view of life as a sustained performance, and since it abolishes conventional distinctions between 'public' and 'private', then 'it probably provides the ideal subject matter'. From this perspective, however, what the film suggests is a disintegration of borders between public and private in which documentary is complicit as both witness and agent, as if it is drawn to those situations where the dividing line is already thin, where the subject is already in a state of agitation, producing signs of inner life that normally remain inward; and in treating this kind of subject matter the documentary magnifies and projects it, sending it into the public sphere, where it starts by offending decorum, but also raises critical questions about the forms of socialisation by which this decorum is constructed.

We need to add a crucial rider. Like the mental patients in *Titicut Follies*, or indeed the traumatised soldiers in *Let There Be Light*, the boys in *Warrendale* didn't have the right not to be filmed. These are places of detention, institutions controlled by authorities on whom the film-makers depend for permission to film, and where the defence for their invasion of privacy is the claim that the film is in the public interest because society has a duty of care to these citizens. Winston, who analyses the legal ins-and-outs of this claim and the attendant questions of consent in considerable detail, argues that the law is often found wanting because it has failed to balance the old right of free speech against the new mass media and their intrusive technologies; instead it has taken a piecemeal approach to problems as they arise.[26] But there are complications and contradictions. *Titicut Follies*, for example, was banned in part over the issue of consent – not all the participants had signed consent forms – but there was a Catch 22, since there was also a question of whether someone locked up as mentally incompetent could be regarded as competent to sign a consent.

To put it another way: new media have placed the old definition of privacy in crisis precisely because they have created new ways of trespassing on privacy (obviously this doesn't only apply to the film camera). But the privacy they trespass on is not a unitary or homogeneous zone, any more than this is true of the public domain. For one thing, public and private are not fixed quantities but relative points on a continuum. Public space, for example, ranges from the open air, like the street, the park and the beach, to enclosed spaces where the public has the right of entry but the place is private property, like shops and art galleries and pubs. Private space also has its gradations. The asylum, the detention centre and the prison are all private, in the sense of being closed off to the public, but the inmates are not in control of their own space. The private house, where people do control their own space, is shut off from public access, a place where guests and strangers (including the camera) enter only by invitation, and are then usually restricted to certain rooms, where in other words certain rooms are more private than others (indeed this also applies to those who live within it, with adults exercising the right to enter the space of the children but not necessarily vice versa). Sometimes a space is ambiguous, like the box in a theatre which is reserved for the exclusive use of a particular party of people who nonetheless remain in public view. Should we perhaps see the effect of the incursion of the documentary camera as analogous, turning a private place into a space that the public can see into, albeit in a controlled and partial way?

IV

If one of the appeals of observational documentary is going 'behind the scenes', into the semi-private space of the public personality when they are not on direct public display, this is the promise of entering what Erving Goffman calls the backstage zone where behaviour often contradicts the impression cultivated by the public performance, and where the very language that is spoken is significantly different.[27] Goffman offers examples like the way that hotel staff chat about the guests behind their backs, or an executive relaxes in his office, where 'he can take his jacket off, loosen his tie, keep a bottle of liquor handy, and act in a chummy and even boisterous way with fellow executives of his own rank'[28] – situations that have ironically come to serve as subjects for television docusoaps. But similar disparities occur with all sorts of social actors, between saying what they think they ought to say in public, and the language in which their daily business gets conducted. The problematic here is not individual but is lodged in the life of the institution to which they belong, as if every habitus has an off-stage doppelgänger. It is not surprising that the social life of the institution, and the intricacies of its open and hidden hierarchies, also becomes an attractive subject to observational film-makers of various different kinds.

Social institutions from every sector of society are the invariable setting for the work of Frederick Wiseman, whose films, after *Titicut Follies*, have generic titles which indicate their subject matter: education in *High School* (1968), the police in *Law and Order* (1969), health care in *Hospital* (1970), the military in *Basic Training* (1971), the legal treatment of youth offenders in *Juvenile Court* (1973), the welfare system in *Welfare* (1975). For Wiseman, the institution is a social microcosm that reveals an inevitable gap between aims and practices which can be 'dramatised' through observational cinema. The scenes that have been captured can be organised into an intelligible form (usually a kind of mosaic pattern, as Nichols has observed)[29] which presents itself without the need for an explanatory commentary. A form of documentary dramaturgy which Wiseman himself has called 'reality fictions'. The resulting film comes to be read on an iconic level, according to documentary's dialectic between particular and universal, as a synecdoche, in which, for example, New York's Metropolitan Hospital comes to signify the problems of illness in American society. In Wiseman's own words, 'each film explores a different aspect of the relationship of the individual to the state in a democratic society'.[30] His justification for invasion of privacy is always public interest, originally on the basis that if an institution receives public funds, then citizens are entitled to know what goes on there. His fly-on-the-wall method, the absence of commentary and thus avoidance of explicit interpretation, is geared to justifying the justification, a strategy that has enabled him to expand his subject matter. Essene (1972) is the portrait of a monastery, Primate (1974) focuses on a scientific research laboratory working with monkeys, Meat (1976) on a meat-packing plant, Store (1983) a department store in Dallas. Each offers its own social metaphor. Like Coutinho, the basic condition for the film is that the subject is contained in a specific location – 'institution' is understood in its physical manifestation in the world, as 'a place that has certain kinds of geographical limitations and where at least some of the people have well-established roles'.[31] In these situations, according to Barry Keith Grant, Wiseman believes that people do not significantly alter their behaviour for the camera and the camera is therefore capable of capturing truths of human character. In his view, if people are made self-conscious by the camera, then they will fall back on behaviour that is comfortable 'rather than increase the discomfort by trying out new roles. This means they will act in characteristic rather than new ways.'[32] This is the opposite of the Rouch of cinéma vérité and the psychodramas, but then Rouch uses the camera to provoke his subjects, where Wiseman is self-effacing; which shows that the question at issue is not just the camera, but also the behaviour of the persons behind it.

There is an unspoken condition. The camera, having entered into a private or semi-private place, must not violate people's personal space. If privacy implies a sense of boundaries not to be crossed, this is not just a matter of fixed spaces separated by a threshold, but also the sense of personal space that the individual carries around with them, so to speak, and which expands or shrinks according to circumstance. It is well established (in the work of social psychologists like Michael Argyle, for example) that personal space is culturally variable and partly defined by gender, class and social hierarchy. I recall Argyle describing the proverbial diplomatic cocktail party where the reserved Englishman kept backing away from an Italian who kept approaching him just a little too closely. Goffman offers the amusing example of passengers in an elevator, who have to allocate space equably. 'The first few individuals can enter without anyone present having to rearrange himself, but very shortly each new entrant – up to a certain number – causes all those present to shift position and reorient themselves in sequence.'[33] The highly restricted space of the elevator provides the scenario for the delightful Lift (2001), where director-cameraman Mark Isaacs installs himself for days on end in the lift of a typical London tower block, filming people riding up and down. At first people ignore him or greet him with indifference, but then they start talking to him and we discover something of their lives. Doubtless, this film was only possible because of the miniaturised digital camera with which it is shot, which allows the film-maker to occupy little more space than anyone else, even, it seems, to shrink into the corner.

Respect for personal distance allows the film-maker to obtain results of the greatest interest even when entering situations governed by complex and intricate power structures. It is essential in an example like Our Friends at the Bank (1997), a film by director-cameraman Peter Chappell following a round of negotiations between Uganda and the World Bank over a period of eighteen months, which according to one reviewer reveals a series of discrepancies between the rhetorical comments of the two sides – the Ugandan government on the one hand, and the Bank, the IMF and donor governments on the other (each of which has their own agenda). Politicians, functionaries, bureaucrats, economists and civil servants of several different nationalities are cast 'almost as chess pieces', as they shuffle between meetings 'in a game played on a shifting board' – sometimes Uganda, sometimes New York or the Bank's headquarters in Washington – and as negotiating sessions alternate with private meetings often characterised by jokes and jibes.[34] The first thing to be said is that this kind of access to affairs normally conducted in full secrecy is extremely rare, and the film came about, according to Chappell, when Wall Street banker James Wolfensohn took over as President of the World Bank, because of concern at the Bank over the bad shape of its image under his predecessor.[35] Both sides granted the film-maker privileged access, in return for editorial review for factual inaccuracies only. Very occasionally, says Chappell, he was excluded from one meeting or another, 'but it would be fair to say that people on both sides pretty much observed the ground rules'. The film is not purely observational, insofar as it carries a judicious commentary by the film-maker informing where we are and who is who as we move backwards and forwards between continents, and explaining the relevant background to what we're seeing. But instead of the conventional format for this kind of subject – press conferences, interviews, the speculations of experts and journalists – here we enter the discursive universe of the politicians and global bureaucrats themselves, and discover how they really talk to each other, how their different agendas are encoded in verbal communicative action. In other words, this is a film which listens, and is also unusual for sustaining these scenes of detailed discussion over sequences that run for several minutes each.

An institution like the World Bank is interesting, says Chappell, because it often brings people into a proximity with others which would be unusual in their own cultures. Chappell speaks of his concern while filming for reading and respecting the subjects' personal spaces, not only in terms of not bringing the camera too close to people to discomfort them, but also in the framing which communicates the scene to the viewer. By maintaining a certain distance and mostly eschewing the use of the zoom for close-ups, the film's varied cast of characters are always seen in the proper setting of their interpersonal behaviour, which helps to reveal the power structure not only through their speech but also differences in body language, as well as factors like the degree of deference or self-confidence that the same person manifests in different situations and places. Like the Ugandan Minister of Finance a little overawed by New York compared to his self-assurance back in Kampala.

The hierarchy of power within an institution is key in determining interpersonal relations. Chappell says he was always amazed to see someone who was self-confident and assertive on his own patch becoming quiet and subservient in the company of Wolfensohn, a man, he says, who is highly tuned to the character and personality of people in his company, and able to adjust his behaviour accordingly. 'The only time you see him wrong-footed – for a moment – is during his first meeting in New York City with Museveni, who is of course an absolute master at handling people of all ranks, class and cultures.' (He was also wrong-footed, however, in a recent press photo, which showed him taking off his shoes to enter a mosque and revealing a large hole in his socks.) This hierarchy also governs the way people respond to the camera's presence: 'If Jim has allowed Peter into this meeting I cannot say I don't want this meeting to be filmed, because Jim is my boss.' But the film-maker has to work for this kind of trust, to overcome the disadvantages of being an uninvited guest. On the one hand, the camera wields a certain power as the agent of public scrutiny; on the other, 'it's not just a camera, it is seen as "Peter's camera" and its presence is allowed or accepted because of who I am to them. In other words, we trust that Peter will represent us fairly.'

The response which Chappell reports after the film was shown to the various parties involved gives food for thought. President Museveni 'thought it might be advisable to remove a comment concerning the military budget of Kenya, which I did as it was peripheral to the argument of that particular sequence'. Wolfensohn gave it his blessing and instructed all the vice presidents to watch it. Talking separately to two of the Bank's functionaries, Chappell found that each considered himself to be fairly represented, but thought the other had been acting up to the camera. One functionary felt he was shown in a light that could be detrimental to his career prospects in the Bank. 'The staff association took up his concerns and questioned the right of management to make an agreement with the producers that overrode individual staff rights.' The Bank's public affairs people requested Channel 4 to have a particular scene edited. 'Legally there was no requirement for them to accede but they did so anyway,' but the Franco-German channel Arte refused, and transmitted the director's cut.

V

Many of the same elements come into play when the camera crosses the threshold into the more intimate personal space of the domestic realm, and it was not long, of course, before this happened. Allan King's film of a marriage in trouble, *A Married Couple*, appeared in 1969, followed in 1972 by a television series by Craig Gilbert called *An American Family*, and in Britain, Paul Watson's series *The Family* two years later, all of which invade the privacy of ordinary folk with no public persona beyond their everyday lives of family, work and neighbourhood, but inevitably turning them into public personalities. These films can hardly be justified under the public right-to-know but answer a different agenda, the voyeurism inherent in the idea of crossing boundaries and witnessing the intimate. Yet the result, as Paula Rabinowitz writes, was that the family was 'acknowledged to be a public institution, like schools and courts', and a means of political and social control – like one of Louis Althusser's Ideological State Apparatuses, through which subjects were 'interpellated' as individuals.[36]

Rabinowitz sees this as re-enacting in a new context what Barthes perceived as a novel form of social experience brought about by photography, 'the publicity of the private', in which the private exploded into public view. In line with the feminist critique of the public sphere, she interprets this as 'a collapse of the gendered and spatial conventions of bourgeois culture' which divided the public and political from the private and domestic, thus delineating the position of women.[37] By bringing the domestic into public view, the boundaries of different realms of life – not just public and private but the political, the social and the economic – are shifted and become fuzzier, because each is seen to include behaviour akin to the other. Indeed, in light of the call of women's liberation to make the personal political, the living room was as likely to reveal the contradictions of capitalism as the boardroom. In this way, says Rabinowitz, 'Craig Gilbert's decision to move into the home, positioning living cinema in the living room of middle-class suburbia, suggested that the erasure of the divide between public and private, a dream of cinéma vérité, had been achieved.'[38]

Vaughan sees 'the appropriation of the domestic realm – the conquest of an area hitherto "accessible" only to fiction –' as 'both a fulfilment and a crisis for documentary'.[39] He offers a filmic definition of the domestic realm 'as comprising those areas of human activity which are (a) most difficult to shoot without interference, since they are not public, and (b) least susceptible to re-enactment, since they are not in any simple way repetitive'.[40] The purpose of this negative phrasing, he says, is to denote a space of personal and intimate behaviour, normally hidden 'though not quite clandestine', which contrasts with 'those repeatable or public events which have formed documentary's traditional sources' – events on which the paraphernalia of film-making has been assumed not to exercise any significant influence. In the domestic setting, where it is difficult to see how it couldn't do so, life has its patterns but events are unique. Fredric Jameson comments on *An American Family* that it not only captured dramatic changes in the Loud family over the course of a year or so, 'but also, and very importantly, the influence of the making of the documentary itself on all of that: so the camera became very much a character in what was happening in this family'.[41] At all events, by effectively turning the lives of the Loud family inside out, placing their private life on public view even as they were living it, the public image of the family as a social institution was transformed. As Rabinowitz puts it, the film-makers sought a family with no special defining characteristics of race or class – a myth, of course – but then undermined their normality: 'Even within the norm, disturbances occur. The centre still holds, but just barely: a marriage on the verge of break-up, a son in drag, a daughter having sex – cracks in the structure.'[42]

Thirty years odd after these first 'living room' films comes a film about a couple who seem to be living their lives for the media. In *When Louis Met the Hamiltons* (Will Yap, 2001) the camera crosses the threshold between public and private several times, as it follows the Hamiltons through their front door to escape the reporters and cameras besieging them on the street outside. Or more precisely, as it follows Louis Theroux following the Hamiltons, because this is an episode in the kind of television series that relies on the personality of the reporter to disarm the subjects, inveigling them out of their reticence and into revealing themselves; in Theroux's case, his elaborately awkward persona is like a parody of the 'friend of truth', and the film promises to coax, beguile, cajole and ensnare the notorious couple. Neil Hamilton is a former MP disgraced for allegedly taking bribes in exchange for asking parliamentary questions, who went to court to try to salvage a reputation that had become synonymous with Tory sleaze, but ended up being forced to withdraw his libel action. Bankrupted when the action collapsed, but with his formidable wife Christine always by his side, he continued to protest his innocence to anyone who would listen, and as the Hamiltons became regular guests on daytime television, they thought they saw an opportunity for a media career. Indeed when Hamilton is asked by Theroux near the start how he now earns his living, he replies, 'as a professional object of curiosity'; adding later on that 'to most people we're like a celluloid couple – we're not real'.

The style of the film is a long way from the classic observational documentary, in the first place because of the presence of the reporter, but also as a product of camcorder film-making, where the film crew is replaced by a single person operating a miniaturised camera with microphone attached (we see him in the images taken by the news crews of the Hamiltons' comings and goings accompanied by Theroux). Like many other forms of journalistic reportage that have appeared over the last few years, the approach owes something to the video diary, which is filmed without a script but records events as they unfold from the perspective of a particular observer; although in this case, Theroux's first-person and self-reflective commentary is not spoken to camera but is added afterwards as voice-over ('I was now four days into the story, and had been absorbed into the Hamilton household. I feared I was losing my bearings as a journalist').

The premise of this kind of film could be described as situational, based on putting the subjects into the situation of encounter with the reporter's personality. The thing is contrived, but this encounter is not fictional. In this case, luckily for the film but not the Hamiltons, shortly after shooting has started, unforeseen events erupt into the scenario and the Hamiltons are plunged into a new scandal by an accusation of sexual harassment against the two of them. Theroux sticks with them as the media circus descends on them; he himself becomes a part of the story when the press pack sees him riding in the Hamiltons' car with his cameraman, and accompanying them into the apartment where they live. The privacy of the home is thus juxtaposed directly with the public sphere coming home to roost on the pavement outside; or when they retreat to their country house, at the bottom of the drive.

In the kitchen of the London flat, Christine is overcome after they watch themselves returning home on the television news, which then goes to a live reporter on the spot. 'It can't be real,' she says, to which Neil responds, 'but this is television', a quip which misfires if you take it as a sign of his own confusion. It is here that Theroux makes the remark that got him into trouble with a number of reviewers, when, urging her to respond to a question, he says 'This is me, Christine, I'm not a journalist, I'm a friend.' For my part, I was struck by the echo in this scene of a book I was coincidentally reading around the same time, Derrida on the politics of friendship, a meditation on the different possible interpretations of the enigmatic remark of the ancient philosopher 'O my friends, there is no friend', which Montaigne attributed to Aristotle. In addition to the various possible readings Derrida rehearses, here was another. The friend, says Derrida, is the ideal other, but friendship is a political issue because it implies responsibility and a certain concept of virtue. It also gives rise to the question of 'what are the political consequences and implications, notably with regard to democracy, of . . . a rupture of reciprocality'.[43] Or its mere simulation. When Theroux was subsequently cornered by a journalist, he conceded

> that there is something contrived in how he relates to his subjects on camera, saying that, like prostitution, journalism can involve 'professional manipulation': 'Prostitutes and journalists are not that dissimilar, especially when it comes to human interest journalism that involves a little bit of beguiling and seduction. You have to become intimate in a slightly fake way with people.'[44]

Here, the narcissism of the subject finds its match in the narcissism of the television journalist and vice versa – it is difficult to say which comes first.

Notes

1. Dai Vaughan, *For Documentary* (Berkeley and London: University of California Press, 1999), p. 76.
2. Vaughan, *For Documentary*, p. 71.
3. Edgar Morin, 'Chronicle of a Film', in Jean Rouch (ed.), S. Feld (tr.), *Ciné-Ethnography* (Minneapolis and London: University of Minnesota Press, 2003), p. 232.
4. Emanuel Berman, Timna Rosenheimer and Michal Aviad, 'Documentary Directors and Their Protagonists: A Transferential/Counter-transferential Relationship?', in Andrea Sabbadini (ed.), *The Couch and the*

Silver Screen: Psychoanalytic Reflections on European Cinema (Hove and New York: Brunner-Routledge, 2003), p. 213.

5. Berman *et al.*, 'Documentary Directors and Their Protagonists', p. 221.

6. Vaughan, *For Documentary*, p. 77.

7. Brian Winston, *Claiming the Real* (London: BFI, 1995), p. 230.

8. Jeanne Hall, '"Don't You Ever Just Watch?" American Cinema Verité [sic] and *Don't Look Back*', in Barry Keith Grant and Jeannette Sloniowski (eds), *Documenting the Documentary: Close Readings of Documentary Film and Video* (Detroit, MI: Wayne State University Press, 1998), p. 224.

9. Mary Ann Watson, 'Adventures in Reporting: John Kennedy and the Cinéma Vérité Television Documentaries of Drew Associates', *Film and History* vol. 19 no. 2, 1989.

10. Ibid.

11. Erving Goffman, *The Presentation of Self in Everyday Life* (Harmondsworth: Penguin, 1971).

12. Stephen Mamber, *Cinéma Vérité in America: Studies in Uncontrolled Documentary* (Cambridge, MA, and London: MIT Press, 1974), pp. 117–18 and *passim*.

13. Personal communication.

14. Mamber, *Cinéma Vérité in America*, p. 129.

15. Hall, "Don't You Ever Just Watch?", p. 224.

16. Hall, "Don't You Ever Just Watch?", p. 228.

17. Paula Rabinowitz, 'Wreckage upon Wreckage', *History and Theory* vol. 32 no. 2, May 1993, p. 131.

18. William Rothman, *Documentary Film Classics* (Cambridge: Cambridge University Press, 1997), pp. 144–210.

19. Jay Cocks, 'A Fine Romance', *Time*, 10 March 1975, <www.time.com/time/magazine/article/0,9171,917162,00.html>.

20. Jay Cocks, *Time*, 21 October 1974.

21. *New York Magazine*, Tom Allen, 22 September 1974.

22. Personal communication from Ambrosio Fornet. See also Michael Chanan, 'Play It Again, or Old-time Cuban Music on the Screen', *New Left Review* no. 238, November–December 1999.

23. See <www.salon1999.com/ent/music/feature/1999/03/09feature.html>.

24. Stanley Kaufman, 'Allan King's *Warrendale*', in Jacobs, *The Documentary Tradition* (New York: W. W. Norton, 1979). p. 464.

25. Jan Dawson, 'Warrendale', *Sight and Sound* vol. 37 no. 1 Winter 67/68.

26. Brian Winston, *Lies, Damn Lies and Documentaries* (London: BFI, 2000), p. 87.

27. Goffman, *The Presentation of Self in Everyday Life*, pp. 114, 129.

28. Ibid., p. 127.

29. Cited by Barry Keith Grant, *Voyages of Discovery: The Cinema of Frederick Wiseman* (Urbana, IL: University of Illinois Press, 1992), p. 21.

30. Quoted in Grant, *Voyages of Discovery*, p. 42.

31. Quoted in Grant, *Voyages of Discovery*, p. 26.

32. Quoted in Grant, *Voyages of Discovery*, p. 14, quoting Wiseman.

33. Charles Lemert and Ann Branaman (eds), *The Goffman Reader* (Oxford: Blackwell, 1997), p. 47.

34. Chidozie Ugwumba, 'Behind the Scenes: Uganda Negotiates with WB & IMF', *Economic Justice News Online* vol. 4 no. 3, October 2001, <www.50years.org/cms/ejn/story/114>.

35. Personal communication.

36. Paula Rabinowitz, *They Must Be Represented: The Politics of Documentary* (London: Verso, 1994), p. 134.

37. Rabinowitz, *They Must Be Represented*, p. 87.

38. Rabinowitz, *They Must Be Represented*, pp. 136, 134.

39. Vaughan, *For Documentary*, p. 66.

40. Vaughan, *For Documentary*, p. 55.

41. Michael Chanan, 'Talking Film with Fredric Jameson', in Douglas Kellner and Sean Homer (eds), *Fredric Jameson: A Critical Reader* (Palgrave Macmillan, 2004), p. 137.

42. Rabinowitz, *They Must Be Represented*, p. 134.

43. Jacques Derrida, *The Politics of Friendship* (Basingstoke and London: Verso, 1997), p. 64.

44. Sathnam Sanghera, 'Louis Theroux', <www.sathnam.com/Features/72/louis-theroux>.

14 After Vérité

The film-maker in person

I

One of the critical problems in documentary representation, according to Fredric Jameson, is its susceptibility to the clichés and stereotypes which are always already present in the afilmic world, shaping the story the film wishes to tell.[1] The documentarist, says Jameson, is like an agent with a mission, and the resulting film can thus be seen as a kind of dramatic act in a larger unfilmed story, which is that of the film-maker going into the field and trying to do something with and to these clichés or conventions. This is to say that behind the primary level of the documentary's subject matter there is another level, which we don't normally see, which shapes the film by conditioning who, where and what the film-maker is able to shoot. This level is inhabited by another kind of social actor – the television executives and panel members who award the commissions and provide the funds for production (and their counterparts who give and withhold permissions to film). As Winston puts it, the documentarist, like the journalist, is not an entirely free agent 'but rather a cultural worker doing the bidding, at least in some measure, of management, commissioning editor, sponsor or funder'.[2] On this level, the individual film is less an aesthetic text sufficient unto itself, but an episode in a bigger story of assumptions and presumptions about the what, where and who of the world of public representation.

The figure of the documentarist as an agent with a mission is illustrated in the example of Michael Rubbo, an Australian director working in Canada with the National Film Board. In 1974, Rubbo went to Cuba in the company of two big-shots, a socialist politician and a media magnate, with a plan to conduct an interview with Fidel Castro. *Waiting for Fidel* is the humorous title of a film both amusing and serious, as the men enter a curious limbo in which waiting for the interview – which never happens – becomes the subject of the film, with Rubbo himself entering the frame as they argue the pros and cons of the Cuban Revolution and of making a film about it without its central figure. Four years later, Rubbo turns up in a documentary by the Chilean exile Raúl Ruiz, who is commissioned by French television to film a report on the French presidential elections from the perspective of the Paris district where he now lives; this is *De grands événements et de gens ordinaires* (Of Great Events and Ordinary People, 1978), which the television people found upsetting and declined to transmit. The difficulty for Ruiz was getting behind the surface of a deceptive normality; Rubbo is visiting Paris and Ruiz asks him on camera for his reflections on the problems of shooting documentaries in foreign countries. These two films make an apposite pair, because both portray the breakdown of documentary conventions in the face of an ostensible subject that escapes the lens. When Rubbo appears in another film, four years after the second, again personifying the documentarist, this time it's a film that rejects the conventions which have broken down in the first two. The film is Marilú Mallet's *Journal inachevé* (Unfinished Diary, 1982), where he turns up as the film-maker's husband.

Jameson suggests that we look at documentary discourse in terms of the different levels shaping the film-maker's endeavour. If the first level is the ostensive subject, a film about such-and-such (and the clichés and commonplaces which normally obscure it), then the second level, which is usually unseen, although it's present the whole time behind the camera, is the drama of the film-maker in the process of making the film (manoeuvring through the system and trying to deal with the clichés and stereotypes at the same time).[3] In *Waiting for Fidel*, the ostensive subject refuses to cooperate, and the film-maker decides to turn the camera on himself and his companions as they're taken off on revolutionary tourist excursions – to the Lenin High School, a mental hospital, the Technical University – and then return to the protocol house where they're lodged, to discuss what they're seeing.

Joey Smallwood, former Premier of Newfoundland, a liberal politician who thinks of himself as a socialist, rehearses his questions to Castro, and argues socialist values with Geoff Stirling, millionaire owner of Canadian radio and TV stations, who has also put up the funds for Rubbo to make this film in which he now appears as himself. As the days pass, Stirling objects to Rubbo spending his money in what he regards as a pointless manner. The resulting film collapses the first level into the second, the drama, normally unseen, of the making of the film we're watching. In the process, the film adopts a first-person narration, with the film-maker bringing himself into the picture, and thus becomes roundly self-reflexive. The result is to question both a number of clichés about Cuba and Socialism – the ostensive subject – and at the same time the conventions of documentary representation. In doing the latter, it not only reveals the drama of the set-up, the tussle between the film-maker and his sponsor. In offsetting Smallwood against Stirling and both with Rubbo's own self-portrait, all of them belligerent and macho in their own way, it also offers a study in the narcissism of the documentary subject as white English-speaking educated male.

If *Waiting for Fidel* turned the documentary inside out, nevertheless it still delivers the perspective of the First World on the Third, the characteristic stance of documentary as a form of knowledge ensconced in the public sphere of Western democracy. Ruiz's *De grands événements* . . . is one of the very few films that see the world the other way round. The film takes the form of a playfully narrated voice-of-the-film-maker diary covering the run-up to the election; if the television station that commissioned the film and then refused to transmit it, because it seems they were upset by its less than flattering portrait of French democracy in action, then perhaps, given the penchant for mischief of this hugely prolific film-maker, this was only to be expected. Ruiz can only make the film from the viewpoint of a Latin American exile, who is not a participant observer within the electoral process in the same way as a French film-maker would be, but an outsider and, moreover, an exile, someone who is dislocated, their political identity held in suspension. Nor can he escape being cast in the role of a kind of ethnographer from the periphery, and inevitably, in this reversal of the familiar perspective, his subjectivity breaks through to the surface, especially when he discovers that he is not in fact in a position to carry out this ethnography.

Ruiz begins by showing us the courtyard of the house where he lives, and then proceeds to street interviews, one of them with the local newsagent, about people's responses to the elections, interviews that often conceal as much as they reveal. That is to say, they show people concealing their opinions through evasions or circumlocutions (in bourgeois democracy, your vote is your own private affair; most people don't mind telling the opinion polls, because they're anonymous, but here Ruiz discovers that those who aren't members of political parties prefer not to confess to a camera). In between these snippets of interviews, the commentary explains the film's title: it is derived from a remark of John Grierson's, when he says that we look to cinema to show us an event, preferably a great event, which involves the dramatic needs of ordinary people. Immediately, and in thoroughly novel fashion, the film begins to comment on itself, by the novel device of splitting the commentary into two voices. The second voice describes the film's procedure: 'During the pan around the courtyard we could have the credits' – actually we just had them – and a little later, 'a series of shots, always in the same order, are inserted from time to time to convey the closed space of the neighbourhood'. Later the second voice will add – and we will see – that these shots can be augmented, and the space 'completed', by means of reverse shots.

The film proceeds day by day. Friends are brought in to help try and understand the process, as the film-maker begins to doubt his capacity to penetrate the surface of reality. On the third day, a sociologist talks about a report by the Trilateral Commission on the 'ungovernability' of democratic societies, which always need a degree of apathy to work smoothly, otherwise the system may become overloaded. (This is Armand Mattelart, who taught in Chile before the coup, but along with other participants, Rubbo included, his name is withheld, and only his social role is given.) Another day brings a strangely set-up shot, where a speaker is commenting on left politics while the producer is on the phone, with the camera panning round from one to the other. The producer (whom we've previously seen trying to set up an interview over the phone with the town clerk), interpolates a comment:

There was a series of TV programmes based on a revealing if slightly dubious idea. People were interviewed not knowing the camera was on. Then they were made to speak with a clapperboard so they knew the camera was running. What was revealing was that in the first part, when they didn't know the camera was running, they spoke freely, but in the second part they censored themselves.

On the sixth day, the commentary announces that 'Attention is shifting to documentary as such. The theme is no longer elections but documentary.' (A curious slippage occurs here in the subtitled print of the film: the French voice speaks of 'le direct', which the subtitles translate as ciné-vérité, in French. This is the 1970s and something odd has happened. The French, who devised the term cinéma vérité, now speak of the style using the English term 'Direct', while the subtitlers assume that the appropriate term in English is the French one, condensed to occupy less screen space.)

We are now halfway through the film, and the rest of it is indeed a deconstruction of what the commentary subsequently calls the 'sterility' of documentary conventions, in the process bringing up a number of problems already familiar to us from the present study. A discussion ensues about what the documentary form gained by incorporating sync sound and avoiding scripted dialogue. For example, the spectator hopes for mistakes, preferably stupid statements, in which people betray themselves. One of the speakers interrupts himself as he tries to light a cigarette – 'I'm having trouble with my matches . . . that's an event produced by ciné-vérité . . .' Warming to the theme, he proposes:

One can say it isn't true that in fiction cinema the camera creates the event, whereas in ciné-vérité it doesn't, for if the matches business means anything, it's because there's a camera here filming it, so in documentary cinema too, although it's usually concealed, the camera's presence acts as a shifter.

It doesn't just frame the event, he says, it creates it, adding that this has become something of a platitude. Most documentaries, he continues, 'pretend the camera isn't there, that the same events would happen if it wasn't, but they know that the camera being there creates special conditions . . .'. As he pauses in his speech, the commentary interpolates 'The subject of the film is ciné-vérité', and then he continues '. . . so people don't act and talk, and *aren't* in their normal conditions'. With the consequence that things happen as a result of the presence of the camera 'and the anticipation of those being filmed that they will be seen on the screen'. These 'special conditions' are illustrated here by the fact that the camera is doing something very odd for a documentary, namely, continuously panning round the scene so that the participants come in and out of frame arbitrarily.

This Brechtian gesture only goes to demonstrate that conventional documentary already creates special conditions and artificial situations, and these include the peculiar form generically known as the interview, a situation where someone is invited to speak about something in a considered way without quite knowing who it is they're speaking to. The interview involves a kind of unwritten contract whereby the interviewee accedes to the power of the camera, but the situation is also like a game (tennis, perhaps, or chess). The art of the interviewer is to appear to the interviewee as their complete interlocutor and a friend of truth. At the same time both of them know that this is a performance for the benefit of the camera, and thus there is always the anticipation of being seen on the screen; or as Derrida put it, the speaker is haunted by this future moment in which this image will be reproduced in their absence. From this future perspective, what the speaker is about to say is unforeseeable, even when prepared or rehearsed, but as long as the interviewee is spontaneously following a particular train of thought and could therefore always say something different. In political interviewing, and especially in an age when politicians no longer give unscripted speeches, the proper function of this kind of documentary interview (which it shares with television current affairs) is to force them into some kind of dialogue, thereby to reveal their real thinking through spontaneous speech; not unrehearsed, because politicians are always prepared, but at least by means of unwelcome or crafty questions which might throw them off balance. The unpredictable and spontaneous element is a crucial part of its documentary quality, to the extent that it's unrepeatable (shoot it again and it will never be quite the same). And this remains, even though in the finished film it has already been subsumed into an organised discourse which is often quite different from the context in which the remarks were first generated, where the peculiar dialogue of the interview is replaced by the dialogical alternation of the film's various different voices.

At this point in *De grands événements . . .*, Ruiz encounters Rubbo, who tells him about a Canadian politician he once filmed who protested that the film would only misrepresent him, objecting that he was 'not a sausage, which you can slice into little pieces', and Rubbo's exasperated reply, 'look here, I've never been accused of manipulating material, I have a reputation to protect, the Film Board has a reputation to protect, we can't afford to do things like that, to manipulate you in this way.' How to interpret what Rubbo is saying here depends on the level on which one reads it. On the ostensive level, Rubbo acts out his indignation for the camera – after all, he's telling a story. 'There are rules,' he declares, 'and I obey them.' On the second level, it is the politician in the tale who is guilty of stepping outside the conventions of the public representation of politics, implicitly questioning the rules which have been spelled out in institutional codes of practice.

Doubtless the rules could be different, but it's not as if they could be discarded altogether. Here the problem is larger than the documentary idiom as such. As Jameson explains, the very organisation of society imposes universals and categories, normative classifications, which not only serve as means of power and control, but derive from the increasingly complex organisation of knowledge, and this, he thinks would be difficult for the documentarist to escape. You may decide, for example,

> that the stereotypes of the homeless are wrong, you want to show some newer kinds of realities that these people live in, but you're still caught in the category of 'the homeless', and you can't get out of that no matter how specific and particular the images are.[4]

Why? Because the categories are everywhere, and the portrayal of particulars (what Deleuze calls singularities) cannot escape them. Why not? Because the image is index and icon at the same time, and can hardly avoid evoking public connotations, starting with its place within the categories of knowledge.

This is to say – as we've already seen – that by its very nature documentary is a form of discourse which can only speak of the universal through the particular, and contrariwise, where the particular is liable to be read as a universal. If this reciprocal reading is poorly balanced, the film may come unstuck as a result – it's not an uncommon experience. This is what happened, for example, with a BBC *Panorama* report a few years ago about single mothers, which was roundly criticised in the press because it chose to follow a single case in a small town which was widely regarded as untypical. Doubtless the mistake was not to have included other comparative single mothers of different social backgrounds and in different circumstances. By contrast, and with none of the BBC's resources, a pair of my own students made a film about homelessness that almost escaped the prison of categories. The film was made for a charity, to be used as a trigger for discussion in group training and public meetings, and what the charity wanted was precisely to destroy certain stereotypes of the homeless. So the students went looking for homeless people who could tell stories of how they became homeless which countered the stereotypes, and they found one: an amnesiac, someone who got off the commuter train one morning having forgotten who he was when he got on it, and because he wasn't your typical lumpen but an educated and articulate man, his account of finding himself homeless and living in a hostel did indeed undermine the stereotypes – but only up to a point. Their other two subjects – a bag lady and a bewildered youth – fitted the bill of typical characters, thus confirming what Jameson suggests, that it's probably impossible to escape the categories altogether. The question therefore becomes one of filmic artistry, of montage and narrative or poetic structure: does the film close back in on itself, intentionally or unintentionally, or does it manage to destabilise the categories to allow an open ending which leaves certain questions hanging around in the viewer's head?

De grands événements . . . deals with this issue by turning itself into a film about how to conceive of making such a film, that is, by portraying the trials and tribulations of the film-maker in the process of shooting, like Rubbo in *Waiting for Fidel*. Both films break open and render visible the conventional forms of construction of documentary discourse, exposing the codes which normally determine the reading of the representation. But with the Chilean exile, the situation of the film-maker is the opposite to that of Rubbo, and in Ruiz's film, the Third World he has left behind is a structuring absence right until it breaks through towards the end, bringing the periphery back into the picture in a series of library images. The result is a paradigm of the documentary of scepticism, a critique of documentary as a mirror of the world; we often forget that what mirrors do is reverse the symmetry, but this is exactly what happens here. Ruiz accordingly treats us in his commentary to an explicit critique of the Griersonian tradition, which ends up in his interview on the run with Rubbo in his real-life role of a Canadian film-maker who is also covering the election, and in comparing notes with Rubbo, he comes to understand that it's easier for a First-Worlder making documentaries in the Third World than the reverse.

There is a crucial qualification to all this. Rubbo and Ruiz succeed in breaking open the closed discourse of documentary convention by putting themselves and the problem of making the film into the picture. But those second-level dramas behind the making can never be fully represented – something necessarily always escapes. In a way, Rubbo's protesting politician is not mistaken, because this is one of the fundamental conditions of the documentary endeavour: it is logically impossible for an instrument, a technique, a form, which depends on the fragmentation and segmentation of the social world to do otherwise. In short, and to recall the formulation in an earlier chapter, the documentary that we see is always only one version of the documentary it could have been. Why? First, because it could have been edited differently, and all the other versions are lying on the cutting-room floor (as it used to be said). Second, because the documentary that was shot is in any case only one version of what could have been shot: the camera could always have been turned on and off at different moments, or pointed somewhere else; and anyway, whichever way it was pointing, there was always whatever was going on behind it at the moment of filming. You can only indicate these other putative versions by some kind of reflexivity or deconstruction, or by some kind of metaphor, precisely because you can never show them. There will always be things that remain invisible, a condition which may turn them into structuring absences.

II

Rubbo and Ruiz present the persona of the film-maker, but Mallet in *Unfinished Diary* goes further. She not only puts herself in the picture and speaks in the first person, but by adopting the form of the diary, she takes the documentary into the terrain of the autobiographical, providing us with a subtle account of exile as a struggle for a sense of reality and identity. And there's more, because she explores the question of identity with a feminist sensibility that insists on holding the concerns of the public and private domains together, however difficult it is to do so. The film thus encompasses both the privacy of domestic life, with its intimate relations of mother, child and husband – and a disintegrating marriage – and the demands of the outside world, the strains of adaptation to a foreign culture and the problems of the exile community.

The diary is a chronotope which allows the fluid mixture of the ongoing present with memories of the past; its film version also invites the inclusion of a disparate range of material, both visual and auditory. Like Ruiz, Mallet begins by showing us where she lives, an apartment house in a residential

neighbourhood of Montreal; we will realise that this location means that the film speaks three languages – Spanish, French and English – and that this polyglot world is one of the symptoms of exile.
She proceeds to expand the family environment, where she tends to husband and child, by introducing two fictional characters, the brother, who plays the guitar, and the mother, an artist; both are seen
during the film practising their vocations, their music and artworks contributing their sensibilities to
Mallet's world. A more enigmatic figure who appears several times is that of a solitary organ-grinder;
for Zuzana Pick, he is at different moments an evocation of childhood memories, and by means of
montage, a mute bystander to political violence, symbolising 'the fear that gripped Chile' in 1973.[5]
The third main element consists of images invoking the trauma of the *golpe de estado* which drove
them all into exile, which therefore serve as a bridge between private memory and public history.
The link becomes explicit when Mallet receives a visit from a family friend, Salvador Allende's daughter Isabel, who recalls the last conversation she had with her father. The friendship between their two
fathers is seen in family photographs, and Allende's untimely end through public images of the bombing of the Moneda Palace where he perished. The archival images are more than historical records,
but the markers of loss and trauma both national and individual.

Mallet, says Pick, 'has imagined exile as a scrapbook in which memory is constantly being recom-
posed'.[6] Several elements invoke the world of Chilean popular culture which had been such a prominent current within the cultural politics of Popular Unity. At one juncture, where as Pick describes it,
Mallet struggles with her husband's ideas about rationality ('Without it, everything would be confusion
and disorder'), the camera pans slowly over a tapestry made with scraps of fabric, of the kind known as
the *arpillera*, a traditional form of folk artistry which after the coup became a symbol of quiet resistance
into which Chilean women sewed the memory of their disappeared relatives and the reality of life under
military rule.[7] Here it also serves as a metaphor for the film's own method of collage, its approach to
montage as a stitching together of scenes and images whose place is defined by the hole they fill in the
overall shape. There is also the *pava* in which the gathered company of friends improvise coarsely joking
verses to the accompaniment of a guitar. Here, husband and son are spectators, outsiders. Lacking the
language to participate or understand, their silence enacts a gulf between cultures, their exclusion an
ironic comment of the displacement of the others. As Pick sums up, by staging or restaging moments
where social, cultural and political experiences enter into conflict, Mallet constantly stresses difference.

Mallet's argument with Rubbo in the kitchen goes to the core of the contradictions the film
addresses. She has put herself in a position which forces her to explain her ideas about the film, seeking
his advice only in order to reject it. She criticises him for criticising her, on the grounds that his 'ration-
alist' theory of film-making is not relevant to what she's trying to do. It is ironic that he espouses here
the kind of well-behaved documentary that depends on keeping certain things out of frame, out of the
range of the camera, which he sidestepped in *Waiting for Fidel*. Pick comments that Rubbo's performance in this film (both as husband and as a documentary film-maker who has located himself in his own
work) foregrounds Mallet's own concept of film-making; without, however, naming it or pinning it
down. Her emotional breakdown in this scene is all the more unsettling not only because it is 'uncanny
in its spontaneity', as another commentator puts it, a heightened moment 'in which the director appears
to lose control over her object, the representation of her image',[8] but precisely because she has propelled

herself into it herself, using the film camera as an instrument of self-assertion, as if to recreate herself and thus reclaim her identity in full public view. Yet in order to do this, she has to assert herself against what is closest to her, even if this means owning up to the breakdown of her marriage. In this way, *Unfinished Diary* ends up speaking for more than the particular displacement of the Latin American exile, but for the broader experience of women across different cultures whose sense of identity is frustrated and demands recognition.

Renov remarks that autobiographical film-making finds a particularly rich strain in works that explore the identity of the exile, citing both Ruiz's *De grands événements* . . . and Mallet's *Unfinished Diary* as examples in a line of films going back to the avant-gardist diary films of Jonas Mekas. The exile is a figure marked by dislocation and displacement, who becomes a partial and divided subject, constituted by spatial and temporal distance from that lost object of desire called the homeland. Once described by Brecht as 'the bringer of bad news', the exile is defined by their politics (whereas the terms refugee and migrant also speak of other possible causes): a political subject deprived of political rights, accepted by the host country on sufferance (the question Derrida calls 'hospitality'). Inserted into the interstices of the host society, the exile is 'deterritorialised', but as Hamid Naficy sees it, remains in the grip of both the before and the after, susceptible to 'ambiguity and doubt about the taken-for-granted values of [both] their home and host societies'.[9] The resulting films have a curious effect: they often seem to be addressed to an impossible audience, and yet they hold up a mirror to growing alienation within the host society itself, at a moment of cultural crisis and shifting paradigms of identity and knowledge.

III

These three films can be taken as emblematic of a crucial shift in the documentary idiom, almost an epistemological break, in which the old idea of objectivity is seen as naive and outmoded, and is revoked by asserting the subjective identity of the film-maker within the body (or 'text') of the film. This is what Michael Renov calls 'performing the self', through which the portrayal of the historical world (the traditional subject matter of documentary) becomes inextricably bound up with the self-inscription of the film-maker.[10] This is not to disavow the documentary status of the image, but to add a new dialectic to it, in which the embodied film-maker acts explicitly as the filter through which the world enters discourse (as opposed to the previous condition, where it is also true that the film-maker filters reality, but the discourse is impersonal, and hides the signs of authorship).

Renov associates the shift with the concept of local knowledge advanced by the anthropologist Clifford Geertz, who in the early 1980s suggested that the predilection for general theories in the social sciences had given way to a 'scattering into frameworks', a movement away from 'universalist' modes towards what he called 'a keen sense of the dependence of what is seen upon where it is seen from and what it is seen with', a description that transfers well to the documentary film.[11] (In another theoretical framework, this is the same as the end of the 'grand narrative' in which Lyotard sees the transition to postmodernism.) On this reading, says Renov, one could see the observational cinema of the 60s as still caught up within the universalist discourse that Geertz disparages, and which is gradually displaced by the disparate cultural identities of the new, where a personal perspective is substituted for the old impersonal mode of address, foregrounding the film-maker's stake in their subject matter. If this shift was an incipient move since the film-maker first stepped in front of the camera in *Chronique d'un été*, it occurred in the 70s through the cross-fertilisation of several currents. A paradigm is found in the diary films of Jonas Mekas, coming out of the New York underground, from *Diaries, Notes and Sketches* (1964–9), to *Lost, Lost, Lost* (1975) and beyond, in which the home movie is inflected by an avant-garde poetic sensibility. There is also, however, a remarkable but paradoxical oddity, a film in which the first-person documentary was satirised even before it properly existed: Jim McBride's *David Holzman's Diary* of 1967 is a fake documentary – one of the first of its kind – where the film-maker, whom only the closing credits reveal as fictional, is an obsessive who places himself bodily in the picture, taking himself and above all his private quest as the very subject of the undertaking. Yet what is prophetically parodied here as an exhibitionist enlargement of the film-maker's ego is translated over the coming years into an emphasis on the film-maker's real individuality, which could be plucked like an instrument to resonate with wider social changes.

This is to speak of a major shift over the last decades of the twentieth century in political culture – and cultural politics – across the globe, but differently manifest in different parts of it. What unfolded in the heartlands of capitalism was a passage from the politics of class to the identity politics and social movements which followed the feminist turn of the 70s, in which the conventional boundaries of social identity were dissolved and subjective selfhood was asserted in forms which challenged old certainties. If the reasons for this shift are complex and fundamental, there were several currents in play, each with its own focus, history and moment.[12] In the US, for example, the old class consciousness which flourished in the 1930s was undermined by factors like McCarthyism, union corruption and the very success of postwar capitalist reconstruction. But the latter largely excluded African Americans, with the result that the Civil Rights movement, which began to take shape in the 1950s, held out the promise of a separate politics which succoured the idea of black pride, with corresponding cultural implications. Eventually this would produce new modes of black film-making, both fiction and documentary.

Capitalist expansion also produced the invention of the teenager, symbolised in the birth of rock 'n' roll: a paradoxical new identity because it represents a transient state, rebellious but unfocused (*Rebel without a Cause* dates from 1955). As teenage culture and music spread, what followed was the world-wide student movement of the late 60s – itself a sign of the growing globalisation of the public sphere – which connected with both the protest movement against the war in Vietnam and the hippy subculture which descended from the beatniks of the 50s. The great novelty of the student movement was the fusion of anti-capitalist and libertarian currents in an attack on the conformism of what Galbraith called 'the affluent society' of Western capitalism, in the name not only of social justice but also of the imagination. (Typical graffiti on the streets in May 1968 included 'Power to the imagination', 'Those who lack imagination cannot imagine what is lacking' and Breton's 'Imagination is not a gift, it must be conquered'.) Hobsbawm remarks that the students of the 60s were motivated by a new configuration of concerns, where 'personal liberation and social liberation went hand in hand',[13] and of course the same can be said of the new wave feminism of the 70s, with its slogan 'the personal is political', as well as the emergent gay rights movement which shared the feminist concern with questions of sexuality. All these currents were particularly attracted to documentary, and would progressively reshape it as the century grew old.

IV

If the new social movements, from feminism to environmentalism, produced a re-evaluation of the categories that organise the experience of everyday life, what interests us here is how this translated into a struggle for documentary representation which had to be conducted on two fronts – the effort to acquire public visibility and simultaneously to counter the stereotypes and clichés which inevitably accompanied such visibility. Here we find a dialectic that moves back and forth between personal and social identity, the self-inscription of the film-maker in an act of self-assertive presence, and the re-interpretation of historical imagery by recontextualising it. In other words, there is also a pull to the kind of film that in Latin American terms comes under the rubric of *cine rescate* – the recovery of history.

The histories to be recovered have been systemically and repeatedly repressed. There is, for example, a long unknown history of black documentary film-making in the US, which, according to a recent study, goes back before World War I and, after the war generated scores of shorts exhibited in 'race theatres' and community meeting places.[14] These films are mostly lost and forgotten because there was no organised distribution network, and no library or repository that preserved them – the early African-American film-makers operated entirely on the margins, sometimes selling prints outright, or taking their films round a circuit of towns and cities like the early film showmen.[15]

If this is the same kind of artisanal mode of production that characterised the early years of cinema, it also arose in subsequent periods in peripheral countries across the world, especially the countries of the South, where it always struggles to survive, a form of marginal, alternative film-making which was refashioned and remediated in the last decade of the twentieth century through the spread of digital video. In the African-American case, the early wave of activity tailed off after the introduction of sound, and for many years after World War II there were only isolated efforts. In the 1960s, as the Civil Rights movement gathered momentum, questions of black politics first entered the ken of documentary in the form of television reportage from a white perspective – the Drew Associates film *Crisis*, of 1963, is an early example but, according to one account, there were more than three dozen television documentaries over the next five years on topics related to African Americans.[16] In 1968 – the year after the assassination of Martin Luther King – when the activities of the Black Panthers in California prompted several independent documentaries, again they were made by white film-makers, albeit in close cooperation with their subjects. They were also ideologically aligned, on the wider front, with everything that Solanas and Getino grouped together under the rubric of third cinema.

The San Francisco Newsreel group made its début with *Black Panther*, which includes a prison interview with Huey Newton, the Black Panther leader arrested for allegedly shooting a policeman; the charges were eventually dropped. Rallies calling for his release are featured in two films both called *Huey!*, and thus confused with each other: one released by American Documentary Films 'in cooperation with the Black Panther Party', and directed by Sally Pugh, the other by Agnès Varda. If these films reflect a particular moment of solidarity between radical white film-makers and black politics, ironically it was television that provided the opportunity for a new generation of African-American film-makers, through commissions for the newly created public television network. PBS responded to black unrest as if Stokely Carmichael was referring to television when he declared, at the rally in the ADF *Huey!*, that 'A lot of people in the [black] bourgeoisie tell me they don't like Rap Brown when he says "I'm going to burn the country down" but every time he says "I'm going to burn the country down", they get a positive pro-gramme.' Indeed one of those programmes, in Carmichael's political sense, was *Black Journal*, a PBS monthly magazine funded by the Carnegie and Ford foundations in response to the report of a Com-mission on Civil Disorders. The Kerner Commission judged that lack of access to the media by black com-munities was one of the major factors in the disorders, and from 1968 to 1970 *Black Journal* provided black film-makers with the first sustained opportunity to represent a black point of view on society in the wider public sphere. Moreover it was to do so in conditions of creative freedom, where the pro-gramme's executive producer William Greaves likened the kind of film-making he wanted to encourage to the liberating aesthetics of jazz.[17]

The opening was brief. The US mass media adapted to widening ethnic participation but on con-ditions that removed its sting. This left plenty of work to be done by independent producers. A signal example is *Eyes on the Prize*, a chronicle of the Civil Rights movement from 1954–65 in the form of a six-part series shown on PBS in 1987, combining photographs, historical footage culled from the archives and music, with the testimony of protagonists coming from divergent viewpoints: a basically orthodox approach which nonetheless made for what the producer Henry Hampton called 'messy history', history that doesn't resolve into neat stories with clear conclusions.[18] It is telling, then, that despite its popular and critical success, Hampton had difficulty raising funds for a sequel, since the closer it came to the present, the more controversial it was for potential funders. The result was that the second series, once made, would then all but disappear, because half of every episode was archive footage, most of it from commercial sources, and the producers could only afford to pay archive rights for the minimum five-year period.[19] Poor transfers of illicit copies now circulate on the internet, orphaned from the company that made them, testifying to a need to recover once more this lost recovered history.

V

Messy history is still history and feminist films like *The Life and Times of Rosie the Riveter* (Connie Field, 1980) demonstrate how it was possible to work within the realist tradition, in a critical and double-edged kind of way, to deconstruct historical imagery of the situation of women. The voice in these films is first person but not autobiographical on the part of the film-maker – it is the collective of voices in the film who tell their own stories. In *Rosie*, US wartime propaganda documentaries promoting the massive incor-poration of women into factory production lines are 'rewritten' by counterposing them with the testi-monies of some of the same women years later recalling their experience of the time, confronting the historical images and the official version with what then happened – their massive removal from these jobs when the menfolk returned from the front at the end of the war. By opening a space for the women who were once the object of media attention to speak of their own fortunes, they are able to shed light on the use of the old images, and the film ingeniously exposes the hypocrisy that underlay the official discourse, demonstrating the manipulative power of mass propaganda at the same time as deconstructing it. Films like this use oral history to construct their narratives, but in doing so are not beyond criticism, especially from a historian's point of view. As one of them writes, 'While oral history subjects are frequently both engaging and uniquely informative, their accounts . . . can be partial, frag-mentary, idiosyncratic and sometimes – deliberately or unintentionally – misleading.'[20] There's a strange paradox at work here, because *Rosie* is one of those films that rescues unheard voices and propels them into the public sphere, yet one of the reasons for its success as a film was that Field trawled through over 700 women in order to select the five who become so engaging on the screen; these five – Jewish, black, white and Asian American – were ethnically representative for the susceptibilities of the time the film was made, not the times it portrayed (when most of the Rosies were white and Christian); and two of them were members of the Communist Party, but their politics are kept out of it. This is not necessarily to impugn this kind of film, but certainly to point to the role of hidden second-level judgments in selecting and shaping the material.

A similar critical realism characterises one of the films which marks the emergence of gay cinema, *Before Stonewall* (Robert Rosenberg, John Scagliotti and Greta Schiller, 1984), which uses archive footage and oral history (and music, of course) to chronicle the evolution of gay culture in the United States from the early l920s to the moment in 1969 when patrons of the Stonewall Inn in New York's Greenwich Village decided to fight back against harassment, transforming a police raid into three nights of rioting that signalled the public arrival of the new gay liberation movement. Like *Rosie*, the archive isn't limited to documentary footage, but takes in clips and photographs from a variety of sources over five decades to give them a double reading, as it explores the gay underground of the 20s and 30s, the situation of gays in the military and workforce during World War II, and their persecution by the US State Department and Senator McCarthy as 'subversives' and 'sexual perverts' in the 1950s. This is a film in which modern history is recovered in the interests of remaking it on a double level, personal and collective. In the new mode of identity politics, of identity as identification, your identity is not simply something passively received but something you choose to assert. Indeed the function of 'coming out' in the gay and lesbian movement is that of making difference visible, and this is exactly why documentary film should become a privileged medium for the purpose.

The 60s already demonstrated how identity finds expression in everyday life through dress, clothes and fashion – typical subjects of early investigations by semiologists like Barthes – which as visual signs provide the media with rich nourishment, and this extends to other aspects of performative behaviour in public by people who are not public figures. Hobsbawm, for example, emphasises the role of the 'newly extended field of publicly acceptable behaviour, including the sexual . . .' which in the US contributed to 'the public emergence of an openly practised homosexual subculture'[21] – especially in the two trend-setting cities of San Francisco and New York. As the subculture transformed into the 'political pressure group' and a new identity politics, the gay film movement developed, for which the autobiographical film proved a highly attractive mode of expression and a field of open filmic experiment. Here one of the paradigms is Marlon Riggs' *Tongues Untied* of 1989, depicting an identity and subculture both black and gay through a tapestry of poetry, performance, personal testimony, musical numbers, documentary footage and media clips. The *Los Angeles Times* called it 'poetic, lyrical, poignant, funny, rapping, street-talking raw art', adding that it could well provoke the homophobic racism it wanted to expose, and indeed its broadcast by PBS television in 1991 provoked a howl of fury from the defenders of decency, who condemned the film as 'indecent', 'graphic' and 'obscene'. 'The vice squad of American culture was once again on the attack,' wrote Riggs himself in response, pointing to a flaw in the mainstream media: '"minorities" might be granted the right to speak and be heard, but only if we abide by the "master codes" of courteous speech, proper subject matter, conventional aesthetics and "mainstream" appeal. Disobey this often unquestioned rule and you risk banishment into cultural oblivion.'[22]

VII

Self-inscription and, more radically, autobiography, redefines the representational space of documentary from a personal position. By presenting a chronotope that declares 'this is my world at this moment', the represented world transcends the opposition between objectivity and subjectivity by including the subjective sense of the pictured world as an objective datum. Simply put, the documentary is here an objective rendering of someone's subjectivity. To an extent, this shift rehearses a withdrawal of documentary from the rhetoric of the public world into a space of personal preoccupations, which would seem to be a de-politicisation of documentary screen-space. But on another level, it invites the embodiment through the camera-eye of the personal as political, proclaimed by the new feminism and transferable to the whole arena of identity politics, and covering a whole range of confessional and activist approaches. The paradoxical result was that the individual voice of first-person documentary marked the emergence into public space of new social collectivities, becoming maps of the habitations of these new social actors and subcultures.

For Pat Aufderheide, first-person film-making, fuelled since the 80s by the flood of camcorders into the consumer market, is both 'symptom and response to the challenge of social location in postmodern society'.[23] A genre somewhere between the essay, reportage and the well-told tale, it is not only marked by personal testimony, it also brings the viewer into the world of the film-maker's experience, less concerned with making an argument than inviting the viewer to recognise the videographer's reality, and incorporate it into their own worldview. Similarly, Catherine Russell sees it as an exploration of the fragmented and dispersed identities entailed by the pluralist societies of the late twentieth century.[24] An 'art of memory' invoked as protection against the homogenising tendencies of modern culture, it becomes ethnographically interesting, she thinks, at the point where the film-maker understands their personal history to be implicated in larger social formations and historical processes.

One of the films which fits this bill is Andrés Di Tella's *La Televisión y yo* (Television and Me, 2003), an exemplary film for its dialectic between the private sphere of family history and the public domain of national history in the South American country of Argentina. We begin in an empty room, unpacking family memorabilia, a first-person voice-over saying he wanted to make a film about television and what it signifies in people's lives, but it came out differently. Meanwhile, the film proceeds to investigate the effects of television, Di Tella talking to friends and television personalities, going back to its beginnings before he was born. He meets Sebastian, grandson of one Jaime Yankelevich, the entrepreneur who set up the first television station in Argentina in 1951, and he discovers curious parallels with his own grandfather, who was also a pioneering entrepreneur. Among other things, Torcuato Di Tella manufactured the television sets that received the broadcasts of the station founded by Yankelevich. Halfway through his investigation, the grandson decides he ought to be making a film about his own family. As he turns his attention to investigating his grandfather, he enters into a dialogue with his father, a sociologist who has written the grandfather's biography, about what it means to write family history. Can a son know his father? Can a family recount anything other than family legend? The questions remain open, but what he shows in the process, taking advantage of archive footage, is how the two entrepreneurial grandfathers both crossed paths with General Perón, and his family history is thereby interpolated into the country's political history. (And because the grandfathers were public figures, this is why there is archive for him to use in this film.)

In formal terms, it's like watching a spiral expand. Setting out to make a film about television, it immediately becomes a film about memory, because he thinks about his first memory of watching television. This turns out to be a political event, Onganía's military coup in 1966, when he was seven. This event is immediately inscribed in his personal history because it prompted his father to resign his post at the university and take the family abroad for seven years, first to the US then to England. The result for the young boy, among other things, was missing out on seven years of Argentinian television which belong to his generation's collective memory, which is consequently half-lost to him, as if part of his cultural identity is missing, and therefore becomes an object of fascination. On the other hand, there are certain television memories they all share, because they had global reach, like *The Dick van Dyke Show* and the moon landing.

Thus, with a few deft steps, the film stakes out an autobiographical position in the historical world which jumps back and forth in time, like private memory, and vaunts across the globe and back, and this fluidity is somehow implicated by his thinking about television, which of course does something very similar. Dick van Dyke and the moon landing. It's all very disorienting. Like cinema but in your own home, television has the capacity to transport you to different spaces, both real and imaginary, both outside and inside your own head at the same time. *Television and Me* reproduces this condition on the formal level, mapping out the strange cultural space of televisual society, full of any images whatever, as Deleuze might say, Dick van Dyke and the moon landing, using all sorts of found material – newsreel, television and movie clips along with family photographs and home movies – intercut with informal interviews and with a first-person commentary, backed by appropriate music to evoke the period.

The diversity of material is familiar from many other autobiographical films as is the looseness of the narrative. Di Tella meanders his way through a series of chapters which pursue various lines of enquiry only to come up with a blank or a gap, in which the film-maker shares his haphazard journey of discovery with the viewer, instead of welding the results into a coherent tale. But these parallel lines of enquiry conspire to invade each other. The stories of the two entrepreneurs, both self-made immigrants, one Italian and one Jewish, run in parallel, and illuminate each other almost like a pair of Shakespearian characters. Important men, patricians, businessmen with powerful connections in society and politics. And the grandsons. Di Tella and Sebastian form a bond because they are both the grandsons of prominent modernising entrepreneurs whose empires both disappeared. What is it like to have almost inherited a fortune? Neither shows any resentment, but they wonder how come it got away. After first meeting Sebastian, Di Tella wanders through a flea market where he finds worthless share certificates for his grandfather's company, which he buys for five pesos. SIAM Di Tella was once the country's largest manufacturer of refrigerators, cars and TV sets, and a kind of national symbol, but then it fell into almost terminal decline. Like Yankelevich, who created an empire of radio stations and built up the first national network, Radio Belgrano, except that Yankelevich's empire came to an end when Perón nationalised it.

The story of the two entrepreneurs, he muses, 'is also the story of a national project that lost its way'. Indeed the film struck one Argentinian film critic as 'an assembly of stories all marked by loss',[25] and according to Di Tella himself, it's really about failure – the failure of the film-maker to make the film he set out to make, and of documentary as a medium for recounting history; the loss of the first ten years of Argentinian television, which was simply discarded – practically nothing survives in the archives; the family's loss of its heritage; and in fact the economic and political failure of the country itself.

It is precisely by pointing all the time to the gaps in the various stories, the family secrets, the mysteries about exactly what happened and how, that Di Tella prises history open a little, and the lacunae of forgetfulness begin to give up something of what they hide. The Spanish film scholar Maria Luisa Ortega draws an interesting comparison between Di Tella's film and Patricio Guzmán's procedure in *Chile, la memoria obstinada* (Chile, The Obstinate Memory, 1997), in which Guzmán goes back to Chile with his film, *La batalla de Chile*, which has never been shown there, to find out what memories or impressions it evokes in viewers old and young. Both these films draw on archive images and use first-person narration, the presence of the film-maker within his own film, and a self-reflexive mode of filmic construction, in order to re-enter history.[26] The difference is that Guzmán, working to recover the memory of those who lived through the *golpe de estado* of 1973 for a new generation from whom the historical truth has been hidden, uses images from his earlier film as a catalysing agent, to re-establish connection between past and present. In other words, Guzmán is borrowing his own images whereas Di Tella borrows the images of others, including the family's home movies. In effect, Guzmán is re-entering a history that he himself has lived from behind the camera, while Di Tella is investigating a history that came before him. Di Tella is moving from the personal, through the family, to the social. Guzmán is moving in the opposite direction, from the historical evidence back to its impact in the domain of the personal, but with the effect, of course, of taking up the personal only in order to politicise it.

VIII

For Jon Dovey, whose concern is what happens when the turn to the first-person reaches the mass media in the 1990s, in the form of the video diary, klutz films, camcorder cults, reality television and docusoaps, there is a 'lurch towards the private in public speech' which upsets the inherited sense of what counts as public.[27] As documentaries inhabit these particular and peculiar worlds, a double process occurs. 'The rhetoric by which individual stories relate to social praxis is being lost (as the common language of the public sphere is being lost), to be replaced by a rhetoric which privileges individual subjectivity as an essential component of social praxis.'[28] In other words, the space is filled 'by voices proclaiming and celebrating their own "freakishness", articulating their most intimate fears and secrets', performing the ordinariness of their own particular subjectivity. If the performance and display of difference has become a driving force in people's aspirations, the questions at stake

> have implications for the wider polity as a whole: what kind of collective identities and common symbolic patterns emerge from a public speech increasingly rooted in local and particular speaking subjects, from 'Other' people who speak intimately and incessantly of their profound difference to an assumed 'public'?[29]

Dovey was writing only a few years ago – at the turn of the millennium – but now there are new questions which can be added here, about the internet as a medium for the dissemination of video, and a new space for the assertion and articulation of both individual and collective identities.

The different tendencies of first-person film-making are difficult to differentiate because they leak over into each other, but we had better admit that the results of self-enquiry can also lead to confusion, where the subject perceives themself as occupying a strange and impossible habitus, divided between several different cultural discourses – ethnic, national, sexual, racial, class – which vie to challenge all received or imposed forms of identity. But whether we're looking at the naivety of the television video diary, the sophisticated diarising of a Ross McElwee, or the social enquiry of the Latin American examples, one question remains insistent. If the film-maker is a construct within the body and text of the film, then is the persona they adopt on the screen not some kind of fiction, or at least invention? Or is this too crude a way to put it, merely inviting a return to the terms of the debate back in the 60s around the emergence of the new subject?

The documentarist as their own subject is doubly self-fashioning – self-inscription means that the film-maker steals their own identity in the act of filming, in order to write a script for themselves in the process of editing. The result is both the creation of a persona and a writing of the self. This is fuzzy territory. Take the case of Nanni Moretti's entrancing *Caro Diario*, which shares the elements of both autobiography and documentary as quest. Here Moretti has a different persona in each of the three parts. The first, filmed with breathtaking control from his scooter, presents us with the film-maker-as-author in his native habitat, observing the city he lives in (this is like a homage to the city film of old). The second part is a video diary of an island trip with a friend in which both are acting up for the camera, which becomes an exquisitely shaped, anecdotal narrative, a kind of moral tale about escaping from the images that assault us back home. The third part, in which Moretti tries to track down the diagnosis and cure of his own skin ailment, adopts another stance. At the outset Moretti declares that in this section of the film, nothing is invented – but what we see here looks like re-enactment. What can this mean? Interviewed by a journalist, Moretti denied that the film was a documentary, but the fact remains, *Caro Diario* is a model of the diary film, and it's Moretti's persona that is written by his own camera-pen.

Perhaps we must start to think of a new and paradoxical kind of representational space which incorporates various different elements of both fiction and documentary without falling back into either. In some films, like Ruiz's *De grands événements . . .*, the generation of a paradoxical space on the screen is a way of saying something about paradoxical spaces beyond it. In others, the film-maker toys with the charge that documentary is after all a type of fiction by driving a wedge between a documentary space on the screen and a fictional space on the soundtrack. The effect can be found in two films, one English and one Chilean, where the visuals are documentary but the soundtrack carries a narration by a fictional voice: Patrick Keiller's *London* and Ignacio Agüero's *Sueños de hielo* (Dreams of Ice, 1992). For a screening of the former on Britain's Channel 4, one newspaper listing called it a 'drama documentary', which hardly seems right, since this is a genre that implies re-enactment and there is none of that here. There is nothing either enacted or re-enacted, but impeccable observational shooting of London scenes, taken by a static camera but hugely engrossing for their decentred perspectives on the familiar. The soundtrack, however, is a monologue, a first-person narrative about the speaker's friend's reflections on the city, delivered in the marvellously gruff voice of a well-known actor (Paul Scofield) who never appears in the picture (and nor does his friend). The Chilean film, which portrays the transportation of a large lump of Antarctic ice to Seville for the World's Fair, has exactly the same form – a fictional narrative told by an unseen voice over observational images, though rather more stylised. The aesthetic of both films consists in the teasing disparity between image and word, the tension between them, the ambiguous mental space which they map out before our eyes.

These are films that transgress the conventional rules of the screen as a representational space, fusing spaces which are conventionally opposed. There is clearly something about them of the documentary essay, but this is not what documentary normally means, nor do they follow the dramatic conventions of docudrama or drama documentary. Perhaps we should think of this as a radical new chronotope, neither fiction nor documentary but both and neither. One of the best-known examples would be Kiarostami's *Close Up*, which was shown in London a few years ago in a season called 'Fake Documentaries', except that this doesn't capture it either. Kiarostami had read a story about a young man, Sabzian, who had impersonated another Iranian director, Makhmalbaf. He arranged to shoot Sabzian's trial and then reconstructed, with the same people, the events that brought him to court, embedding the trial into a circular narrative. Kiarostami himself said he set out 'to keep reminding the viewer that they are watching the filmed version of a real story'. These are characters playing themselves, and doing it very well – in both the documentary events the camera witnesses and those which are re-enacted for it.

IX

We arrive in the late 1990s at a series of films in which an Israeli film-maker performs the occupation through his own divided persona. According to a writer in the newspaper *Ha'aretz* in 2002, Israeli documentarists have been caught in a bind. To succeed internationally they must make films that deal with either the Holocaust or the Israeli–Palestinian conflict, topics which local television, says the writer, prefers to avoid.[30] The result is that abroad they win prizes and get screened on television, but not at home. Avi Mograbi is one of them, with three oddly titled films called *How I Learned to Overcome My Fear and Love Arik Sharon* (1997), *Happy Birthday Mr Mograbi* and *August: A Moment before the Eruption* (2002). The mode employed by all three is the parody of the video diary, in which Mograbi plays his own central and semi-fictionalised character, that of a documentary film-maker trying to confront the everyday reality of the conflict in a highly ironic attempt to get underneath the skin of the Israeli psyche. In a word, these films are not conventional documentaries, but the staging or performance of the problem of documentary in the context of a national political disaster. Mograbi himself calls them 'fictional documentary', but this should not be allowed to disguise the veridical value of their documentary dimensions.

How I Learned . . . takes the form of a documentary about a leftwing documentarist trying to make a film about a rightwing politician in an election campaign, who is decidedly uncooperative about being filmed. Mograbi's persona is reminiscent of Nick Broomfield going after his prey, in which the quest is framed by the film-maker's personal diary-style confessions to camera. What unfolds is not just an amusing tale about the excitement and frustrations of the chase. These confessions even include his dreams (in which the autobiographical facts are those of the real Mograbi) where we witness the way the politician enters the film-maker's psyche as he tries to get close to him. Where journalists universally keep their backstage relations with their subject out of the camera's eye, here everything is turned inside out, and the backstage story becomes the framing narrative of the film, which as a result takes on the tone of a black comedy. Is the Avi Mograbi in this film an authentic self-representation? As Mograbi later explained, 'I was forced to play the part of somebody who is not really me, and getting as close as possible to him made me play the part even harder.'[31]

Happy Birthday Mr Mograbi is the most complex of these films in narrative terms. Mograbi plays a film-maker who is commissioned to make a happy film about Israel's 50th anniversary. At the same time he is asked by a Palestinian television station to shoot footage for a film they're making on the Naqba, or Disaster, as the Palestinians call the founding of Israel in 1948, when they were driven from their homes. Halfway through the film, Mograbi discovers that Israel's Independence Day, which follows the Hebrew Calendar, this year falls on the same day as his own birthday according to the international calendar – a fact that seriously discombobulates him. Intertwined with the stories of the two films he's supposed to be making is a third, in which Mograbi recounts his attempt to sell a half-finished house on a plot of land he bought ten years earlier. Once again, the convoluted details of this third story provide a tone of black humour which pervades the entire film. Mograbi's persona in this film veers closer to Nanni Moretti, but his narrative method is that of constant self-interruption. The result of this manic montage of disparate elements is a caustic view of the nationalism of the Israeli jubilee (which was clearly shared by the audience at the documentary film festival in Tel Aviv where I first saw it).

The parody, the self-interruption, the style of video filming which emphasises its rawness – this is a Brechtian aesthetic, but very different from the third figure with whom Mograbi suggests comparison, namely Michael Moore. Mograbi is not aiming to rouse our emotions and indignation, still less tell us how to vote, but wants to tease us into questioning the very nature of the representation. According to Mograbi, reality is never there in itself, it is always being represented by someone, typically by 'forces . . . that interpret reality for us all the time, and thus the meaning of reality has become a tool in their hands to promote their agenda'.[32] In other words, Jameson's second level. The madness in Mograbi's method is that whether the scene is fictionalised or belongs to public reality, whether the camera is interacting with the subject or merely observing, the constant shifting back and forth between different scenes and different styles of filming demonstrates the elusive nature of historical and social truth.

The third of these films, *August: A Moment before the Eruption*, tries to confront this problem directly. Here again there is a three-stranded narrative, with Mograbi this time playing three different characters – himself, his wife and his producer. Avi wants to make a film about the month of August, when it's too hot for comfort, and which he sees as a metaphor for everything hateful in the State of Israel. His wife gets caught between him and his producer, who is trying to get him to make a film about Baruch Goldstein, the West Bank settler who massacred twenty-nine Palestinians in Hebron in 1994. The film we're seeing moves back and forth between Avi's home, a series of unconvincing auditions for an actress to the play the role of Goldstein's wife and his sorties with his camera onto the streets. Here, in a disconnected series of scenes, we become increasingly disconcerted by the aggression we discover on the streets which is occasioned by the mere presence of the camera itself. Filming a demonstration of settlers, he's beset by a stream of questioning about who he's filming for; some of his interrogators interpret his reply, 'For myself, I'm independent', as meaning that he's a stringer for one of the international news agencies, freelancing for the police. He encounters the same suspicious questions from a bunch of casual labourers waiting on the roadside for jobs, working-class North African Jews on one side of the road, Israeli Palestinians on the other, and no love lost between them. At a religious revivalist rally in a stadium where the rabbi arrives by helicopter, he is soon stopped from filming. Later, he is stopped from filming a demonstration outside the Ministry of Defence, and yet again in the street where a motor cavalcade for the King of Jordan is about to pass by.

These scenes are paradoxical. On the one hand, one would suppose that people who are ready to challenge the camera understand something about the uses of the image for propaganda and surveillance and are not entirely wrong to be suspicious. On the other hand, this suspicion comes across as paranoia. On the one hand, a justified fear of misrepresentation, and on the other, aggression. A very social paranoia of which the film is a cognitive mapping. And to top it all, in one extraordinary scene, they not only want to argue with the camera but they want to direct it as well. In the Old City of Jerusalem, when Mograbi finds himself filming the arrest of a couple of Palestinian youths, he is surrounded by a bunch of hostile onlookers who complain that he didn't film the youths when they were throwing stones and why doesn't he point his camera in a different direction. Finally a policeman removes him from the scene.

In the Sharon film we see evidence of the discrepancy between politics as spectacle and what is hidden behind closed doors, a gap the camera places in evidence but is not allowed to cross. In *Happy Birthday* we witness the discrepancy between official public celebration and the hidden angst of the Palestinian people, the hopes buried under the sabra bushes which mark the sites of forcibly abandoned villages. The discrepancy addressed in *August* is if possible even more disturbing: it is the disparity between the external and internal image of the same people. People who think of themselves as a reasonable and democratic nation but behave towards each other (let alone the Palestinians) with mistrust and aggression. Repeatedly obstructed from filming in public places where everyone always demands that he explain himself, the film-maker documents his own failure, the impossibility of making such a film as this in Israel today. But the very encounters of the camera with these people on the streets who try to impede it become themselves the primary evidence of the condition of the country which the film wants to document – a condition, in Mograbi's words, of 'constant anger, bitterness, suspicion'. None of these films is about solutions, or the prospects for peace. They are ironic calls for Israel to wake up to itself. As Mograbi puts it, 'Life in Israel is oppressive and sad enough even without the August heat.'

A growing number of Palestinian documentaries that portray the Occupation from the perspective of the Occupied are evidence of the way that digital video has extended access to those who were previously invisible. Along with a number of striking fiction films, they comprise a new cinema of urgency created in the most remarkable circumstances, because they emerge from a population besieged and cut off from the rest of the world, their physical isolation breached by their access to the virtual world of electronic communication and hence their insertion in the same global cultural space as their oppressors. But here I want to mention another Israeli film, Yoav Shamir's singular *Checkpoint* (2003), an exercise in observational reportage that demonstrates a radical shift in the relation between camera and subject in the times of globalising media diffusion. Filmed over the course of a year at different checkpoints that control the movement of the Palestinians around the Occupied Territories, at different times of day and in all weathers, nothing here is staged and there are no interviews, but from time to time, people address themselves to the camera of their own accord. At the start of the film we see lines of Palestinians waiting outside Nablus to be allowed past the barrier; split into two – one line of men, one of women and children – penned into a narrow space while the Israeli soldiers keep pushing them back, the camera settles on a well-dressed man wearing Western-style jacket and tie, who shakes his head and speaks in English: 'Nobody knows about us here,' he says, 'Nobody'. But everyone here is aware of being filmed, and they regard the camera as a witness of their situation: neither are they passive subjects any longer, nor the naive realists of former times – they are perfectly aware that the film-maker has a point of view and is capable of slanting the argument this way or that. This emerges most remarkably in the entreaty of one of the Israeli soldiers at the end of a long sequence in which an Israeli Palestinian pleads to be allowed through to return to Jerusalem. After finally letting him pass, one of the soldiers half turns to the camera and says, 'Try to make me look good, not like the bad guy. I'm going to look very bad.' 'How can I make you look good?' says the voice behind the camera. 'Try', says the soldier, 'Blame it on the higher ranks, not on me.'

What is happening here is extraordinarily revealing: clearly this soldier feels ashamed of what he is seen to be doing, and wants to communicate his discomfort. In the process, he signals an awareness of the power of representation but also of his own capacity, even prerogative, to intervene and to represent himself. I found something similar when we were shooting our film on Detroit a couple of years ago. Like so many mid-sized American cities, Detroit is almost devoid of pedestrians, but whenever we stepped out on the streets to film one of the innumerable ruins, someone would appear and ask us what we were doing. On hearing that we were a couple of academics making a documentary about Detroit, they would immediately launch into their own rap, hardly even waiting for me to turn on the camera. My collaborator, George Steinmetz, summed up by alluding to Marx's famous phrase about the French peasantry, 'since they cannot represent themselves, they must be represented', but here in Detroit, he said, 'they *want* to be represented'. This is clearly different from earlier times when people were mystified by the documentary camera and the rituals of the film crew, and then when they grew increasingly sceptical of their intentions. Today it would seem that the ubiquity of the video camera, and dissemination of its imagery by satellite and the internet, is in process of demystifying the medium, at least to the point where people being filmed are no longer subdued by it, but ready to have their say.

Checkpoint's remarkable climactic sequence demonstrates another quality. Here we're at the entrance to Ramallah after a heavy snow fall. A Palestinian man hands over his pass with the words, 'Let us past this time, look at the weather.' An Israeli soldier walks away from the camera with the comment 'Let him film. What do I care? I don't care what people think.' A moment later, they're all throwing snowballs at each other, the Palestinians crying 'Allah Akbar', as one man shouts 'You can see that you went through an Intifada', and another replies 'Come on, we'll give you an Intifada'. The scene transcends itself to become a powerful, intensely poignant, and poetically ambiguous symbol of the physical violence, which throughout the film remains off-screen but which the viewer knows is going on. In the process, it exemplifies one of the most profound capacities of documentary cinema, which goes beyond the representation of the way things appear, to become a metaphor for what is going on behind and beyond the image which the camera records. In a strangely understated kind of way, the snow-fight in *Checkpoint* is cathartic, precisely because it doesn't invent or fictionalise but simply points beyond to the wider and deeper tragedy.

Notes

1. Michael Chanan, 'Talking Film with Fredric Jameson: A Conversation', in Douglas Kellner and Sean Homer (eds), *Fredric Jameson: A Critical Reader* (Basingstoke and New York: Palgrave Macmillan, 2004).
2. Brian Winston, *Lies, Damn Lies and Documentaries* (London: BFI, 2000), p. 128.
3. Chanan, 'Talking Film with Fredric Jameson'.
4. Chanan, 'Talking Film with Fredric Jameson', p. 132.
5. Zuzana Pick, *The New Latin American Cinema: A Continental Project* (Austin: University of Texas Press, 1993), p. 165.
6. Pick, *The New Latin American Cinema*, p. 167.
7. Pick, *The New Latin American Cinema*, p. 165.
8. Brenda Longfellow, quoted in Pick, *The New Latin American Cinema*, p. 166.
9. Hamid Naficy, *An Accented Cinema: Exilic and Diasporic Filmmaking* (Princeton, NJ: Princeton University Press, 2001), pp. 12–13.
10. Michael Renov, *The Subject of Documentary* (Minneapolis: University of Minnesota Press, 2004), p. 176.
11. Quoted by Renov, *The Subject of Documentary*, p. 176.
12. See, for example, Stanley Aronowitz, *The Politics of Identity: Class, Culture, Social Movements* (New York: Routledge, 1992).
13. Eric Hobsbawm, *Age of Extremes: The Short Twentieth Century 1914–1991* (London: Michael Joseph, 1994), p. 333.
14. Janet Cutler and Phyllis Klotman, *Struggles for Representation: African American Documentary Film and Video* (Bloomington: Indiana University Press, 1999).
15. Pearl Bowser, in Cutler and Klotman, *Struggles for Representation*, p. 6.
16. Tommy Lee Lott, 'Documenting Social Issues', in Cutler and Klotman, *Struggles for Representation*, p. 74.
17. Lott, in Cutler and Klotman, *Struggles for Representation*, p. 77.
18. See Elizabeth Amelia Hadley, '*Eyes on the Prize*: Reclaiming Black Images, Culture, and History', in Cutler and Klotman, *Struggles for Representation*, p. 104.
19. See Jack Ellis and Betsy McLane, *A New History of Documentary Film* (New York: Continuum, 2005), p. 275.
20. Sonya Michel, quoted by Paula Rabinowitz, 'Wreckage upon Wreckage: History, Documentary and the Ruins of Memory', *History and Theory* vol. 32 no. 2, May 1993, pp. 133–4.
21. Hobsbawm, *Age of Extremes*, p. 333.

22. Marlon Riggs, 'Tongues Re-tied?', *Current*, 12 August 1991, <www.current.org/prog/prog114g.html>.

23. Pat Aufderheide, *The Daily Planet: A Critic on the Capitalist Cultural Beat* (Minneapolis: University of Minnesota Press, 2000), p. 215.

24. Catherine Russell, *Experimental Ethnography* (Durham, NC: Duke University Press), p. 276.

25. Clara Kriger, 'Andrés Di Tella' in Paulo Antonio Paranagua (ed.), *Cine Documental en América Latina* (Madrid: Cátedra, 2003), pp. 264–5.

26. María Luisa Ortega, 'Rupturas y continuidades en el documental social', mss.

27. Jon Dovey, *Freakshow: First-Person Media and Factual Television* (London and Sterling, VA: Pluto Press, 2000), p. 3.

28. Dovey, *Freakshow*, p. 34.

29. Dovey, *Freakshow*, pp. 3–4.

30. Sara Leibovich-Dar , 'Screen Test', *Ha'aretz*, 9 June 2002.

31. 'A Conversation with Avi Mograbi', in Avi Mograbi, *(Fictional) Documentary* (Oldenburg: Edith Russ Site for Media Art, 2003), p. 33.

32. Mograbi, *(Fictional) Documentary*, p. 24.

15 History and Memory

The paradoxes of the archives

I

In 1939, on the eve of World War II, Paul Rotha made a big and expensive documentary for and about *The Times*, called *The Fourth Estate*, which remained unseen for thirty years. This was not just because the outbreak of war rendered a film about a newspaper in peacetime outdated before it had even been shown, and then it was just forgotten. According to Rotha himself,[1] the paper disapproved of his mildly satirical vision of its establishment role (so mild it hardly registers nowadays) and withheld the film (until the paper was taken over by the Thomson organisation who let it be shown). Given an outing in a screening in 2003, in a double bill with a short called *Book Bargain* by Norman McLaren, made for the GPO Film Unit a couple of years earlier, about the manufacture of the London telephone directory, the contrast between the two films is striking. Rotha was a leftwing social democrat, McClaren a member of the Communist Party who had just been to Spain with Ivor Montagu to shoot a film about the defence of Madrid against the Fascists. Rotha tries to beat the system and fails, McLaren doesn't try and succeeds – that is, he turns out a simple factual film, beautifully photographed, which in eight minutes unpretentiously reveals a slice of social and industrial history about the spread of a crucial modern technology of communication. Where the first London telephone directory in 1878 had no more than 200 entries, the 1937 directory listed 850,000 subscribers, ran to 2,500 pages, and its production required a dedicated printing operation as complex as that of a newspaper but with its own specialised machinery. We also learn, in the course of the film, that in one section of the production line the women swap their jobs around in order to try and alleviate their boredom a little, which nearly seventy years later prompts the response that such flexible labour practices are difficult to imagine under twenty-first century managerialism. There is nothing about such things in the Rotha film, which is lacking in perspective and paints a portrait of an entirely patriarchal world where it wouldn't be playing the game to talk about what goes on on the shop floor.

If forgotten documentaries like these contribute to our knowledge of recent history then they do so on different levels, in different ways, and unevenly. Sometimes, like *Book Bargain*, they reveal signal bits of information, indicative facts about the way things were. At the opposite pole, while a film like *The Fourth Estate* has little by way of hard empirical content, it presents an historical picture of a social institution at a certain moment, in a peculiarly synthetic form that can still be very revealing. In the words of a producer of historical compilation documentaries, all sorts of films, including newsreels, public information documentaries and works of propaganda, may not only capture 'an impression of what an event looked like' but give 'a topical and often revealing interpretation of that event, which is, in its own way, a historical document itself'.[2] Indeed there is no film that is not a document in and of itself, being inevitably inscribed with the conditions and circumstances of its production (which also means the nega-tive imprint of certain structuring absences). This is why historical footage sometimes says more about the past of cinema and its way of seeing than it does about what it pictures; it is also why documentaries quickly become dated, leaving the ideology which informed them looking threadbare. On the other hand, the corollary is not that the documentary image is historically superficial and unreliable, and of no real interest to historians, but something more elusive, namely, that the film as such becomes a strange new form of historical evidence which gives us the immediate sight of the recent historical past embed-ded in what is always already a partial perspective on it: a veridical social and historical world as inter-preted by the film-maker just a moment before it becomes historical, for, as Derrida has it, the act of recording or photographing immediately turns the subject into a non-presence, a 'past present'. Almost as if it were the act of filming that made it historical.

Because we are speaking of documentary, we know that the historical worlds depicted here are taken from social reality (allowing for episodes of contrivance and re-enactment), and that those who are pictured in them are social actors, appearing as themselves, by name or anonymously. In 1953, BBC Television carried out an unusual exercise. They screened another film by Rotha, *Total War in Britain*, from 1945, introduced by questions to the viewers. Were you there? Do you see yourself in this film? What are you doing now? The response from people who saw themselves doing war jobs in the film was so large, says Jay Leyda, that it was shown again, stopping at certain frames to show interviews with people seen in them.[3] In short, documentary is related not only to history but often also to memory, and to ask about the one is also to raise questions of the other. The two are separate but related phenom-ena which overlap, one being public and collective, the other private and individual. But if documentary is a medium which can encourage people to see themselves in relation to history, this is precisely because it becomes a space of interaction between the two.

At least the field is clearly delimited, since we're talking of a period that for cinematic purposes stretches back little more than 100 years. The filmic representation of history before the moment when cinematography was invented either has to be enacted, therefore fictionalised, or else to dispense with flesh-and-blood, and content itself with artefacts and their interpretation by the living, and of course there are many documentaries that have done this (though nowadays, they often make up for the lack by means of digital fabrication). But even within this delimited period, to pose these questions is to ask about what Derrida calls 'the economy of memory', which directs us to the archives, the place where society's memory is stored away.[4] Since the functioning of the archive, however, cannot be separated from its material substrates, it is therefore also a question about how these substrates are stored and what the act of retrieval consists in. Hence, we would have to speak of the archive as an institution with a certain structure and economy, and retrieval as a process of research and investigation. And discoveries.

The archive is a space of paradox, a repository of objects of memory where they can be safely left and forgotten. The first thing that it turns out has been forgotten in this way is the history of docu-mentary itself. If the computer screens which nowadays display the catalogues reveal the history of documentary as a history of forgetfulness, this is not just a question of unremembered names and titles, but what else is being let slip along with the forgotten films – not just unremembered, but repressed. This word, which so readily offers itself in this context, inevitably takes us in two directions. On the one hand, into the territory of psychoanalysis, which has a fundamental involvement with all questions of memory, and from which we know, first and foremost, that memory is always selective, and it cannot be addressed without incurring its corollary, forgetting. And on the other, towards the domain of politics, where repression is not only administered directly through censorship, constraint and suppression, but also more subtly, by means of ideological dissuasion, the pressures of conformism and conventional wisdom, the doxa of self-censorship. Both are at issue in the construction of history through film.

II

If we remember to think of documentary as Wittgenstein thought of games – as an extended family in which various features are shared out among them in such a way that some relatives may not resemble each other at all – then new variants are like the arrival of new generations of cousins. Meanwhile, older members pass away and are unceremoniously buried in the archives. The result is that documentary is continually reinventing itself, for better or worse, and contemporary practitioners are much less con-nected than directors of fiction to the history of cinema. If nowadays the diffusion of DVD means a growing supply of contemporary documentaries – many from independent sources – and their circu-lation beyond both cinema and television, nonetheless the older films, except for a few 'classics', even the ones that were maintained in circulation by 16mm distribution libraries, are now stashed away, mostly forgotten, reappearing on DVD in dribs and drabs. However, because they were archived, they also become liable to return to us as images retrieved and inserted into other films. Indeed this is one of the essential qualities of the archive, what Derrida calls the archive as 'pledge', its orientation towards the future, as if the archived film is a kind of keepsake or souvenir which has been mislaid but is bound to turn up again.

Here we should speak of the paradox of the archive as a locus both physical and conceptual. There is the place you can go and visit, an organised collection – perhaps dedicated to a particular field, although much material will be missing, and certain items might be deliberately rejected or kept from access for various different reasons. And then there's the archive as a virtual space of historical imagery, from which nothing can in principle be excluded (although it may still be lying forgotten in someone's attic or the junk dealer's back room). Both are liable to yield unexpected finds and produce the return of the repressed. As a place of consignment, says Derrida, the archive incites forgetfulness and amne-sia; it is the site of the loss and breakdown of memory. But this also makes it a source of discovery. (Archivists are wont to tell stories of the joys of discovery. Finding something, especially when you don't know what you're looking for or you're looking for something else, is one of the greatest pleasures for the documentary film-maker who goes looking in the archives, and there are those who dedicate their professional careers to such pleasures, specialising in picture research for the wide range of films that nowadays regularly make use of archive material.)

However, the process of retrieval is far from straightforward, but first of all a problem of the struc-ture of the archive: how things were stored, what classifications were used and what information was recorded about the materials (what the modern archivist now calls metadata). In short, how the techni-

cal structure of the archive also decides the structure of the archivable. Second, things have to be identified. The archives record no film images of George Orwell, for example, but that doesn't mean there
aren't any there. A television documentary made for George Orwell's centenary in 2003 showed a newsreel of the traditional Wall Game at Eton College taken in 1921 when Orwell was in his final year at the
school; the commentary explained that although he was not to be seen in this piece of footage, he might
have been. It seems they weren't looking in the right place, however, since a few months later a pair of
researchers thought they found him in another shot, not of the boys actually playing the game but strid-
ing through the school grounds beforehand.[5] Then there is the problem of misattribution, not just of
authorship but also metadata like place or time. One of the most poignant examples is the Soviet
footage shot at Auschwitz, used in countless films over the years, which was assumed to date from
around the time the camp was liberated. But as the history films' producer Jerome Kuehl has recounted,
this was an event which happened during the middle of winter, 'and it was not until fairly recently that
someone spotted a previously unnoticed clue. There are leaves on the trees in the film; it must date from
some months later.'[6] Taking this into account, the footage is no less horrific but reveals a new facet: it
becomes evidence of how long it took the Soviet forces to find somewhere for the inmates to go.

The archive constitutes a space of aporia, but also a site of potential interaction between history and
public memory. This is precisely the domain of the historical-compilation documentary, which renders
the excavation of the archive public. Nor did it take cinema very long before this promise occasioned a
response. The first compilation films, which appeared in the latter part of World War I, were not yet
properly historical in their mode of discourse – the events whose unfolding they chronicled were not yet
complete. This is why the credit goes to Shub for producing the first historical compilation films ten years
later – even before there were any film archives to collect the material. *The Fall of the Romanov Dynasty*
(1927) can be called the first historical archive film because it proves the virtual existence of the archive
which is waiting to be created and organises its entirely pre-1917 material into a cogent discourse in
which each scene contributes to the historical narrative and its interpretation.

This film occupies a special place in the theory of montage. The family resemblance between the
montage theories of Eisenstein, Pudovkin and Vertov was due in part to the shared influence of Marxist philosophy and the concept of the dialectic, which each interpreted freely according to their own
predilections, but it was left to Walter Benjamin, in another context, to speak of the 'dialectical image'
as such, and for Shub, in her historical reconstructions, to discover its properties in practice. Benjamin
proposed the idea of the dialectical image, which he noted could be applied to film, in his unfinished
Arcades Project, an account of Paris as the capital of the nineteenth century, for which he assembled
over 1,000 pages of research notes, which survived, and an album of images, which didn't. The idea
derived from the Arcades themselves, where it was possible to observe a kaleidoscopic and fortuitous
concurrence of window displays and shop signs which created bizarre juxtapositions. Benjamin,
according to Susan Buck-Morss, was drawn to concrete graphic representations in which images of
particular phenomena or moments pointed to larger historical truths. He also thought that 'the technique of montage has "special, perhaps even total rights" as a progressive form because it "interrupts
the context into which it is inserted" and thus "counteracts illusion"'.[7] In short, he was interested in
images as emblematic traces removed from the historical continuum, which could be reactivated

through juxtaposition. The crucial quality of the dialectical image was its historical resonance. The concept is a fuzzy one, because the dialectical image is necessarily ambiguous, but it points to the space
of history because the image represents a momentary aspect of a dialectical process – 'the figurative
appearance of the dialectic, the law of the dialectic at a standstill'.[8] This is precisely the way that Shub
approaches the footage she discovered in the rusting cans stored in those Leningrad cellars, weaving
a sustained tapestry from fragmented snippets by treating them as historical data.

After Shub, the compilation genre never entirely disappeared, although sustained historical narratives were for some time less common than the rather looser contemporary survey, especially those covering the Spanish Civil War and World War II which followed. These are not exactly archive films, but
rather compilations of contemporaneous material from different sources which have been intercepted,
so to speak, on their way to the archives. One of the first was produced as early as 1936 by none other
than Buñuel, working for the Republicans in Paris, cutting together newsreel footage from Spain for a
film to counter the distortions of the cinema newsreels. Sundry such compilations were distributed
through the working-class film club movement which flourished in several countries in the 30s, a milieu
that was thoroughly internationalist in outlook. Many of their scenes would become, through continual
borrowing and repetition thereafter, the iconic images of the Spanish events – everywhere except Spain
itself, where General Franco banned them.

Spain offers an interesting example of the intermittent circulation of archive footage. Here one of
the forgotten names is that of the Russian cameraman Roman Karmen, who set the standard for war
reportage in his work in Spain and China in the 30s and the Russian home front during World War II,
who is the author of many of the best-known icons of anti-Fascist struggle. The footage he shot during
the year he spent in Spain (while Ivens and Montagu, with their cameramen Ferno and McLaren, came
and went) was not only used for a series of newsreels for home consumption in the Soviet Union, but
also in documentaries for foreign distribution with titles like *In Defence of Madrid* (1936). The same
material was quickly incorporated into other films produced elsewhere in solidarity with the Republicans,
including the compilations put together in Paris by Buñuel and in New York by Helen van Dongen.
Back in Russia, Shub used Karmen's footage to make *España*, released in 1939 soon after the Civil War
ended; this film enshrines the official Soviet version of events although in Shub's highly skilled hands, it
is the images which drive it. Many years later Karmen's images would reappear in Frédéric Rossif's documentary *To Die in Madrid* (1965). Two years later, Karmen himself returned to Spain to make his own
retrospective documentary on Spain, *Granada, My Granada* (1967), but the film which people remember is Rossif's.

Rossif was an experienced and respected French television documentarist who discovered how much
material existed on the Spanish Civil when he participated in a television programme in homage to Ernest
Hemingway following his suicide in 1961. Here we see a new logic emerging. The branch of television
known as current affairs develops a huge hunger for historical images, but can only make cursory use of
them when it finds them. Rossif collected everything he could find, ending up with material from Pathé,
Gaumont and Éclair in Paris, Visnews and Movietone in London, Moscow's Sovexportfilm, the East
German archives in Berlin, and more. (This is like a map of newsreel production centres in the 30s. What
would it look like today?) From this abundance of footage he selects the most graphic and photogenic

to construct a narration of the Civil War which has enormous visual impact on the cinema screen; the archive is supplemented by contemporary scenes of Franco's Spain for which he got permission to shoot by cunningly submitting a script for a television programme quite different from the film he intended to make. Premièred at Cannes, banned in Spain, the scandal it caused brought it international distribution (the English-language version is beautifully narrated by a cast of actors led by John Gielgud and Irene Worth). The commentary guides us through the background and events of the conflict, there are episodes dealing with the assassination of García Lorca, the International Brigade and Guernica. The relationship between the verbal and visual texts is exemplary in achieving a balance between image as illustration and as substantiation. Furhammer and Isaakson call it 'solemn and serious', but with an underlying passion which 'plays on our emotions'.[9] They also register the criticism that it tended to 'aestheticise' – a problem that is always a liability of a film as beautifully crafted as this one, where the 'raw' source material (which of course is not raw but always already crafted) is integrated and meshed into a unified historical narrative. Criticism of the film by the right need not detain us, but it also met with criticism from the left. Catalan anarchist Frederica Montseny accused the film of Communist propaganda which deliberately ignored the Barcelona Anarchist movement which figures so strongly in Orwell's *Homage to Catalonia* and Loach's *Land and Freedom* (1995). But there are also other omissions, like French involvement, or the French government's abstention, or any allusion to the fortune of Spaniards who took refuge in France at the beginning of 1939, most of whom ended up herded into concentration camps. Nevertheless, *To Die in Madrid* stands as a paradigm of filmic history at the peak of the art – just before Ophuls comes along to turn that kind of sure-footed history inside out with *Le chagrin et la pitié*.

III

The archive compilation genre had come back gradually after World War II, especially in the now-forgotten work of Andrew and Annelie Thorndike in East Germany in the 1950s, who assimilated the methods of Shub, Vertov, even Cavalcanti and Capra, to provide the new East German state with a myth of origins in films like *Du und mancher Kamerad* (aka 'The German Story', 1956), a big expensive piece of work in which three million feet of archive footage were cut down to ninety-nine minutes and, as if this were not enough, also included a fake actuality of Friedrich Engels (who died in 1895) addressing a political meeting. Two years later they came up with a film that would find a furtive place in the annals of documentary in England. *Operation Teutonic Sword* (1958) caused an international rumpus by revealing the Nazi past of the then commander of NATO ground forces in Europe, one General Speidel. This included his involvement in the assassination in 1934 of the King of Yugoslavia and the French Foreign Minister, captured on film by Pathé because it happened during a state visit, which the Thorndikes use to great effect along with a host of other footage and documentary evidence. In the felicitous description of Jay Leyda, the film traces

the busy though concealed career of Speidel (whose dislike of cameras did not defeat our researchers) through Poland, into the Soviet Union with the Wehrmacht, into occupied France to wipe out the Resistance, back to Germany to play a role in the suicide of Rommel and then to his post-war glory with NATO.

Detailed visual analysis of film footage and photographs

> gives the spectator the stimulating sensation of a good detective novel . . . A sharp, animated arrow or a sudden freezing enlargement will pluck Speidel for us from the camouflage of a group of officers watching a military operation (such as the destruction of Ukrainian factories), or from a crowd at a ceremony which thereupon immediately gains in significance.[10]

In short, the film was a model of the investigative documentary, not unlike the kind of thing that would be fostered by Granada Television's *World in Action*. But here it also demonstrates something suggested just a few years earlier by Arthur Elton, one of Grierson's team back in the 30s, when he explained that historical documentary was not so much the image of history as its palimpsest.[11] In other words, the historical value of its images was the same as any other artefact from the past – fragments, sometimes fragments of fragments, often blemished or defaced by time – which are employed by the film-maker to reconstruct the past by reading into them as much as reading from them what is inscribed therein. In short, the evidence doesn't interpret itself, it has to be interpreted.

It is in the nature of the beast that the evidence assembled might remain circumstantial, as the English distributors, Plato Films, discovered when Speidel sued them for libel. As Plato's managing director Stanley Forman later recalled the affair, the case took three years to go through the courts. 'It went to the House of Lords on a legal point and we never lost, we never won.'[12] The problem, in a nutshell, was that British law would not accept proof made up of photocopies of documents discovered by East German spies in Bonn. Perhaps you can't blame them, but the affair revealed the blindness of legalistic judgment about the nature of documentary film evidence, simply because the judges had to allow the possibility that something seen on the screen might have been faked (did they know this was something the same film-makers had done already?).

Most documentaries are never required to pass such stringent tests, but are subject instead to codes of practice, either implicit or explicit, which always allow a certain leeway. Conventions were either sanctioned by tradition (which effectively means the practice of the previous generation) or officially spelled out in various advisory documents (like the BBC's *Principles and Practice in Documentary Programmes* introduced in the early 1970s). For current affairs, there was always a limiting factor in the risk of libel, but the arrangements left open the general question of accuracy at the very moment that television was taking up archival techniques. Two main modes of usage quickly developed. On the one hand, the illustrative trope, widely used in many different subgenres, where archival images are inserted into a contemporary narrative to represent what the narrative tense of the film designates as the past. On the other, the sustained historical discourse of the compilation film, favoured by major television documentary series on subjects like the world wars, for which the archives are particularly extensive, where the narrative is the unfolding of a past which doesn't yet have a future – a kind of historical present tense but narrated from a position of hindsight.

In both of these modes, however, the generalised use of illustrative images which serve as simple tokens of history permits them to remain partly unanchored and allows numerous slippages to occur, which are generally hidden under the semantic domination of the commentary. Taylor Downing cites the case of the sinking of an Austro-Hungarian battle-cruiser in 1918 which was filmed from an escort vessel: the dramatic shots of the hull keeling over and of sailors running to escape across the sinking deck have been used, it seems, to illustrate countless episodes at sea, from the Battle of Jutland to Pearl Harbor.[13] Dai Vaughan, writing in 1986 about 'ferocious rows which break out in cutting rooms over questions of authenticity', spoke of 'a recent TV programme on Jewish history' which used footage of the Warsaw Uprising of 1944 for a sequence on the earlier uprising of 1943.[14] These practices continue unabated; another producer mentions the antics of his office cat, who

> unlike human film researchers, knows how to find film even when it doesn't exist . . . One of the cat's ancestors discovered film of the iceberg which sank the Titanic, another found the Wright Brothers' first flight, and a third discovered film of Hitler marrying Eva Braun.

Recently, the cat found some lovely colour shots of American P-47 fighters being loaded onto merchant ships. Said the cat:

> The colour was so good I simply wouldn't allow the fact the P-47 didn't enter service until 1942 to stand in the way of my using them to illustrate events in 1941 . . . But my motto has always been: What the producer wants, the producer gets.[15]

The historical compilation documentary was standard fare on US television by the early 60s. Leyda cites a week in March 1961 when US network television was transmitting three major series using newsreel archives. CBS was running *The Twentieth Century* – the episode that week was on New York City in the 1920s – and ABC had two series on World War II, *The Other Adolf*, occasioned by the pending trial of Adolf Eichmann, using captured films of Nazi atrocities, and the BBC's *Winston Churchill – The Valiant Years*. A few weeks later, *The Twentieth Century* was dealing with Paris in the 20s, and another series called *Not So Long Ago* was covering 1945–50. The contrast between these chronicles of war and peace is first of all an effect produced by television itself, and its peculiar relationship to time and temporality: the way the flow of television produces an antinomy between regularity and disruption, normality and crisis, in which catastrophe is the moment of rupture when normal schedules are suspended. Back-projected onto history, this produces a structural opposition between the calamity of war and the normality of peace which belies historical realities. On television, war is all action, battles, explosions, advance, retreat, death and destruction. Peace is regular, reliable – history becomes the trivia of everyday life, through which the steady progress of the good society can be charted. But this antinomy disguises the fact that history is not generally punctual, does not mainly consist in separate and discrete events, it takes time to develop and evolve before overflowing into crisis and war.

Television histories of the war began by performing similar ideological services to the state in the Western democracies as examples like the films of the Thorndikes in Communist countries; at any rate, they affirmed the authority of the state by providing what Kuehl has called mandarin history, in which 'a revered figure, or perhaps even a controversial figure, but at any rate a *public personality* . . . tells the audience *what to think*'.[16] Or simply the authoritative voice of the actor reading the commentary.

The tone was set by the BBC series *The Great War*, which appeared in 1964: twenty-six episodes of film footage and photographs of the 14–18 War, with one of those classic authoritative commentaries beautifully delivered by Michael Redgrave, and a matching cast of classical actors intoning the words of historical characters, occasionally interspersed with old soldiers on camera speaking their well-rehearsed reminiscences. According to Downing, this was the first time in a popular television series that the archive film was step-printed to compensate for the jerkiness of silent film speed, to make it supposedly more natural at the same time. The films freely intercut feature-film footage, such as close-ups of explosions, to extend the limited material actually shot at the front.[17]

Ten years later, *The World at War* from Thames Television on World War II modified the formula by relinquishing pundits and experts in favour of eyewitnesses. The series was organised thematically rather than just chronologically, in workable storylines accessible to effective narration using archive and interviews, occasionally supplemented by location shooting 'to establish atmosphere and to fill a gap where archive film did not exist'. According to Kuehl, the associate producer on the series, they followed the principles of never using known film footage where there was fresh unknown film newly available, and of never knowingly misidentifying a shot through laziness or any other reason. But mostly the originality of the series stemmed from the relation of the moment when it was made to the shifting social memory of the war as it receded. On the one hand, it was made by a team who in the main were too young to have participated in the war as combatants – 'an advantage because it means we were not settling old scores'.[18] On the other, they went for interviewees 'who we thought would talk and say something fresh', who fell into two groups – 'those who had to say it before they died and the younger participants who were now mature enough to look back reflectively on what had happened to them'.[19] Kuehl gives the credit to the series producer, Jeremy Isaacs. By using 'ordinary people' to tell the story – in other words, embedding within the films the texture of an oral history – he 'translated a mandate to make a shoot-'em-up' – which is what the television company thought they were paying for – 'into a populist, popular, and popularizing visual history of the Second World War'.[20]

The two series remain unsurpassed – they are available everywhere on video, and regularly reappear in the schedules; the week in which I write these sentences, BBC2 is near the end of the latest repeat of *The Great War*. In short, they also performed an ideological service to the institution of television itself, by establishing its role as 'popular historian' of the contemporary world, of greater reach and efficacy than formal education and written history. This needs a rider, however. To call it 'populist, popular, and popularizing' means it is being addressed to the widest possible audience, and therefore being cast in terms of being comprehensible and appealing to the layman. But this is not the same as representing popular memory. On the contrary, the great flaw in this form of historical discourse is that in the end, as Foucault once put it, 'people are shown not what they were, but what they must remember having been'.[21]

The response to television history came from independent film-makers working on the margins of the industry to explode the linear one-dimensionality of the official version, even in its revisionist forms. Here we should speak of the exemplary films of Emile de Antonio, who reconstructed the contemporary political history of the United States with almost every film he made. In 1963 there is *Point of Order* which takes the 1954 Army–McCarthy hearings and edits them down into a demonstration of political theatre. Five years later, in the heat of the anti-war movement, *In the Year of the Pig* explodes myths in reprising the history of how the US got embroiled in Vietnam. In 1989 comes *Mr Hoover and I*, a film in a wryly autobiographical mode which recounts how the FBI considered him a dangerous subversive, a duly ironic comment on his genius as a political film-maker. But I want to move quickly back to Spain, where in 1971 Basilio Martín Patino picked up the story where Rossif left off in the extraordinary *Can-ciones para después de una guerra* (Songs for after a War), prohibited from viewing in Spain itself until 1976, the year after Franco's death. Where de Antonio is sober and rational and given to passages of disruptive formalist montage to express his anger, often through ironic juxtapositions, with Patino it's as if the whole film is made up of ironic juxtapositions, as he recounts the history of Franco's Spain using only the films and music which circulated freely in the public sphere of the times (times that were still in progress when the film was completed).

We hear a huge range of songs – military anthems, satirical political ditties, popular versions of fla-menco and other folklore styles, dance music, clips from musicals – everyday music,' says Patino in his notes on the film, 'in bad taste, affected, smelling of the sacristy or aggressively patriotic, by everyday singers,' 'not a Juliette Gréco, an Yves Montand or an Edith Piaf among them'. No narration, but once or twice an anonymous voice, male or female, speaking of the distance of memory or the uses of music to make the world bearable. We see images of street parades, bombardments, hunger, queues for social security, theatre, dance, fragments of Spanish movies, newspaper advertisements, men leaving prison to be greeted by their families at the prison gate, evacuated children returning to their parents, religious pro-cessions, bull fights, the funeral of the matador Manolete, football, the streets of the city. Sometimes these visual fragments come attached with their own piece of sound but mostly not; often he takes a Francoist NO-DO newsreel, for example, and, removing its post-synchronised soundtrack of music and commen-tary, liberates the images – which were originally mute – to recombine with music of his own choosing, often in satirical and poignant juxtaposition. Mixed in with this oneiric mix of reality and fantasy are Hitler, Mussolini, Stalin, the Nazi concentration camps and the atomic bombs over Hiroshima and Nagasaki.

Spanish film critics took the film very personally, in many cases seeing it as the re-creation of their own childhood. Francisco Umbral wrote of it in 1971 as a film which rewrites 'all our memories', encom-passing 'our family photos, the comic books we read, the films we saw, the triumphalist teaching' – it was like the collective autobiography of a whole generation.[22] Five years later, José Luis Guarner likened it to exorcism:

Through its somewhat complex structure, this unique film, in which each section contrasts with the following to provoke new meanings, goes beyond the usual limits of documentary. It becomes an almost Pavlovian experiment, in which the spell of the images and sounds set the mechanisms of memory in motion.[23]

Josep M. Català, writing in 2001, explains that the songs work as mnemonic devices, reviving memories which are given objective shape in the archive images.[24] For most of the film's first viewers, who lived through the period which it narrated, especially those who grew up in it, the realism of the film lay in the songs, which comprised a landscape of memories which everybody shared and which is what the

266 THE POLITICS OF DOCUMENTARY

film documented. They carried an emotional charge which transferred to the images, especially when either the music or the image sparked off in the viewer a private and intimate recollection. Patino him-self imagined the effect as a filmic version of Proust dipping the madeleine in the tea and provoking the subconscious, through a mixture of images and sounds belonging to different, even conflicting seman-tic registers, to explode into a forgotten richness of feelings and memories.[25] Distance and the Solidarity syndrome alter the relationship of the film to memory, but what the censors wanted to suppress remains a powerful film which communicates across time, a cultural psycho-social history which disturbs the viewer with its contradictory emotional power, its sense of the in-between-the-lines of the images, and the humorous dialectic of the spirit of resistance with which the film was lovingly made.

IV

A new DVD arrives. The British Film Institute have issued a bunch of documentaries made in the 1950s under the Free Cinema banner, several of them supported by their own experimental production fund but previously unavailable on video. I pick out three to look at straight away, which I remember seeing some time past: two films by Robert Vas, *Refuge England* from 1959 and *The Vanishing Street* three years later, and *March to Aldermaston*, dating from 1959 and released without credits, but made by a team of thirty film-makers headed by Lindsay Anderson. I have chosen the films by Vas because they por-tray the London I grew up in at the moment in my teens when I first acquired a wider knowledge of the city, and the Aldermaston film because if it had been made a year or two later, I might have been in it. I find myself gripped as I watch all three by an unusual kind of apperception, which is neither nostalgia nor *déjà vu* (I am not nostalgic about 1950s' London, and the sight of it doesn't take me by surprise) but which forces me to try and remember. (But remember what?)

It strikes me that the three films each have a different temporality, and as a result they work on dif-ferent bits of memory. The most paradoxical is *Refuge England*, in which Vas recreates the day he arrived in London as a Hungarian refugee in 1956, with no English and an incomplete address written on the back of a photo, and succeeds in creating a portrait of the city which I feel like saying that only a Londoner can fully appreciate. The narrative mode is low-key reconstruction: an actor plays Vas to a first-person voice-over narrator with the appropriate accent (an early example of first-person documentary narration); London 1958 stands in for London 1956 (not much change there). But it isn't fiction: it has the look and feel of documentary, indeed of the oldest tendency – the city film of the 1920s – combined with the testimony of the narrator's individual memory. I am seeing it again now through the prism of my own memory. In the course of the day, as the speechless foreigner searches for the correct street, criss-crossing the city from the teeming West End to the quiet leafy streets of the semi-detached in the suburbs, then on to the run-down terraced rows of the inner city, the film takes me back to the London I knew, in the same grey tones as I remember it, and not just the sight of it but the feel, a London that corresponds to my own teenage cognitive map of the city. At the same time, because all this is shown through a stranger's eyes, the city sheds its familiarity, and even a Londoner is forced by this estrangement to re-evaluate.

There is no commentary in the case of *The Vanishing Street*, which portrays the disappearing world of Hessel Street, a Jewish neighbourhood street in London's East End, with its market and shops, con-demned by a redevelopment scheme. Since the film ends with the bulldozers moving in, the film is explicit in declaring not 'here is . . .', but 'here was . . .', where the fact of being filmed means it has come to an end, gone into history. But this corresponds exactly to the old Yiddish culture of my memory as a Jewish lad whose family had moved out to the leafy suburbs glimpsed in *Refuge England*. This is documentary as memorial to a vanished past, which makes me feel both connected and disconnected at the same time. Something similar is true of *March to Aldermaston*, but the temporal projection is different, since this film is not about what passes into history, but in portraying the birth of the Campaign for Nuclear Disarmament, projects a present moment into an unknown future.

Three ways of reading documentary time – as memory, as loss and as what Derrida calls the unknowable promise of what is yet to come. Perhaps this is inevitable in a medium which separates the viewer from what it represents at the same time that it connects. I think of a moment at a docu-mentary conference which illustrates the complexity of the relation between the viewer and the screen, and the process that goes on in the space between the screen and the viewer's eyes – in this case, my own. The viewing facilities were of a high quality and conference speakers were able to show audiovi-sual material of any format on a very large screen above them. This setting gave enormous impact to the images with which Frances Guerin opened her presentation, 'Recycling to Forget', by showing silent colour footage of the Warsaw Ghetto, taken from a recent television documentary with the awful title 'The Third Reich in Colour'. Then she showed it again, this time with the soundtrack of the documen-tary turned up – its commentary and music – in order to analyse the way the television programme revis-ited these mute amateur 16mm images of the past only to close off the histories they narrate. The footage is not used to remember or understand, challenge, open up or investigate the unspeakable his-tory of the Third Reich, but rather to confirm 'a historical narrative that has been told countless times elsewhere' in such a way that 'the original footage is pressed into the service of a . . . narrative nowhere identifiable in the images themselves' but contained entirely in the commentary and its assumptions. The result is that the historical images are 'closed down, delimited, forgotten' by a documentary that is intent primarily upon confirming its own authority.[26]

On an intellectual level I am happy to agree with the analysis, but because of an accident of history I find myself seeing these images in a way she has not allowed for. This is footage I haven't seen before, and immediately and involuntarily I find myself scanning the large clear picture for the possible sighting of my paternal grandparents. I never met them – they perished in the Ghetto, or at Auschwitz, we don't know where or when – but I know their appearance very well from family photographs. And as my eyes quickly take in every face I can see, jumping over figures too small or turned away, they fill with a film of tears. My reaction, in short, is both interrogative and emotional – the latter with a force that reminds me that emotion is perforce a bodily experience.

Because the context of the screening was a conference, which encourages an analytic attitude, this moment immediately suggested to me a whole series of implications. For one thing, the incident con-firmed that a reading of the images depends on the position of the viewer, but that this position has mul-tiple determinants of a contingent nature: not only the physical space and circumstances of viewing but the viewer's disposition, which includes external knowledges and personal memories.

The experience also made me think, inevitably, of Benjamin's remark which came up earlier, that the newsreel offers everyone the opportunity to rise from passerby to movie extra. However, here the footage was deeply problematic, to be held under suspicion because it is known to have been taken by a Nazi playing the role of ethnographer studying an alien caste. But to me this did not destroy the transparency of the image – it doesn't mean that the people in the scene are film extras acting the part, as they are in Roman Polanski's *The Pianist* (2002) which recreates the Ghetto as a quite convincing fiction but where the viewer wouldn't imagine they might catch a glimpse of a relative. This is more like the black-and-white footage of the Ghetto in Ilan Ziv's self-reflexive documentary *Tango of Slaves* (1994), footage that again is known to have been shot by the Nazis for propaganda purposes, and which he examines with a film archivist at a viewing table in an effort to detect the signs of Nazi ideology in the construction of the image. There is evidence of course of selectivity, including certain ways of framing the subject, and certain scenes were probably set up, but these are not studio sets and those who appear in them are not character actors. On the contrary, some of them – the community leaders – are identifiable. Even if they were sometimes acting in the sense of performing actions devised for the camera, their body language and comportment are not invented. This is a socio-historical reality. Of course it's only a fragment, historical cause is invisible, and Guerin is right that the images in themselves have very little narrative or explanatory content. The question becomes, what are you looking for?

V

The archive is full of films and images which are used to construct audiovisual histories, usually along national lines, and to evoke what are thought of as social memories; or they become the iconic signifiers through which national and social memory is mediated, or better, remediated. Does this mean the archive is part of something called national or social or collective memory? What can this mean when its contents mostly remain unseen? And when they do get screened, one is reminded that the memory they proffer is both partial and fragmented. If you went back to Britain in the 1930s, for example, and added in the films of the workers' film movement (part of the ETV collection which has recently been deposited in the National Film Archive), then the picture becomes less partial but it remains fragmented. And anyway, since this history is not in the films, which are merely its symptoms or traces, is this not inevitable? Which raises the question, what exactly is being remembered? All this brings up another puzzle, this time about the word 'memory', which, after all, is highly ambiguous.

For one thing, there is a dichotomy which Derrida reminds us is already present in Freud, but that we can add is also the bane of the neurosciences. On the one hand there is memory as a reservoir, a place where memories are stored, the psychic archive, on the other, memory as the act of recalling, the process of remembering. How can you have the recovery of a memory if there isn't a trace that is stored somewhere? Perhaps on this reading we can think of the film archive as the set of traces, but not the memory itself, in active form, as what Derrida calls 'spontaneous, alive and internal experience'. This might be achieved, however, through the film which uses the archive to reconstruct the historical as a symbolic domain in which the viewer is invited to identify with the situation of the social actors pictured therein. But in that case, and in this way, the memory becomes socialised, it becomes part of public discourse, simply because, after all, film is a form of social communication. And documentary even more so, because it is not addressed to the interior sentimental life of the spectator as a private individual, but to their sociality, to the viewer as citizen, as a member of the social collective, as putative participant in the public sphere.

Freud discovered that people were suffering not from their memories but from their forgetting. The psychic archive isn't passive: memories that are repressed have a habit of returning in disguise, in dreams and waking life, as symptoms and obsessions, or just as screen memories – memories that screen off other memories. Indeed a memory always belongs to a chain of memories, in which it is not only itself but also a symptom of something else, yet to be remembered. The object of psychoanalysis is to return the patient to themselves in such a way as to allow them to acknowledge the forgotten without having to repeat the symptoms of their forgetting in the form of neurosis. Now film isn't psychoanalysis, but perhaps the film archive has similar properties. In Derrida's account, the Freudian analogy is always slippery, because it risks eliding the individual and the social, sometimes leading to mysterious notions like the collective unconscious, but it invokes the problem of how and why certain memories are conserved and others repressed, and makes it clear that this has to do with the structures that control the configurations and dynamics of lived experience; in other words, the domain of ideology and hegemony. If this means that memory is also a site of cultural conflict, then where it turns on questions of power and authority, there is also a politics of memory, in which the interpretation of historical experience is contested, and the relative priority of different memories comes to be challenged.

The psychoanalytic must therefore be complemented by the sociological. In one of the first such attempts, written before World War II, Maurice Halbwachs argued that memory is socially constructed, not only by the social properties of language but also because it is always generated and sustained within the context of social groups, especially the enduring groupings of family, social class, religion and people or nation.[27] The memory of the group realises and manifests itself in individual memories, but individual memories become intelligible only through the discourse of the social group. Since the individual belongs to several different social groups at the same time, on different levels, this is a highly complex process of psychic negotiation – and some of these levels are more widely reinforced than others. For the politics of memory, the most critical question is what happens when individual memory contradicts the collective? Or when the memory of a subaltern group contradicts the hegemonic version? Documentary is a form where the public construction of history takes over from living memory even as it incorporates it, but which, as it does so, also enlarges the space of public memory both in the present and in the archive of the future.

Memory is dialogical. It depends on the telling, and the telling depends on the setting, the situation and the medium. It is one thing to receive the memory of a grandparent from their own mouths, another to see someone who might be your grandparent talking in a film, which has a different status ontologically. Your grandparent arouses your empathy, even while their experience remains beyond reach. But to follow Elizabeth Cowie, the world shown in the actuality of documentary film is presented as knowable – although the terms of knowability are organised by the film, not by reality or history.[28] This may occur in different ways. Visually, in taking up the view presented by the camera, the spectator adopts its look as their own, 'and thus participates as a seeing subject who controls and possesses what is shown'.[29] This is aided by the explicit controlling discourse of titles, commentary, presenter and more surreptitiously, music, which usually all induce identification with the figure of the-one-who-knows. But the direct speech of someone remembering is capable of cutting through all the framing devices that encode it, and fulfil the Deleuzian role of telling stories without being fictional, which connects the viewer directly with their subjectivity. In this way, the film memory, which is separate and other, some-one else's memory, comes to clothe and configure the social memory which is collective, and which the viewer can thereby adopt as an integral part of their own sense of historical comprehension and even identity. This would bring us to a view of memory itself, as well as the archive, as a space of flux, an unfinished process, not just a place of dormant remnants of the past, but a collaboration between past experience and present consciousness. But this again needs a crucial rider: it all depends how open the process of identification is allowed to be, or contrariwise, how manipulative the controlling hand. If tele-vision documentary has indeed taken over the role of popular historian of the contemporary world, then it is ideologically safe as long as the history in question is treated as over and done with, foundational but fully assimilated, and this indeed is the mode of historical documentary which has recently featured in the broadcasting schedules. On the other hand, the continual arrival of new films on certain subjects which refuse to go away, like the Holocaust, or on suppressed episodes which insist on returning, like the Armenian genocide, only testify that history remains problematic.

Freud liked to compare the excavation of the psychic archive to archaeology. The analyst is like an archaeologist 'excavating some dwelling place that has been destroyed and buried' who reconstructs it from its traces. His task is 'to make out what has been forgotten from the traces which it has left behind or, more correctly, to construct it'. This is not always based on the patient's recollection.

> Quite often we do not succeed in bringing the patient to recollect what has been repressed. Instead of that, if the analysis is carried out correctly, we produce in him an assured conviction of the truth of the construction which achieves the same therapeutic result as a recaptured memory.[30]

Perhaps, although Derrida remains a little sceptical, this might well serve for the documentary history film. But then there is no conclusion to be reached. The work of memory is continuous and unending, the archives are growing, and history continues to be made.

Notes

1. Paul Marris, 'Interview with Paul Rotha', in Paul Marris (ed.), *Paul Rotha*, BFI dossier no. 16, 1982.
2. Taylor Downing, 'History on Television: The Making of *Cold War*, 1998', in Marcia Landy (ed.), *The Historical Film: History and Memory in Media* (London: Athlone Press, 2001), p. 298.
3. Jay Leyda, *Films Beget Films* (London: Allen & Unwin, 1964), p. 135.
4. Jacques Derrida, *Archive Fever: A Freudian Impression*, trans. Eric Prenowitz (Chicago, IL, and London: University of Chicago Press, 1996).
5. 'Orwell Film Footage Found' (3 September 2003), <www.theage.com.au/articles/2003/09/03/1062515434408.html?from=storyrhs>.
6. Penelope Houston, *Keepers of the Frame: The Film Archives* (London: BFI, 1994), p. 96.
7. Susan Buck-Morss, *The Dialectics of Seeing* (Cambridge, MA: MIT Press, 1991), p. 67.
8. Walter Benjamin, *Charles Baudelaire: A Lyric Poet in the Era of High Capitalism* (London: New Left Books, 1973), p. 171.
9. Furhammer and Isaakson, *Politics and Film* (London: November Books, 1971), p. 54.

10. Leyda, *Films Beget Films*, p. 85.
11. Arthur Elton, 'The Film as Source Material for History' (London: ASLIB Proceedings, vol. 7 no. 4, November 1955).
12. Stanley Forman, Interview by Tony Pomfret and Tom Fogg, <www.netribution.co.uk/features/interviews/2000/stanley_forman/6.html>.
    In the end, said Forman, the East Germans 'got fed up' because they realised the case could never be won without presenting the originals of the evidence, 'and we realised that we could never get [them]'. Eventually Speidel settled out of court, renouncing financial claims in return for the film's withdrawal from circulation. Meanwhile, to protect its valuable film library, Plato Films turned into ETV, the name under which it survived in business till 2002, when the library was deposited in the National Film and Television Archive.
13. Downing, 'History on Television', pp. 296–7.
14. Dai Vaughan, *For Documentary* (Berkeley and London: University of California Press, 1999), p. 85.
15. E-mail to friends and colleagues from officecat@kuehl.tv, 2 October 2003.
16. Interview with Jerome Kuehl in Alan Rosenthal (ed.), *The Documentary Conscience: A Casebook in Film Making* (Berkeley and London: University of California Press, 1980), p. 40.
17. Downing, 'History on Television', p. 295.
18. Kuehl, in Rosenthal, *The Documentary Conscience*, p. 44.
19. Kuehl, in Rosenthal, *The Documentary Conscience*, p. 38.
20. Kuehl, in Rosenthal, *The Documentary Conscience*, p. 40.
21. Michel Foucault, 'Interview', Edinburgh '77 Magazine (no publication details), p. 22; also in *Radical Philosophy* no. 11, trans. Martin Jordin, from *Cahiers du cinéma* 251/2.
22. Francisco Umbral, *La Voz de Asturias*, 21 November 1971, <www.basiliomartinpatino.com/critica02.htm>.
23. José Luís Guarner, *Cuadernos para el Diálogo*, 1976, <www.basiliomartinpatino.com/critica02.htm>.
24. Josep M. Catalá, 'La crisis de la realidad en el documental español contemporáneo', in Josep Catalá, Josetxo Cerdán and Casimiro Torreiro (eds), *Imagen, memoria y fascinación, Notas sobre el documental en España* (Madrid: Ocho y Medio, 2001), p. 40.
25. Basilio Martín Patino, 'Sobre Canciones para después de una guerra', <www.basiliomartinpatino.com/escritos.htm>.
26. Frances Guerin, 'Recycling to Forget: A Contemporary Re-presentation of Amateur Nazi Film Footage', Visible Evidence, Marseille, 2002.
27. Maurice Halbwachs, *On Collective Memory*, trans. Lewis A. Coser (Chicago, IL, and London: University of Chicago Press, 1992).
28. Elizabeth Cowie, 'The Spectacle of Actuality', in Jane M. Gaines and Michael Renov (eds), *Collecting Visible Evidence* (Minneapolis and London: Minnesota University Press, 1999), pp. 19–45.
29. Ibid., p. 29.
30. Sigmund Freud, 'Constructions in Analysis', 1937, Standard Edition, Vol. XXIII, pp. 258–9.

Index

List of Illustrations

While considerable effort has been made to correctly identify the copyright holders, this has not been possible in all cases. We apologise for any apparent negligence and any omissions or corrections brought to our attention will be remedied in future editions.

With Captain Scott, R.N. To the South Pole, Gaumont Company; *Trials and Tribulations of a Cameraman*, Educational Film Corporation of America; *The Bridge*, CAPI; *Man with a Movie Camera*, VUFKU; *K.Sh.E.*, Esfir Shub; *We Are the Lambeth Boys*, Graphic Films; *Primary*, Time-Life Broadcasting/Drew Films (from Peter Wintonick, *Cinéma Vérité: Defining the Moment*, 1999); *Salesman*, © Bible Salesman Company, re-copyrighted 2001 © Maysles Film, Inc. (from Wintonick, 1999); *El Mégano*, Julio García Espinosa/Tomás Gutiérrez Alea (from Michael Chanan, *New Cinema of Latin America*, 1983); INCINE newsreel crew (from Chanan, 1983); Mexico City (from Chanan, 1983); ICAIC newsreel (from Chanan, 1983); *Thames Film*, William Raban; *Cinéma Vérité; Defining the Moment*, National Film Board of Canada/Peter Wintonick; Washington DC (from Michael Chanan, *Human Wrongs*, 2001).